SÁNDOR FERENCZI

The Psychotherapist of Tenderness and Passion

SÁNDOR FERENCZI

The Psychotherapist of Tenderness and Passion

by Arnold Wm. Rachman, Ph.D.

JASON ARONSON INC.
Northvale, New Jersey
London

This book was set in 10 point Goudy by TechType of Ramsey, New Jersey, and printed and bound by Integrated Book Technology of Troy, New York.

Library of Congress Cataloging-in-Publication Data

Rachman, Arnold W.
   Sándor Ferenczi : the psychotherapist of tenderness and passsion / by Arnold Wm. Rachman.
      p.   cm.
   Includes bibliographical references and index.
   ISBN 1-56821-100-7
   1. Ferenczi, Sándor, 1873-1993. 2. Psychoanalysis. I. Title.
   [DNLM: 1. Ferenczi, Sándor, 1873-1933. 2. Psychoanalysis.
   3. Psychoanalytic Theory. WM 460 R1188s 1995]
   RC438.6.F47R33   1995
   616.89'17'092 – dc20
   [B]
   DNLM/DLC
   for Library of Congress   94-32540

Manufactured in the United States of America. Jason Aronson Inc. offers books and cassettes. For information and catalog write to Jason Aronson Inc., 230 Livingston Street, Northvale, New Jersey 07647.

I dedicate this book to my Austro-Hungarian Jewish heritage, passed down through my grandmother, Bertha Metsch-Beispiel, my mother, Sally Beispiel-Rachman-Grossman, and my father, Max Rachman. Although they are all gone now, they live on in my heart and mind, providing inspiration for my attempts to understand and help others.

Do not believe anything on hearsay: do not believe traditions because they are old and handed down through many generations; do not believe anything on account of rumors or because people talk much about it; do not believe simply because the written testimony of some ancient sage is shown thee: never believe anything because presumption is in its favor or because the custom of many years leads thee to regard it as true; do not believe anything on the mere authority of teachers or priests. Whatever according to thine own experience and after thorough investigation agrees with thy reason and is conducive to thine own will and to that of all other living things, that accept as the truth and live so accordingly.

—*Gautama Siddhartha Buddha*

Any method of teaching is good insofar as it humanizes, refines, undermines authority and makes slaves ripe for freedom. And any teaching method is bad insofar as it blocks action.

—*Thomas Mann*

Amor est forma omnium veritutum
(Love is the form of all virtues).

—*St. Thomas Aquinas*

CONTENTS

ACKNOWLEDGMENTS

My connection to Ferenczi is personal, intellectual, emotional, and analytic. Both my grandmother, Bertha Metsch-Beispiel, and my mother, Sally Beispiel-Rachman-Grossman, were born and lived in the city of Chernovitz, Bukovana, which was in Austria near the Hungarian border, being part of the Austro-Hungarian Empire during Hapsburg rule (Chernovitz is now part of the Ukraine). My paternal home was Vienna.

Emotionally, I feel most connected to Ferenczi of any psychoanalyst because of his warmth, friendliness, liveliness, flexibility, responsiveness, and empathy. He was the lovable analyst. Intellectually, his ideas and methods appeal to my intellectual and academic heritage of phenomenology, pragmatism, democratic and liberal pedagogy, and humanistic psychology.

I can trace my analytic heritage to Ferenczi as being a fifth-generation analysand of Ferenczi's as follows: Ferenczi analyzed Clara Thompson, who in turn analyzed Lewis Wolberg, who in turn analyzed Betty Feldman, who in turn analyzed me.

At different periods over the last eighteen years, from when I first began my study of Ferenczi until the present, my relationships with colleagues have been the intellectual, interpersonal, and emotional mortar from which I could create this book.

Michel Larivière has become, in recent years, my "Paladin et Grand Vizir Secret." During a difficult period in the early 1980s, when I was unsure if I should continue with my Ferenczi project, Alexander Wolf was crucial in helping me renew my commitment and hope. When I turned to him one day and asked him if he would coauthor the book with me, he warmly said, "Arnold, if you want me to write it with you I will, but I think you should write it yourself. That would be better for you." His empathy, encouragement, and faith in me were rejuvenating. I never turned back from that point forward.

My professional and personal experiences with Esther Menaker have furnished both historical continuity and contemporary creativity through her humanistic functioning as a psychoanalyst.

There have been a number of individuals who have encouraged and supported my dissidence and creativity during the years, for which I am very grateful: Janet Baumann, Beatrice Beebe, Thomas Bratter, Velleda Ceccoli, Abe Fenster, the late Alice Hampshire and Asya Kadis, Sheila Kaplan, Robert Kennedy, Robert Marshall, Paul Mattick, Monica Moser, Joyce Nathan, Robert Prince, Richard Raubolt, Peter Schlachet, Samuel Slipp, and Saul Tuttman.

My emotional, interpersonal, and intellectual debt to my analyst, Betty Feldman, M.S.S., is great. My experience with her initiated my analytic awareness. She helped me gain personal understanding, encouraged me to write my first paper, and provided emotional and interpersonal experiences that have sustained me.

Sylvie Teicher-Kamens was enormously helpful. At a time when the Ferenczi materials were sequestered at the Library of Congress, she helped me obtain and translate much of this material, which became available in the early 1980s, from the French. Sylvie bought many of these materials for me during a trip to France and diligently helped me translate *The Clinical Diary* and the Ferenczi/Groddeck correspondence, as well as articles available only in the French journal *Cahiers Confrontation*.

The dedication, reference research, and hours of editorial help by Sharon R. Kahn were essential to the final version of the book. The editorial help of Judy Cohen is gratefully acknowledged. Norma Pomerantz was very helpful in applying for permissions. I am very grateful to the librarians of the A. A. Brill Library of the New York Psychoanalytic Institute.

First Aron Shor and then Joellyn Ausanka transformed my "antique" handwritten text into the required modern form of word-processed, laser-printed manuscript. I am most grateful to them for this necessary help.

There have been many analysands from whom I have learned so much. I consider it a sacred trust to be a clinician. These mutual experiences of healing and learning are interwoven into the fabric of this book.

A special note of gratitude to Barbara-Ellen, a one-of-a-kind woman, whose dramatic presence enlivened my life and my work.

Finally, I wish to acknowledge my children, Rina Beth and Marc Joseph. They are in my thoughts each day, framing my research, writing, and clinical work with their never-ending support, good wishes, and inspiration.

INTRODUCTION

MY DISCOVERY OF FERENCZI

In or about the spring of 1976, I stumbled upon Sándor Ferenczi's work for the first time. I was searching the literature for any analytic precursors for the encounter and human potentiality movement with which I had become active. I wished to ground and integrate what I felt was positive and meaningful about the then burgeoning methods of encounter and marathon group psychotherapy into the history of psychoanalytic method.

I ran across Ferenczi's name for the first time in an article about active psychotherapy in the *American Journal of Psychotherapy* sometime in the mid-1970s. Ferenczi was mentioned in the paper as an early advocate of active techniques, and listed in the bibliography was one of his papers (Ferenczi 1920).

I went to the library to look up Ferenczi's paper, with no special feeling that I was going to find anything of note. But when I began quickly to read, I felt an immediate rush of excitement. I was excited by the idea that at last, I was reading a psychoanalyst with whom I could identify. Finally I had found a bridge between my training and education in humanistic psychotherapy and psychoanalysis, an experience I was awaiting all through my Analytic Institute training. I decided to pursue a study of Ferenczi's work, which I found in the original Hogarth Press three volumes of the *First, Further,* and *Final Contributions* (Ferenczi 1952, 1950, 1955). Looking through these three volumes in 1976, I discovered an interesting fact. When I looked at the book card, which indicated the dates when these books previously had been taken out of the Institute library, I found that I was only the second person who had taken out these Ferenczi volumes in about thirty years.

I never realized the journey of intellectual, emotional, interpersonal, and personal growth that I was about to take when I researched the first Ferenczi article. Examination of the three volumes of his *Contributions* convinced me that Ferenczi was a clinical genius, a significant figure in psychoanalysis, and a forgotten pioneer who deserved the attention of contemporary psychoanalysis.

So I embarked on an intensive study of Ferenczi's work and on a one-man mission to make Ferenczi known to, at the very least, my colleagues, students, analysands, and teachers. I began to include reference to Ferenczi in my presentations. During the next ten years I gave lectures, talks, and seminars on Ferenczi on a limited basis, since I did not feel there was much interest in or understanding of his work (Rachman 1977b, 1978a, 1980a, 1982, 1984a,b, 1987). The unavailability of Freud's papers in the Library of Congress and the unpublished Ferenczi materials hampered my research in the early 1980s. A breakthrough occurred in the mid-1980s when the French translations of the Ferenczi/Groddeck correspondence, his *Clinical Diary*, articles in *Cahiers Confrontation*, and some books on Ferenczi by French authors became available. Then, using the information gathered from these new sources, which amplified and extended the previously available material, I began to give talks to wider psychoanalytic audiences and to publish papers on Ferenczi.

During these last eighteen years of research, teaching, and writing, I have clarified my mission regarding Ferenczi:

1. To retrieve something of value to the analytic and psychotherapy communities that has been lost. Ferenczi's work is part of the lost history of psychoanalysis, as well as a missing link in contemporary clinical theory and practice.

2. To right a wrong in the history of psychoanalysis and psychotherapy. A conspiracy among Freud, Jones, and other members of the original analytic community was successful in suppressing Ferenczi's work, importance, and influence. Were Ferenczi's ideas, methods, and presence so unsettling that he had to be suppressed?

3. To demonstrate that the suppression of Ferenczi's ideas created a vacuum in psychoanalytic thought and practice, so that the link between his work and contemporary frameworks such as interpersonal/humanistic, object relations, and self psychology can be understood.

4. To rediscover Ferenczi's contributions to working with the so-called "difficult cases" (narcissistic, borderline, and psychotic conditions), much needed in contemporary psychoanalysis.

5. To reinstate Ferenczi as a role model for contemporary analysts who wish to be flexible, creative, and innovative.

6. To reintroduce the lost theory of the "Confusion of Tongues," which can inform the contemporary treatment of the incest trauma, as well as provide insights into understanding the psychodynamics of any dyadic relationship, such as teacher/student, or peer to peer, where issues of power, control, and status predominate.

When I first began to look for articles and books about Ferenczi's life and work to inform my understanding of his ideas and methods, it was clear that there were very few resources and materials. Each time I located an article or, much less frequently, a book or chapter, it felt like panning for gold. Each find, however, was a compromise between the excitement of the discovery of some new detail or perspective and the disappointment of knowing that there were significant missing links in my research. Very early in my undertaking, it became clear to me that there was a serious gap in the Ferenczi materials and in the theory and methodology of his last clinical period, 1928 to 1933, the relaxation therapy phase. It became clearer and clearer over the years of my research that there was at first a suppression of ideas and methods, followed by a conspiracy of silence and a deliberate removal of Ferenczi's relaxation therapy from mainstream psychoanalysis. Ferenczi's last clinical period, roughly from 1928 to1933, when he began to deviate from Freud and struggle to resolve his own confusion of tongues and become less tongue-tied, constitutes his most important work. His humanistic psychoanalysis is a legacy of unparalleled emotional courage, flexibility of functioning, clinical genius, and such a reservoir of theoretical ideas that we will have material to study, research, and teach for the foreseeable future.

PSYCHOANALYSIS'S DARKEST HOUR: THE SUPPRESSION OF SÁNDOR FERENCZI

It is now a matter of record that Ferenczi's clinical work and theoretical ideas were suppressed, censored, and removed from mainstream psycho-analysis (Masson 1984, Rachman 1989a, in press, Roazen 1975, Sylwan 1984). Freud's once favorite son, most devoted pupil, and paladin and secret grand vizier suffered Freud's scorn and rejection, was derided by his analytic colleagues, and was denounced by Freud, Ernest Jones, and Max Eitingon as an emotionally sick person.

Jones's condemnation of Ferenczi as a madman, as chronicled in his influential Freud biography (Jones 1953–1957), put the official seal of disapproval on Ferenczi's personality and clinical work. Freud's turning away from Ferenczi (Fromm 1959) and Jones's condemnation of him created a taboo against the study and appreciation of his work. Michael Balint, Ferenczi's analysand, student, and close friend, was present at Ferenczi's last presentation at the 12th International Psychoanalytic Congress at Wiesbaden in 1932, when Ferenczi gave his "Confusion of Tongues" paper against Freud's objections to it (Ferenczi 1933). Furthermore, during the next thirty-odd years, Balint, who had left Budapest for London, observed the trauma created in the analytic community as a result of the Freud/Ferenczi conflict. As one of the founders of the middle group of the British Psychoanalytic Society, Balint experienced the impact of the traditional analytic community's continued suppression of Ferenczi's work in the post-pioneering period.

Balint felt like an outsider because of his love for Ferenczi and his work and because of his own deviations from classical analysis (Balint 1968b). Neither Balint's love and respect for Ferenczi's work nor his own significant extensions of it, as well as his unique contributions, created a new respect or reevaluation of Ferenczi's contributions. In 1965, when Paul Roazen interviewed Balint for his revisionist history of psychoanalysis, *Freud and His Followers* (Roazen 1975), the following remarks indicate the negative climate that prevailed, thirty-three years after the Wiesbaden Conference.

> I had seen Dr. Michael Balint in July 1965, and . . . late fall of 1966; he was in full agreement with me about the immense distortions that Jones's biography had imposed on the historical record. Balint was regarded as a free spirit in the field, but he knew where the power lay in London and in the international psychoanalytic movement. He simply could not believe that I proposed to rectify Jones's biased version of Ferenczi's last days. As Balint said when it dawned on him that I would not be intimidated: "Anna Freud will destroy you." [Roazen 1993, p. 120]

These words of Balint's, now published for the first time, help explain why he was so hesitant in defending Ferenczi, when Jones's biography so clearly distorted history and biased the legacy of Ferenczi as containing madness.

> It is striking that Balint was so prudent about Anna and willing to conform to pressures from the psychoanalytic powers that be, especially since he was neither a member of Anna's circle nor of Melanie Klein's group. . . . Balint knew intimately how difficult it had been for Ferenczi's work to gain acceptance because of Ferenczi's personal problems with Freud. Since Anna Freud had never forgiven Ferenczi, even though he had been dead for over three decades, it had taken years for some of his most brilliant papers to be translated into English. . . . [Roazen 1993, pp. 120–121]

SILENCING FERENCZI

The attempts to suppress Ferenczi's ideas and methods constitute the darkest moments in the history of psychoanalysis. Originally growing out of the Ferenczi/Freud conflict, the events of suppression and censorship were:

1. The attempt to suppress the presentation of the confusion of tongues ideas in 1932 (Masson 1984, Rachman 1989a).
2. The embargo on publishing "The Confusion of Tongues" paper in English from 1932 until 1949 (Masson 1984, Rachman 1987, 1988c, 1989a, 1991d, 1992c, 1993a, in press).
3. The denunciation of Ferenczi's relaxation therapy and later clinical experiments in analytic technique (indulgences, analyst self-disclosure, mutual analysis) as not being psychoanalysis (Masson 1984, Rachman 1982, 1988b, 1989b, 1990a, 1993c, Roazen 1975).
4. Freud's open criticisms of Ferenczi's non-interpretative behavior with analysands (e.g., the "kissing letter" [Jones 1957, p. 197]) as being irresponsible and encouraging acting out.
5. Jones's mean-spirited and deliberate character assassination of Ferenczi, labeling him as manifesting latent psychotic trends and explaining his deviations from Freudian theory and method as a function of this psychopathology (Dupont 1988a, Jones 1957, Masson 1984, Rachman 1989a, 1994b).

6. The institutionalization of Ferenczi in mainstream psychoanalysis as a fringe and negative figure. There was continuation of the suppression and censorship in which Ferenczi's name, ideas, and methods were not mentioned or studied in traditional analytic institutes. Balint (1988), outlining the difficulties he encountered in saving Ferenczi's work from destruction during World War II and then the further difficulties in publishing them after the war ended, has clearly noted Jones's continued attempts at suppression: "After the War my first concern became to translate and edit all the important papers by Ferenczi which had not yet appeared in English. After overcoming some resistance by Ernest Jones . . . *who wanted to omit from the English edition all the papers written by Ferenczi after 1928*, the *Final Contributions* appeared in 1955 (p. 220).

The original voices that rose up in protest of Ferenczi's mistreatment by Freud and Jones as well as in praise of his work, most notably Balint (1958), De Forest (1942, 1954), Fromm (1959), Lorand (1966), Thompson (1942, 1943, 1944, 1950c, 1964a,b), did not belong to the traditional analytic establishment, and so they did not have the power and influence to reverse the trend toward ignoring Ferenczi's work and ideas. Also, Anna Freud's attempts at suppression cannot be minimized. Although she had a personal liking for Ferenczi, she clearly identified with her father's continued need to maintain Ferenczi as an outsider to mainstream psychoanalysis once their personal relationship deteriorated. Roazen (1993) wrote, "Even without Balint's warning to me about Anna, and despite her personal charm, she represented an enormous obstacle to historical inquiry by an outside researcher" (p. 121).

THE CONSEQUENCES OF THE SUPPRESSION OF "THE CONFUSION OF TONGUES" PAPER

The proof that Freud and the orthodox analytic community were successful in suppressing and censoring Ferenczi's "The Confusion of Tongues" (as well as his relaxation therapy theory and method) can be outlined.

The first English translation of "The Confusion of Tongues" did not appear until 1949 (Balint 1949), seventeen years after the paper was delivered at Wiesbaden and sixteen years after it was first published in

German (Ferenczi 1933). Therefore, Jones, by reneging on publishing the paper in English, was successful in delaying its publication for a generation of psychoanalysts. The unavailability of "The Confusion of Tongues," which describes the culmination of Ferenczi's relaxation therapy, deprived the analytic community of his last and, some analysts feel, greatest, contribution (Fromm 1959, Rachman 1989a, 1992c,d, 1993a,b,c,d). The deliberate unavailability of the paper had these very specific consequences for analytic theory and technique:

1. Ferenczi's attempt to reintroduce the seduction theory was successfully suppressed.

2. Psychoanalysis was not challenged to examine either the oedipal conflict theory of neurosis or the role of the drives in motivation.

3. Ferenczi's trauma theory of human relations would have to wait for Balint to help introduce it into the development of the object relations perspective of the British middle group (Balint 1968a).

The suppression of Ferenczi's work is also clearly illustrated in the conspiracy of silence that continued into the 1970s and 1980s and, in some instances, until the present. Ferenczi's ideas and methods are not mentioned in instances in which he pioneered the study of the area. The most dramatic example of this omission, or deliberate silence, is Heinz Kohut's treatment of the issue of empathy. Kohut does not credit Ferenczi as being a significant figure in the introduction and elaboration of the concept of empathy in clinical psychoanalysis. This is clearly one of the most serious omissions in the history of psychoanalysis (Rachman 1988a, 1989b). Furthermore, an argument can be mounted that Ferenczi is one of the precursors for the development of self psychology (Rachman 1989b).

Ferenczi's work in the area of sexual trauma is so significant that I cannot imagine "The Confusion of Tongues" not being cited in any meaningful discussion (Ferenczi 1933). Ferenczi's theory and clinical method are actually based on case after case of incest survivors (Ferenczi 1932c). Yet, in a recent publication that attempted to understand the issue of aggression in sexually abused girls (Larson 1993), the author does not cite Ferenczi in the discussion, even though his confusion of tongues theory was the first attempt to examine the dynamic impact on the child's developing ego, an issue to which this paper is addressed. There is no discussion of Ferenczi's concept of identifying with the aggressor, which is a meaningful explanation for aggression in children who have been molested (Ferenczi 1933, Masson 1984, Rachman 1989a).

These pages, which represent almost fifteen years of work using English, French, and German sources, are at one and the same time an expression of an all-consuming passion for the study of Ferenczi's life and work and a personal odyssey. During these fifteen years I became more connected to my Austro-Hungarian heritage and systematized my professional thinking and functioning. This book also represents my attempt to present Ferenczi to a professional and lay audience, not as a saint but as a totally human figure, with a message relevant to clinicians, scholars, researchers, trauma survivors, and anyone interested in the study of a clinical genius who fell from grace in the psychoanalytic establishment.

1

FAMILY BACKGROUND, PERSONALITY, AND TRAINING[1]

HUNGARY AT THE TIME OF FERENCZI'S BIRTH

Sándor Ferenczi was born on July 7, 1873, into the Fränkel home in Miskolc, a city of 60,000 citizens not far from Budapest (Lorand 1966), at a time when Hungary was in the midst of great political and social turmoil. The country was in a state of crisis and transition for many reasons, and the crisis was to last until World War I and beyond. Hungary was also undergoing an industrial revolution, which had far-reaching consequences for its political and social equilibrium. Politically, Hungary was part of the Austro-Hungarian Empire, under the monarchy of the Hapsburgs. As the industrialization of Hungary was accompanied by a renaissance of national feelings (expressed in various movements such as literature, music, science, and medicine), the precarious balance of the dual regime that governed the two countries was threatened. Dissension between the two nations began around 1870. Other consequences of industrialization were the growth of a middle class that called for democratic freedom and the intensification of conflicts among the working class, the peasantry, and a socially and politically repressive monarchy. In addition, there were the problems of the influence of Austria and the difficulty of integrating a great number of national minorities (Serbs, Slovaks, Ukrainians, Romanians, and Germans). It was in the midst of

---

1. I am grateful to Giselle Galdi, Judit Mészáros, André Haynal, and Ernst Falzeder for their clarification and information on Ferenczi's background.

such intense conflicts, constant government changes, political strikes, and repressions that Hungary was searching for a national identity. The Hungary in which Ferenczi was born and in which he began his work as a psychiatrist was not a haven of peace. His early and mid-career paperswere introduced during this period of political unrest. Claude Lorin (1983) wrote:

> The remedy chosen for an illness reveals the face and intellectual life of men who created it. . . . This medical response, this "remedy" precisely uncovers the need for an intellectual understanding of "madness" as a confrontation to the repressive demands of the Hungarian society in crisis and transition. . . . Most of Ferenczi's papers are produced at a key moment in this history. That is why their chronology must be respected. . . . the image that psychoanalytical writings have built of this man till now is mythical, in other words, it is apolitical. But Ferenczi, on the contrary, knew very well whom he represented and to whom he spoke. [p. 41]

THE FERENCZI CHILDREN

Bernát Fränkel and Róza Eibenschütz were married in 1858. There seems to be some confusion among modern scholars as to whether Ferenczi's parents had eleven or twelve children. Judith Dupont (1982) however, notes that the confusion "seems to be a result of the death of one of Ferenczi's sisters, when he was five years old" (p. 28). Of those older than Sandor, Henrik was the eldest, followed by Miksa (Max), Zsigmond (Sandor's favorite brother), Ilona, Mária (first name Rebus – probably for Rebecca), then Jacob (Joseph), and finally the little Gizella. During the next ten years, four more children were born: Moritz-Karoli, Vilma (who died during her first year), Lajos, and finally Zsófia (Sabourin 1985). Sandor was the third (Balint 1970) or fifth son (Lorand 1966). The latest modification places him as the eighth of twelve children and the fifth son (Falzeder 1995, Haynal 1993b, Mészáros 1995).

    Of this group of children and their progeny, many were murdered during the Holocaust of World War II. Others were scattered around the world, to Berlin, London, Rome, New York, and New Zealand. But all six brothers remained in Hungary: Henrik, the eldest, and Lajos stayed in Miskolc; Joseph, Károly, and Miksa remained with the family bookstore (Barande 1972).

His favorite brother, Zsigmond, worked as a chemist in a paper factory close to Vienna. Both brothers loved mountain climbing and often took hikes together.

Freud (1923a) commented upon the rivalry toward his siblings related to his middle position:

> Ferenczi, who, as a middle child in a large family had to struggle with a powerful brother complex had, under the influence of analysis, become an irreproachable elder brother, a kindly teacher and promoter of young talent. [p. 268]

This large family, with Ferenczi arriving during the period when his mother had seven other children to cope with, no doubt left some psychological mark on his personality. There could not have been sufficient physical or emotional time for him from his mother, no matter how giving and empathic she may have been. Ferenczi had additional difficulty adjusting to this maternal deprivation, when three other siblings were added to the family. It is safe to speculate that this family situation left Ferenczi with significant feelings of maternal deprivation. Two of his closest students and friends have verified his special needs for affection on this basis of his early experience of maternal deprivation (Balint 1949, Thompson 1944). His own description verifies the experience with a difficult mother (see Grubrich-Simitis 1986).

THE FERENCZI HOME AND FAMILY BOOKSTORE

There was always a great deal of activity in the Ferenczi home. The bookstore was on the first floor, to which the elder Ferenczi added a printing shop, and the building also housed a concert agency. He organized concerts featuring artists of international renown and was also the publisher of Mihály Tompa (one of the main poets of the Hungarian resistance). On the second floor was the family apartment, run by the industrious Madame Fränkel.

All the important problems of the time were discussed in the Ferenczi home: art, literature, political theories. The family also played chamber music (Sabourin 1985). The Ferenczis led a rich and full life that must have been intellectually very stimulating for the children, but, because there were so many of them, there was little time for each one individually (Sabourin 1985).

FERENCZI'S FATHER: BARUCH FRANKEL

As a young man of 18, Baruch Fränkel, a Polish Jew, emigrated from Krakkó to Miskolc to join the fight against the Hapsburgs. He obtained permission after the 1849 defeat to settle in Miskolc. He magyarized his name from Frankel to Ferenczi in order to assimilate (Jones 1955) and omitted the aristocratic y at the end, which he had refused as a true democrat (Barande 1972, Sabourin 1985). In addition, Baruch became Bernát. Pierre Sabourin (1985) wrote, "In their efforts to assimilate they wanted to integrate into a country they felt was theirs and for which many of them had fought with distinction" (p. 20) as had Baruch Fränkel. The father settled first in Eger and then became a proprietor of a bookstore in the small provincial town of Miskolc.

According to his younger sister Zsofia, Sándor was his father's favorite, but the elder died in 1888, when Sándor was 15 and needed his father to work through the identity and authority issues that were to play such an important role later on in life in the reenactment of a paternal relationship with Freud.

The father's bookstore contained a great number of both Hungarian and foreign works, which certainly had a major influence on Sándor (Lorin 1983). Among the writers were Vörösmartis, author of a call to the people that became the national anthem; Sándor Petöfi, Hungary's most revered poet; Shelley; and important French writers (Sabourin 1985). Thus, Sándor was exposed as a young man to political and revolutionary ideas, identifying with his father's freethinking spirit. The adolescent Ferenczi, who cherished and idealized his father, assimilated this intellectual revolutionary spirit. His position as the "enfant terrible of psychoanalysis" easily suggests this connection to his father (Balint 1933).

Ferenczi's cherished relationship to his father was revealed recently through the research of one of the leaders of Hungarian psychoanalysis, Livia Nemes. References occur directly and by inference in two of his scientific papers. The indirect reference was noted in a 1909 paper, where he stated that he had more success with hypnotizing apprentices in his father's bookstore than he did as a doctor with his patients. He said, "I lacked later the absolute self-confidence which can come only through ignorance" (Ferenczi 1909, quoted in Nemes 1988, p. 245). Nemes (1988) believed that it was his special relationship to his father that made the difference: "I think it is possible that the absolute self-confidence he describes here was founded not just on his ignorance but also on the admiration that this feat inspired in his father" (p. 245).

The second and more direct reference occurred in his paper "Criminality and Psychoanalysis" in which he demonstrated his remarkable capacity for self-analysis. The episode involved a bonfire in the lavatory. He began the revelation by talking in the third person.

> One day after the death of his beloved father, he was fifteen at that time—he could not resist the temptation. As an experiment, he pinched a bottle of ether which had been used for the resuscitation of his dying father, locked himself in the lavatory, and lit a bonfire with it. . . . He was fully aware that his act was a forbidden one and sacrilegious. Afterwards he felt remorse and made a resolution to keep the memory of his father alive by thinking of him at least once a day until the end of his life. [quoted in Nemes 1988, p. 245]

Ferenczi concluded his self-analysis in the first person (Nemes 1988): "In unfavorable circumstances all these features could have led to more culpable deeds. Merciful fate was satisfied by making me a doctor and a psychoanalyst" (p. 245).

Perhaps, in this episode and self-revelation, we have some understanding of Ferenczi's tendency toward combining something daring with a cherished figure. First it showed itself with his father (Nemes 1988), then Miksa Schächter, his medical role model (Ferenczi 1993) and then later in his relationship to Freud.

FERENCZI'S MOTHER: ROZA EIBENSCHÜTZ

In all the biographical materials of Ferenczi, his father is clearly mentioned first because he was the more cherished parent. His mother, Roza Eibenschütz, was from a Polish family that settled in Vienna. She efficiently managed the household and assisted her husband and was also president of the local union of Jewish women. After she was widowed, she was perfectly able to take care of the bookstore and her many children. She also generously entertained their friends and the intellectual society of writers and artists who passed through Miskolc (Sabourin 1985).

Difficulties in the relationship with his mother are evident in Ferenczi's writings. A glimpse into the Freud/Ferenczi correspondence reveals "Ferenczi, son of an 'otherwise harsh mother' . . ." (Letter from Ferenczi to Freud of October 30, 1912, cited in Grubrich-Simitis 1986, p. 274). Sándor will tell later how much he suffered from deprivation (Ferenczi and Groddeck 1982):

> According to my memories, it is certain that as a child, I received from her too little love and too much rigor; sentimentality and caresses were unknown in our family. And feelings such as modesty and respect toward the parents were jealously cultivated. [pp. 55–56]

The letter also revealed Ferenczi's need for a responsive adult, which he would later convert into an empathic attunement of the adult (analyst) for the child or child-in-the-adult (Ferenczi 1933).

Recent evidence also suggests a more tender and loving feeling for his mother. The following poem was written to her on the occasion of his 24th birthday in 1897. The poem was addressed to her, from Vienna. Writing poems was something he did frequently, according to his sister Zsofia (Sabourin 1985):

> At the edge of a new life, I salute you, my mother.
> Only you, no one else can understand when I cry.
> And today, I shed warm tears,
> Real tears, earnest tears;
> My twenty-four years are lying here
> In the coffin.
> [Ferenczi and Groddeck 1982, p. 57]

MEDICAL STUDENT AND ARMY PHYSICIAN

In 1890, at the age of 17, Ferenczi began to study medicine (Bergmann and Hartman 1976). As a medical student he became interested in psychic phenomena. He tried hypnosis—at first with his sisters, who were not good subjects, and later with a 17-year-old clerk in the family bookstore (Lorand 1966). Ferenczi graduated from medical school in 1894 (Sabourin 1985). In 1896 he did his military service in the Austro-Hungarian Army (Barande 1972). As Michael Balint said (Barande 1982), "He often told us that during his school days, he wasn't a very serious student. At the university, he preferred to have a good time" (p. 9).

After serving his compulsory military service for one year, he interned in the various hospitals in Budapest. In 1899–1900 he worked in the section reserved for prostitutes at St. Rokus Hospital. Then, in 1901, he entered the neuropsychiatric section of St. Elizabeth Hospital for the poor. There he specialized in neurology and neuropathology, also developing his skill in hypnotism and autosuggestion (De Forest 1954). In 1905, he was a trial medical consultant (Barande 1972, Mészáros 1993).

FERENCZI'S COURTSHIP AND MARRIAGE

The story of Ferenczi's courtship and marriage to Gizella Pálos is a tragic one. Apparently, Sándor and Gizella met in Miskolc through their parents, who were friends. Sándor must have been an adolescent at that time and Gizella a young bride. It was a long time before they met again, since their marriage was not possible until after the death of Gizella's first husband in 1919 (according to Balint, Gizella's husband refused to divorce her) (Barande 1972).

Ferenczi maintained the outward appearnace of a bachelor, becoming an active member of the coffeehouse society of Budapest. A few intimates knew, however, that he maintained a long-standing relationship with Gizella Palós, née Altshol (1863–1949). She was an attractive and charming woman, about ten years his senior and the mother of two daughters. Although Gizella had separated from her husband, he refused her a divorce. Unable to marry Gizella and wanting a family produced a significant amount of disturbance for Ferenczi (Balint 1970).

The marriage did not occur until March 1919, when Ferenczi was in his mid-forties. This meant that the courtship had lasted eighteen years. Freud approved of the marriage and was fond of Gizella, describing her to Jung as "thoroughly versed in our lore and a staunch supporter" (Roazen 1975, p. 358).

Gizella has been described as having similar traits to Ferenczi; she was kind and sentimental. At first, the Ferenczis lived in Pest. Then, realizing his dream, they owned a house with a garden overlooking the Danube, in Buda.

The final episode of the tragedy occurred on Ferenczi's wedding day.

They were going to the wedding ceremony when they were informed of Géza Pálos's death. There is a question as to whether it was a heart attack or suicide (Jones 1957). After their having had to endure many years of frustration in being apart, their marriage began on this tragic note; however, it was a successful marriage. There were no children from the union, but Mrs. Ferenczi's two daughters by her former marriage were a joy to Ferenczi (De Forest 1954). The younger daughter, Magda, married Ferenczi's younger brother, a baker in Budapest (De Forest 1954, Roazen 1975). The Ferenczi marriage was not without an element of strain, however – the triangle between Ferenczi, Gizella, and the other daughter, Elma.

It was with Elma that a darker episode in Ferenczi's life occurred. The first hint of a romantic link between Ferenczi and his future wife's daughter was suggested by Paul Roazen (Roazen 1975). The material that contains this information was not revealed in Ernest Jones's biography of Freud; what is more, Jones said in a letter to Balint (who was Ferenczi's literary executor) that he took great pains not to discuss Ferenczi's private life, his relation to Gizella, and his intimacy with Elma (Jones 1957, Roazen 1975). Roazen speculates that Jones felt justified in attacking Ferenczi as a madman because he (Jones) showed discretion and restraint in dealing with his private life.

The first concrete evidence of the Ferenczi/Elma romance was chronicled in the French translation of the Ferenczi/Groddeck correspondence, edited by Judith Dupont, in a letter from Frederick Kovács to his future wife Vilma (mother of the Ferenczi portrait painter Dormándi), dated January 8, 1927 (Dupont 1982). However, we now have the most direct evidence of their romance, published in the first volume of the Freud/Ferenczi correspondence: *Letter Ferenczi to Freud – December 3, 1911.*

> Things are proceeding more rapidly than I imagined they would. I was not able to maintain the cool detachment of the analyst with regard to Elma, and I laid myself bare, which then led to a kind of closeness which I can no longer put forth as the benevolence of the physician or of the fatherly friend – I know and share your view of the Janus character of the neurotic, and it is precisely this connection that toughened my resolve, again and again, to resist temptation. . . Frau G.'s incomparably kind, unstintingly kind and loving attitude toward me – she has been told everything. I harbor the most tender feelings toward her – I feel terribly sorry for her.

> She knows that I am writing to you and asks you through me
> to compel me to make a quick decision. . . Perhaps you can call my
> attention to something that could be of use to me in my struggle to
> decide. [Brabant et al. 1993, p. 318]

The problem was further complicated by Elma's treatment by both Ferenczi and Freud. On July 14, 1911, Ferenczi told Freud that he had begun to analyze Elma, the daughter of his friend Gizella (Haynal 1993). From New Year's Day 1912 to Easter 1912, Elma was in analysis with Freud. Then she returned to Ferenczi for analysis (Haynal 1993).

> He [Ferenczi] repeatedly begged Freud to take over Elma's analysis.
> Reluctantly, Freud agreed. On this note, Elma's psychoanalysis
> begain, with many indiscretions between the two men, and with
> extreme oscillations in the attitude of Ferenczi, who at times de-
> clared a wish to marry her and at other times wanted to resume
> analysis with her . . . until at Easter 1912, she came to the end of her
> analysis in Vienna with Freud, having reached the narcissistic stage.
> In short, we see the entire imbroglio, all the evidence (if any were
> needed) that Freud would later bring to bear in determining if the
> love involved in the transference is a genuine love (see Freud 1915
> [1914] p. 168). [Haynal 1993, p. xxiii]

EARLY CLINICAL INTERESTS

Ferenczi's early contact with the Freudian system was not favorable. At the turn of the century, when Ferenczi finished medical school, he first encountered rare essays by Freud, but claimed that he wasn't very affected by them (Barande 1972). Next came Ferenczi's response to Freud's land-mark *The Interpretation of Dreams*. There is disagreement among Ferenczi scholars as to his reaction to this work. Izette De Forest (1954) suggested, "This book was the turning point in his career; for its original and exciting ideas so impressed him that he immediately began using the psychoana-lytic method in the treatment of his patients" (p. 2). Ferenczi received the book from the Hungarian medical journal *Gyógyászat (Art of Healing)*, edited by his friend Max Schächter. After giving the book a quick scanning, he is supposed to have said, "It isn't worth the effort" (Sabourin 1985, p. 24). In one of his first writings, he spoke of his reaction to Freud's works:

> In 1893 I had read the article of Breuer and Freud on the psychic mechanism of hysterical symptoms; later on, I read a paper written by him alone, in which he demonstrated that early sexual traumas were at the root of psychoneuroses. Today, having had too many occasions to be convinced of the truth of Freud's theories, I have to ask myself this question: why did I immediately discard them; why did I find them a priori improbable and artificial; and why did this theory of the sexual origin of neurosis trigger in me so much displeasure and aversion that I did not find it necessary to verify if, perchance, there were some element of truth in it! [Ferenczi 1908b, p. 31]

Strangely enough, on the title page of his copy of *The Interpretation of Dreams* were written the words "Aere Perennius" ("more lasting than bronze").

PRE-FREUDIAN FERENCZI

The overwhelming tendency in Ferenczi biographies has been to stress the enormous influence that Freud had on Ferenczi's life and work. By so linking these two men, it appeared that Ferenczi was unaccomplished and insignificant and did not have a singular voice before his collaboration with Freud. Fortunately, this false assumption has been eradicated with the recent discoveries and research of the French psychologist Claude Lorin. He has located all of the pre-Freudian publications and discussed them from the involution of Ferenczi's own personal and professional development (Lorin 1983).

During Ferenczi's pre-analytic clinical work, he was involved in the study and treatment of issues and cases that foreshadowed his later work: he was intimately involved in treating nontraditional cases at St. Rokus Hospital and St. Elizabeth Hospital. In this work, one can see the embryonic seeds of his interest in disenfranchised and marginal people, his belief in the need for a politics of health, and his technical research to find a communality between the role of the psychoanalyst and the role of the physician (Sabourin 1985). These early trends are expressed by Lorin (1983).

> He asserts the human adventure against the human nature. He does not seek to keep but to conquer; trained as a doctor, he nevertheless goes exploring psychology, literature, politics, and law. . . . His comprehension of psychoanalysis is ascentional instead of magic. His first essays show that he did not cross out the analytical thought that was growing in him. His work is not without contradictions and lacks cohesion, but it is the sum of a thought in movement. [p. 36]

Lorin also sees the trend toward dissidence in Ferenczi's early work, such as in his 1899 paper, "Spiritism" (Lorin 1983). In this paper, he challenged the dogma behind established ideas and incurability that are too often linked to cultural prejudices (Sabourin 1985). As has been pointed out, Ferenczi's dissident views in psychoanalysis were not just his personal and intellectual views, but also reflected the Zeitgeist of the Hungarian revolutionary spirit. There were cultural movements that pointed in the same direction that Ferenczi was heading. Sabourin (1985) wrote:

> From 1900, successive attempts were made to found a literary journal that would reflect this change . . . the outcome of which was *Nyugat* (West), a synthesis of the new trends. The director and theoretician of this review was Ignotus, who was a friend of Ferenczi. The poet Endre Ady wrote in 1906: "I think and boldly proclaim that I am the spokesman of the Hungarian European soul. Perhaps not brave enough, or discouraged enough yet, but nevertheless, a spokesman. My Mecque is in the place where souls are more refined and where human culture projects a sacred light." [p. 26]

As Sabourin points out, it would be premature to establish dominant patterns in Ferenczi's early work, but there are certain essential ideas and tendencies (Sabourin 1985). In "Spiritism," Ferenczi "appears as a precursor of active psychiatry, working at eroding pre-established certitudes, so that prognostics will cease to be destinies" (Lorin 1983, pp. 72–73). In this early paper, Ferenczi theorizes about the "division of the functions of the mind": "What we know in fact shows clearly that there are

in the human mind unconscious and subconscious elements which participate in their functioning. We accomplish innumerable logical things which our consciousness has not apprehended" (Lorin 1983, pp. 72–73).
He related this to occult phenomena.

> It is highly probable that a great number of these occult phenomena are also the expression of these diversions of the mind; one or several parts of the minds are reflected in the consciousness while others function outside of the field of consciousness and in a way automatically. [Lorin 1983, pp. 72–73]

Ferenczi was the first to raise questions as to the differences among belief, faith, observation, and telepathy, questions that Freud considered thirty years later.

In his paper "Two Mistaken Diagnoses" (1900), Ferenczi focused on the psychological phenomena that are not well known, referring to this work as unconscious work: "the elaboration within myself of the diagnosis" (Ferenczi 1902, in Lorin 1983, p. 19). This phenomenon Lorin believes would later be described as countertransference.

On the eve of Ferenczi's first contact with Freud, he was immersed in the beginnings of his analytic activities. This was his fascination with Jung's word association technique.

> He bought a stopwatch and after that, no one could escape his zeal. Writers, poets, painters, rest room attendants, or waiters, anyone he could get his hands on in the cafes of Budapest was subjected to the "associations test." In this manner, he came to repair the omission of the past and read from beginning to end all the psychoanalytic literature available at the time. [Sabourin 1985, p. 27]

It was not until that fateful meeting with Freud in 1908 that Ferenczi's early revolutionary spirit, enthusiasm for healing, concern for the less fortunate, and intellectual daring were to become devoted to psychoanalysis.

2

FERENCZI'S EARLY HUMANISTIC PSYCHOTHERAPY

FERENCZI'S CONTRIBUTION TO SEXUALITY

Ferenczi made remarkable contributions to the study and treatment of sexuality, an aspect of his work that is not fully understood. His contributions to the study of human sexuality have been addressed by several authors (Masson 1984, Rachman 1993a, Stanton 1991, Vida 1991). It is fitting that a study of Ferenczi's long overlooked contributions to the study and treatment of sexuality be undertaken. Recently, the author outlined Ferenczi's overall contributions to sexuality (Rachman 1993a). The present discussion will focus specifically on the area of homosexuality.

Ferenczi's early clinical work, before collaborating with Freud, indicates a young psychiatrist with talent, daring, and creativity—an innovator and humanist. This "pre-Freudian Ferenczi" indicates that "the young Ferenczi" (Lorin 1983) could function independently of Freud to produce theoretical advances and clinical innovations. Ferenczi's emotional dependence upon Freud, in the light of his own special capacities, seems all the more puzzling.

The compelling presence of a genius whose personal authority mesmerized not only Ferenczi but all his followers is part of the answer. The other part is Ferenczi's need for a father figure. His childhood was characterized by both maternal deprivation and a close, loving relationship with his father. They shared many qualities, and, when his father died in Ferenczi's adolescence, an intellectual, emotional, and interpersonal vacuum was created. It was inevitable that not only would Ferenczi be attracted to Freud, but that his unresolved need for tenderness and responsiveness in a paternal figure (since the father served as the nurturing figure) would be reenacted in their relationship.

An earlier paper has been discovered that presents Ferenczi's treatment of a female homosexual transvestite. "The Case of Rosa K." was very significant for its time, as Ferenczi struggled to free himself from the medical conventions of this era and develop a humanistic approach. Ferenczi's struggle at that time can provide inspiration for clinicians, and his empathic method has relevance for the treatment of homosexuality and transvestites in contemporary psychoanalysis.

FERENCZI'S EARLY TREATMENT OF A FEMALE HOMOSEXUAL TRANSVESTITE: "THE CASE OF ROSA K."

Ferenczi's first statements about sexuality appear in this 1902 paper, which was called "Homosexualitas feminina" (Female Sexuality) which appeared in the Hungarian medical journal Gyögyaszat, Number 11.[1] That paper was a prelude to his 1914 paper "The Nosology of Male Homosexuality." "The Case of Rosa K." was the first paper written in Hungarian with the purpose of having the medical world accept the duality of human sexuality (Lorin 1983). The theories of degeneration, prevalent at the turn of the century, were part of Ferenczi's thinking, although he did struggle to free himself of them and move toward a humanistic view of homosexuality. Rosa K. was a female homosexual transvestite whom Ferenczi treated as part of his clinical work as a hospital psychiatrist at St. Elizabeth's Hospital. Lorin characterized this woman as the Joan of Arc of Hungarian psychiatry (Lorin 1983). Ferenczi described the sad fate of Rosa K. in an empathic way. It is clear that he was attempting to understand her, not to judge or categorize her.

Hunted, incarcerated, and oppressed, she found herself in social isolation and emotional instability when she met the young Ferenczi. The attitude toward Rosa K. was universally negative, rejecting, and con-

---

1. I am grateful to Dr. Judith Dupont for sending me a copy of the original article on Rosa K. and to Gabor Kalman for translating the Hungarian material into English: "Female Sexuality," Gyógyászat, Number 11, 1902.

demning by the community, her family, the medical establishment, and society at large. But Ferenczi viewed this cursed woman as a person.

Ferenczi asked Rosa K. to write an autobiography so that he could understand her difficult life,[2] and he incorporated this autobiographical material into his description of the case. He began the case discussion by describing her in the medical style of the turn of the century, which viewed homosexuality as a degenerative disease. This orientation searches for evidence of degeneration in physical and psychological attributes.

> Rosa K., alias Robert, 40 years old, unmarried domestic—whose portrait I am presenting here—is one of those unfortunate creatures whose inborn perverse tendencies attracts them towards members of their own sex with irresistible force, while the satisfaction of the natural, i.e. heterosexual, instinct leaves them cold or even disgusted. Such cases are not particularly rare; anyway, the weedlike proliferation of "scientific" literature of sexual perversity which is bringing rich financial rewards to both authors and publishers saw to it that the medical readership is much better informed about every detail of this chapter of psychopathology than about many other, more significant subjects. If I still publish these observations briefly, I do it only because they serve an opportunity for a few remarks.
>
> Rosa K.'s biography is a real Odyssey. Particularly because of her inborn restless nature, but mostly because of the animosity of others, she could not stay long at any one place. Her folks would have nothing to do with her, people made fun of her, they would not employ her, some even took advantage of her degenerate tendencies and blackmailed her out of her saved pennies. Most often, she had run into difficulties with the police. In Vienna and Budapest, she was jailed for wearing men's clothing, and in Esztergom she was incarcerated, for she was taken for a man in women's clothing. Finally the police headquarters thought she would cause less consternation if she wore men's clothing; she was even given a written permission, and this was perhaps the greatest joy in her life.
>
> In her autobiography, which she has written on my request, considering her meager education, she presents her life with surprising logical chronology and style. Her memory is unusually sharp.

---

2. Unfortunately, in my recent inquiries to Drs. Dupont, Haynal, Hidas, and Lorin, Rosa K.'s autobiography has not been located.

She shows particular preference toward music, and because she had no opportunity to study piano or voice, she begged 50 Forints and bought a hurdy-gurdy. Her musical pitch is indeed uncommon. Such singular talent is a common phenomenon in connection with sexual perversity. Already in her teens she liked to associate only with girls, which her parents found rather conspicuous. At parties, she only enjoyed dancing with her girlfriends. She preferred rougher, manlier activities to womanly needlework or household chores. Her manner of walking, too, was virile, with long strides, which made her quite conspicuous in women's clothing.

The coldheartedness of her parents forced her to leave her home, and she was charged with vagrancy and expelled from Vienna to Budapest. From time to time she sneaked back into the city of her birth and on one occasion she worked as a head waiter in a small restaurant for two years. This was the scene of the story of her only true love, which she still remembers with aching heart. The subject of her attraction was the young cashier of the restaurant, who seemingly out of greed gave in to "Robert's" requests, and they entered into a common household.

Naturally, the marital relationship was rather platonic, and it is understandable that in a few months the unfortunate Rosa K. found out that her lover was unfaithful to her – with a man! This was the end of this peculiar liaison.

Once more she was expelled and sent to Budapest, where the officials placed her in the poorhouse, but the constant ridicule she was subjected to from the other residents irritated her a lot and she was transferred first to the observation ward, then to one of the government insane asylums. She was freed a few months later, when she resumed – as she continues today – her eternal wanderings with sojourns in the poorhouse, jail, halfway house, and the mental institution.

In regards to R. K.'s bodily sexuality, there are no perceptible irregularities. Both external and internal genitalia are normally developed female reproductive organs. Her voice is soprano, windpipe small, breasts not particularly atrophied, and the dimensions of her hips are somewhat feminine. Her gestures and gait are rather masculine, her hands and feet are large, facial features and profile are rugged. She has no abnormal hair anywhere.

Her psychological sexuality—as I mentioned—manifests towards the same sex exclusively. It happened though—about ten times altogether—that she had contact with men, but she did it only out of need for money.

In normal sexual contacts she felt no libido. "Ich habe eben nur für Damen Interesse," she says in her biography. Otherwise her mental capacity surpasses that of other women of similar social standing, she is excellent in doing math in her head, possesses an extraordinary memory, and she has satisfactory legal and moral concepts. She is subject to mood swings, with a special tendency to be overemotional and depressed.

Among the so-called degenerative physical characteristics—or inherited developmental defects—the gothically hollow upper palate, the protruding lower jaw (prognathia) and irregularly grown teeth are notable, as well as two symmetrically located belt shaped pigment atrophy around the hips. Her face is quite ugly and rather repulsive; such degree of ugliness could be considered as degenerate, for the impression given by ugliness is actually nothing else but the aesthetic affect of not separately considered irregularities.

We should give particular thought to two questions related to this case. The first one is, where could we put such an individual. Because of her conspicuous behavior, her weakness for life's struggle, and unexpected and temperamental mood swings she cannot fit into society without support and protection. On the other hand, there is no place for such an individual, either in prison or in a mental institution. In the meantime, until separate institutions are established to house such "débiles" and "déséquilibrés", perhaps the best solution is to place them in the village poorhouses where they can enjoy some liberty, perhaps work and are more or less protected from the malice and harm of others.

The other question, how such and similar individuals could be prevented from procreation, was answered by Nature itself. Experience proves that the more severe the physical and mental deviation the less these degenerate individuals are capable for procreation. For example, idiots with few exceptions are sterile. From this perspective, sexual perversity, similar to our case, is beneficial to society: it helps to prevent such an individual burdened with such degenerate physical and mental symptoms from creating progeny.

All sexual aberrations are abnormal only because they differ from the mode of sexual contact which is appropriate for the continuation of the race, and homosexuality creates a mode of contact which is least appropriate for the continuation of the race.

Homosexuality, therefore—in the case of degenerate individuals—is not a thing without a purpose; it improves the next generation. And it is not mere coincidence, perhaps, that these degenerate individuals are willing participants in the aberrations of sexual life. Perhaps we can see in this a phenomenon of omnipresent theology, or "automatic regulation" of nature.

The "survival of the fittest" is valid not only in the continuation of the race, but also in the selection of sexuality. The aggressive, normally developed representative of the race has greater attraction toward the opposite sex, and thus has a greater chance for progeny. On the other hand, the degenerate, the ugly—if other less natural motifs such as self-interest or money don't play a part—are excluded from participating in the creation of the next generation. Altogether, however, exclusion through sexual selection is not entirely reliable. As a one time hospital physician to prostitutes I had cause to believe that neither the lack of an eye or a leg, nor spinal deformities, old age or ugliness were any hindrance to continuing in that profession—and as the frequent infections indicated—with success.

It is useful and necessary, therefore, that nature takes care of the exclusion of deviant individuals, and does not leave the task to unreliable humans. [Ferenczi 1902, pp. 167-168]

Meaning of Rosa K. Case Study

What makes this case study so remarkable is that it clearly indicates Ferenczi's attempt, in a era of psychiatry when homosexuality was seen as a sign of physical, intellectual, and emotional degeneration, to bring a humanistic perspective to the study and treatment of these problems. Lorin (1983) wrote, "Although he is influenced by the theories of Morel on degeneration, Ferenczi is critical of . . . forms of writing that exploit the perverse fascination of the public for this kind of woman" (p. 206). The study of Rosa K. encouraged Ferenczi to change his use of the term homosexuality to *homo-eroticism*, because it implied the concept of "psychological sexuality" (Ferenczi 1914).

The word comes from Karsch-Haak (Das gleichgeschlectliche Leben der Naturvölks [1911]), and is in my opinion preferable to the amibiguous expression homosexuality, since it makes prominent the psychical aspect of the impulse in contradistinction to the biological term "sexuality." [p. 299 n9]

As Lorin points out, Ferenczi *did not* use the Hungarian term *romlott*, which is pejorative and means perverse or depraved. Rather, he used the word *perfverz*, which means inverted or out of order, an equivalent to the Freudian expression "verkehite Sexualimpfindring" (inverted sexual feeling) (Lorin 1983). Ferenczi, therefore, attempted not to attach a moral denunciation to homosexuality.

Asking Rosa K. to write her autobiography so that he might better treat her was a significant technical innovation that still has contemporary application. What better way to gain an empathic perspective of an individual's subjective frame of reference than to ask the analysand to form her life story—her struggles for sexual identity and self-definition in her own words? It is the exact opposite of a diagnostic framework, so much a part of psychiatry, where the physician forms his or her opinion of the meaning of a person's problems and life's struggles from the physician's frame of reference. In the case of Rosa K., Ferenczi began to search for the perspective of the patient and concentrate on the patient's view of her experience. This early perspective of the other in the treatment process became a significant theme in Ferenczi's clinical work. In 1928, he introduced the concept of empathy into psychoanalysis in "The Elasticity of Psycho-Analytic Technique" (Ferenczi 1928b). His empathic studies consumed him during his final clinical period of humanistic pschoanalysis, culminating in his mutual analysis technique described in his *Clinical Diary* (Ferenczi 1932c).

Later, in April 1908, Ferenczi presented a paper to Budapest physicians entitled "Intermediary Sexual States," where he openly advocated the defense of homosexuals. He uged his colleagues to "take sides against the unfair penal sanctions which homosexuals are subjected to in many countries, especially in Germany, but also in our country" (Lorin 1983, p. 211). Ferenczi also urged his colleagues to join the Berlin Humanitarian Scientific Committee, of which he became the Hungarian correspondent.

3

FREUD AND FERENCZI: THE HISTORY AND MEANING OF THEIR RELATIONSHIP

THE TRAGEDY OF FREUD AND FERENCZI'S RELATIONSHIP

The relationship between Freud and Ferenczi is a fascinating, controversial, and creative contact between two pivotal figures in the history of psychoanalysis. Ferenczi's relationship with Freud bears study because it helped shape the course of psychoanalysis for two decades, particularly during the development of psychoanalysis as an international movement in psychology, psychiatry, and psychotherapy. Furthermore, Ferenczi had a remarkable influence on Freud as well as on psychoanalysis. For the first ten or so years of their friendship, roughly 1909–1919, they were inseparable. Ideas about human behavior, theories about the development of psychopathology, technical recommendations about therapy, discussions about the lives of psychoanalysts, and the development of an international movement flowed back and forth between them, making it safe to say that the demarcation between Freud's thoughts and Ferenczi's is not always clear. Freud has acknowledged, for example, that his New Introductory Lectures were strongly influenced by talks that Ferenczi and he had as they walked the paths of Clark University before each lecture (Freud 1933c).

What began as an instant and electric friendship that captivated the minds and souls of these two pioneers of psychoanalysis ended in tragedy. Toward the latter part of his career, Ferenczi's daring clinical experiments in active and humanistic psychoanalysis puzzled, displeased, and finally alienated Freud. Freud disassociated himself from Ferenczi's work, turning his back on his once favorite pupil. Ferenczi was devastated and never recovered personally or professionally.

De Forest (1954) wrote

> The long and close friendship of Ferenczi and Freud is a fact and tradition of which the psychoanalytic school can be proud. That the threatened "fatal break" did not occur is a second fact for which it can be thankful. Both the long friendship and the avoidance of its destruction stand out as exceptional occurrences in the early years of psychoanalysis in Vienna. [p. 6]

Erich Fromm suggested that Freud's treatment of Ferenczi was one of the great shames in the history of psychoanalysis (Fromm 1959). Clara Thompson believed that Ferenczi was, in part, responsible for the tragedy because he couldn't break away and found his own movement (Thompson 1944).

The tragedy of Freud and Ferenczi's relationship has greatly influenced the development of psychoanalysis and Ferenczi's place in its history. It has

1. blurred the history of psychoanalytic theory and technique
2. robbed analysts of a meaningful role model for active and humanistic behavior
3. encouraged orthodoxy and discouraged clinical experimentation and elasticity
4. robbed Ferenczi of the special place he deserved in history of psychoanalysis and psychotherapy
5. removed Ferenczi's work from study by psychoanalysts and psychotherapists.

Both men contributed to this tragedy: Freud because of his authoritarianism, intolerance of criticism, and need for total devotion, and Ferenczi because of his timidity, need for approval, and denial of his differences with Freud. The unraveling of this tragedy can contribute to our understanding of the history of psychoanalysis and the place Ferenczi played in its development. The relationship deserves greater attention, and, it is hoped, that when the Freud/Ferenczi correspondence is fully published during the next several years, the history and meaning of their relationship will be more fully illuminated. The following is a chronology of the important events in the Freud/Ferenczi association to begin the process of developing an overview of the accomplishments and conflicts of their relationship.

THE CHRONOLOGY OF THE FREUD/FERENCZI RELATIONSHIP

Ferenczi was asked to review Freud's *Interpretation of Dreams* in Hungarian. Ferenczi paid casual attention to it and found it unscientific. However, as mentioned, he became fascinated with Jung's word association test, which led to his interest in psychoanalysis (Balint 1970).

Ferenczi read the existing literature in psychoanalysis (Balint 1970). He was encouraged to meet with Freud by a fellow Hungarian, Dr. F. Stein (Jones 1955).

The Fateful Meeting: "The Effect Was Electric"

On Sunday, February 2, 1908, shortly before the Salzburg Congress, Ferenczi met Freud for the first time. Jones (1955) wrote

> . . . [Ferenczi] had read *Interpretation of Dreams* on its appearance, but had dismissed it with an shrug of his shoulders. In 1907, however, Dr. F. Stein of Budapest, a psychopathologist who, through an introduction from Jung, was slightly acquainted with Freud personally, induced Ferenczi to give him another chance, and *this time the effect was electric.* He wrote to Freud and accompanied by Stein who introduced him, called on him on Sunday, February 2, 1908, shortly before the Salzburg Congress. [p. 34, italics added]

"My Dear Son"

The bond that was established was immediately positive and intense. Jones (1955) wrote, "The impression he made was such that he was invited to spend a fortnight in August with the Freud family, with whom he soon became a special favorite, on their holiday in Berchtes-Garden" (p. 34).

Freud addressed Ferenczi as "My dear son" (Jones 1955, p. 89) and wished him to marry his oldest daughter Mathilda. From then on they would be close friends until nearly the end of Ferenczi's life (Lorand 1966).

It is clear that Freud's immediate, positive response to Ferenczi was a rare occurrence, since he was generally reluctant to be involved with outsider and rarely received guests from abroad (Jones 1955).

Ferenczi Becomes Freud's Alter Ego

Ferenczi joined Freud as one of the first analysts to visit America. G. Stanley Hall, the first president of Clark University, Worcester, Massachusetts, invited Freud to lecture for the Twentieth Anniversary Commemoration of the university. Although Jones and Jung also accompanied the master to America, Ferenczi became Freud's alter ego in the preparation of these lectures, which introduced psychoanalysis to America. Freud wrote:

> I invited him to go with me to Worcester, Massachusetts, when in 1909 I was called upon to lecture there during a week of celebrations. In the morning, before the time had come for my lecture to begin, we would walk together in front of the University building and I would ask him to suggest what I should talk about that day. He thereupon gave me a sketch of what, half an hour later, I improvised in my lecture. In this way he had a share in the origin of the *Five Lectures*. [Freud 1933c, p. 227]

The Clark lectures not only introduced psychoanalysis to America, but also established Freudian psychology as a legitimate area of academic study. Ferenczi shared in this momentous accomplishment by his behind-the-scenes influence on Freud's lectures. Furthermore, it is likely that Freud needed Ferenczi's emotional support and friendship to make the trip and to turn it into a triumph for psychoanalysis.

Although Freud was unimpressed by America and had little good to say about his stay (Koelsch, 1970), Ferenczi would return to America for an extended stay years later and teach, analyze patients, train lay analysts, and influence an alternative psychoanalytic movement in America (see Chapter 19, this volume).

Ferenczi and Freud became inseparable. Their work and life become intertwined. For many years they traveled and took vacations together, discussing psychoanalysis and cases. These informal jaunts inspired future papers by both men (Freud 1933c).

Freud Asks Ferenczi to Help Found the International Psychoanalytic Society

Ferenczi's closeness to Freud was instrumental in the founding of the professional association of psychoanalysis. In 1910, at the Nuremberg Congress, Freud "charged Ferenczi with the task of making the necessary proposals for beginning a psychoanalytic society." (According to Jones, Ferenczi's "dictatorial side" caused the Viennese analysts great distress. It was only Jones's interventions that prevented a split in the ranks. See Chapter 6.)

"The Sicily Trip": The First Emotional Difficulty in Their Relationship

By 1910, Ferenczi was firmly established as Freud's closest friend in psychoanalysis. When Freud took his cherished vacations, he brought Ferenczi along as his traveling companion.

It was not until the Sicily trip a year later that Ferenczi and Freud experienced the first serious rift in their relationship. Jones was very critical of Ferenczi's behavior (Jones 1955, also see Chapter 6) and asserted that this trip was fateful for their relationship. Furthermore, Jones used the difficulties as the first indication that Ferenczi was mad. The difficulty was an indication that he was not a fit personal partner for Freud and that his work was an indication of his madness, not his clinical genius (Jones 1955).

The incident seems to be an indication of Ferenczi's desire to move emotionally closer to Freud, both in a personal and professional way. Freud was weary of emotional ties that were eventually disappointing and hurtful, especially since the Fliess affair (Freud 1954, Jones 1953, 1955). Freud apparently wanted a traveling companion with whom he could share the sights, as well as have a period of rest and protection (Schur 1972). Ferenczi wanted more: to continue the sharing of dreams, the continuation of self-analysis, a growing sense of emotional communion, and closeness. Freud wrote Ferenczi on October 6, 1910, in response to an apologetic letter from Ferenczi after his return to Budapest (Jones 1955).

Dear Friend:

You not only noticed, but also understood, that I no longer have any need to uncover my personality completely, and you correctly traced this back to the traumatic reason for it. Since Fliess's case, with the overcoming of which you recently saw me occupied, that need has been extinguished. A part of homosexual cathexis has been withdrawn and made use of to enlarge my own ego. I have succeeded where the paranoiac fails.

So when you look at it more closely you will find that we haven't so much to settle between us as perhaps you thought at first.

I would rather turn your attention to the present. [pp. 83–84]

One can safely conclude that Ferenczi's need for emotional closeness was expressed in a manner and at a time that encouraged a defensiveness in Freud. The master was not willing to tell his favorite pupil all his personal secrets or fully discuss his soured relationship with the person Ferenczi replaced in Freud's favor, Fliess. Ferenczi's push toward intimacy also encouraged a homosexual concern (Schur 1972).

Jones's version of the first difficulty in the Freud/Ferenczi relationship has been challenged. What Jones labeled Ferenczi's immaturity was actually Freud's authoritarianism. Ferenczi believed that he and Freud were going to author a paper jointly. On the first evening of the Sicily trip, Freud asked Ferenczi to take his dictation, not to jointly author the paper. Ferenczi refused. There was then a coolness between them (Grosskurth 1991).

Ferenczi Becomes an Ardent Practitioner and Teacher of Freudian Psychoanalysis

Freud proposed the basic rules of psychoanalytic technique between 1912 and 1915. Ferenczi immediately applied these rules to his understanding and practice of psychoanalysis (Ferenczi 1919a,b, 1920, 1924b, 1925a,b). There was not at the time, nor since, a more eager student or enthusiastic clinician of psychoanalysis. Freud began to turn his attention to theory, feeling that Ferenczi would become the master of technique.

The Establishment of the Hungarian Psychoanalytic Society

Ferenczi began to play a significant role in what Freud called the external affairs of psychoanalysis (De Forest 1954, Roazen 1975). The first meeting of the Hungarian Psychoanalytic Society had been held in 1913 under Ferenczi's leadership. Freud (1923a) stated that under Ferenczi's guidance it became "a center of intense and productive work and was distinguished by an accumulation of abilities such as were exhibited in combination by no other Branch Society" (p. 268).

The Committee of Ring Holders

In May 1913, Sigmund Freud gave each of his small group of associates, who had organized into a committee to assist him, a Greek intaglio from his private collection. The members of the committee, who by 1920 had increased to seven, had these intaglios mounted in gold rings. Freud had such a ring, with an intaglio of the head of Jupiter. These rings became valued possessions of the members of the committee (Freud Museum 1987, Jones 1955, Roazen 1975).

Ferenczi Enters Analysis with Freud

Ferenczi became one of the first analysts to undergo a personal psychoanalysis as part of his professional training. According to Jones, Ferenczi underwent an analysis with Freud for three weeks in October 1914 and for another three weeks (with two sessions daily) in June 1916 (Freud 1933c, Jones 1955, 1957, Roazen 1975). Formal analysis of the kind and duration as we now know it was not yet in place. Freud's analysis of Ferenczi was necessarily incomplete, as witness Ferenczi's criticisms of it in the *Clinical Diary* (Ferenczi 1932c). Ferenczi at one point offered to analyze Freud and Freud did not resent it.

There is a very illuminating glimpse into their analysis as chronicled in a disguised example in Freud's "Analysis Terminable and Interminable." In one example, Freud (1937) talks about "a certain man, who had himself practiced analysis with great success," who had "neurotic impediments" and entered analysis with "someone . . . he regarded as superior to himself" (p. 221). Jones suggested that these quotes referred to Ferenczi and Freud (Jones 1957). Freud went on to illuminate what seemed like a transference/countertransference bind. After what Freud termed a successful analysis— " . . . this critical illumination of his own self had a completely successful result" (p. 221)—Ferenczi "for no assignable externable reason . . . reproached him [the analyst, Freud] for having failed to give him a complete analysis" (p. 221). Freud was shocked and apparently hurt that his favorite son was accusing him of not paying "attention to the possibilities of a negative transference" (p. 221). He defended himself against the accusation by pointing out that the negative transference wasn't obvious in the analysis and that to point it out, if he was aware of it (which he wasn't), would have been to violate the patient's frame of reference. Finally, Freud questioned whether the analytic difficulty was a result of transference.

Ferenczi Establishes Budapest as a World Capital of Psychoanalysis

In this year, 1918, Ferenczi was elected president of the International Psychoanalytic Society. The Budapest Congress marked a turning point for Freud's movement. Budapest gave psychoanalysis a remarkable welcome. It was a milestone in the history of psychoanalysis (Roazen 1975). The bond between Freud and Ferenczi strengthened still further.

The Budapest Congress: 1918.   The Congress, held in the second half of September 1918, was in every respect a great success. The festive spirit that pervaded it was in marked contrast to the country's expectation of the imminent collapse of the Hapsburg Empire.

After the Congress, Freud wrote Ferenczi a glowing letter (Schur 1972):

> Do you remember the prophetic words I uttered before the first Congress in Salzburg, when I said that we expected great things from you?
>
> I am reveling in satisfaction, my heart is light since I know that my problem child, my life's work, is protected by your interest and that of others, and its future taken care of. I shall be able to see better times approaching, even if I do so from a distance. [p. 316]

Freud's dream of establishing the analytic capital of Europe outside Vienna seemed to be on the verge of reality. He had been severely disappointed when he had failed to achieve this dream with Jung in Zurich (Roazen 1975). However, with the advent of World War I, the Hapsburg Empire collapsed, isolating Hungary from the rest of the world. Ferenczi resigned from the presidency of the International Psychoanalytic Association. In addition, Anton von Freund, a wealthy Hungarian who was to finance a psychoanalytic institute in Budapest, died in January 1920 (Roazen 1975). Freud's dream of establishing Budapest as the capital of the psychoanalytic world and of placing Ferenczi as his heir apparent came to an end.

Ferenczi became the first university professor in psychoanalysis at the University of Budapest (March–August 1919). When political difficulties arose, Ferenczi lost his professorial chair, and the center of psychoanalysis returned to Vienna (Roazen 1975).

Freud Passes the Mantle to Ferenczi

In his last paper on technique, Freud made a dramatic and daring declaration for the future of psychoanalysis. In so doing, he passed the mantle to Ferenczi.

> Developments in our therapy therefore, will no doubt proceed along other levels; first and foremost, along the one which Ferenczi, in his paper "Technical Difficulties in an Analysis of Hysteria" (1919) has lately termed "activity" on the part of the analyst. [Freud 1919 [1918], pp. 161–162]

With this declaration, Freud established Ferenczi as the heir apparent to psychoanalysis (as Jung had once been in an earlier time). He also helped establish *active analysis* as the next direction for the evolution of psychoanalysis. Freud left technical recommendations to Ferenczi to develop and from then on concentrated on theory (Roazen 1975). Ferenczi became the foremost clinician in psychoanalysis, fully supported by Freud. No doubt many analysts both envied and hated Ferenczi for this special place at Freud's side and the status, power, and recognition it afforded him. It is conceivable that among these detractors was Jones, who believed that Freud had a special mission for him within the psychoanalytic movement.

Ferenczi Develops *Active Psychoanalysis* with Freud's Support and Approval

In a series of innovative and daring clinical experiments, Ferenczi began to alter the role of the analyst, the participation of the analysand, and the process of the therapeutic interaction, contributing new dimensions to psychoanalytic therapy. Initially, Ferenczi was excited by Freud's paper "On Transference Love," which introduced "the rule of abstinence" (Freud 1915 [1914], p. 165). He used Freud's notions of withholding premature gratification of neurotic needs to experiment with the interaction within an analytic session. In a series of daring clinical experiments, he outlined the use of activity by the analyst to directly prohibit the analysand from receiving emotional gratification from neurotic symptoms (Ferenczi 1919a,b, 1920, 1924b, 1925a,b).

Ferenczi pushed the active role of the analyst, as regards the prohibition of premature neurotic gratification, as far as he could, before realizing its limitations (Ferenczi 1925a). He was also concerned about the criticisms of his active method by members of the analytic community (Glover 1924).

Ferenczi began to receive negative reaction from conservative analysts who saw his clinical experiments as a serious deviation from Freudian psychoanalysis (Glover 1924). These criticisms labeled Ferenczi as a dissident and radically set him apart from the conservative members of Freud's inner circle. From that moment onward, some of his peers—notably Abraham, Jones, and Glover, who were influential both within the psychoanalytic community and with Freud—encouraged a negative view of Ferenczi as a dissident analyst. This label was then, as it now, a serious blow to one's status and influence within the mainstream of the psychoanalytic community, which has always maintained a decidedly conservative stance. These groups of analysts who became overtly critical of Ferenczi did so without actually reflecting Freud's sentiments, even though part of their motivation may have been to please him by criticizing anyone who did not strictly maintain his rules of technique. Their vehement criticisms of Ferenczi were actually without Freud's approval, since he supported and approved of these clinical experiments in "activity" and the active method of psychoanalysis. Actually, Freud himself began the deviation from his own method (see Chapter 7).

There were some, like Jones, who used the opportunity of Ferenczi's clinical experiments to begin a campaign to discredit him as a significant influence in psychoanalysis. Jones had his own personal reasons for attacking Ferenczi. Others, like Abraham and Glover, were reflecting their own conservatism in thinking and clinical functioning. These criticisms of Ferenczi's deviations ushered in the infamous phenomenon in psychoanalysis that is still present today. There are those analysts who designate themselves "the keepers of the keys"; they will keep psychoanalysis pure and clean from any contaminating influence. They believe that they alone know what Freud had in mind when he founded psychoanalysis, using him as a vehicle for their own conservative and even reactionary thinking and political maneuvers. Ferenczi suffered an irretrievable blow to his reputation, and person because of this type of repressive and overly conservative thinking.

The *Rundbriefe* (Circulating Letters)

The Committee of Ring Holders wrote *Rundbriefe* (circulating letters) to one another on the suggestion of Sigmund Freud:

> If the letters are read as a record of scientific discussion they would be disappointing. . . . The true importance of this correspondence is very different and in character twofold:
> The Ring Holders kept their watch for the Professor and for the psychoanalytic movement through times in which all concepts of established existence were shattered by inflation and world crises. . . .
> The second importance of these documents is the candid insight into such a rare and unique group of creative people who kept working together for these years and then continued in different forms for many years afterwards until death. [Grotjahn 1973, p. 85]

The Developmental Aims of Psychoanalysis

In collaboration with Rank, Ferenczi published the first book to be critical of psychoanalysis by members of the inner circle. This book, *The Developmental Aims of Psychoanalysis*, was, however, not a polemic against psychoanalysis. It was a landmark exposition of the shortcomings of psychoanalysis as it had developed up to the 1920s and pointed the way for a new theory and technique of the treatment process.

Ferenczi and Rank (1925) were concerned that psychoanalysis had failed to evolve with experience and had become fixed. Their greatest fear was that psychoanalysis had overemphasized the intellectual reconstruction of early childhood at the neglect of emotional experiencing." The book went on to reintroduce the emotional component in psychoanalytic therapy Ferenczi and Rank were attempting to emphasize a neglected area of therapy and suggested that psychoanalysis should evolve in this direction. Although one could view the reemphasis on the emotional component as the necessary holistic approach to a deeper and more emotionally meaningful analysis, Ferenczi and Rank placed additional emphasis on the interpersonal component, a radical departure for psychoanalysis.

Apparently, the beginning of Freud's concern about his favorite pupil's work surfaced with this publication. Although Freud was generally supportive of the book, both Abraham and Jones were not (Roazen 1975). They felt the book contained heresy and warned Freud of a revival of Jung's ideas in a new guise. Freud shared Abraham's and Jones's concerns with Rank, who in turn told Ferenczi. Both Rank and Ferenczi became angry. Ferenczi, however, also felt hurt and rejected by Freud's reservations (Roazen 1975). But Freud wrote to reassure Ferenczi on February 4, 1924.

> I know that I am not very accessible and find it hard to assimilate alien thoughts that do not quite lie in my path. It takes quite a time before I can form a judgement about them, so that in the interval I have to suspend judgement.
>   . . . That you or Rank should in your independent flights ever leave the ground of psychoanalysis seems to me out of the question. Why shouldn't you therefore have the right to try if things won't work in another way from that I had thought? If you go astray in so doing you will find that out yourself some time or other, I will take the liberty of pointing it out to you as soon as I am myself sure about it. [Jones 1957, pp. 57–58]

This letter is significant in the history of psychoanalysis, because it clearly stated Freud's endorsement of an evolutionary attitude toward both psychoanalytic theory and technique, which Ferenczi and Rank's book represented. What is more, it marked a special aspect of Freud's openness and flexibility to two pupils who dared to deviate from his thinking. It suggested a warmer, humanistic side to the master's relationship with his dissident pupils. This particular affection and respect for his favorite pupil prevented a split at that time.

However, Freud's special relationship with Ferenczi apparently did go through a transformation after this period. It is conceivable that events that were to unfold had begun to take shape during the period of controversy stirred by *The Development of Psychoanalysis*. Although Freud was not interested in a break with Ferenczi, others were preparing for this prospect.

Thalassa: A Theory of Genitality
(Freud/Ferenczi Collaboration)

Ferenczi reluctantly published his speculative theory on the origins of the human psyche (Ferenczi 1924a) following Freud's urging (Freud 1933b, Gedo 1976). Freud (1933c) would later praise *Thalassa* as the apogee of Ferenczi's scientific accomplishments.

It is clear that *Thalassa* was a collaborative effort between Ferenczi and Freud. This essay was developed from the 1915 Hungarian translation of Freud's "Three Essays on the Theory of Sexuality." *Thalassa* was originally discussed with Freud as early as 1919, but Ferenczi could not bring himself to write down the material (Simon 1984).

In a letter from Freud to Abraham, dated November 11, 1917, the collaboration is confirmed (Schur 1972).

> Have I really not told you anything about the Lamarck idea? It arose between Ferenczi and me, but neither of us has the time or spirit to tackle it at present. The idea is to put Lamarck entirely on our ground and to show that the "necessity" that according to him creates and transforms organs is nothing but the power of unconscious ideas over one's own body, of which we see remnants in hysteria, in short the "omnipotence of thoughts." This would actually supply a psycho-analytic explanation of adaptation; it would put the coping stone on psycho-analysis. . . . [pp. 312–313]

Freud was clearly enamored of his favorite pupil during this period and saw Ferenczi's bioanalysis as the future direction of psychoanalysis, just as he had earlier suggested that Ferenczi's active method would be (see "Freud Passes the Mantle to Ferenczi," this chapter). Freud's (1933c) own words pay the fitting tribute to their relationship as well as to his own relationship with the material:

> But he was holding back his most brilliant and most fertile achievement. I knew of it, and in the closing sentence of my contribution I

urged him to give it to us. Then, in 1924, his *Versuch einer Genital-theorie* appeared. This little book is a biological rather than a psychoanalytic study; it is an application of the attitudes and insights associated with psychoanalysis to the biology of the sexual processes and beyond them, to organic life in general. . . . We lay the little book aside with a feeling: "This is almost too much to take in at a first reading; I will read it again after a while." But it is not only I who feel like this. It is probable that some time in the future there will really be a "bio-analysis" as Ferenczi has prophesied. . . . [Freud 1933c, pp. 228–229]

Freud's reference to other analysts who shared his enthusiasm for *Thalassa* included Federn (1933) and Rado (1933) (see Gedo 1968, pp. 376–377, for a negative reaction).

Ferenczi Returns to America without Freud

Ferenczi came to New York City for an eight-month stay to lecture at The New School for Social Research, apparently with Freud's approval (Roazen 1975). There were several important activities that Ferenczi participated in that had a great influence on the development of American psychoanalysis.

1. Lecturing at the New School and promoting interest in psychoanalysis in America (Quen and Carlson 1978).
2. Giving classes on treatment techniques for the New York Psychoanalytic Society (Quen and Carlson 1978).
3. Conducting several analyses while in New York City. There is a documented account of one such experience by a patient (Mrs. F. H. 1952, 1954). Another analysand is likely to have been Izette De Forest (De Forest 1954).
4. Lecturing at St. Elizabeth's Hospital in Washington (Quen and Carlson 1978).
5. Training lay analysts (Quen and Carlson 1978).

These activities influenced the direction of American psychoanalysis (Quen and Carlson 1978): "Sullivan had been favorably impressed by Ferenczi's lectures in the United States during his 1926–27 visit. When

Clara Thompson decided to journey to Europe for personal analysis, Sullivan recommended that she go to Ferenczi. Later, Sullivan briefly became a psychoanalytic patient of Thompson" (p. 104). Ferenczi's ideas and methods, no doubt, found their way into Thompson's analysis of Sullivan, as well as their theoretical and clinical discussions at weekly seminars.

Thompson (1950a) indicated Ferenczi's influence in the development of her interpersonal approach to psychoanalysis.

> In 1928, I went to Budapest to study with Ferenczi and found myself in the midst of his experimentation with his "relaxation" therapy. I found Sullivan's and Ferenczi's approach more in keeping with my own way of thinking than the classical Freudian methods. [p. v]

Ferenczi Offers to Analyze Freud

Ferenczi offered to come to Vienna to analyze Freud (Jones 1957). It was a tribute to their loving relationship that Ferenczi felt free to make the offer on the basis of concern and that Freud was not offended by it. The reason for the offer and Freud's reaction are chronicled by Jones (1957).

> On February 17 and 19 Freud suffered in the street mild attacks of angina pectoris (steno-cardia); the pain was not accompanied by any dyspnoea or anxiety. On the second occasion he found himself only a few steps away from the house of a friend, Dr. Ludwig Braun, a well-known physician, so he managed to get there [Letter to Felix Deutsch, March 17, 1926]. Braun made the diagnosis of myocarditis and advised a fortnight's treatment in a sanitorium. Freud resisted the advice and was for once optimistic about his condition, which, doubtless correctly, he attributed to an intolerance of tobacco. He had been smoking some de-nicotined cigars, but even these had produced on each occasion some cardiac discomfort; he regarded it as an ominous sign that he was not finding abstinence at all hard [Ferenczi, February 24, 1926]. Ferenczi was convinced that the condition was psychological and offered to come to Vienna for some months to analyze him [Letter to Freud from Ferenczi, February 26, 1926]. Freud was touched by the offer and in thanking him added:

There may well be a psychological route and it is extremely doubtful if that can be controlled through analysis; then when one is three score and ten has one not a right to every kind of rest? [Letter to Ferenczi February 27, 1926] [p. 120]

Ferenczi Turns Away from Freud

In 1927, Ferenczi returned to Budapest from his successful stay in America. Freud was irritated that Ferenczi did not directly visit him on his return to Europe (Roazen 1975). Freud later described Ferenczi as seeming changed after his return from the United States. He found him to be more withdrawn, less inclined to share his clinical functioning and ideas. Freud speculated that in retrospect it was at this juncture that Ferenczi began to be concerned with creating a more emotionally tender climate in psychoanalysis (Freud 1933c).

The Emergence of Humanistic Psychoanalysis: The Ferenczian Alternative to Freudian Analysis

Although he did not intend to produce an alternative method to Freudian psychoanalysis, Ferenczi's departures from tradition, his dedication to work with difficult cases, his growing independence from Freud, and the conservative analytic community's desire to censor his work produced a force that separated Ferenczi from the mainstream of psychoanalysis. Wounded but undaunted, Ferenczi, with the support of his grateful patients and dedicated analysands and pupils, pursued an alternate, dissident form of psychoanalysis. It combined the departures he had pioneered in the use of activity with developments in the empathic method and use of the humanistic/interpersonal aspects of the psychoanalytic situation. There were five significant papers and a clinical diary that signaled the advent of this humanistic psychoanalysis: (1) "The Elasticity of Psychoanalytic Technique," 1928; (2) "The Principle of Relaxation and Neo-Catharsis," 1930; (3) "Child Analysis in the Analysis of Adults," 1931; (4) Clinical Diary, 1932; and (5) "The Confusion of Tongues between Adults and Children: The Language of Tenderness and of Passion," 1933.

The "Elasticity" paper introduced the empathic method in psychoanalysis. Ferenczi, building upon Freud's notion of tact, developed the notion that resistances, difficulties in the psychoanalytic situation, and patient complaints should be dealt with by empathy. It signaled a departure from the Freudian tradition of interpretation and encouraged a two-person view of resistance and the analytic relationship.

Freud was not only pleased with Ferenczi's new developments, but saw the employment of empathy as within the province of Freudian psychoanalysis. He wrote:

> Your accompanying production ["Elasticity" paper] displays that judicious maturity you have acquired of late years, in respect of which no one approaches you. *The title is excellent and deserves a wider provenance. . . . The only criticism I have of your paper is that it is not three times larger and divided into three parts. There is no doubt that you have much more to say on similar lines, and it would be very beneficial to have it.* [Jones 1953, p. 241, italics added]

There was a gentle reproach in Freud's letter, however, where he expressed concern about the departure from interpretation and the analysis of resistance.

> . . . but I have some misgivings about the manner in which you make those concessions. All those who have no tact will see in what you write a justification for arbitrariness, i.e., subjectivity, the influence of their own unmastered complexes. . . . But with beginners, one therefore has to rob the idea of "tact" of its mystical character. [Jones 1953, p. 241]

In "The Principle of Relaxation and Neocatharsis," Ferenczi began to expand on his dissident view by presenting a radical departure from the Freudian method. His ideas and practices centered around democratizing the relationship between the analyst and analysand and creating an emotionally open and accepting atmosphere. This revolutionary work did have its adherents among the developing liberal wing of second generation psychoanalytic pioneers (Alexander 1933).

With the publication of "Child Analysis in the Analysis of Adults," Ferenczi expanded his humanistic psychoanalysis still further. He began to theorize about the development of psychopathology in childhood as springing from parental rejection and a lack of loving, nurturant contact. Therapy of the adult would then involve a corrective emotional experience, where the analyst would provide the necessary love and affection to heal the ailing child in the adult.

Ferenczi's *Clinical Diary*, written in 1932 and known only to those closest to him, was kept secret from Freud. The *Diary* was not completed because Ferenczi had to interrupt his practice due to his terminal illness. In it, Ferenczi chronicled his advanced clinical experiments with narcissistic, borderline, and psychotic cases, extending his empathic method to mutual analysis (Ferenczi 1932c). Ferenczi knew that Freud would not approve of his forays into therapist self-disclosures, revealing countertransference reactions, allowing the patient to be the therapist to the analyst, and a variety of indulgences (parameters) to meet the intense emotional needs of difficult cases.

The *Diary* was not published until 1985, an amazing fifty-two years after Ferenczi's death, and then only in French (Ferenczi 1932b). The English version of the *Diary* was published in 1988 (Ferenczi 1932c). Why such a delay in publication? As with the "Confusion of Tongues" paper (Ferenczi 1933) and the Freud/Ferenczi correspondence, the *Clinical Diary* contains controversial material that the ruling body in psychoanalysis did not wish to confront. Witness the discussion by Ferenczi's literary executor not to reveal the *Diary* upon his death in 1933.

> After his death, at least three among us, Vilma Kovacs, Alice Balint and myself [Michael Balint], read considerable excerpts from *The Diary*. The unanimous advice we gave Madame Ferenczi, and she followed this advice, was to postpone its publication for the time being. We thought it would be preferable to wait until the immediate repercussions of the disagreement between Freud and Ferenczi had quieted down. This would give time during which a more favorable atmosphere could be created—more favorable to the objective evaluation of Ferenczi's ideas, which are contained in this Diary. [Balint 1988, p. 219]

Balint (1988), in his introduction to the *Diary*, made what seems like a remarkable statement regarding Freud's approval of Ferenczi's ideas.

> During the few years that followed, the three of us devoted our energies to gather, edit, and translate the materials corresponding to Volumes II and IV of the *Bausteine*. Of course, not only did we

inform Freud of our intention, but we sent him all the material then not published. *We can assert that he followed our work with interest and did not have a single objection to any part of the text we proposed; on the contrary, he expressed his admiration for Ferenczi's ideas unknown to him till then.* [italics added] [Balint 1988, p. 219]

But whatever favorable reaction Balint credits Freud with having, he judged that the analytic community was not ready for the *Diary* until 1969, when he was under the impression the material would be published.

"The Confusion of Tongues between Children and Adults: The Language of Tenderness and Passion" brought Ferenczi into the final stages of dissidence in psychoanalysis. In this paper, he made his most radical departure from Freud's method. In fact, the revolutionary ideas he proposed could not be tolerated by either Freud or the analytic establishment. Ferenczi's proposal reintroduced Freud's original "Seduction Theory" into psychoanalysis. He postulated that Freud was correct in hypothesizing that the origins of neurosis were connected to sexually abusive behavior by adults toward children. Freud was clearly angry with Ferenczi and wished him not to deliver or publish this paper. Ferenczi's notions have serious consequences for rethinking Freud's oedipal theory of neuroses (Masson 1984).

On August 24, 1932, Freud asked Ferenczi not to publish the paper. Roazen (1975) wrote that "Freud thought the paper could do his reputation no good . . . begged him not to read it" at the Wiesbaden Congress of that year (p. 368).

Jones (1957) reported that the analytic community also had its concerns: " . . . other leaders in the movement thought it would be scandalous to read such a paper before a psychoanalytic congress"(p. 173).

J. M. Masson has recently thrown some additional light on Freud's reaction to Ferenczi's last paper. Janet Malcolm (1983b) wrote

Eissler did to me what Freud did to Ferenczi. This was one of the things I found in Anna Freud's house that appalled me so much. I found evidence of how Freud dumped Ferenczi. I found a packet of letters in Freud's desk between Freud and Jones and Eitingon showing how they ganged up on Ferenczi and tried to prevent him from reading his last paper at the Wiesbaden Conference of 1932. [p. 101, quoting Jeffrey Moussaieff Masson]

Freud Openly Criticizes Ferenczi's Interactions with Patients

Freud and Ferenczi's relationship was beginning to show signs of strain and conflict. Freud wrote to Ferenczi beginning to express his displeasure about reports he had heard that Ferenczi was kissing his patients. The famous "kissing letter" indicates Freud's concern with Ferenczi's clinical experiments with "the tender mother transference," especially the use of the physical parameter. Although Freud was comfortable with the issue of parameters, he was critical of Ferenczi's physical behavior with patients. However, Freud failed to make the crucial distinction between maternal touching and erotic contact. There is no evidence to suggest Ferenczi had sexual contact with patients. Perhaps Ferenczi's behavior stimulated some conflictual sexual issues for Freud, which will be discussed more fully in subsequent chapters.

Following is the the "kissing letter" from Freud to Ferenczi, on December 13, 1931 (Jones 1957):

> I see that the differences between us come to a head in a technical detail which is well worth discussing. You have not made a secret of the fact that you kiss your patients and let them kiss you; I had also heard that from a patient of my own. Now when you decide to give a full account of your technique and its results you will have to choose between two ways: either you relate this or you conceal it. The latter, as you may well think, is dishonorable. What one does in one's technique one has to defend openly. . . . Now I am assuredly not one of those who from prudishness or from consideration of bourgeois convention would condemn little erotic gratifications of this kind. I am also aware that in the time of the Nibelungs a kiss was a harmless greeting granted to every guest. I am further of the opinion that analysis is possible even in Soviet Russia where so far as the State is concerned there is full sexual freedom.
>
> But that does not alter the facts that we are not living in Russia and that with us a kiss signifies a certain erotic intimacy. We have hitherto in our technique, held to the conclusion that patients are to be refused erotic gratifications. You know too that where more extensive gratifications are not to be had milder caresses very easily take over their role, in love affairs, on the stage, etc.

Now picture what will be the result of publishing your technique. There is no revolutionary who is not driven out of the field by a still more radical one. A number of independent thinkers in matters of technique will say to themselves: why stop at a kiss? Certainly one gets further when one adopts "pawing" as well, which after all, doesn't make a baby. And then bolder ones will come along who will go further to peeping and showing and soon we shall have accepted in the technique of analysis the whole repertoire of demiviergerie and petting-parties, resulting in an enormous increase of interest in psycho-analysis among both analysts and patients. The new adherent, however, will easily claim too much of this interest for himself, the younger of your colleagues will find it hard to stop at the point they originally intended, and God The Father Ferenczi gazing at the lively scene he has created will perhaps say to himself: maybe after all I should have halted in my technique of motherly affection before the kiss. [pp. 163–164]

Freud's letter does not yet reach the proportions of criticism and hostility he showed in the past to other dissidents. The fight with Adler was a serious example of Freud's anger and rejection (Quen and Carlson 1978):

Once Freud decided that the follower had turned into a dissenter, his fundamental tactic was all-out war, and his wrath was ill-concealed. Of Adler, after their break, Freud said to Fritz Wittels, "I have made a pygmy great." To Abraham, Freud wrote about Adler's "venom and meanness." To Lou Andreas-Salome, he declared that Adler was "a loathsome individual." Hanns Sachs, a devoted disciple to the end, stood in awe of Freud's battle with Adler: "In the execution of this duty he was untiring and unending, hard and sharp like steel, a 'good hater' close to the limits of vindictiveness." [pp. 15–16]

Freud apparently did not wish to alienate Ferenczi and did not possess the same venom for him that he had for Adler. He was aware that Ferenczi's clinical experiments with physical activity were still an attempt to expand the Freudian method of psychoanalysis. Ferenczi, in turn, was following his own ideas and feelings, never believing that Freud would break away from him.

The Final Hours: Freud Turns His Back on Ferenczi

On August 24, 1932, the two men met for the last time. The meeting was strained. Freud told Ferenczi not to publish the "Confusion of Tongues" paper. As the meeting ended, Ferenczi put his hand out to shake the master's hand. Freud did not shake hands. Ferenczi was crushed (Fromm 1959, Roazen 1975). So ended in tragedy one of the most loving and special relationships in the history of psychoanalysis. Recently, Grünberger (1980) reported this tragic ending through the eyes of an eyewitness.

> . . . when Ferenczi developed his clearly dissident views, Freud's reaction was extremely harsh. A characteristic episode in this connection has been reported by the journalist Zsofia Denes (1970), a niece of Ferenczi's wife; by Izette [D]e Forest (1954), an analysand of Ferenczi; and also by Erich Fromm (1959). According to these accounts, when Ferenczi explained his new psychoanalytic views to Freud (this took place in the villa at Semmerring where Freud was spending his summer holiday), the master listened to him with irritable impatience, made a few dry remarks, and, when Ferenczi extended his hand to say good-bye, Freud turned his back and precipitously left the room. Denes, who had earlier been introduced to Freud by Ferenczi for a consultation and then for an interview, and who was waiting for Ferenczi in another room, was struck by Freud's extreme coldness in contrast to his first reception of her, and she could not help feeling that something fundamental had occurred in the relationship between the two men. An intimate in the household, whom Freud used to call "my dear son," Ferenczi had had to have himself announced this time and was granted only a brief and formal audience. Only Gizella was given a friendly smile, and it was she who, on leaving, dissolved in tears. [p. 138]

Freud's Obituary of Ferenczi

Freud returned to his affectionate thoughts about his favorite pupil in his glowing eulogy of Ferenczi. Some additional material not previously quoted indicates the lasting tribute to Ferenczi, his and Freud's incredible relationship, and his place in psychoanalytic history.

> . . . It fell to me in January, 1926, to write an obituary of our unforgettable friend, Karl Abraham. A few years earlier, in 1923, I could congratulate Sándor Ferenczi on the completion of his fiftieth year. To-day, scarcely a decade later, it grieves me that I have outlived him too. In what I wrote for his birthday I was able to celebrate openly his versatility and originality and the richness of his gifts; but the discretion imposed on a friend forbade my speaking of his lovable and affectionate personality, with its readiness to welcome everything of significance.
>
> Since the days when he was led to me by his interest in psycho-analysis, still in its youth, we have shared many things with each other. . . . at the Nuremberg Congress of 1910, I arranged that he should propose the organization of analysts into an international association—a scheme which we had thought out together. With slight modifications it was accepted and is in force to this day. For many successive years we spent the autumn holidays together in Italy, and a number of papers that appeared later in the literature under his or my name took their first shape in our talks there. When the outbreak of the World War put an end to our freedom of movement, and paralysed our analytic activity as well, he made use of the interval to begin his analysis with me. This met with a break when he was called up for military service, but he was able to resume it later. The feeling of a secure common bond, which grew up between us from so many shared experiences, was not interrupted when, late in life unfortunately, he was united to the outstanding woman who mourns him to-day as his widow.
>
> Ten years ago, when the *Internationale Zeitschrift* [and the *International Journal*] dedicated a special number to Ferenczi on his fiftieth birthday, he had already published most of the works which have made all analysts into his pupils. But he was holding back his most brilliant and most fertile achievement. I knew of it, and in the closing sentence of my contribution I urged him to give it to us. Then, in 1924, his *Versuch einer Genitaltheorie* appeared. This little book is a biological rather than a psycho-analytic study; it is an application of the attitudes and insights associated with psycho-analysis to the biology of the sexual processes and, beyond them, to

organic life in general. It was perhaps the boldest appliation of psycho-analysis that was ever attempted. Ferenczi has prophesied, and it will have to cast back to the *Versuch einer Genitaltheorie.*

After this summit of achievement, it came about that our friend slowly drifted away from us. On his return from a period of work in America he seemed to withdraw more and more into solitary work, though he had previously taken the liveliest share in all that happened in analytic circles. . . . Shortly before completing his sixtieth year he succumbed to pernicious anaemia. It is impossible to believe that the history of our science will ever forget him. (Freud 1933c, pp. 227–229).

FREUD AND FERENCZI: THE MEANING
   ## OF THEIR RELATIONSHIP

The years from 1924 to 1933 marked a period of emotional and professional upheaval for Ferenczi. This change was brought about by several factors, both positive and negative. Ferenczi needed to pursue his own theoretical and clinical ideas. He was an innovator, as was Freud. Both his personality and his intellectual interests moved him in the direction of change, experimentation, and innovation. Like Freud, he was a man who had a mission. Freud could not rest in his search to systematize man's unconscious behavior. Ferenczi could no sooner abandon his search for the techniques of how to cure emotional illness than could Freud give up his quest. In that enduring search to unravel the mysteries of human misery and its amelioration, they were very much alike. This quest was one of the forces that attracted these two great men to one another and kept their emotional bond cemented. Roazen (1975) pointed out the significance of the extended relationship that existed between Freud and Ferenczi: "That Freud took to Ferenczi in the first place, so many years earlier, and held him in the movement as long as he did, should be considered as least as important as Freud's final rejection of him" (p. 368).

Freud understood Ferenczi's need to pursue his own quest. After all, it was Freud who first suggested that Ferenczi develop the active method. But neither of them could have foreseen where this experimentation would eventually lead. It has been suggested by Ferenczi's enemies that the road toward his interpersonal and humanistic psychoanalytic method was taken because he was driven by an emotional disorder. But this journey was the expression of his creative, not pathologic, urges. It was a combination of political and sibling rivalry as well as the pressure to adhere to the orthodox position that gave rise to Ferenczi's enemies. Ferenczi's primary rival for Freud's affection and status within the inner circle was Jones. There were many factors in the Jones/Ferenczi rivalry. Jones apparently never recovered from Freud's rejecting him for analysis and rather displaced that anger onto Ferenczi. His analysis with Ferenczi did not adequately work through his negative transferences to Freud or Ferenczi. There are no materials available that delineate Ferenczi's analysis of Jones (except an unrevealing segment in Jones's autobiography – see Chapter 6). In any event, Ferenczi should have analyzed Jones's disappointment in not being able to have Freud as his analyst and should have uncovered the negative transference toward him. The analysis took place prior to Ferenczi's humanistic method, so he used an active Freudian approach. But we know from Freud's analysis of Ferenczi that this method produced serious shortcomings in the analysis of negative transferences (Freud 1933c).

The master's relationship to his followers was complicated by both Freud's personality and the personal and political factors that were so much a part of the psychoanalytic movement. Several analysts have commented on these factors. Grotjahn (1971) listed his notion of the Freud/follower dynamic: "He considered himself a patriarch to his sons and he may never have fully realized his role as a nursing mother to a group of grown children" (p. 15).

Fromm (1959) raised the issue of Freud's authoritarian side in his relationship with Ferenczi.

An interesting issue has also been raised regarding the inherent conflict that arises in psychoanalytic work. Lorand (1975–1976) wrote:

> . . . my friend Bertram Lewis many years ago drew my attention to what he considered a major divisive element within the psychoanalytic movement. Inevitably, he felt, dissension and discord arise among those who work with unconscious material for any length of time. . . . [p. 706]

Hanns Sachs (1944) noted that the analyst may be all too human in his or her "repressed affect" against a substitute father, with rebellion, hate, resentment, and other petty spites playing all sorts of nasty tricks.

Individual personality issues abound in the history of the psychoanalytic movement. Jones, the outstanding critic of Ferenczi, demonstrated many personal conflicts with colleagues.

> In 1923, for example, my old friend Ernest Jones would find it "monstrous that personal factors should be pushed into scientific movements like ours." Yet, Jones himself proved to be extremely jealous about his position in English psychoanalysis and kept competitors at a distance. When Reik wanted to move to England, he prevented it, and he also effectively kept Eidelberg from settling in London, urging him to settle in Oxford instead. It was Jones also who ruled that no qualified analyst could give lectures on psychoanalysis in London without his approval. [Lorand 1975–1976, p. 706]

Ferenczi's "Madness" (Regression) and His Conflicts with Freud

The meaning of the Freud/Ferenczi conflict has been the subject of much debate. By now, we have several conflicting proposals by his analysands, students, and detractors as well as champions (Balint 1933, 1949, 1968b, Covello 1984, De Forest 1954, Dupont 1988a, Fromm 1959, 1963, 1970, Gedo 1968, 1986b, Grünberger 1980, Haynal 1987, Jones 1955–57, Ludmer 1988, Masson 1984, Nemes 1988, Rachman 1984a, Roazen 1975, Thompson 1942, 1944). Ferenczi's detractors, claim, in essence, that his "madness" was at the heart of the conflict with Freud. Historically, this argument was first established by Jones in his obituary of Ferenczi (Jones 1933) and then carefully elaborated on in his Freud biography (Jones 1955–1957).

Jones asserted that Ferenczi was psychotic during the latter part of his life. According to Jones, this mental derangement explained the deviations from Freud in theory and technique, as well as Ferenczi's personal conflicts with Freud and his alienation from the analytic community (see Chapter 6 for a discussion of Ferenczi's "madness"). Although eyewitness reports disagree with Jones's accusations (Balint 1958, De Forest 1954, Fromm 1959, 1963, 1970, Thompson 1944), there continues to this day the idea that Ferenczi's conflict with Freud (as well as his dissident work) was a function of his psychopathology (Grünberger 1980; Nemes 1988). One wonders if there is a continuing need to assert Ferenczi's "madness" in order to remain in good standing in the psychoanalytic establishment. The contemporary euphemism for Ferenczi's madness is *regression*–that he was in a regressed state of personality functioning during the time that the conflicts with Freud became exacerbated (Grünberger 1980, Nemes 1988).

Ferenczi's "Regression"

The issue of Ferenczi's "regressive" behavior as a causal factor in his conflicts with Freud has been recently suggested. Grünberger (1980) concluded that Ferenczi lapsed into a regression in his relationship with Freud: " . . . although Ferenczi was perhaps not clearly psychotic, he nevertheless showed unmistakable signs of deep regression" (p. 139).

Livia Nemes, president of the Hungarian Psychoanalytic Society, has recently offered her formulation of the Freud/Ferenczi relationship. She first states that no one has paid sufficient attention to the traumas that occurred in Ferenczi's life in 1919. There were three traumas that year: (1) the death of his wife's ex-husband on Ferenczi's wedding day; (2) his dismissal from his post as the first university professor of psychoanalysis; and (3) his resignation as president of the International Psycho-Analytical Association because of the collapse of the Hapsburg regime, which isolated Budapest (Nemes 1988). Nemes (1988) then makes her point about the Freud/Ferenczi conflict–that the traumas of 1919 produced a regression: " . . . his regression shook his relationship with Freud. The repeated traumas strengthened his desire to replace the lost father with Freud and, via the ambivalence, to lose him as well" (p. 243).

In fact, Nemes's (1988) interpretation of Ferenczi's entire relationship with Freud is based on the regression theme. She claims the following.

1. Ferenczi unconsciously wanted Freud, his father figure, to be an indulgent mother, as indulgent as his wife.
2. The cause of Ferenczi's regression was that that he expected, even demanded, from Freud this indulgent behavior.
3. This expectation can be traced back to his therapeutic innovations and to the idea that the therapist should allow the patient everything, even the utmost regression.

Ferenczi's devoted pupil, analysand, and leader of the British object relations school, Michael Balint, had a completely different version of the issue of regression in the Freud/Ferenczi relationship. Balint (1968) believed that the conflict between the two was based upon their different technical and emotional view of the role of regression in the therapeutic process: "The technical problem of how to respond to a regressed patient who had developed an intense transference, was perhaps the major cause of this tragic disagreement" (p. 149).

But Balint's focus was on the way in which Freud was uncomfortable with regressive patients and his concern that Ferenczi was overlooking the dangerous effects of treating such cases. Balint in no way suggested, however, that Ferenczi was in a regressive state during his final clinical period when he worked exclusively with difficult cases. He did remark that Ferenczi was carried away by his successes and his enthusiasm in helping patients who had failed in classical analyses of ten years or more.

> The immediate results of this technical approach were encouraging. His patients—most of them with more than a decade of treatment by other analysts behind them—came to life again, their state improved . . . . [Balint 1968, p. 151]

As Balint (1968) saw it, the problem arose in Ferenczi's new technical innovations, his principle of indulgence, and his relaxation therapy.

> . . . he came to the conclusion that if a patient was willing to come regularly to analysis, the analyst must find techniques to help him. In his sincere belief in this principle, he went to really incredible lengths to meet his patients' expectations. . . . This, however, meant abandoning the principle of abstinence. [p. 151]

Freud saw in Ferenczi's clinical experiments "the same morass from which he [Freud] could escape only by a supreme effort . . ." (Balint 1968, p. 150). Balint (1968) suggested that this concern for treating regression in an indulgent rather than abstinent manner (classical [Freudian] vs. humanistic [Ferenczian] analysis) prompted Freud to "become alarmed, critical and—what is very rare indeed for Freud—somewhat insensitive" (p. 150). Unfortunately, Balint argued, although Freud could correctly see dangers in Ferenczi's technique and the emotional toll on his personal functioning, he did not appreciate the breakthroughs that were being made. In essence, then, the Freud/Ferenczi conflict was based upon the following (Balint 1968):

1. Ferenczi, because of his own uncertainty, could not make use of Freud's well-meant and well-founded criticisms and saw in them only a lack of understanding.
2. Freud was still influenced by his disappointing experiences (case of Anna O., sexual manifestations of patients in hypnotic trance, sexual trauma reports of hysterical patients) and found in Ferenczi's experiments confirmation for his cautiousness.

The tragedy of this disagreement (Balint 1968b) "acted as a trauma on the psychoanalytic world. . . . Freud and Ferenczi, the two most prominent psychoanalysts, were not able to understand and properly evaluate each other's clinical findings, observations and theoretical ideas; the shock was highly disturbing and extremely painful" (pp. 151–152). The end result of the Freud/Ferenczi tragedy was that classical analysts declared Ferenczi's clinical findings unacceptable (Balint 1968): "By tacit consent, regression during analytic treatment was declared a dangerous symptom and its value as a therapeutic ally completely or almost completely repressed. . . ." (pp. 151–152).

No one has been more critical of Freud's behavior in the Freud/ Ferenczi controversy than Erich Fromm. Fromm had contact with one of Ferenczi's pupils, Clara Thompson, in their joint effort in founding the William Alanson White Institute. He also knew another of Ferenczi's analysands and students, Izette De Forest. It was these informants, as well as Fromm's theoretical formulations regarding political and ideological functioning, that led to his criticism of Freud. Having discussed the Freud/Ferenczi issue in three of his books (Fromm 1959, 1963, 1970), Fromm made it clear that he was taking Freud to task for his harsh and insensitive treatment of Ferenczi.

Fromm believed that, although Freud began the psychoanalytic movement as a reformer, he became a leader of an orthodox group who were chosen for their loyalty to Freud and the movement (Fromm 1970): " . . . many of them possessed characteristics of bureaucrats . . . [and] were men without any capacity for radical criticism" (p. 7).

When these faithful followers found the courage and independence of mind to deviate, there were only two courses open to them: to leave the fold or to mend their ways and repudiate their errors. Ferenczi attempted the latter when he realized that his use of activity had begun to produce a negative therapeutic effect (Ferenczi 1925a). But it was his work with difficult cases, his need to work with regressive states, and his dedication to his innovative clinical experiments that moved him to continue his dissidence, even in the face of Freud's seemingly insensitive and mean-spirited criticisms. It was this independence of functioning, coupled with his need to be loved by Freud, that produced the intense conflict.

Fromm makes a significant and useful point regarding the adherence to orthodoxy that even affected Ferenczi's devoted pupil Balint, himself a dissident who felt ignored by the classical analysts (Balint 1968, Fromm 1970). Balint felt rejected by the "massive centre of psychoanalysis" because he as well as other analysts who believed in therapeutic regression (Khan, Little, Searles, Winnicott) belonged "to the fringe. We are known, tolerated, perhaps even read, but certainly not quoted" (Balint 1968, p. 155). But when it came time to answer Jones's accusations that Ferenczi was psychotic, Balint bowed to orthodoxy. Instead of vigorously defending Ferenczi against this damning accusation, his reply to Jones was a lesson in politics. His letter was a mild-mannered, almost apologetic note, deferring to Jones's greater knowledge of Ferenczi's life and work (Balint 1958). He seemed to ignore his own expertise as a physician, as well as his personal experience as an eyewitness to Ferenczi's last days. He suggested that the next generation should be entrusted with finding the truth (Balint 1958). Fromm's (1970) conclusion is that Balint bowed to the analytic establishment:

> If such a tortuous and submissive letter had been written by a lesser person than Balint, or if it had been written in a dictatorial system in order to avoid severe consequences for freedom or life, it would be understandable. But considering the fact that it was written by a well-known analyst living in England, it only shows the intensity of the pressure which forbids any but the mildest criticism of one of the leaders of the organization. [p. 12]

It is very difficult to be critical of Balint, since he was a devoted friend and pupil of Ferenczi and championed his cause in these critical years after his death, when the analytic establishment attempted to remove his name and influence from mainstream psychoanalysis.

Ferenczi's Deviations

Another viewpoint in the Freud/Ferenczi conflict centers around Ferenczi's deviations in theory and technique as the reason for the strain in their relationship. Paul Roazen, a controversial historian of psychoanalysis, presented a thoughtful and scholarly defense of Ferenczi in his conflict with Freud. Roazen's discussion was based on interviews with analysts, patients, and interested parties who had contact with and knowledge of Freud and Ferenczi and the early pioneering days. Roazen (1975) believes that "the central issue between Freud and Ferenczi was the question of activity in the analyst's technique" (p. 367). The specific activity that Roazen feels Freud was most concerned with was Ferenczi's theory of motherly affection and his kissing technique.

According to Roazen, Ferenczi took Freud's criticism as a "personal slight and not just the result of a scientific controversy" [letter from Michael Balint to Ernest Jones, January 22, 1954, Jones Archives] (p. 368).

Masson, who alienated the entire analytic community with his behavior associated with the Freud archives and his vehement criticisms of Freud (Malcolm 1983b), has also come to Ferenczi's defense in the Freud/Ferenczi controversy. He is convinced that the conflict between the two pioneers was centered on still another controversial issue in psychoanalysis. Masson (1984) believes that the issue that tore their relationship apart was the seduction hypothesis. The controversy came to a head in Ferenczi's last paper, "The Confusion of Tongues" (see Chapter 13). Masson (1984) chronicled the Freud/Ferenczi materials he uncovered in Freud's desk at Maresfield Gardens and his conversations with Anna Freud regarding their publication:

> I showed Miss Freud the 1932 correspondence I found in Freud's desk concerning his close friend Sandor Ferenczi's last paper which dealt with this very topic [seduction theory]. Clearly, I thought, it was her father's continued preoccupation with the seduction theory that explained his otherwise mysterious turning away from Ferenczi.
>
> Miss Freud, who was very fond of Ferenczi, found these letters painful reading and asked me not to publish them. But the theory, I insisted, was not one that Freud had dismissed lightly as an early and insignificant error, as we had been led to believe.
>
> Anna Freud urged me to direct my interests elsewhere. In conversations with other analysts close to the Freud family, I was given to understand that I had stumbled upon something that was better left alone. . . . But the seduction hypothesis, in my opinion, was the very cornerstone of psychoanalysis. . . . Freud was the first

psychiatrist who believed his patients were telling the truth. [pp. xvii–xviii]

Why Didn't Ferenczi Break Away from Freud to Form His Own School?

It is apparent that Ferenczi's deviation from and adoration of Freud had a crippling effect on the elaboration of his own method of psychoanalysis, his leadership in the analytic community, and the development of his true self. According to De Forest, Ferenczi had no desire or intention to break away. His only desire was to be a loyal disciple of Freud. De Forest (1954) wrote, "In spite of their many fundamental differences of opinion, Ferenczi revered Freud's brilliant genius. His capacity for love and loyalty was unusually genuine and profound . . . he must simply have loved Freud too deeply to break with him" (p. 12).

What is more, De Forest (1954) suggested that Ferenczi was demonstrating his loving maternal technique in the way he handled the criticisms and rejection by Freud:

> . . . he listened to Freud's criticism, though its bitterness wounded him deeply, examined it, and accepted and acknowledged whatever seemed to him applicable; hoping against hope that, as with his patients, his beloved friend would, in time, finally reestablish his trust in him. . . . Ferenczi, in preserving both his integrity and his friendship with Freud, created a shining example of his own most deeply felt precepts and beliefs . . . he was being quite simply himself; it was a full expression of his whole way of living, he fulfilled his personality at the height of its maturity. It was the triumphant affirmation of his extraordinary capacity to give love. [pp. 13–14]

Freud's Transference to Ferenczi

There is another point of view in the Freud/Ferenczi conflict that suggested that the issue is one of transference. Many analysts have noted that Freud was involved in a transference relationship with his disciples (Balint 1968b, Fromm 1970, Haynal 1987, Nemes 1988). Another opinion cites Freud as being a stern father or even a tyrant toward his disciples (Fromm 1959, 1963, 1970). The problem was that Freud did not treat the rivalry, which seemed so obvious to his disciples, as a manifestation of transference (Haynal 1987). In addition, Freud failed to analyze the situation. He made an error that he would have chided any first-year analytic candidate for making. Instead of recognizing the interaction as transference and analyzing it, he played into it, using his authority and stern father role to resolve it (Haynal 1987, Nemes 1988).

Thompson (1944) viewed Ferenczi's devotion to Freud as limiting to his own potential as a leader and independent thinker. She felt that Ferenczi's personality traits contributed to his conflict with Freud: "In his devotion to Freud and because of his naturally timid and modest nature, for many years he did not strongly assert his own point of view except where it coincided with Freud's" (p. 245).

Another personality issue was Ferenczi's need to be accepted and loved. Balint (1958) wrote, "Despite Ferenczi's obviously lovable qualities, he suffered during life from a need to be accepted and loved" (Balint 1968b, p. 68). Thompson (1944) noted that Ferenczi's need to be loved played a role in his relationship to Freud: "Because of this need, his personal relationship to Freud was more than his own independent thinking. He was the type of man who is happy in working for a strong person. Freud was that strong person in his life" (p. 245).

Fromm, as has been noted, made this a keynote of his argument for Freud's mistreatment of Ferenczi (see previous section on Ferenczi's "regression"). Ferenczi's devotion to Freud prevented him from being himself. He was a secret rebel who harbored anger against the master, but could not freely express it. The need to court Freud's approval, combined with his seething anger, produced an ambivalence.

> This ambivalence, I believe, can be seen in his writings . . . his need for submission and conformity all too often dominated the picture. . . . So, I believe, Ferenczi was impeded in developing his own thinking by the nature of his attachment to Freud—an attachment compounded of admiration, dependence, fear of disapproval and veiled rebellion. [Thompson 1944, pp. 245–246]

Ferenczi's True Self

Freud was aware and concerned that their relationship was undergoing a transformation. He worked with the memory of their past glories together and perhaps the unresolved transference elements when he entreated Ferenczi to stay in the inner circle. In 1929, they were still in meaningful contact, as seen in a letter from Freud to Ferenczi in December 1929.

> You have without doubt withdrawn yourself outwardly from me in the past few years, but not so far, I hope, that a move toward creating a new oppositional analysis has to be expected from my Paladin and secret Grand Vizier. [Jones 1957, p. 147]

So it was not just Ferenczi's inability to break away from Freud to form a new school (Balint 1968b, Fromm 1970, Thompson 1944) that was the problem. Freud did not want Ferenczi to leave the fold, and Ferenczi did not want to leave. Ferenczi wanted to continue the evolution of psychoanalysis, keeping true to Freud's tradition. He did not want to begin an oppositional analysis. But the dilemma was how to be true to one's own self and yet be faithful to one's mentor. In that situation, there are only three choices: convince your mentor of your position, abandon your position, or fulfill your own needs. Ferenczi attempted to convince Freud of his humanistic method, but Freud could not accept it as part of his own method. Also, he could not tolerate deviation. Ferenczi did abandon, for a time, his active method, but this eventually became transformed into his humanistic method. Ferenczi tried to be true to his own convictions by pursuing his new method, but not in opposition to Freud.

Ferenczi's dedication to his humanistic method may be seen as an attempt to develop his true self.

> As a pupil, Ferenczi had to free himself of his adoration for his analyst [Freud], of his fear and hatred of him, in order to stop being oblivious to his true self . . . to disclose his struggle to elevate his own voice above the authority of the man he once called his "honoured master." [Ludmer 1988, p. 235]

Ferenczi's true self began to emerge in his last clinical phase, when his empathic and humanistic method predominated (Ferenczi and Rank 1925; Ferenczi 1928b, 1930b, 1931, 1932c, 1933). The final emergence of his true self is chronicled in his *Clinical Diary* (Ferenczi 1932c) and his "Confusion of Tongues" paper (Ferenczi 1933). In his *Clinical Diary*, Ferenczi expressed his dissident views in secret. Apparently, Freud never knew of and never saw this material. But in the "Confusion of Tongues" paper (see Chapter 13), Ferenczi made his thoughts known to Freud and the analytic community. What is more, he asked Freud to approve of his new views. Freud not only disapproved, but attempted to censor Ferenczi's paper. Ferenczi, in asking for Freud's approval, obviously was saying that he wanted to remain in Freud's good graces and maintain a position in the psychoanalytic mainstream. When this was not possible, he remained true to himself, refusing to waver in his beliefs. It is a sign of the strength of his ego and mature personality that he maintained his independence.

Freud's increasing negative reaction to Ferenczi's humanistic method had a profound emotional effect upon Ferenczi. Freud's growing impatience, criticism, and eventual hostility and rejection of him was traumatic. The great tragedy in their relationship was that Freud could not allow Ferenczi to deviate from him without punishment and that Ferenczi could not deviate without needing Freud's approval. In this sense, both men were victims of their own neuroses.

Balint's Wish for a Ferenczi Revival

It is time to fulfill Balint's wish that a newer generation of analysts will rediscover Ferenczi and help promulgate his ideas and techniques. To this end, I wish to emphasize the following points as a summary of the Freud/Ferenczi controversy as well as to advance a positive viewpoint of Ferenczi.

1. Ferenczi was not psychotic or mentally deranged, either during the course of his lifetime or during his final days. The testimony of eyewitnesses (Balint 1949, 1958, De Forest 1954, Fromm 1959, 1963, 1970, Thompson 1942) outweighs the mean-spirited and false accusations of Ferenczi's chief rival and political enemy (Jones 1957).

2. Ferenczi's conflict with Freud was not a result of his psychosis or neurosis. The conflict that led to their relationship difficulties was a result of differences about theory and technique (Balint 1968b, De Forest 1954, Dupont 1988a, Gedo 1986b, Lorand 1966, Masson 1984, Roazen 1975, Thompson 1944).

The issues regarding theory center around the issue of trauma in the development of psychopathology (Dupont 1988a), the centrality of sexual seduction in the ontogensis of personality disorders (Masson 1984), the conceptualization of childhood emotional trauma due to empathic failures by parental figures (Rachman 1988a), and the issue of regression in the transference (Balint 1968a).

What Freud did not understand or accept was that Ferenczi was experimenting with techniques to reach the difficult cases (narcissistic, borderline, and psychotic conditions) with which he specialized during the latter part of his career. It is now known that variations on Ferenczi's techniques are necessary in order to reach difficult cases (Kernberg 1975, Kohut 1984a, Masterson 1976, Winnicott, 1965a).

3. Ferenczi's technique was the expression of his creativity (Gedo 1968, 1986, Ludmer 1988). He was a highly creative, original thinker who appealed to Freud because of his speculative turn of mind. Freud made Ferenczi his favorite son because he realized that Ferenczi was the most creative and dedicated of the inner circle. Ferenczi was Freud's speculative and expansive alter ego.

4. Ferenczi did suffer from neurotic symptoms during his lifetime, most notably a special need for affection and recognition (Balint 1949, 1968, Thompson 1944). But why hasn't anyone suggested that Freud's neurosis was at the root of his oedipal theory, as it has been suggested that Ferenczi's neurosis is at the root of his seduction/trauma theory? It is possible that no psychoanalyst dares to make this association for fear of being ostracized from the analytic community for defaming the master and icon of psychoanalysis.

Ferenczi's neurosis also contributed to his empathic understanding of patients, especially difficult cases (Rachman 1988a). Ferenczi's theories and techniques constitute an original, creative contribution to psychoanalysis that began the tradition of dissidence within psychoanalysis (Gedo 1986b) and also established the first alternate school of psychoanalysis.

4

FERENCZI AND JUNG: FAVORITE SONS OF THE MASTER

FERENCZI'S INTRODUCTION TO PSYCHOANALYSIS BY JUNG

It was in keeping with Ferenczi's active nature that Jung's method would initially be more appealing than Freud's approach. In the years following, Ferenczi integrated his active nature into the Freudian method, which changed the face of psychoanalysis. Freud's attraction, first to Jung and then to Ferenczi, was to their active, creative temperaments and intellects. This was just one way in which Ferenczi and Jung were kindred spirits.

Jung was instrumental in another significant way in paving the road to psychoanalysis for Ferenczi. As mentioned in Chapter 3, Dr. Philippe Stein of Budapest, a Hungarian psychiatrist who studied in Vienna, had also studied at Burghölzli, the famous Swiss clinic where Jung had trained. Stein, who was acquainted with both Ferenczi and Jung, encouraged his Hungarian colleague to give psychoanalysis a second chance and contact Freud, with Jung as the conduit. On June 28, 1907, Jung wrote to Freud.

> Dear Professor Freud,
>   First some "business" news. Dr. Stein of Budapest and another mental specialist, Dr. Ferenczi, want to visit you sometime in Vienna and have asked me to inquire when it would be most convenient to you. . . . [McGuire 1974, pp. 65–66]

Freud took over six months to reply, but, on the basis of Jung's recommendation, agreed to meet the two Hungarian psychiatrists on

Sunday, February 2, 1908, shortly before the Salzburg Congress. Freud and Ferenczi formed an immediate bond that developed into a close friendship and professional collaboration that lasted for about twenty-five years. Freud shared the special developments in their relationship with Jung, writing to him on August 13, 1908 (McGuire 1974): "Our colleague Ferenczi, who has great personal charm, is now in Berchtesgaden and comes to see us often. He goes mountain-climbing with my boys . . ." (p. 169).

As indicated in this letter, Ferenczi had become a member of the Freud family. Jung was apparently delighted with the special relationship that had developed between Ferenczi and Freud. The second prince of psychoanalysis now helped form a golden triangle—Freud/Jung/Ferenczi. On August 21, 1908, Jung wrote to Freud (McGuire 1974): "Please give Ferenczi my very cordial regards. He is highly deserving of your goodwill" (p. 170).

FREUD/JUNG/FERENCZI: THE KING AND HIS TWO PRINCES

It is well known that Freud anointed Jung "the crown prince" of psychoanalysis. But when the relationship with Jung soured and Jung left Freud's inner circle, Ferenczi became the heir apparent, making him the second prince of psychoanalysis.

Freud had chosen Jung to be his "Gentile prince," to spread the word of psychoanalysis beyond the parochial walls of Vienna to the shores of greater Europe. Jung was to legitimize this "Jewish science" of psychoanalysis to the world of psychiatry (Roazen 1975). Freud saw in Jung a brilliant intellect and an inquiring mind. It has also been suggested that Freud was attracted to Jung because he sensed the heretic, a trait he acknowledged he possessed (Roazen 1975).

Ferenczi was the "Hungarian Jewish prince." The charming, gregarious psychiatrist from Budapest had distinguished himself as a champion of the underpriviliged prior to meeting Freud. As seen, Ferenczi did pioneering work with nontraditional patient populations, developing humanistic treatment for the poor, criminals, and homosexuals. Freud saw in Ferenczi a daring, experimental, and healing doctor. No doubt he also sensed Ferenczi's rebellious nature. Freud's attraction to these two unconventional thinkers and clinicians seemed to satisfy the daring and adventurous side of Freud's personality. But Freud had difficulties with his princes when they wished to have a more democratic or mutual relationship. He also wished to be the master of his disciples.

Freud's controversies with both Jung and Ferenczi suggest oedipal struggles. He wished to have a favorite son with whom he could be intimate friends, and then he was threatened by the son's desire for equality. The relationship was strained to the breaking point, when Freud expressed a need to vanquish the son as he became the rival and enemy. Freud's relationships with Fliess, Adler, Jung, and Ferenczi followed a similar pattern (Roazen 1975).

> He sometimes extended himself to people too enthusiastically and tended to idealize them. He then later blamed them for not having qualities which he himself had imputed to them, for having failed to live up to his fantasized conception of them. [p. 242]

Jung was not entirely comfortable with the designation as Freud's crown prince. In September 1909, he shared his concerns with Ferenczi.

> Whether I am recognized or not recognized as the "crown prince" can at times annoy me or please me. . . . It is really of greater importance to me to see clearly in scientific matters and work ahead for the future than measure myself against Freud. . . .
>   In the end it is always the one who really is or was the strongest that remains king, even if only posthumously. As always, we have to submit trustingly to this natural law, since nothing avails against it anyway. [Donn 1988, p. 120]

Jung's Father Complex

Ferenczi was a witness to the interaction between Freud and Jung that revealed what some scholars have called Jung's father complex. When Ferenczi came on the scene, Freud and Jung had already established a bond. In a letter of October 28, 1907, Jung confessed his trauma of childhood seduction and suggested the psychodynamic of his father complex.

... my veneration for you [Freud] has the characteristic of a passionate "religious infatuation" . . . . [it] doesn't cause any discomfort, it is repulsive and ridiculous to me, because of its undeniable erotic connotation. This abominable feeling has its source in the fact that as a little boy I succumbed to a homosexual attack from a man I had previously venerated.

Practically, I feel repulsion in my relationships with colleagues who transfer strongly to me . . . I fear your trust. I fear also the same reaction with you when I share with you intimate details. [McGuire 1974, p. 95]

Freud admitted he was overanxious in his response to Jung, especially when Jung was late in responding to his letters.

As Freud's relationship with Ferenczi began to take shape, he began to take some emotional distance from Jung. Freud was uncomfortable with Jung's latent homosexual confession. Eventually, Ferenczi would take the baton from Jung and become Freud's intimate friend and heir (Sabourin 1984).

Ferenczi's Brother Complex

Freud characterized Ferenczi "as a middle child in a large family, [who] had to struggle with a powerful brother complex [and] had, under the influence of analysis become an irreproachable elder brother, a kindly teacher and promoter of young talent" (Freud 1923a, p. 267). Thus, Freud suggested that he cured Ferenczi of his brother complex.

Ferenczi had a pivotal role in the relationship between Freud and Jung. While Jung was the crown prince, Ferenczi had to accept the role of the second son. Out of his respect and admiration for Freud, the analysis of his brother complex, and a genuine admiration and liking for Jung, Ferenczi was able to control his jealousy. He was aware of these feelings and told Freud, " . . . I am not jealous of Jung" (Donn 1988, p. 120).

On January 3, 1910, Ferenczi wrote to Freud about Jung's capacity to be a leader.

Obviously as a fullblooded human being [Jung] also has to struggle with his temperament and especially with his hunger for power and ambition. Most likely, this will be the last thing he will overcome.

But these affects are very well suited to the work we expect from him, provided that he does not let himself be dominated by them. . . .

I have to concur with you about Jung's future role in psychoanalysis. His two great achievements: his courageous and independent stand in acknowledging your ideas, as well as the first experiments in psychoanalysis [word association test] secure this role for him, even if he were to accomplish nothing more. [Ferenczi to Freud, January 3, 1910, Freud Collection, accession number 19042—quoted in Donn 1988, p. 122]

Ferenczi did, however, struggle with his feelings of jealousy and sought out a psychic regarding his relationship with Jung.

"What is to be recommended regarding my relationship with Jung?" Ferenczi asked Frau Jelenek [the psychic]. Her answer was, Ferenczi recalled, "It will work out all right. He is, to be sure, irritable and violent." (Ferenczi was not certain he remembered this last word accurately.) But in the end, Frau Jelenek said, "You will come together in collaborative work" [Ferenczi to Freud, October 24, 1909, Freud Collection, accession number 19042—quoted in Donn 1988, p. 12]

The Freud/Jung/Ferenczi Triangle

Ferenczi's *Clinical Diary* gives us insight into the triangular relationship between Freud, Jung, and Ferenczi. Ferenczi's (1932c) own words tell of his suppressed feelings toward Freud surfacing, as he joined Jung in his criticism of Freud.

Contrary to all the rules of technique that he established himself, he adopted Dr. F. [Ferenczi] almost like his son. . . . he regarded him as the most perfect heir of his ideas. Thereby, he became the proclaimed crown prince, anticipating his triumphal entry into America. (Fr. [Freud] seems to have expected something similar of Jung years ago; hence the two hysterical symptoms observed with him): (1) the fainting spell in Bremen, (2) the incontinence on Riverside Drive, added to the bit of analysis he gave us; dying as soon as the son takes his place, and regression to childhood, childish embarrassment, when he represses his American vanity. (Possibly his contempt for Americans is a reaction to this weakness which he could not hide from us and himself. . . .)

The anxiety-provoking idea, perhaps very strong in the unconscious, that the father must die when the son grows up, explains his fear of allowing any one of his sons to become independent. At the same time, it also shows us that Freud as the son really did want to kill his father. Instead of admitting this, he founded the theory of the parricidal Oedipus, but obviously applied only to others, not to himself. Hence the fear of allowing himself to be analyzed. [pp. 184–185]

VOYAGE TO AMERICA:
THE CLARK UNIVERSITY LECTURES

In what has been described by many scholars as a milestone in American intellectual history and in the history of psychoanalysis, Freud, Ferenczi, and Jung visited America in 1909 to help commemorate the twentieth anniversary of Clark University in Worcester, Massachusetts. Freud shared his delight about the Clark lectures with Jung, writing to him on June 18, 1909, saying they would discuss the material on the voyage.

> Of course your joy is now beginning to be clouded by the same concerns as mine, . . . What am I to say to those people? . . . I have a saving idea, which I shall not keep secret from you. . . . we can think about it on shipboard, on our long walks round the deck. . . . the audience is now at our mercy, under obligation to applaud whatever we bring them. [McGuire 1974, p. 234]

Freud could have had no idea when this letter was written that their discussions aboard ship would turn into a crisis that would fuel the eventual break with Jung.

The three met in Bremen and sailed on the steamship *George Washington* on August 21, 1909. But before they left for America, a strange event occurred. Freud hosted a luncheon, and conversation during the meal turned toward the mummified corpses of prehistoric man still being found in northern Germany. Jung was an expert on the subject and went into great detail about the corpses. Freud became angry at Jung, saying: "Why do you keep talking about these corpses? You are wishing my death?" Jung replied: "My dear Professor, can't you stop such funny interpretations?" Freud then fainted (Clark 1980b, Jones 1955).

Various explanations have been given for Freud's reaction. Jung said that Freud believed his talk about corpses meant that he harbored a death wish toward him. The oedipal struggles between Freud and Jung were evident from the first. Binswanger, who witnessed Jung's first visit with Freud in February 1907, reported that Freud asked the two to tell their dreams. When Jung told his, Freud's interpretation was that Jung wished to dethrone him and take his place (Roazen 1975).

The luncheon meeting conflict was a portent of further difficulties. On the trip, Freud, Jung, and Ferenczi passed the time by analyzing each other's dreams. Once again Freud and Jung clashed, but this time an incident occurred that became one of the keys to the eventual emotional estrangement between Jung and Freud. Ferenczi was witness to this event, but could do nothing to prevent it. In the light of Ferenczi's eventual estrangement with Freud, almost twenty years after Jung's break, one wonders whether Jung's oedipal struggles with Freud were shared by Ferenczi.

During a dream analysis session, Jung asked Freud for some associations. Freud refused to respond, because he did not wish to undermine his own authority as the leader of the psychoanalytic community. Jung was livid and described his reaction to this refusal. Roazen (1975) quotes Jung as saying

> And so, when Freud told me the dream in which his wife and her sister played important parts I asked Freud to tell me some of his personal associations with the dream. He looked at me with bitterness and said, "I could tell you more, but I cannot risk my authority." That, of course, finished my attempt to deal with his dreams. [p. 246, f17]

Ferenczi continued this kind of informal dream analysis. While on vacation, he developed such dream-telling interactions (Ferenczi 1916–1917): "I once spent several weeks at a spa and was able to collect a little series of such easily interpreted dreams at meal-times" (p. 346).

Freud delivered his five lectures at Clark, which were published as *The New Introductory Lectures to Psychoanalysis* (Freud 1915–1916). Ferenczi played a crucial role in these lectures. Freud (1933a) described Ferenczi's contribution to this remarkable event.

Each lecture, covering such concepts as free association, dream interpretation, repression, hysteria, infantile sexuality, and neurosis, was delivered without any notes and, according to contemporary accounts, in a modest, convincing, and conversational manner (Koelsch 1970).

Jung lectured on the word association test and also received an honorary degree from Clark University. James J. Putnam, the Boston psychiatrist who helped establish psychoanalysis in America, reflected on his experience as a member of the audience at the event. "Dr. Jung's observations, full of personality, fire, and life, have already excited much comment. . . . Dr. Ferenczi has written a number of admirable papers, partly in Hungarian, which are bound soon to bring him prominently into notice" (Putnam 1909, p. 2).

The Clark lectures did much to accelerate the spread of the psychoanalytic movement in America and introduced psychoanalysis as a field of study in an academic institution.

THE CONTRAST BETWEEN FERENCZI'S AND JUNG'S CONFLICT WITH FREUD

The Jung/Freud Conflict

It is clear that Jung had the capacity to be direct with his dissatisfactions, his criticisms, and his anger toward Freud. Witness the difference in expression of feelings between Jung and Ferenczi as they communicated with their master.

On December 18, 1912, Jung wrote from Zürich. At first, he asked Freud's permission to be honest, but he didn't hesitate to speak his mind (McGuire 1974):

> . . . I admit the ambivalence of my feelings towards you, but am inclined to take an honest and absolutely straightforward view of the situation. If you doubt my word, so much the worse for you [p. 534]

Jung went on to be blatantly direct with Freud, holding back none of his anger and outrage, in a way that no other of his followers dared to do, either during that early period of psychoanalysis or subsequently (McGuire 1974):

> I would, however, point out that your technique of treating your pupils like patients is a *blunder*. [Freud had made a comment on a slip of the tongue (pen) he noticed in Jung's behavior.] In that way you produce either slavish sons or impudent puppies.

Jung continued, holding back nothing of his anger and outrage:

> I am objective enough to see through your little trick. You go around sniffing out all the symptomated actions in your vicinity, thus reducing everyone to the level of sons and daughters who blushingly admit the existence of their faults. Meanwhile you remain on top as the father, sitting pretty. For sheer obsequiousness, nobody dares to pluck the prophet by the beard and enquire for once what you would say to a patient with a tendency to analyze the analyst instead of himself. You would certainly ask him: "Who's got the neurosis?"
>
> You see, my dear Professor, so long as you hand out this stuff I don't give a damn for my symptomatic actions; they shrink to nothing in comparison with the formidable beam in my brother Freud's eye. . . . If ever you should rid yourself entirely of your complexes and stop playing the father to your sons and instead of aiming continually at their weak spots take a good look at your own for a change then I will mend my ways. . . .

Jung finished this amazing letter with a manifesto of independence.

> I shall continue to stand by you publicly while maintaining my own views, but privately shall start telling you in my letters what I really think of you. I consider this procedure only decent. [pp. 534–535]

Ferenczi's temperament and relationship to Freud produced a different response. Although Ferenczi and Jung were both dissidents of psychoanalysis, Jung was the overtly rebellious son, who openly criticized and fought with the father and then was able to break with his mentor/father-figure and go on to develop his own intellectual system. Jung spoke in a clear, loud, independent voice (putting aside any issues of Jung's possible defensiveness regarding his slip of the tongue).

Ferenczi spoke in a muted voice, not wanting to precipitate a break with his cherished master. At about the same time as Jung's letter, Ferenczi also wrote to Freud. He was dissatisfied with the interaction between Freud and himself on the Sicily trip. Contrast Jung's direct anger and criticism of Freud with Ferenczi's plea for understanding (see Chapter 3).

The Ferenczi/Freud Conflict

Ferenczi's correspondence is an indication of someone who bent over backwards to please the master. In the following excerpts, he is distressed to hear that Freud has some criticisms of his revolutionary work, co-authored with Rank, entitled *The Development of Psychoanalysis*. Freud wrote to Ferenczi on January 22, 1924:

> . . . I do not agree with everything in your common production [Ferenczi and Rank 1925], although there is a good deal in it that I appreciate. . . . I prefer to keep in the background so as not to disturb you all in your productivity. In this way I hope to render harmless my continued presence in old age.

Ferenczi answered Freud's letter on January 30, 1924. It is clear that Ferenczi does not show the directness in his feelings that Jung demonstrated.

> Your letter upset me not a little. For the first time in our acquaintance—that you soon elevated to a friendship—I hear words of dissatisfaction from you.
> . . . your remark that you do not agree with everything in the joint book struck me quite unexpectedly. . . . I . . . was concerned to avoid anything with which you might not agree. . . . and because you read proofs and gave us valuable advice (gratefully accepted and made use of) . . . we believed ourselves correct in thinking you had no objections to the content. . . .
> Had you voiced any further misgivings we would certainly have considered them with the utmost care and in all probability, also have taken them into account. . . .

> Allow me . . . [to] ask you to convey to me all your objections to my work. . . . We neither can nor wish to do without your criticism and guidance. After so many years of working together under your direction you should not, even though politely, leave us to rely on ourselves. [Grubrich-Simitis 1986, pp. 265–266]

Ferenczi's "secret rebellion" becomes evident when one reads his *Clinical Diary* (also a secret document, written without Freud's awareness during 1932). In this remarkable document, he begins to sound like Jung of 1912. In an entry dated May 1, 1932, he wrote (Ferenczi 1932c)

> It should not be forgotten that Freud is not the discoverer of analysis but that he took over something readymade, from Breuer, . . . he only analyzed others but not himself. . . . I tend to think that originally Freud did believe in analysis . . . [but] the problems of countertransference opened up before him like an abyss. . . . Freud no longer loves his patients. . . . he still remains attached to analysis intellectually, but not emotionally. . . . [pp. 92–93]

This is the same criticism Jung voiced in the 1912 letter previously cited.

Ferenczi's (1932c) criticisms in the *Clinical Diary* are more revealing of his feelings.

Clinical Diary March 17, 1932
>   My own analysis could not be pursued deeply enough because my analyst (by his own admission, of a narcissistic nature), with his strong determination to be healthy and his antipathy toward any weaknesses or abnormalities, could not follow me down into those depths. . . . [p. 62]

Clinical Diary July 19, 1932
>   *In opposition to Freud* I developed to an exceptional degree a capacity for *humility* and for appreciating the clearsightedness of the . . . (patient). [p. 160]

Clinical Diary October 2, 1932
>   I did indeed also feel abandoned by colleagues (Radó, etc.) who are all too afraid of Freud to behave objectively or sympathetically toward me, in the case of a dispute between Freud and me. A

more restrained circulation of letters between Freud, Jones, and Eitingon has certainly been going on for a long time now. I am treated like a sick person who must be spared. My intervention will have to wait until I recover, so that the special "care" becomes unnecessary. [pp. 212–213]

FERENCZI AND JUNG'S SHARED CLINICAL IDEAS

There are two significant areas of clinical thinking and practice where Ferenczi and Jung had similar ideas: empathy and the subjective experience and the analyst's role in the analytic process. Both these subject matters indicate the parallels in Jung and Ferenczi's approach to psychoanalysis and their natural tendencies to deviate from Freud. From early in their careers, both Ferenczi and Jung had a tendency to view the psychoanalytic situation differently from the master. Both were more comfortable with the subjective experience. Ferenczi was always looking to respond more empathically to an analysand, while Jung was looking to better understand the experience.

Empathy and the Subjective Experience

Ferenczi's contribution to psychoanalysis could be measured by his focus on empathy. It was clear to him that a certain kind of humanistic response was necessary. His humanism, early in his career, was very evident in the empathic way he both understood and responded to Rosa K. (Ferenczi 1902, Lorin 1983). In this case, Ferenczi pioneered the empathic approach to the therapy of homosexuals, which was at odds with the prevailing notion at that time (see Chapter 2).

When Ferenczi became a Freudian, he brought this humanistic view of treatment to psychoanalysis. He had been a psychoanalyst less than five years when he began to introduce an experimental approach. The role of activity, which will be discussed more fully in Chapters 7–10, was Ferenczi's first formal attempt to open up the Freudian method to a more experiential, less intellectual approach. Having broken with tradition, it was inevitable that Ferenczi's personality and his clinical approach would move him toward empathy as the major focus in psychoanalysis. He sensed intuitively and understood intellectually that difficult cases needed to be viewed in a new way. His introduction of the active dimension contributed to making the analytic process more fluid and encouraged a more responsive orientation to the analytic situation.

Although Ferenczi's clinical experiments with activity came to an end, they had helped establish the analyst's concentration on the subjective experience of the analysand rather than on the analyst's theoretical orientation. By attuning to the response of the analysand to the analyst's interventions, analysts could begin to frame their responses from the analysand's frame of reference. This kind of clinical functioning led Ferenczi to formally introduce empathy into psychoanalysis (Ferenczi 1928b). Freud had actually suggested to Ferenczi, according to his report, that he experiment with the psychoanalytic method. It was to Freud's credit that he sensed that psychoanalysis needed to expand its capacity to deal more effectively with neurotic conditions and that he had the foresight to anoint Ferenczi as the chief innovator in psychoanalysis.

After the introduction of empathy in 1928, Ferenczi devoted the rest of his clinical career to developng his empathic method. The elaboration of his work involved changes in the process of an analytic session (Ferenczi 1930b), development of the process of empathic communication (Ferenczi 1931), focus on the analyst's contribution to empathic failure (Ferenczi 1928, 1931, 1932c, 1933), and development of psychopathology based on empathic defects in childhood (Ferenczi 1932c, 1933). These aspects of Ferenczi's empathic method are elaborated on in Chapter 13 of this volume. As we shall see in Chapter 18 of his *Clinical Diary*, Ferenczi was willing to go to almost any length to respond empathically to an analysand, including jeopardizing his own functioning.

Jung believed that all inquiry into psychological processes was basically a subjective process (Corbett 1989). To understand another human being, one must attempt to know his or her subjective world, which cannot be done through an objective analysis. He said (1960), "If we want to understand anything psychological, we must bear in mind that all knowledge is subjectively conditioned" (p. 182).

Jung, like Ferenczi, put his emphasis on trying to understand the subjective meaning of an analysand's associations. "As analysts we should attempt to discern the goal and meaning of each communication; and we do this 'in and through ourselves'—the empathic method" (Corbett 1989, p. 35).

Jung amplified the potential meaning and direction of man's subjective experience by his study of symbol, religion, mythology, and alchemy.

In this study, Jung courageously opened up new vistas of subjectivity, realizing he was going against scientific tradition. His journey into the symbols of subjectivity brought new meaning to the psychotic process in both neurotics and seriously disturbed individuals.

The statement of Jung's (1969) view on empathy is clear:

> If the doctor wants to guide another . . . he must *feel* with that person's psyche. He never feels it when he passes judgment. . . . It is a human quality—a kind of deep respect for the facts, for the man who suffers from them, and for the riddle of such a man's life. [pp. 338–339]

The Analyst's Role

One of Ferenczi's great contributions to the psychoanalytic method is that he added the human dimension to the analytic process. This was a remarkable departure from the Freudian method, which in his time had emphasized a neutral, detached observer role for the analyst. Freud stressed noninvolvement—what he called an objective approach.

But Ferenczi was different in both temperament and ambition from Freud. He was warm, friendly, lively, and romantic. These special and positive qualities of personal functioning were an integral part of who he was as a clinician. The same Ferenczi who entered a room and kissed his colleagues who were in assembly also pioneered the therapeutic use of touch in his clinical practice. Ferenczi's use of touch—that is, to allow an analysand to hug or kiss him—was not, as Freud suggested in the famous "kissing letter" he sent to Ferenczi on December 13, 1931, an indication of erotic intimacy. Touching for Ferenczi was a part of the tender-mother transference he wished to establish. His own words clearly state the distinction between affection and eroticism, which Freud was unable to discern (Ferenczi 1931):

> It is important for the analysis that the analyst should be able to meet the patient as far as possible with almost inexhaustible patience, understanding, goodwill, and kindliness. . . . The patient will then feel the contrast between our behavior and that which he experienced in his real family and knowing himself safe from the repetition of such situations. . . . [p. 132]

The analyst's behavior is thus rather like that of an affectionate mother, who will not go to bed at night until she has talked over with the child all his current troubles, large and small, fears, bad intentions, and scruples of conscience and has set them at rest. [p. 137]

Ferenczi's idea of a tender-mother transference herein described has parallels in contemporary clinical thinking, in both Winnicott's concept of "good enough mothering" (Winnicott 1960c) and Kohut's selfobject transference (Kohut 1978b).

Jung was likely to be closer in his clinical practice to Ferenczi than to Freud, as is witnessed by Freud's admonitions to Jung about his more humanistic practice. On December 13, 1911, Freud wrote to Jung with this advice.

I gather that neither of you [Pfister] has yet acquired the necessary objectivity in your practice, that you still get involved, giving a good deal of yourselves and expecting the patient to give something in return.

Permit me . . . to say that this technique is invariably ill-advised and that it is best to remain reserved and purely receptive. We must never let our neurotics drive us crazy.

Freud then finishes this portion of the letter with a special invitation to develop a method to deal with the difficulties that patients present to their analysts:

I believe an article on "countertransference" is sorely needed; of course we could not publish it, we should have to circulate copies among ourselves. [McGuire 1974, p. 476]

Ferenczi would take Freud's recommendation most seriously, even though the suggestion was made to Jung. As an integral part of Ferenczi's humanistic method of psychoanalysis, he placed countertransference analysis in the center. He became devoted to recognizing, taking responsibility for, and analyzing his own personal reactions to an analysand, as an integral part of the analytic process.

Jung also did not accept the analyst as a neutral observer. Corbett (1989) wrote, " . . . he insisted that therapy is a dialectic, reciprocal interaction between two psychic systems" (p. 42). In a similar fashion, Jung (1966) stressed the importance of the personal contribution of the analyst, his countertransference reactions, and the mutual influence that occurs in the therapy.

Jung used the metaphor of a chemical reaction, suggesting that if change were to occur, both participants would be transformed, because their behavior is so mutually interactive (Corbett 1989). Of this mutual interaction, Jung (1966) said the following: "In any effective psychological treatment the doctor is bound to influence the patient; but this influence can only take place if the patient has a reciprocal influence on the doctor. You can exert no influence if you are not susceptible to influence" (p. 71).

Jung (1969) was quite emphatic on this point, indicating Ferenczi's sentiments on the analyst's active involvement in the treatment process:

> We could say . . . that a good half of every treatment that probes at all deeply consists in the doctor's examining himself, for only what he can put right in himself can he hope to put right in the patient. It is no less either, if he feels that the patient is hitting him, or even scoring off him: it is his own hurt that gives the measure of his power to heal. This, and nothing else, is the meaning of the Greek myth of the wounded physician. [p. 71]

THE OCCULT

After Freud and Ferenczi returned from America, they visited a female medium in Berlin whom Ferenczi knew. Her performance stimulated Freud's interest in thought transference. But Freud, knowing he could not take the journey into the occult himself, encouraged Jung and Ferenczi to go where he could not go. Ferenczi's interest was piqued by such visits to a medium.

Jung wrote to Freud on May 8, 1911, of his desire to delve into the occult.

> Occultism is another field we shall have to conquer—with the aid of the libido theory. . . . I am looking into astrology, which seems indispensable for a proper understanding of mythology. There are strange and wondrous things in these lands of darkness. Please don't

worry about my wanderings in these infinitudes. I shall return laden with rich booty, for knowledge of the human psyche. For a while longer I must intoxicate myself on magic perfumes in order to fathom the secrets that lie hidden in the abysses of the unconscious. [McGuire 1974, p. 421]

Freud, realizing he could not hold back this interest in the occult in his two favorite sons, encouraged them to collaborate. On May 11, 1911, he wrote to Ferenczi:

Jung writes to me that we must conquer the field of occultism and asks for my agreeing to his leading a crusade. . . . I can see that you two are not to be held back. At least go forward in collaboration with each other; it is a dangerous expedition and I cannot accompany you. [McGuire 1974, p. 421]

Apparently, Freud's interest in the occult did continue, although he made no public acknowledgement of it, because he did not want psychoanalysis to be identified with the occult. However, he told Jones in 1926 that he harbored a "favorable prejudice in favor of telepathy." Furthermore, he confessed that he was involved in experiments with Ferenczi and his daughter Anna that apparently were related to thought transference (Gay 1988), "the transferring of psychical processes through space to other people" (Roazen 1975, p. 240, n47). Freud was searching for an understanding of unconscious processes.

Ferenczi never relinquished his interest in the occult, believing in telepathy. He even invited a telepathist to a meeting of the Vienna Psychoanalytic Society and had the medium divine written messages of the members. Imagine such a meeting in contemporary psychoanalysis.

Freud once singled out Ferenczi's occult studies as evidence that he was able to grow independently within psychoanalysis, "succumbing neither to rebelliousness nor undue submissiveness" (Roazen 1975, p. 233). Ferenczi called himself "Freud's court astrologer" (Sabourin 1985).

Jung made attempts to understand graphology, astrology, alchemy, mysticism, and ancient religions. In his later years he was interested in flying saucers (Roazen 1975). These studies can be viewed as Jung's attempts to understand man's creations as "mediators of the extrapsychic experience of the self" (Corbett 1989, p. 27). For example, in alchemy, he viewed these traditions as (Corbett 1989)

. . . a very old record of the structure and dynamics of the psyche in projected form. . . .

The alchemical "gold" made out of lead was, in reality, the alchemist's attempt to experience the self, as he struggled to emerge from his initial psychological state of chaos and depression. Alchemical texts are therefore seen as symbolic representations of unconscious processes projected onto the operation of the laboratory. [p. 28]

THE HEART AND SOUL OF PSYCHOANALYSIS

Although Freud chose two heirs to the throne of psychoanalysis—Jung and Ferenczi—they have not been regarded with the honor, status, and appreciation they deserve. It would be interesting to speculate about how psychoanalysis would have developed if Ferenczi and Jung had stayed within the fold or mainstream. Psychoanalysis would have maintained its heart and soul. Ferenczi would have supplied the heart, by virtue of his focus on empathy, his analysis of difficult cases, and his unfailing belief in the curative powers of psychoanalysis and the mutuality of the psychoanalytic situation. Jung, of course, would have supplied the soul by his focus on the collective unconscious and archetypes and by his studies of ancient beliefs, alchemy, and man's symbols and artifacts.

Unfortunately, Jung left the fold and Ferenczi went underground. Psychoanalysis has suffered not from their dissidence, but from a lack of appreciation and acceptance of their ideas and clinical methods.

5

FERENCZI AND GRODDECK: KINDRED SPIRITS

THE "WILD ANALYST": GEORG GRODDECK

Georg Groddeck referred to himself as a "wild analyst" (Grossman and Grossman 1965). He has also been referred to as the "untamed analyst" (Grotjahn 1945). In a history of the pioneers of psychoanalysis, he was described as ". . . unsystematic, disorganized, and inspired" (Roazen 1975, p. 331). In a more positive vein, this complicated individual has been lauded as "the father of psychosomatic medicine," a term he despised as shallow and misleading (Grotjahn 1945).

Grotjahn (1966) wrote about him:

> Georg Groddeck was born in Baden-Baden in 1866. He had a distant relationship with his mother and a close relationship with his sister, Lina. The relationship with the latter he credits with helping him understand the bi-sexual nature of man, pregnancy/envy in men, creativity, and the ability to be a healer ("mother-father").
>
> While in medical school he was required to sign up for eight years of Army reserve. After marrying, he moved back to Baden-Baden, where he became Medical Director and owner of a sanitarium founded by his teacher Schweninger. Groddeck remained there and developed the Baden-Baden sanitarium into a famous treatment center where he pioneered the combined use of physio-therapeutic treatment, such as diet, massage, with psychoanalytic understanding. [p. 308–309]

Grotjahn (1966) lovingly sums up Groddeck's formative years and significant influences. Groddeck's early history paralleled Ferenczi's. They both had emotionally unresponsive mothers, which marked their personality development. Their family experiences in childhood left them not only with a significant need for responsiveness, but also with a special sense of empathy for those who also shared this need.

Groddeck and Ferenczi also shared similarities in their adult experiences. Both men turned to married women for their permanent relationships, perhaps looking, at least in part, for the fulfillment of childhood frustrations. Both men pioneered the understanding of the role of preoedipal maternal issues in psychoanalysis. Furthermore, they both shared an interest in and understanding of the psychology of women. In the original Freudian circle, Groddeck and Ferenczi could be said to be especially empathic to women analysands and colleagues.

Ferenczi and Groddeck saw themselves primarily as healers, doctors whose mandate was to cure human misery. They allowed their creativity, spontaneity, and passion to become part of their clinical method. They helped to pioneer the role of the active and compassionate analyst.

Their early backgrounds also influenced their treatment philosophies. Both men sought to integrate their personalities into their therapeutic method. Both had engaging, active, and emotionally spontaneous personalities, and their psychotherapies reflected this: Groddeck's direct treatment of the body, mind, and spirit, and Ferenczi's active method and humanistic relaxation therapy. They were both men of passion and were intensely devoted to their clinical work as well as to the people they served. Everyone either loved them or wished to be free of them; it was not possible to be neutral about Ferenczi or Groddeck. They channelled their need for maternal love into their form of psychoanalysis. They were different versions of Ferenczi's concept of the tender mother. Groddeck was the tender mother who involved himself in the total treatment of his sanatorium clients, making sure that their analytic cure was focused on a sound mind in a sound body with a sound spirit. Ferenczi pioneered the tender-mother transference, emotionally holding the analysand in an empathic ambience until he or she was cured. Both analytic pioneers were daring, experimental, and fearless clinicians. Groddeck's hands-on clinical approach literally meant physical touching via massage. Ferenczi also used noneroticized, affectionate touching to heal the trauma of maternal deprivation (Rachman 1993a).

Their kindred clinical spirit was also evident in this tribute to Groddeck by Ferenczi.

The relaxation-technique which I am suggesting to you assuredly obliterates even more completely the distinction between the analysis of children and that of adults — a distinction hitherto too sharply drawn. In making the two types of treatment more like one another I was undoubtedly influenced by what I saw of the work of Georg Groddeck, the courageous champion of the psychoanalysis of organic diseases, whom I consulted about an organic illness. I felt that he was right in trying to encourage his patients to a childlike naiveté, and I saw the success thus achieved. [Ferenczi 1930b, pp. 122-123]

FREUD AND GRODDECK

Groddeck had an interesting relationship with both Freud and Ferenczi. What is even more interesting is that Freud's initial relationship with Groddeck was more cordial than Ferenczi's. But this was later reversed, and Ferenczi and Groddeck became kindred spirits (Dupont 1984).

The relationship between Ferenczi and Groddeck can be viewed through their correspondence (Ferenczi and Groddeck 1982, published in French; as of now still untranslated into English). The Freud/Ferenczi correspondence, which is just beginning to be published (Vol. I, Brabant et al. 1993a,b,c,d; Vol. II, Brabant et al. 1994), will shed further light on the relationship as well as Freud's contribution to it. The correspondence between Ferenczi and Groddeck extended from August 1921 until April 1933. There is a quick change in salutation: Ferenczi moved from using the salutation "Sehr Geehrter Herr Kolleg" (My distinguished colleague) on August 17, 1921, to "Lieben Freund" (Dear friend) at Christmas of the same year, to "Dear Groddeck" on February 27, 1922 (Dupont 1982).

When Groddeck first wrote to him, Freud felt that this physician might be an interesting ally in the medical field. In a letter dated May 27, 1917, Groddeck outlined his concept of psychotherapy (Grossman and Grossman 1965). Groddeck also apologized for having written unfavorably about psychoanalysis, stating that his attack was rooted in envy (Grotjahn 1966).

It was from Groddeck that Freud borrowed the term *id*. Freud acknowledged that he used Groddeck's term *das es*, the It, rendered into *id* in English-speaking countries. (In turn, Groddeck, as Freud knew, had borrowed the term from Nietzsche.) In the "Traumbeit und Arbeit des organischen Symptoms" (The Effect of Dreams and of the Organic Symptom), Groddeck noted Freud's acknowledgment (cited as such in Schachet 1977):

> Freud honored me by drawing attention to me in his book *The Ego and the Id* as the person who was the first to use the expression "the It" and said that he had taken it over from me. This is true, except that the term "It" as used for my purposes was unusable to him and he turned it into something different from what I meant. As far as I can see he chose the expression in order to illustrate his ideas about his conception of what he calls topic. Yet he has not changed the nature of psychoanalysis with it, neither adding nor subtracting anything. It remained what it was, the analysis of the conscious and of the repressed parts of the psyche. But the It cannot be analysed, whether it is Freud's Id or mine which share a common name, any more than can Ferenczi's Bios. [pp. 14–15]

Groddeck's professional sense of self was very similar to Ferenczi's. ". . . to be a physician was for Groddeck, a special application of being human – passionately devoted to helping and to curing" (Grotjahn 1945, p. 11). Apparently, this was not the usual philosophy of the medical community. " . . . not sharing the dominant feeling of the Berlin analytic community which regarded Groddeck as something of a fool, both Erich Fromm and his wife admired his originality and urge to heal" (Roazen 1975, p. 512). Tribute to Groddeck's originality and importance can be found in several sources (Grossman and Grossman 1965, Grotjahn 1945, 1966, Roazen 1975, Simmel 1926). Groddeck's own works can also be consulted (Groddeck 1928, 1928/1929, 1929, 1933, 1934).

Freud's original affection for Groddeck was clearly evident when he invited him to be part of the "Wild Hunt," Freud's designation for psychoanalysis's conquest of the mind, with his followers as part of a horde (Roazen 1975). Freud's reaction to Groddeck is contained in a letter of June 5, 1917, which was a response to Groddeck's letter of May 1917, initiating their relationship.

> It is a long time since I received a letter which has pleased and interested me so much, it also tempts me to replace in answering it the normal politeness due to a stranger with analytic candor.

I will do my best: I note that you urge me to confirm to you officially that you are not a psychoanalyst, that you don't belong to the flock of disciples, but that you may be allowed to consider yourself as something apart and independent. I evidently would be doing you a great favor by rejecting you to the place where Adler, Jung and others stand. But this I cannot do; I must lay claim to you, must insist that you are an analyst of the first order who has grasped the essence of the matter once for all. The man who has recognized that transference and resistance are the hubs of treatment belongs irrevocably to the "Wild Hunt." Whether he give the "UCS" [Unconscious] the name of "Id" as well makes no difference. [Roazen 1975, p. 332]

Freud's optimism about Groddeck cooled as he realized that he didn't have a company man in this untamed clinician. He could not rein in this free-spirited person and make him a conforming member of his circle.

Freud is increasingly irritated by Groddeck's lack of rigor, by his public effusion, his whimsical approach, his "follies." Progressively, he comes to the conclusion that Groddeck is a friendly joker. And . . . he will always keep him at a distance. Never will he accept Groddeck's repeated invitations to vacation in Baden-Baden, and even more, to seek a cure there. [Dupont 1984, p. 33]

Freud's negativism toward Groddeck, once aroused, never seemed to abate. Ferenczi's valiant attempts at subduing his friend, the wild analyst, did not placate Freud. Freud felt that in Groddeck he had another untrustworthy member in the psychoanalytic movement. He seemed to compare him to Stekel, who was discredited because he was suspected of confabulating case material (Roazen 1975).

Freud wrote to Ferenczi on June 3, 1917, mentioning a "very interesting German physician whose ideas are close to Ferenczi's 'patho-neurosis,' and to their shared ideas regarding Lamarck" (Dupont 1984, p. 34). In response, Ferenczi wrote to Freud on June 13, 1917, concerning Groddeck's initial contact with Freud and indicating a negative view of this new analytic adherent. "[There was] dubious value of this method of examination. . . . Dr. Groddeck must live in a world of fantasy. . . . He obviously does not work with our psychoanalysis . . . [he has a] tendency to mysticism and dogmatism" (Dupont 1984, p. 35).

According to Dupont (1984), on October 19, 1917, Freud sent Ferenczi a publication by Groddeck and requested him to write a detailed and friendly review, which Ferenczi did. The publication was "Die Psychische Bedingheit Und Psychoanalytische Behandlung Organischen Leiden" ("Psychoanalysis of Organic States").

The review (Ferenczi 1917) seemed to be an exercise in obedience to Freud, since it extolled Groddeck's theory of the psychological basis of organic disease and clinical capacities:

> Dr. Groddeck is the first to make the courageous attempt to apply the results of Freud's discoveries to organic medicine. . . . He reports that in a great number of purely organic illnesses . . . he has succeeded in demonstrating that the illness has developed as a defence against unconscious "sensitivities" . . . He has even succeeded through psychoanalytic work . . . in improving, even curing, very severe organic illnesses . . . by [creating] more favourable conditions "for the *it* [unconsious] by which one is lived." [Ferenczi 1917, pp. 342–343]

Ferenczi (1917) also manages to take a swipe at Adler, "Freud's whipping boy":

> The sober way, free from all "finalistic" philosophizing, in which Groddeck treats the teleology demonstrable in the organic (a teleology which is determined causally) must be stressed. In this way he happily avoids the rocks on which Adler's research foundered after a promising beginning. [p. 343]

However, on June 14, 1918, Ferenczi wrote to Freud that it was more and more probable that Groddeck did not cure at all through analysis and that he did not even analyze.

> The attached letter . . . brings us an interesting perspective on the therapeutic methods of Dr. Groddeck. This man must greatly lack in judgement to let a patient . . . know about his correspondence with you. Besides, I feel it is more and more probable that Groddeck does not cure at all through analysis, and that through transference,

he utilizes the physical energy of hysteria to serve the tendency of organs toward recovery. If he can achieve such results, it's precisely because he doesn't analyze. . . . [Dupont 1984, p. 38]

At the beginning of 1921, Ferenczi reviewed a novel by Groddeck entitled *Der Seelensucher* (Soul Searcher). Ferenczi now tempered his criticism of Groddeck:

I have no knowledge whether other physicians have examined these remarkable therapeutic results and have proved or disproved them, and so for the time being I cannot say definitely whether we have to do here with a really new therapeutic method of genius or with the suggestive power of a single extraordinary medical man. On no account, however, could the consistency of the author's arguments or the sincerity of his main idea be doubted. [Ferenczi 1921a, p. 345]

Ferenczi basically praised the novel by saying:

The educational value of the book lies in the fact that the author, like Swift, Rabelais, and Balzac in the past, has torn the mask from the face of the pious, hypocritical spirit of the age and has exposed the cruelty and lust hidden behind it while at the same time comprehending its inevitability. [p. 346]

THE FERENCZI AND GRODDECK RELATIONSHIP

In 1921, Groddeck became Ferenczi's friend with what has been characterized as "a cry from the heart" in the Christmas letter of 1921. Ferenczi pleaded for understanding when he said (Ferenczi and Groddeck 1982), "I want, the ID wants, not an analytical interpretation, but something real: a young woman, a child" (Letter from Ferenczi to Groddeck, Christmas 1921, p. 60).

This plea for help contains a complicated set of issues involving Ferenczi's triangular relationship with his wife, Gizella, and her daughter, Elma (Dupont 1982, Rachman 1993a, Sabourin 1985, Torok 1984); his dissatisfactions with his analysis and relationship with Freud (which he more fully spells out in the *Clinical Diary*); his own personality shortcomings; his desire to have a mutual analytic relationship; and the childhood trauma and the development of his false self.

This letter to Groddeck is a remarkable document of emotional honesty and engagement. Groddeck became the mutual analytic partner for which Ferenczi hungered – the partner Freud could not become. The letter looks into the window of Ferenczi's true self. Ferenczi began by telling Groddeck that his childhood experiences with emotional deprivation, discipline, and prudishness resulted in a hypocrisy. This notion of the discrepancy between what parents say and what they actually do was to leave a mark on Ferenczi's personality. He was to translate this experience into the concept of "clinical hypocrisy" (Ferenczi 1933).

> Never before have I talked so openly to a man, not even to "Sigmund" whose name has caused the spelling error. . . . On several occasions I let myself be analysed by him (once for three weeks, another for 4 – 5 weeks, and for years we've travelled together every summer). But I never felt free to open myself totally to him. He had too much of this "prudish respect," he was too important for me, too much of a father. The result: in Palermo, where he wanted to do this famous work on paranoia (Schreber) with me, I had a sudden attack of rebellion. I jumped to my feet, on the first evening of work, because he wanted me to take down his dictation. I told him that to have me simply take down his thoughts was not writing a paper together.

In the same letter, Ferenczi said his openness with Groddeck has helped him to be open with his wife, especially about his "repressed love" for her daughter Elma:

> I told her again about my dissatisfaction about my repressed love for her daughter (who should have been my fiancée. As a matter of fact, she was my fiancée, until a somewhat disapproving comment from Freud led me to struggle with all my might against this love and to categorically reject this young girl). Between us this kind of confession ends up in a strange manner. I am overwhelmed by her goodness and indulgence, and I feel closer to her again. . . . In any case, ever since the last encounter, I feel less and less cold every night; cold as in death. I also started zealously doing exercise again;

foot massages on my stomach [treatment invented by Grod-deck]. . . . [Ferenczi and Groddeck 1982, p. 55]

Ferenczi had changed his original reservations about Groddeck and began a campaign to convince Freud of Groddeck's "faithfulness to psychoanalysis."

On August 31, 1922, Ferenczi writes Freud that he is doing a little self-analysis in the presence and with the help of Groddeck. He is also retracing, so to speak, previous judgments, and notes that Groddeck proceeds "with caution." . . . He hopes to help dissipate the misunderstanding that made Freud think that Groddeck worked with the Stekelian method.

In a letter of September 21, 1924, Ferenczi writes to Freud that Groddeck [has] "always been faithful to psychoanalysis."

In the memo of August 18, 1925, he attempts to convince Abraham that one shouldn't use essays to intimidate Groddeck; in his letter of August 10, 1925: "He remains, imperturbably, on the grounds of psychoanalysis . . . " and he adds: "a worshipper of" Freud. On September 9, 1926: "He is faithful to our causes, even if he follows his own paths." [Dupont 1984, pp. 39–40]

In two letters in 1925, Ferenczi continued his defense of Groddeck, hoping to convince Freud of his friend's faithfulness to their joint cause and to give Freud alternate material to temper criticisms of Groddeck within the psychoanalytic community.

Ferenczi to Freud: August 1925
My relation to Groddeck is very pleasant. It is very refreshing. On the other hand, I think I have a moderate influence on his intuitive mode of thinking or working. In this manner, I help him remain within the boundaries of science.

Ferenczi to Freud: November 23, 1925
Groddeck has an intuitive spirit. His hunches regarding a possible extension of psychoanalysis to the organic call for more . . . attention . . . his lectures have been very beneficial. Both in the professional and public lectures, however, it must be noted that there were points that went beyond the psychoanalytic point of view. The members of the association participated in a lively con-versation. The physicians among the members had to recognize the

validity of his main criticisms of "organicists." Physicians neglect the personality of their patients. But, they all rejected certain exaggerations in his presentation.

Groddeck seemed more open to our arguments. Personally, I've learned a lot from Groddeck, especially the act of forgetting occasionally what I've learned about medicine. Of course, I consider it to be a necessity to also occasionally remember what was learned. It is from this unique combination of knowing when to remember, when to forget, that can be useful to the psychoanalysis of the organic. [Dupont 1984, p. 40]

Groddeck as Ferenczi's "Analytic Physician"

Groddeck was Ferenczi's healer. Ferenczi became a patient of Groddeck's on the advice of Felix Deutsch (Schachet 1977). Ferenczi had been ill with nephritis in 1921; nephrosclerosis complicated by severe headaches (Grossman and Grossman 1965). According to Schur (1972), it was toxic goiter. In any event, his physician could do no more for him, and Freud's physician, Felix Deutsch, was consulted.

In September 1921, Ferenczi decided to seek treatment at Groddeck's sanitarium at Baden-Baden. Apparently, he believed he had some "Groddeckian Symptoms"—neck pains he attributed to psychological causes (Dupont 1984). The treatment was beneficial, but more importantly, he was engaged by Groddeck's warmth, freedom to fantasize, and independence of thought. Little by little, he sent his family and friends to Groddeck. Grotjahn (1945) wrote, "Ferenczi never tired of singing Groddeck's praises and telling others of the benefit he derived from his regular, annual 'analytic holiday' in Groddeck's sanitarium" (p. 315).

Ferenczi's "Analytic Cure" at Baden-Baden

Ferenczi was a frequent visitor to Groddeck's sanitarium at Baden-Baden, going for the cure as much as to maintain contact with his kindred spirit. Groddeck believed he could contribute to the cure of any individual, whether it was a disease of the body, mind, or spirit.

Ferenczi's visits to Baden-Baden included the employment of one of his famous indulgences. A British ophthalmic surgeon, Dr. William Inman, had sought analysis with Ferenczi on Freud's advice. Inman, a pioneer in psychosomatic medicine, had developed the notion that most patients who consult an ophthalmologist are suffering from some sort of neurotic symptom, especially phobias. Complaints about light or darkness, he reasoned, were rooted in childhood fears. Inman's psychological theory was ignored, and the craze for glasses went on. He was determined to continue research into his theory.

> But research also went on, since the few analysts of that time already had enough to do in mental exploration. . . . Freud directed me to Sandor Ferenczi, a fortunate choice as it happened because a few years earlier the latter himself, apparently incurably ill from kidney disease, had gone for treatment to that master of psychosomatic medicine, Georg Groddeck, and had been cured. [Grossman and Grossman 1965, p. 139]

Dr. Inman was so determined to be trained in psychoanalysis and psychosomatic medicine that, during the customary summer holiday, he did not want an interruption in his analysis. When Ferenczi went to Baden-Baden, Inman took a room in a hotel and had his daily analytic session. C. M. Grossman and S. Grossman (1965) wrote:

> One day when Inman had been indulging on the couch in highly speculative theories about disease and the emotions, Ferenczi exclaimed, "Dear me, this is out-Groddecking Groddeck!" But he would only say of Groddeck, when Inman asked who he was, that they must meet one day. [p. 139]

Among the other European analysts who appreciated Groddeck's artistic and intellectual spirit were Fromm-Reichmann, Horney, Rank, and Simmel. Besides Ferenczi, Horney and Simmel took an analytic holiday at Baden-Baden. In 1933, Groddeck wrote his last book, *Man As Symbol*. He reluctantly sent it to Freud, even though he didn't want to trouble him during the dark time of Nazism. In addition, Groddeck's intuition may have also discerned that his mentor was also enveloped in an inner darkness, as his mouth cancer began to sap his spirit. Sigmund had Anna respond to Groddeck, telling him he had read the book with great interest and reassuring him he was not mentally disturbed.

The year 1933 was also a dark year for Groddeck's friend Ferenczi, who was lying in his sickbed, dying of pernicious anemia. Groddeck had also sent Ferenczi a copy of *Man As Symbol*. Although failing in health, he responded from his sickbed that he loved the book (Grotjahn 1966).

The Impulse to Heal

Both Ferenczi and Groddeck were linked together by their identity as doctors who wished to treat the difficult case and in their belief that they could be the agent for a cure. Groddeck was inventive and daring and would try a method if it promised to help a patient. He was not bound by a theoretical framework and was not as interested in understanding the cure as he was in the cure itself. (A letter of November 12, 1922, from Groddeck to Ferenczi expresses his deliberate effort *not* to understand [Ferenczi and Groddeck 1982]). Ferenczi was also daring, experimental, and interested in understanding. In fact, one could say that his clinical experiments were an attempt to more fully understand both the difficult analysand and the process of analytic cure in preoedipal cases. They both argued that doctors should not try to fit their patients into a theory that does not suit their needs. Ferenczi felt that analysands should not be selected on the basis of whether they were analyzable in the traditional sense. Rather, analysts should adapt their procedures and their functioning to fit the needs of the individuals.

Both were very aware of the personal factor in the analytic cure and that they needed to examine their contribution to the analytic process. They were remarkable in this sense; they were as daring in examining themselves as they were in finding means to help their patients.

In a letter to Groddeck dated October 11, 1922, Ferenczi mentions the ultimate flexibility and daring in the process of examining the analyst's contribution to the treatment process. In this letter Ferenczi alludes, for the first time, to the idea of mutual analysis (Ferenczi and Groddeck 1982). Apparently, the origin of the idea was Groddeck's, in that he had been pursuing a kind of mutual treatment experiment. In Groddeck's "Lectures to the Patients," he spoke a great deal about himself, and he believed that these were a vital component of the treatment provided. Ferenczi's correspondence can be viewed as a form of mutual analysis, as both clinicians reveal themselves to each other and attempt to offer meaningful responses to encourage healing.

Groddeck's last talk was in May 1934, when he lectured on "Eyes,

Vision, and Vision Without Eyes." Grossman and Grossman (1965) wrote, "Afterward, he collapsed . . . yet he seemed to be possessed of endless energies. He planned great things, a treatment which could rid the whole German nation of cancer. . . . Frieda Fromm-Reichman [was ordered] to take dictation . . . a few days later, he was dead" (pp. 195–197).

Groddeck had complete confidence in his approach to healing — one could say a kind of fanaticism. His capacity to heal was significant, and in that he shared a personal and professional gift with Ferenczi. Groddeck's belief in his healing capacity, however, went beyond the more humble and modest claims of Ferenczi. Ferenczi had a complete dedication to healing; he would not give up on a case, no matter how difficult. He felt that there was always a new idea, an innovative technique that could lead to a cure. But Groddeck believed he could cure anyone, including Hitler, to whom he wrote, trying to convince him that he was misled and that he could help him. According to Grossman and Grossman (1965), "When there was no answer, he wrote again. Groddeck could not believe that Hitler was evil or that he wasn't interested in the Baden-Baden cure." (p. 159)

Ferenczi's "Confessor"

This dialogue with Groddeck was the one Ferenczi wished to have with Freud. Groddeck did not evoke a superior or authoritarian attitude, but entered into a peer relationship with Ferenczi, even though Groddeck was the doctor. Groddeck's nonjudgmental and accepting attitude paved the way for Ferenczi to open up, telling him his emotional problems. Groddeck was a "brother confessor" not a "father confessor" (Ferenczi and Groddeck 1982, p. 55).

Ferenczi's Last Days

In the last months of Ferenczi's life, he apparently wanted Groddeck to take care of him. Ferenczi's stepdaughter Elma said (Grossman and Grossman 1965), "I think he would have liked to consult Dr. Groddeck . . . but . . . he was unable to travel, the consultation was postponed — and then it was too late" (p. 192).

Lou Andreas-Salomé told Ferenczi's wife that it was unfortunate that Ferenczi could not be treated by Groddeck. "Groddeck would have saved him," she said to Gizella Ferenczi (Grossman and Grossman 1965) .

However, in the gathering storm of Nazi Germany, Ferenczi, a Jew, would have had difficulty entering the south of Germany to receive treatment at Groddeck's Baden-Baden facility. Nor could Groddeck have gone to see Ferenczi. By 1932, Hitler was in power, travel was restricted, and he may have been prevented from treating a Jewish psychoanalyst (Grossman and Grossman 1965).

A series of letters was exchanged between Gizella Ferenczi and Groddeck regarding Ferenczi's illness and Groddeck's evaluation of their friendship. In December 1933, Mrs. Ferenczi wrote to Groddeck:

> In March he was already so weak that he had to stop giving lessons and we thought that a long rest until September would help him out of this weakness. Unfortunately, his illness, pernicious anemia, does not know mercy, and he became weaker and weaker. . . . He lay in bed for four weeks. On the 22nd of May, the day he died, he still spoke with us, read the paper (which repeatedly fell from his hands) and he called S. to him to tell her: "It will be revised." [Grossman and Grossman 1965, p. 191]

On February 19, 1934, Groddeck wrote to Gizella:

> These last few years I have only been able to think of Sandor's life with a heavy heart. He became a victim of his spirit of scientific investigation, a fate which has been spared to me only by my own lack of thirst for knowledge. I must first speak of myself. Even before I went on to psychoanalysis there was as a basic in my medical thinking the conviction that in the human being, aside from the psyche with which science occupies itself, there exist thousands and millions of more or less independent inner lives which group themselves sometimes this way, sometimes another, working together or in opposition, and are even quite independent at times. With this conclusion I have satisfied myself and I have never tried to study this cosmos. It just isn't in my nature to concern myself with things which I consider inexplicable.
>
> In my close friendship with Sandor I noticed relatively early that he judged these things similarly, but with shock, I saw then that he was about to search in the world of man scientifically even if possible to picture it so that one could take part in this, one might also call it drama. This striving became overpowering with him. To

me he used the expression, "I atomize the soul." However, such atomizing, when it is attempted seriously, can only end with self-destruction, because the other man is and will remain to us a secret; we can only atomize our own soul and that destroys us. The form in which Sandor . . . was finally delivered of the pains of a superhuman struggle is quite beside the point. I tried every now and then to point out the dangers of his ways to him; but just as one cannot stop a raging storm with a bare hand, so I could not help Sandor. When someone says that I might have been able to do it, then is this a mistake? As close as we were, he was already far removed from me in a flight to the stars which I could not and would not join.

Gizella replied a week later:

Your letter, Dear Pat [Groddeck's nickname], has excited and moved me deeply. I can see from it that you also needed quiet and reflection before you wanted to answer me and to make your standpoint clear to me. . . .

The experiences of these last years have shown me that nobody, not even you, could help him. There was a change in him which not only destroyed his body slowly, but also had a great influence upon his psychic life. His "flight to the stars," which you call it so well, flung him to such distances that he himself did not know where the final end was. From this, his desperate searching, his battle with science and conscience, his continually lasting doubts of that which already had been discovered, all this undermined his health in body and soul and caused his destruction. Would you not think that his diseased and with-time-destroyed kidney added to this? If ever someone helped in his battle, it was you, who could be master of yourself for so long. You yourself know how refreshed he always left you, how well he felt with you, and no one had such a long-lasting influence on him as you, my dear Pat. [Grossman and Grossman 1965, pp. 193–195]

THE LAST CONTACT BETWEEN FERENCZI AND FREUD

The Ferenczi/Groddeck correspondence indicates that a real break between Freud and Ferenczi never occurred (see letter of March 20, 1933,

Ferenczi and Groddeck 1982, p. 127 [Dupont 1982] as well the last letters exchanged between Ferenczi and Freud and between Gizella Ferenczi and Freud [see Chapter 3]).

Three weeks before Ferenczi's death on May 4, 1933, he wrote Freud:

> . . . the date of your birthday is still present in our memory . . . my symptoms are unchanged. I try to have faith in the optimistic words of my doctors.
>
> Your Sándor and Gizella Ferenczi

FERENCZI AND ELMA

Ferenczi's triangular relationship with his daughter-in-law Elma and his wife Gizella has been chronicled (Dupont 1982, Masson 1984, Rachman 1993a). Ferenczi referred Elma to Groddeck for a cure, which he mentioned in a letter of May 2, 1922 (Ferenczi and Groddeck 1982).

The Ferenczi/Groddeck relationship is a source of additional information about Ferenczi and Elma Pálos. The information comes from a secondary source, Frederick Kovács, who had undergone a cure at Baden-Baden. Prior to becoming his student, Vilma Kovács, Frederick's wife, was an analysand of Ferenczi's. She later became a member of the Budapest Psychoanalytic Society.

The Kovácses were personal friends of Ferenczi, and, as with his other friends, he recommended them to Groddeck's sanatorium. Frederick Kovács suffered from cardiovascular and digestive difficulties. Toward the end of 1927, he was persuaded to take a cure with Groddeck. The first treatments lasted seven weeks. During this time, he wrote his wife one letter a day. In his letters he detailed, day by day, sometimes hour by hour, his life at the sanatorium and his discussions with Groddeck. These letters give us a view of how Ferenczi valued his relationship with Groddeck. In particular, the Kovacses' letters clarify Ferenczi's relationship with Elma.

Letter from Frederick Kovács to Vilma Kovács, January 8, 1927
    You won't believe . . . what Groddeck told me; . . . Ferenczi first loved Gizella, then got engaged to Elma; . . . the engagement was broken . . . it's after that Ferenczi married Gizella. . . . Gizella's

dearest wish and project . . . is to have Sandor divorce her and marry Elma . . . (Ferenczi and Groddeck 1982, p. 135]

TECHNICAL ISSUES

Ferenczi referred to the technical debt he owed to Groddeck in "Principles of Relaxation and Neocatharsis."

> In a conversation with Anna Freud in which we discussed certain points in my technique she made the following pregnant remark: "You really treat your patients as I treat the children whom I analyse." I had to admit that she was right, and I would remind you that in my most recent publication, a short paper on the psychology of unwanted children who later become subjects for analysis, I stated that the real analysis of resistances must be prefaced by a kind of comforting preparatory treatment. The relaxation-technique which I am suggesting to you assuredly obliterates even more completely the distinction between the analysis of children and that of adults — a distinction hitherto too sharply drawn. In making the two types of treatment more like one another I was undoubtedly influenced by what I saw of the work of Georg Groddeck, the courageous champion of the psycho-analysis of organic diseases, whom I consulted about an organic illness. I felt that he was right in trying to encourage his patients to a childlike *naïveté*, and I saw the success thus achieved. But, for my own part, I have remained faithful to the well-tried analytical method of frustration as well, and I try to attain my aim by the tactful and understanding appreciation of *both* forms of technique. [Ferenczi 1930b, pp. 122–123].

Simmel's ideas and methods were of value to both Groddeck and Ferenczi. As has been mentioned, Simmel was one of Groddeck's champions in analytical circles. Ferenczi, in developing his relaxation therapy, felt that Simmel's analytic in-patient treatment approach had relevance (Ferenczi 1930b).

In "Termination of Analysis" Ferenczi (1927a) said that the "difference between him [Groddeck] and me is that he sets out for his goal straight from the symptoms while I try to reach it by means of the 'orthodox' analytic technique, though at a slower pace" (p. 84).

Groddeck was, in turn, critical of Ferenczi in his conception of bioanalysis (Ferenczi 1924a): "Groddeck . . . attacked violently what he called 'scientification' and the 'rape of the divine' by psychoanalysis, and the appropriateness of the term 'bioanalysis' when 'every analysis was always . . . concerned with Bios, Life' " (Grotjahn 1945, p. 19). Groddeck "criticized Ferenczi's recent coinage of the term Bio-analysis, which 'has enlarged the confusion.' There is no such thing as Bioanalysis . . . life does not let itself be analyzed, one can only speculate about life" (Grotjahn 1945, p. 19).

In "Contra-Indications to the 'Active' Psychoanalytic Technique" (Ferenczi 1925a), Ferenczi compared the differences in active technique between Alexander and Groddeck. Ferenczi said that Groddeck would aggravate a patient's symptoms by offering a transference interpretation that suggested the patient was aggressing against the analyst. Ferenczi made it clear that his active technique was orthodox in comparison to Groddeck's. Yet Ferenczi said in this essay that "the credit of priority belongs to Groddeck, who, when the condition of one of his patients is aggravated, always comes forward with the stereotyped question 'what have you against me, what have I done to you.' " Ferenczi also added, "[a] degree of value placed on the analytic situation is only indirectly concerned with activity . . . no way implies activity in my meaning" (p. 225).

Ferenczi (1926d) discussed the issues of organic development in his "bio-analytical" framework.

> . . . we can accordingly distinguish even in the organic between primary and secondary processes — processes, that is, which in the realm of the mind we regard as stages in intellectual development. That would mean, however, that in a certain degree and sense the organic also possesses a kind of reckoning-machine, which is concerned not simply with qualities of pleasure and 'pain,' but also with quantities. To be sure, organic adaptation is characterized by a certain inflexibility, seen in the reflex processes which are undoubtedly purposive but immutable, while the capacity for adaptation shows a continual readiness to recognize new realities and the capacity to inhibit action until the act of thinking is completed. Groddeck is therefore right in regarding the organic id as intelligent; but he shows bias when he overlooks the difference in degree between the intelligence of the ego and that of the id. [p. 375]

MUTUAL ANALYTIC PEERS

It is clear from the Ferenczi/Groddeck correspondence that Ferenczi took it upon himself to become Groddeck's mentor and help him build and maintain a bridge to the analytic community. Ferenczi recognized Groddeck's special qualities of intuition, spontaneity, and emotionality, as well as his knowledge and appreciation of the organic. In many ways, Groddeck was an example of a holistic clinician, combining the knowledge and appreciation of the body with a willingness to explore the contribution that the personality makes to human behavior. Ferenczi respected Groddeck's intellectual capacities, inviting him to lecture in Budapest in the middle 1920s, at a time when he and Rank had already published the disquieting *Development of Psychoanalysis* and when he himself was beginning to drift toward a dissident view. No doubt his friendship with Groddeck gave him a compatriot with whom he could identify, test the waters of independence, and gain support for unusual views. It is clear that Groddeck, like his friend Ferenczi, was a stimulating presenter, who encouraged new thoughts in his audience and heightened the emotional experience of learning. This kind of learning, which became characteristic of Ferenczi, was the stimulation of the intellect in a heightened emotional atmosphere. It was discussed in *Development of Psychoanalysis* and would become Ferenczi's hallmark of clinical functioning in the psychoanalytic situation as he moved toward the fuller development of his humanistic method.

The degree to which he trusted Groddeck emotionally is clearly indicated in his bold announcement to Freud that he, Ferenczi, was undergoing a self-analysis with Groddeck's assistance. The self-analysis with Groddeck may have been prompted by Ferenczi's need to continue his analysis while he was beginning to feel the deficiencies in the formal analytic experience with Freud, which he revealed in the *Clinical Diary*. Ferenczi and Groddeck were spiritual brothers in their temperament, intellect, manner of relating an independent attitude, and relation to authority. Furthermore, Groddeck's position of not being a member of the "Society of Rings," the inner circle of Freud's faithful, allowed Ferenczi a less risky political and professional experience. The self-analysis, of course, was being carried out in the presence of one another. This condition of a dyad brings to mind a precursor for Ferenczi's mutual analysis that he would conduct later with Elizabeth Severn.

That Ferenczi could be objective about Groddeck's shortcomings is evident from a later correspondence with Freud.

> Even behind the words of Groddeck . . . behind his statements on disease, he is 'Id' and so on. I could detect things that have a real future. But his intuition needs logical direction, more adequate scientific bases. It might be possible to provide him with part of his effort. [Dupont 1984, p. 40]

One of the functions that Groddeck served for Ferenczi was to be an analytic self-help peer or, in Ferenczi's terms, a "mutual analysand." Groddeck was the colleague, peer, and analytic clinician who was his closest emotional partner in the dark period when Ferenczi drifted away from Freud and toward humanistic psychoanalysis. Although there were colleagues who thought highly of his later dissident work—most notably Rank, Alexander, and Simmel—none was able to give him the support he needed during the most difficult period, 1932, when he turned down the IPA presidency, delivered the "Confusion of Tongues" paper, and wrote his *Clinical Diary*. Ferenczi initiated his correspondence with Groddeck in 1921, and it lasted until a month before his death in 1933. During this twelve-year period, Ferenczi "enjoyed the most lasting friendship" with Groddeck (Dupont 1984, p. 34). It was Groddeck, his trusted students, and his self-analysis *(Clinical Diary)* that became the emotional and interpersonal life-saving devices for Ferenczi during the very difficult period of his last clinical phase. Ferenczi was also Groddeck's mutual analyst. In a letter to Freud on May 31, 1923, Groddeck told of his mutual analytic experience with Ferenczi.

> In September 1921 Ferenczi had his first treatment with me and I know that I felt proud and thought to myself: "What stupid people analysts are." I also told him a number of times: "You do things like this or like that, but I . . ." And I made no exception of Freud. . . . Next year, Ferenczi came to me again, I treated him again and was analysed by him about six or seven times. He talked to me very seriously about my father complex. I listened to all this and the result was that a few weeks later I said to his sister-in-law and stepdaughter: "The other paralytics" (instead of analysts), and the unconscious self-mockery of this still makes me laugh. This too happened around the anniversary of my father's death. [Schachet 1977, pp. 81–82]

Beneath both Groddeck's own negative self-evaluation of the Wild Analyst and the negative view of orthodox psychoanalysis is the compelling picture of a passionate, inventive, larger-than-life figure (the experiential reports of his actual physical height vary from 5' 7" to 6' 6"), an emotional dynamo whose direct honesty emerges in the affectionate portraits by Grossman and Grossman (1965), Grotjahn (1945, 1966), and Schachet (1977). It is no wonder that Ferenczi was able to work through his initial negative reaction and finally embrace Groddeck as a kindred spirit, healer, friend, and mutual analytic partner. Groddeck's work, like Ferenczi's, deserves reexamination and reevaluation for the contribution it made to contemporary psychoanalysis. Grotjahn (1966) has outlined the influence of "the untamed analyst" in his respectful and thoughtful examination of Groddeck's contributions.

> Grantly Dick-Read's theory and technique of *natural childbirth* are the final confirmation of some of Groddeck's early ideas. John Rosen has applied Groddeck's approach in the direct analysis of schizophrenic patients. In Switzerland, Madame Sechehaye has followed Groddeck's ways of thinking and acting in her method of *symbolic realization*. Many of Groddeck's thoughts have found their expression in the system developed by Melanie Klein. Still another application of Groddeck's technique led to Jacob Moreno's Psychodrama. The work of René Spitz with anaclitic depression confirms Groddeck's intuition and continues where he left off. The influence of Groddeck's ideas can be seen in Géza Róheim's work. Psychoanalysis has always postulated the pleasure principle as restricted by the reality principle. Recently, a third principle has been formulated, which might be called the principle of magic—mystic, or symbolic, thinking. All human mental activity starts this way, and Groddeck expressed it and applied it consistently in his praxis of healing. [p. 319]

The biographers (Grossman and Grossman 1965) of Groddeck's life and work reached an interesting conclusion about the Ferenczi/Groddeck relationship: "It is interesting to note that Dr. Balint was analyzed by Ferenczi, who must have established some sort of record for analyzing creative, original thinkers. Without exception, Ferenczi's analysands have shown great enthusiasm for Groddeck" (p. 200).

6

JONES'S CHARACTER ASSASSINATION OF FERENCZI: OEDIPAL RIVALRY WITH THE MASTER'S "FAVORITE SON"

THE ANALYTIC COMMUNITY TURNS AWAY FROM FERENCZI

Jones's assertion that Ferenczi was psychotic is one of the most mean-spirited and damaging accusations in the history of psychoanalysis. How Jones came to this assertion is another great mystery that surrounds Ferenczi's life. Whatever the motivation, it is safe to say that Jones's accusations, the political intrigues during Ferenczi's lifetime (Fromm 1959, Roazen 1975), and Jones's assertions of psychosis published in his widely influential biography on Freud (Jones 1953–1957), contributed significantly to a negative view of Ferenczi within the psychoanalytic establishment. Furthermore, it added a new, damaging dimension to the voices that wanted to remove Ferenczi's name and work from the mainstream of psychoanalytic thought and clinical practice.

It is curious that few analysts have risen up and voiced indignation or severe criticism regarding Jones's shabby and unjust treatment of Ferenczi, Fromm's courageous discussions being an exception (Fromm 1959, 1963, 1970). Perhaps they followed Freud's model when he turned away from Ferenczi during the latter part of their relationship. The report of the analytic community's response to Ferenczi's "The Confusion of

Tongues" indicates a uniform negative reaction (including one of his leading students and supporters, Michael Balint) (Masson 1984). One cannot discount the power of Freud's disapproval as a role model for the analytic community to emulate. Esther Menaker, a leading American psychoanalyst who was a student at the Vienna Psychoanalytic Institute during the 1930s, verified the analytic community's turning away from Ferenczi. Ferenczi's death on May 22, 1933, was announced at a seminar conducted by Helene Deutsch. Menaker (1986) remembers that a negative silence filled the room after the announcement was made, as if no one was permitted to express any positive feelings about him.

Jones's case against Ferenczi is cleverly orchestrated. First, he presents material to assert that Freud and Ferenczi always had personal difficulties because of Ferenczi's psychopathology. Then he asserts that Ferenczi had negative personality characteristics, as witness his "dictatorial side." Finally, with these issues established, he asserts that Ferenczi showed signs of psychosis throughout his life, which negatively affected his relationship with Freud as well as his own clinical work. These psychotic trends became more evident, Jones argues, during the latter period of his clinical work, when he tried to establish his own method and move away from Freud. According to Jones, Ferenczi was overtly psychotic when he died.

JONES'S ASSERTIONS ABOUT FREUD
AND FERENCZI'S RELATIONSHIP

The statements about Freud and Ferenczi's relationship are contained in Jones's biography on Freud (Jones 1953–1957). Jones admitted that the disagreements between Freud and Ferenczi were complicated: " . . . so involved as to make it harder to pass an opinion" (p. 162). He also stated that Freud's personality may have contributed to his difficulties with people. "Several times in his writings Freud mentioned his need for a loved friend and hated enemy . . . he could both love and hate passionately" (p. 162).

Jones seemed ambivalent about the nature of the personal relationship between Freud and Ferenczi. On the one hand he clearly stated that the first meeting between the two was "electric" and that Ferenczi immediately became a favorite of Freud and his family. Jones (1955) went on to say that "Freud was attracted by Ferenczi's enthusiasm and lively speculative turn of mind, qualities which had previously fascinated him in his great friend Fliess" (pp. 34–35). However, Jones qualified the relationship as being more of sharing intellectual and scientific interests than personal. Speaking of the contrast in Freud's friendship between Fliess and Ferenczi, he pointed out the following.

JONES'S ASSERTIONS OF FERENCZI'S NEGATIVE PERSONALITY TRAITS

Ferenczi's negative personality qualities became the second level of ad hominum argument that Jones marshalled to prove his ultimate accusation of Ferenczi's psychosis. At the 1910 Congress, Jones (1955) asserted that Ferenzci's "dictatorial side" encouraged "a great storm of protest"

> In his speech he had made some very derogatory remarks about the quality of Vienese analysts. . . . suggested that the center of the future administration could only be Zurich, with Jung as President. . . . Moreover, Ferenczi, with all his personal charm, *had a decidedly dictatorial side to him* . . . [italics added]. Some of his proposals went far beyond what is customary in scientific circles. . . .
> Ferenczi went on to assert the necessity for all papers written or addresses delivered by any psychoanalyst to be first submitted for approval to the President of the Association, who was thus to have unheard of censoring powers. *It was this attitude of Ferenzci's that was later to cause such trouble between European and American analysts which it took me, in particular, years to compose* [p. 69, italics added]

Jones also indicated that the content of Ferenczi's presentations at the 1910 Congress met with Freud's approval, including of his proposal of an elite to lead psychoanalysis. Freud also approved of the proposal that the Swiss analysts be nominated to president and secretary, in order to establish psychoanalysis beyond the province of Viennese Jews. It has been documented in other sources that it was Freud's idea to have Jung become the first president of the Psychoanalytic Society (Roazen 1975).

There were other difficulties at the Congress that related to Adler and Stekel. Freud turned to Ferenczi to unburden himself because of the difficulties that Adler and Stekel were causing him: "The tactlessness and unpleasant behavior of Adler and Stekel make it very difficult to get along together. I am chronically exasperated with both of them" (Jones 1955, p. 30).

This admission appeared to confirm that Ferenczi wasn't totally at fault for the negative reaction at the 1910 Congress. It was a difficult time, as factions jockeyed for position in the newly formed association of psychoanalysis. But Jones chose to highlight Ferenczi's negative behavior and said that it took Ferenczi only two years after having met Freud to display negative personality traits that were to cause difficulty for the psychoanalytic movement.

JONES'S ASSERTION THAT FERENCZI HAD AN EXAGGERATED NEED FOR LOVE AND AFFECTION

Freud wrote to Ferenczi regarding Bleuler's need for love, suggesting it was a natural, not a neurotic, need. Furthermore, Freud asserted that it was the same kind of love he and Ferenczi needed (Jones 1955).

Jones (1955) made a reference to Ferenczi's difficulty in not receiving a positive response from a paper read before the Budapest Society of Physicians in 1911. He used what was a negative climate for psychoanalysis in all medical circles at that time to point out another alleged negative quality of Ferenczi: "For several years Hungary did not seem favorable soil for psychoanalysis, but later on it relieved Ferenczi from his loneliness by providing a number of excellent analysts" (p. 74).

It has been documented that Ferenczi may have had an exaggerated need for love (Balint 1968b, Thompson 1944). But it is only Jones who used this personality issue as ammunition for character assassination. Balint and Thompson cite this failing of Ferenczi in a compassionate manner, attempting to explain one of the personal mainsprings of his clinical functioning.

JONES'S ASSERTION THAT FERENCZI WAS PSYCHOTIC

Obviously, the assertion by Jones that Ferenczi was psychotic was the most serious charge. We need to examine the actual statements by Jones regarding Ferenczi's alleged psychosis, present the rebuttals, and then speculate on the motivations behind this damaging, mean-spirited and unfounded accusation.

The references to Ferenczi's madness began in Volume II of the Freud biography. Jones referred to "severe trouble in the depths" of Ferenczi's personality and how Ferenczi's "stability began to crumble." He began by referring to the Sicily trip, where Freud and Ferenczi had a dispute. Jones asserted that the dispute, which occurred in 1910, was not only the beginning of the manifestation of Ferenczi's pathology, but was "fateful for their subsequent relationship." Since the bond between them was the "most important Freud was to forge in his later years, it is necessary to mention briefly the beginning of their difficulties" (Jones 1955, p. 82).

Jones goes on to describe the "emerging madness" of Ferenczi that became clear in the vacation in Sicily:

> But behind those manifestations lay severe trouble in the depths of his personality. . . . he was haunted by a quite inordinate and insatiable longing for his father's love. It was the dominating passion of his life and was indirectly the source of the unfortunate changes he introduced into his psychoanalytic technique twenty years later, which had the effect of estranging him from Freud (though not Freud from him). [Jones 1955, p. 82]

Let us see what Jones has done with this first reported difficulty in the interpersonal relationship between Freud and Ferenczi. Freud and Ferenczi had been intimate friends and colleagues for about two years at the time of this vacation to Italy. There had been no serious disagreements or conflicts during their 1909 American trip (Clark 1980a, Doorley 1982, Koelsch 1970). In fact, Freud had used Ferenczi as an alter-ego during the Clark Lectures (Freud 1933a), and the pattern for intimacy—a sharing of professional and personal material—had been established on this trip. On the voyage over, Freud, Ferenczi, and Jung shared their dreams with one another, taking turns analyzing them (Sabourin 1984). In analytic terms, nothing could be more intimate. Yet Jones chose to characterize Ferenczi's desire for closeness with Freud as a sign of emerging psychopathology.

That two close friends would have a personal disagreement after two uninterrupted years of friendship is not a serious event. In fact, it is unusual that they did not quarrel sooner. It is also likely that Ferenczi's desire for closeness was not a new phenomenon, but a continued desire and experience reinforced by Freud's need as well.

Jones (1955) also introduced a damaging and misguided assertion that Ferenczi's deivations in analytic technique were the result of his longing for fatherly love. The implication is clear. It is inconceivable to Jones that Ferenczi's deviations from Freudian technique were the result of creative genius. Rather, he believed that Ferenczi's clinical experiments were the product of a deranged mind.

After the incident in Sicily, Ferenczi felt badly about his behavior and feared that it would cause a serious impediment to his friendship with Freud. He wrote Freud a letter expressing his anxiety. Jones referred to the letter without making any overt judgment about Ferenczi's mental health, which is surprising, since Freud seemed to be quite direct and harsh in referring to Ferenczi's instability (Jones 1955).

Freud also seemed to be dismissing Ferenczi's attempts at closeness when he wrote that there were no issues in their relationship (Jones 1955).

Freud offered three explanations for his impatience with Ferenczi's attempt at greater emotional intimacy. He said that there was the matter of the unresolved countertransference issues from his analysis with Ferenczi, the disagreeable mood that his gastrointestinal problem presented while on vacation, and his unwillingness to enter into another totally revealing and devastating relationship of the kind he had with Fliess.

The second reference to Ferenczi's serious emotional problems in Volume II of Jones's (1955) Freud biography is as follows.

> The generosity and tactfulness Freud constantly displayed towards Ferenczi, and his great fondness for him, preserved a valuable friendship for many years until, long after this episode, Ferenczi's own *stability began to crumble.* [p. 84, italics added]

Jones was apparently referring to Freud's willingness to put the unpleasantness of the Sicily trip behind him, once the air was cleared. But Jones could not pass up an opportunity to reinforce the notion that the unpleasantness of this trip was an early indicator of Ferenczi's madness.

In Volume III, Jones mentions Ferenczi's alleged psychosis repeatedly. It first appears as a self-serving statement regarding the mental stability of the founding committee that originally surrounded Freud.

> Adherence to what psychoanalysis had revealed signifies the same as retaining one's insight into the workings of the unconscious, and the ability to do so presupposes a high degree of mental stability. My

hope . . . was that the six of us were suitably endowed for that purpose. It turned out, alas, that only four of us were. Two of the members, Rank and Ferenczi, were not able to hold out to the end. . . . *Ferenczi more gradually toward the end of his life, developed psychotic manifestations that revealed themselves in, among other ways, a turning away from Freud and his doctrines. The seeds of a destructive psychosis, invisible for so long, at last germinated.* [Jones 1957, p. 45 italics added]

There are several significant implications to this first statement regarding Ferenczi's alleged psychosis. Jones makes it appear that he, not Ferenczi, had the original idea for a support group to surround Freud (Jones 1955). He also sets himself up as the epitome of mental health, but, as is documented, Jones had been arrested for child molesting (Roazen 1975).

Of course, the most serious, misguided, and damaging statement was the accusation that Ferenczi developed psychotic manifestations. Apparently, Jones was not aware that he made a blatant, fallacious, and causal connection between Ferenczi's deviations from Freud's doctrines and his psychotic manifestation. The implication in Jones's distorted logic is clear: if one goes beyond Freud to a new direction, one is likely to be psychotic. There is no room for the evolution of psychoanalytic technique and theory. Adherence to Freudian doctrine is not only the standard for professional competence in psychoanalysis, but for emotional well-being as well. It may be one of the few times in the history of science that creative departures in technique (actually originated and supported by Freud (Freud 1919 [1918]) were considered to be the product of a deranged mind.

Perhaps the most damaging of all is Jones's assertion that whatever mental problems existed in Ferenczi's later years, organic or otherwise, they were just the final stages of an ongoing lifetime psychosis.

Jones was more willing to grant to Freud the benefit of the vicissitudes of human functioning than he was to Ferenczi. He blamed Ferenczi for the distress Freud felt for "the evil spirit of dissension" that arose in the committee in 1923. Jones is undoubtedly referring to the presentation of Ferenczi and Rank's 1925 book, *Development of Psychoanalysis*, which criticized psychoanalysis as becoming too cognitive and intellectual, ignoring the emotional component in the transference relationship. In fact, Freud wrote to Ferenczi on February 4, 1924, supporting his thesis and encouraging him to continue his work.

I know that I am not very accessible and find it hard to assimilate alien thoughts that do not quite lie in my path. It takes quite a time before I can form a judgement about them, so that in the interval I have to suspend judgement. . . . That you . . . should . . . ever leave the ground of psychoanalysis seems to me out of the question. Why shouldn't you therefore have the right to try if things won't work in another way from that I had thought? If you go astray in so doing, you will find that out yourself some time or other, or I will take the liberty of pointing it out to you as soon as I am myself sure about it. [Jones 1957, pp. 57–58]

We need to return to Jones's accusation that Ferenczi's deviations were causing Freud distress and were the result of psychosis. *"It was only after a lapse of a few years that the true source of the trouble became manifest: namely in the failing mental integration on the part of Rank and Ferenczi"* (Jones 1955, p. 46, italics added)

Jones does not fail to take every opportunity to create the case for Ferenczi's madness. Besides blaming the dissension in the original committee on Ferenczi, the next evidence of psychosis comes from Ferenczi's sojourn to the United States in 1926 to teach at the New School and train lay analysts, which Jones vehemently opposed.

Ferenczi had for some time been feeling dissatisfied and isolated in Budapest. . . . In April he had received an invitation from Frankwood William to give a course of lectures in the autumn at the New School of Social Research in New York, and with Freud's approbation he accepted it. Some intuitive foreboding . . . made me advise him to decline, but he ignored this and planned to spend six months in New York when he would analyze as many people as possible in the time. . . . *The outcome was to justify my foreboding. Ferenczi was never the same man again after that visit, although it was another four or five years before his mental deterioration became manifest to Freud.* [Jones 1957, p. 127, italics added]

By 1926 there were many factors that were related to Ferenczi's feeling dissatisfied that did not have the implication that his unhappiness was due to personality deterioration. Hungary was no longer the center of psychoanalysis, and Ferenczi wanted to return to the center of psychoanalytic professional and clinical activity. The onset of the First World War had shifted the center of influence in psychoanalysis from him in Hungary to a return to Vienna and Freud's other followers.

Ferenczi was also in a period of clinical unrest. He had taken activity as far as he could go, realized the limitations of abstinence and prohibition as technical interventions, and suffered the criticisms of his peers for his active clinical experiments (Glover 1924). However, he was beginning to move in a new and daring direction. With the publication of his collaborative effort with Rank, Ferenczi initiated the first formal criticism by a Freudian of psychoanalysis. It was also the beginnings of an experiential/relationship-oriented alternative to the traditional psychoanalysis.

Furthermore, Ferenczi's reputation as a flexible, daring analyst had spread to America. He was also willing to train nonmedical analysts, something that Freud was later to champion (Freud 1937), but that Jones vehemently opposed (Jones 1959). It was, no doubt, irresistible to have the opportunity to revive himself professionally and personally. The isolation from the mainstream of psychoanalysis and the absence of Freud's companionship could be alleviated by an extended sojourn to a friendly and receptive community of scholars at the New School (Quen and Carlson 1978, Roazen 1975).

Ferenczi may have realized that Jones and Abraham were talking to Freud about the seeds of dissidence that they believed were contained in *Development of Psychoanalysis* (Roazen 1975). Furthermore, he correctly perceived that he was being pushed further into the background. Jones and Abraham were so inflamed by the critique of traditional analysis that they could not appreciate the attempt at deepening and reorienting psychoanalysis to a more experiential and relationship orientation. This was a legitimate scholarly concern. Fifty years later psychoanalysts were to begin to grapple with these issues. Perhaps they saw in this unusual work an opportunity to express their jealousy of Ferenczi, court Freud's favor, and move Ferenczi further from the center of psychoanalytic prestige and power.

Freud had made it well known that he did not like America (Clark 1980b, Doorley 1982, Koelsch 1970). He also did not want his disciples to go there. He held America's values and its intellectual atmosphere in low regard. Freud felt that Ferenczi could be negatively influenced in such an atmosphere. Jones was eager to share Freud's prejudice and was concerned that Ferenczi would develop a following apart from Freud. Ferenczi could not play the conformist game. He was marching to a different drummer before he joined forces with Freud and continued to do so when they became colleagues and collaborators. He went to America because it was good for him to do so, not because he wanted to alienate Freud.

Jones and Ferenczi were two men of considerably different temperaments, personality traits, professional striving, and clinical functioning. Were they not united by a common bond to Freud, it is unlikely that these two men would have been friends or close colleagues. But their relationship is still more complicated because Ferenczi was Jones's analyst. The analysis did not bring them closer together or bridge the gap in their differences. It may even have driven them further apart, and these differences were not fully worked through as part of the transference relationship.

What were their basic differences? Temperamentally they were opposites. Jones was a reserved, controlled Welshman who did not believe in spontaneous, effusive displays of emotion. His family background and his social and cultural milieu served as a training ground for the formation of an emotionally reserved and somewhat cool individual (Jones 1959). Ferenczi was a spontaneous, warm, effusive individual who would burst into the room and kiss everyone hello (Jones 1957). His family life was a gregarious one, filled with people and discussions (Balint 1949, Lorand 1975–1976; see also Chapter 1). The Hungarian in him was romantic, loving, open, and friendly. The social atmosphere he cherished was characterized by the European coffeehouse as a regular meeting place for social and intellectual contacts. Jones was a company man (Fromm 1959), someone who did not have the intellectual genius of Freud or the clinical genius of Ferenczi. The pathway to fame and status was to court the master's favor.

The next references to Ferenczi's mental state come in Jones's writings about the early years of the 1930s, when Ferenczi began to suffer from pernicious anemia, the physical disorder that was to claim his life. The reference to Ferenczi's emotional condition comes in a cryptic remark, referring to the distress Freud was coping with in 1932: "No honors came this year, but anxiety in full measure to add to the continual physical distress. Its main sources were deep concern over the 'Verlag' and *the progressive deterioration in Ferenczi's mental condition*" (Jones 1957, p. 166, italics added).

Jones intended to discuss the controversy about the *Verlag*, which involved a paper by Reich linking psychoanalysis with Marxism. The controversy was settled by publishing the paper, as well as a rebuttal by Bernfeld. But Ferenczi's suggestion, which hinted of an unnecessary type of censorship, was rejected by Freud. There was no elaboration of the damaging statement "of the progressive deterioration in Ferenczi's mental condition" (Jones 1957, p. 166).

JONES'S ANALYSIS WITH FERENCZI

Jones originally came to Vienna in 1912, bringing his lover, Loe Kann, to be treated for her morphine addiction by Freud. During the period of treatment, Jones began a social relationship with Freud. He quickly became enamored of the master of psychoanalysis (Jones 1959).

Since Jones was free of personal commitments at the time, Freud recommended that he undergo an analysis (the primary training method at the time). Jones interpreted this recommendation as a sign that the master had found a new crown prince to succeed Jung (Roazen 1975). It was clear that Jones felt this way (Jones 1959).

Jones was captivated by Freud and so enjoyed (and perhaps needed) the attention of a father figure that he naively assumed that Freud was as captivated by him. He was also apparently not aware of Freud's growing emotional and intellectual attachment to Ferenczi, which began in 1908, four years before Jones appeared upon the scene. Ferenczi's favored position in the early history of the psychoanalytic movement suggests that Freud, in 1912, had already begun to think about Ferenczi (not Jones) for the coveted position as the heir apparent to psychoanalysis.

Freud recommended that Jones go into analysis with Ferenczi. It is not clear why Freud did not take Jones into therapy—for example, whether he did not have the time or the interest, since he was treating Jones's female friend (although Freud did see both members of a couple for therapy) (Roazen 1975). Jones never revealed any negative feelings about Freud's recommendation of Ferenczi, but it must have been a crushing blow for him. He was already in an intense positive transference to Freud, and he assumed he was going to be groomed to be Freud's successor. Perhaps because he had been in an idealized transference to Freud, Jones accepted the recommendation of Ferenczi as his analyst without complaint. His description of his analysis with Ferenczi sounds positive on the surface. But what he describes seems more like a didactic analysis than a genuine emotional experience. What is more, Ferenczi may not have pierced Jones's intellectual facade, and the displaced angry feelings toward the analyst were never fully analyzed in the transference. Jones (1959) described the failed analysis as follows.

My analysis, like the rest of my life, was intensive. I spent an hour twice a day on it during that summer and autumn and derived very great benefit from it. It led to a much greater inner harmony with myself, and gave me an irreplaceable insight of the most direct kind into the ways of the unconscious mind which it was highly instructive to compare with the more intellectual knowledge of them I had previously had. [p. 199]

According to Schur (1972), Jones had what was a conventional analysis for that early period of psychoanalysis.

Jones was the first of Freud's inner circle to undergo an "analysis" which, of necessity, was experimental in nature. It consisted of one or two hours daily on the couch, followed by endless discussions in the evening at one or another of Budapest's coffee houses. The whole process lasted only a few months. The recognition that a training analysis had to follow the same "ground rules" as a therapeutic analysis came only after decades of trial and error. [p. 283]

In an interesting commentary on the influence of Ferenczi's analysis of Jones, Roazen(1975) wrote:

The four months that Jones spent in analysis with Ferenczi had unfortunate consequences for the Hungarian's future historical reputation. For Jones concocted such an extraordinary account of Ferenczi's last years that one is tempted to agree with James Strachey and Edward Glover who both maintained that Jones never forgave Ferenczi for having been his analyst. [p. 357]

FERENCZI'S SOJOURN TO AMERICA TAKEN BY JONES AS A SIGN OF PSYCHOPATHOLOGY

Jones (1955) marked the year of 1927 as significant because according to him, it was the first indication that Ferenczi's personality changes were producing a disturbed relationship with Freud. Apparently, Jones is alluding to the conflict of training lay analysts that Ferenczi first championed and put in practice when he taught at the New School for Social

Research between 1926 and 1927. Jones (1955) began his discussion of this issue by suggesting that Ferenczi's behavior was inappropriate even before he landed in New York City "because he did not tell the New York analysts he was coming" (p. 133).

But Jones (1957) goes on to discuss Ferenczi's enthusiastic reception in New York as if it were a function of the graciousness of the New York analytic community in spite of Ferenczi's negative behavior and had nothing to do with Ferenczi's warm and friendly personality or the significant intellectual and professional contribution he had made during his stay: "Then came a period of American lionizing and hospitality which stimulated Ferenczi to an excited outburst of energy; every day there was a new engagement for him to speak at both private and public gatherings" (p. 134).

The real problem was not Ferenczi's personality, but his training of lay analysts, which Jones used as an indication of Ferenczi's rebelliousness, problem with authority, and deliberate turning away from the analytic community. Jones was vehemently opposed to training nonmedical analysts, because he was emotionally and professionally dedicated to seeing psychoanalysis as a branch of medicine. He was also in conflict with Freud about the training of lay analysts (Jones 1959), but he would never consider attributing any personality defect to Freud because of his desire to see nonmedical professionals become psychoanalysts. Of course, it was a very touchy personal issue between Freud and Jones, since it meant that Jones was trying to exclude Freud's daughter, Anna, from her father's side.

Ferenczi's interest in training lay analysts was a courageous, humanistic, and prophetic endeavor and was in keeping with his history of championing the causes of deserving minorities. He was not bound by the conventions of either the medical establishment or the analytic community. Is that rebelliousness and indications of negative character traits? Or is it an indication of a creative deviation? This distinction between deviation as a result of psychopathology and deviation as a result of creativity is crucial in understanding Ferenczi's contributions to psychoanalysis. Jones was clearly intent on demonstrating that Ferenczi's contributions were primarily a result of his underlying psychopathology and, subsequently, of the emergence of that pathology, which eventually overtook his personality. Jones was not willing to grant Ferenczi his creative contribution, even though the master, Freud, was willing to do so. It is clearly an indication of some very personal preoccupation that Jones had with Ferenczi and their failed analysis.

Freud encouraged and embraced many lay analysts as part of the inner circle of psychoanalysis. The number of lay analysts who were first- and second-generation members of the pioneering history of psychoanalysis are legion: August Aichorn, Siegfried Bernfeld, Marie Bonaparte, Erik Erikson, Anna Freud, Melanie Klein, Ernst Kris, Otto Rank, Theodore Reik, and Robert Waelder, among others. In addition, Freud defended Reik's right to practice psychoanalysis and to become a member of the American Psychoanalytic Association (Freud 1926).

Ferenczi was serious about training nonmedical analysts and responded to the enthusiasm of this group in New York City that gathered around him. Once again, he was moving in a new direction for psychoanalysis. He was not only responding to the enthusiasm and acceptance of a new circle of individuals interested in his work and him personally, but he was further developing his theoretical and clinical ideas as set forth in his book, *The Development of Psychoanalysis* (Ferenczi and Rank 1925). This book was the first formal statement of a new psychoanalysis, which conceived of psychotherapy as an interpersonal, humanistic interaction between analyst and analysand. It is also likely that his collaboration with Rank, who was a lay analyst, influenced Ferenczi to regard nonmedical analysts with great favor. He also had contact with Anna Freud, who had a very high regard for Ferenczi (Masson 1984). Ferenczi analyzed several individuals who became well-known lay analysts, such as De Forest (De Forest 1954) and Elizabeth Severn (Severn 1934).

The details of Ferenczi's training of lay analysts and the negative reaction of the New York analytic community were outlined by Jones (1955).

> He was at the same time engaged in training analytically eight or nine people, mostly lay. They were necessarily shorter analyses, but the total number was enough for a special group of lay analysts to be formed, which he hoped would be accepted as a separate Society by the International Association. [p. 134]

The politically conservative New York analytic community was apparently angry at Ferenczi for training nonmedical people and, perhaps, for gathering a group around him separate from the New York Psychoanalytic Society. The combination of encouraging intruders and potential competitors in psychoanalysis and separating himself from the New York Society apparently sent an angry shock wave through the New York analytic community. They responded by ostracizing Ferenczi, a fate he was later to suffer again with his "Confusion of Tongues" paper.

A partial explanation for the negative reaction against Ferenczi's deviations from Freud and psychoanalytic customs may be that there was a necessary antagonism caused by his personal ambivalence. He did place himself, Freud, and the analytic community in a bind when he deviated from them, yet he always seemed to want their approval. Unfortunately, he could not break with Freud and found his own school of psychoanalysis, which would have creatively solved the ambivalence issue (Thompson 1944). He could not understand and accept that his deviations would cause severe criticisms. Ferenczi did seem to possess a naïveté and immaturity. His openness and acceptance of others and their positive response to him encouraged him to expect his colleagues to respond positively to him.

Furthermore, there was then, as there is now, a difference between European and American psychoanalysis. American psychoanalysis is more conservative, both professionally and politically. The encouragement of lay analysis that Freud and Ferenczi pioneered took a foothold in Europe, most notably in England. It has been necessary for psychologists and social workers to form their own analytic institutes and associations in order to gain recognition as analysts in the United States.

THE FREUD/FERENCZI CONFLICT AS A SIGN OF "MADNESS"

Jones's writing style insinuated that he had special awareness and information that verified his accusations about Ferenczi. Usually his veiled references to special sources suggest that Freud had told him something about Ferenczi in confidence (Roazen 1975). This method lends an aura of authority and special privilege to Jones's writing that seems beyond questioning, since it cannot be researched and verified, and it uses Freud as the ultimate authority.

Next, Jones (1957) introduced the notion that Ferenczi was paranoid and conspiratorial. First, he presents himself as Ferenczi's friend and champion.

> Ferenczi traveled . . . to England. . . . We received him warmly, which must have been a welcome change after his recent experiences in New York. I gave a garden party and served dinner parties for him, and he spent a couple of days at my country home. [p. 134]

After positioning himself as Ferenczi's supporter, Jones reached the inevitable conclusion he so often developed—that Ferenczi's madness destroyed their relationship. Of course, Jones was never willing to admit that he harbored any ill feelings toward Ferenczi. Jones played the innocent child who is abused by the bad parent. He never took emotional responsibility for being the bad child who is angry at the parent, and we don't know if the parent with whom he was angry was really Ferenczi, his former analyst, or Freud, the analyst who turned him away (Roazen 1975, Sabourin 1985).

Jones (1955) concludes this indictment of Ferenczi with the following.

> I was under the impression that nothing had disturbed our old friendship, and in fact remained under that impression until, as mentioned earlier, I recently read his correspondence with Freud. Yet on that occasion when he asked me if I had been in Italy to meet Brill and I answered in the negative, he wrote to Freud saying he was convinced I was lying and that Brill and I had certainly been together in Italy apparently conspiring on the topic of lay analysis. *Such a remark in itself betokens a serious state of mind,* and it was followed in the next couple of years by a series of similar remarks expressing both suspicion and derogation of my activities. There is evidence in the letters that Freud was thereby influenced unfavorably against me, of course without my knowledge. [p. 134, italics added]

Jones encouraged the notion that it was Ferenczi's madness that led him to complain to Freud about the behind-the-scenes opposition to his clinical and professional work. But it is well documented, including Jones's own words, that he and A.A. Brill and the New York analytic community were vehemently opposed to Ferenczi's training lay analysts (Jones 1959). As is well known, Jones and other conservative analysts were also opposed to Ferenczi's clinical experiments in activity and humanistic psychoanalysis. What Jones failed to mention was that Freud and Ferenczi were in agreement on these issues for many years. Therefore, Jones was actually in opposition to Freud. He never could acknowledge that he had negative feelings toward Freud for disagreeing with him. It was always displaced onto Ferenczi. Jones's position, as the oedipal rival of the master's favorite son, must be considered at least as a partial explanation for his antagonism to Ferenczi. It seems that Jones could never accept rejection by Freud, whether it was the first trauma of refusing to be his analyst, choosing Ferenczi as his "favorite son," or their disagreement over training lay analysts (see p. 105 for a fuller discussion). Jones's autobiography made it quite clear that he was the favorite son in the oedipal triangle of his own family. He tried in vain to re-create that idyllic position in the analytic family with Freud. But Ferenczi's favorite position with the father, Freud, allowed no positive resolution of the oedipal struggle for Jones. What is more, he could not tolerate anger toward the father, for he feared ostracism. It was clear to everyone in the analytic family that Freud was capable of disowning the bad child (Adler, Jung, Stekel, Tausk). Jones could not tolerate this ultimate rejection. But he could work on getting rid of the oedipal rival, Ferenczi. By displacing his rage onto Ferenczi and developing a campaign to discredit him in Freud's eyes, Jones could hope to, once again, become the favorite child. He couldn't fully accomplish this while Ferenczi was alive because Freud was reluctant "to kill off" his once favorite child. But when Ferenczi was dead, Jones was freer to devote his unresolved oedipal energy to "killing off" his brother rival by discrediting Ferenczi's life and work as a product of a deranged personality. In Jones's scenario, Ferenczi never deserved the favorite son position. Jones announced to the analytic community that he deserved the seat next to Freud with his devoted, scholarly, loving, and unblemished biographical tribute to Freud.

The deteriorating condition of Freud and Ferenczi's relationship was the next reference that Jones (1957) used as a basis for further insinuations about Ferenczi's emotional disturbance.

> After their meeting in the previous September Freud and Ferenczi did not again discuss their differences. Freud's feeling for him never changed, and Ferenczi remained on at least outwardly friendly terms. They continued to exchange letters, the burden of which was mainly Ferenczi's increasingly serious state of health. The medical treatment was successful in holding the anemia itself at bay, but in March the disease, as it sometime does, attacked the spinal cord and brain and for the last couple of months of his life he was unable to stand or walk; *this undoubtedly exacerbated his latent psychotic trends.* [p. 176, italics added]

Jones's one-sided statements of the negative changes in the Freud/Ferenczi relationship suggested that the sole responsibility for the deteriorated relationship was Ferenczi's. He cited the Freud/Ferenczi correspondence and his own memory as the indisputable source for this assertion. At the time that Jones wrote his Freud biography, the Freud/Ferenczi correspondence was not available to scholars and the general public. Now we are beginning to have those letters available (Brabant et al. 1993a,b,c,d). But, because we now have available certain other materials that bear on the Freud/Ferenczi relationship, we can see how prejudiced Jones's account was (Covello 1984, Dupont 1988a, Sabourin 1985, Sylwan 1984, Torok 1984).

Jones (1957) went on to discredit any evidence to the contrary regarding Freud's ill treatment of Ferenczi, by saying that there is "no truth whatever in this story, although it is highly probable that Ferenczi himself in his final delusional state believed in and propagated elements of it" (p. 176). Jones (1957) also cited a letter from Freud to Ferenczi dated November 1, 1933.

> You speak of the many years of good understanding between us. I should say it was more than that, rather a close sharing of your life, emotions and interests. When today I have to conjure all this only from my memory the sole consolation I have is the certainty that I contributed remarkably little to the transformation. Some psychological fate has brought it about in you. At all events we are glad to hear of the restoration of your health, a precious price of the more beautiful past. [p. 177]

Jones used this letter to demonstrate that Freud bore no ill will toward Ferenczi. The letter does seem an affectionate statement of Freud's caring for Ferenczi. It also suggested a wistful feeling, that Freud did not feel emotionally connected to Ferenczi at this point in time. Apparently, Freud also felt that the changes in Ferenczi's negative functioning (i.e., transformation) were not of his doing, but some mysterious psychological fate. It suggested that Ferenczi's personality was unraveling, as Jones asserted. Once again, Freud took no responsibility for the interpersonal difficulty between them. Jones used Freud's lack of responsibility to bolster his own negative conclusions about Ferenczi's pathology.

Jones was not above deleting or changing information. For example, in Balint's reply to Jones's assertions in volume III of the Freud biography, he made Balint delete the passage that both of them were analysands of Ferenczi before it was printed (Roazen 1975). We have no way of knowing what other deletions or "corrections" were made by Jones in order to prove his point about Ferenczi's "madness." Jones did not miss an opportunity to point out how emotionally disturbed Ferenczi had been. He even used Ferenczi's concern for Freud's safety as the Nazi persecution of the Jews spread in Germany during the early months of 1933 as a sign of Ferenczi's instability.

> The next letter was written three weeks after the Reichstag fire in Berlin, the signal for widespread Nazi persecution. *Ferenczi in a somewhat panicky letter urgently entreated Freud to flee from Austria . . .* to leave for England at once. . . . *His doctor assured him that his pessimism came from his pathological state but, with our hindsight one must admit there was some method in his madness.* [Jones 1957, p. 177, italics added]

Ferenczi's compassionate pleading to his dear friend to flee the encroaching Nazi madness was prophetic rather than panicky. Freud's reply to Ferenczi on February 4, 1933, the last letter he ever wrote to him, indicated that Freud had no intention of leaving Austria (Jones 1957).

Not only did Ferenczi correctly predict that Freud would resist leaving Austria, he was correct in suggesting England as his new home. However, Freud was not convinced to leave for England until 1938. Would not psychoanalysis and the world community have benefited from Freud's earlier move to England in 1933, as Ferenczi had suggested?

JONES'S FINAL BLOW TO FERENCZI

The final references to Ferenczi's mental disturbance are used by Jones to verify all the preceding accusations about his lifelong psychopathology and the deterioration during the last year of his life. Jones used the last letter written by Ferenczi to Freud to deliver the final psychological blows to Ferenczi's personality. He used several avenues for his emotional attack on Ferenczi in a attempt to destroy his credibility and reputation: the mental deterioration previously observed was continuing its course; Ferenczi was allowing a patient to analyze him; Ferenczi believed in telepathy; "delusions he had about Freud's hostility" toward him; he suffered "violent paranoiac and homicidal outbursts." Jones (1957) wrote

The last letter from Ferenczi, written in bed on May 4, [1933], was a few lines for Freud's birthday. *The mental disturbance had been making rapid progress in the last few months.*

He related how one of his American patients, to whom he used to devote four or five hours a day, *had analyzed him and so cured him of all his troubles. Messages came to him from her across the Atlantic. Ferenczi had always been a staunch believer in telepathy.*

Then there were *the delusions about Freud's supposed hostility.* Toward the end came *violent paranoiac and even homicidal outbursts,* which were followed by a sudden death on May 24 [1933].

That was the tragic end of a brilliant, lovable and distinguished personality, someone who had for a quarter of a century been Freud's closest friend.

The lurking demons within, against whom Ferenczi had for years struggled with great distress and much success, conquered him at the end, and we learned from this painful experience once more how terrible their power can be. I of course wrote to condole with Freud. . . . Freud replied "Yes, we have every reason to condole with each other. Our loss is great and painful; it is part of the change that overthrows every thing that exists and thus makes room for the new. Ferenczi takes with him a part of the old time; then with my departure another will begin which you will still see. Fate. Resignation. That is all. [pp. 178–179, italics added]

FIRSTHAND ACCOUNTS OF FERENCZI'S LAST DAYS

No one who was an intimate of Ferenczi, either before or during his fatal illness, has confirmed Jones's allegations of his psychosis. There are no indications in the biographical material by Ferenczi's colleagues, pupils, or analysands that Ferenczi suffered from a psychotic or borderline condition (Balint 1958, Freud 1933c, Lorand 1966, Thompson 1944). The most severe psychiatric condition that has been attributed to him is that he had some neurotic traits, "among them a touchiness and an inordinate need to be loved and appreciated" (Balint 1958, p. 68). It must be clearly noted that Jones did not see Ferenczi in the last year of his illness (Fromm 1963). Thus, Jones's assertions of Ferenczi's psychosis were not based upon firsthand observations. Jones did not make it clear that he was reporting the notions of a secondhand source, until he replied to Balint's rebuttal of his assertions: "What I wrote about Ferenczi's last days was based on the trustworthy evidence of an eye-witness" (Jones 1958, p. 68).

According to the examination of Jones's correspondence, he implied that Freud, the master himself, was the source of his information about Ferenczi's deterioration (Roazen 1975). A telephone call made to Freud after Ferenczi's death was apparently used as the source of the information. A recent thorough investigation of this early period in psychoanalysis revealed no direct or clear-cut verification of Freud suggesting that Ferenczi was psychotic at the time of his death (Roazen 1975). Even if Freud were to have suggested this, it would only be speculative, since Freud was not present at Ferenczi's death. Furthermore, Freud's conflict and anger at Ferenczi during his last period and the very negative evaluation of the "Confusion of Tongues" paper may have influenced his view of his once cherished colleague as a madman. Ferenczi's deviating from Freud had cost him his personal and professional reputation.

There are, however, firsthand accounts of Ferenczi's mental state during his last days that need to replace Jones's prejudiced and dishonest view. The most clearly stated renunciation of Jones's allegations come from Balint (1958), Ferenczi's literary executor.

> I wish to state that I saw Ferenczi frequently — once or twice almost every week — during his last illness, a pernicious anemia which led to a rapidly progressing combined degeneration of the cord. He soon became ataxic for the last few weeks, had to stay in bed and for the last few days had to be fed; the immediate cause of his death was paralysis of the respiratory centre. *Despite his progressive physical weakness, mentally he was always clear . . . I saw him on the Sunday before his death; even then — though painfully weak and ataxic — mentally he was quite clear.* [p. 68, italics added]

Clara Thompson was with Ferenczi from 1932 until his death on May 22, 1933. She stated that

> except for the symptoms of his physical illness, there was nothing psychotic in his reactions which I observed. I visited him regularly, and talked to him, and there was not a single incident, aside from memory difficulties, which would substantiate Jones's picture of Ferenczi's psychosis or homicidal mood. [quoted in Fromm 1963, p. 139]

Ferenczi's step-daughter, Mrs. Elma Laurvik, also was with Ferenczi until his death and wrote Erich Fromm a statement, confirming Balint's and Thompson's accounts of Ferenczi's last days (Fromm 1963).

The question of Ferenczi's illness is still a complicated one. By 1926, pernicious anemia was treatable. "In January and February of 1926, the beneficial effects of liver were convincingly documented for the first time" (Kass 1976, p. 24). The ingestion of high amounts of liver reduced the symptoms of the disease. By 1927, an extract of liver was developed that could be given to ameliorate the disease. Clearly, by the late 1920s there was a significant treatment for pernicious anemia (i.e., liver therapy) that produced a remission of symptoms and recovery so that death from the disease was not inevitable. In fact, the 1934 Nobel Prize in physiology and medicine was awarded to Minot, Murphy, and Whipple for their 1926 paper that demonstrated hematological improvement in pernicious anemia through the administration of liver therapy (p. 40). (By 1948, Vitamin B_{12} was isolated as the "anti–pernicious anemia factor" (p. 62).)

The availability of a cure for pernicious anemia by the late 1920s brings into question Ferenczi's death from the disease in 1933. Did he receive liver therapy at the onset of the disease? If he did receive liver therapy, why did it not produce a cure? Research into Ferenczi's medical treatment and the European mode of treatment for pernicious anemia shows that liver therapy was being discussed in European (German, French) journals in the 1930s. On December 25, 1930, there was a study of liver therapy in the Hungarian medical journal, *Gyógyászat* (Hajos, 1930), the same journal in which Ferenczi had published his earliest papers (see Chapter 2).

THE MEANING OF JONES'S CHARACTER ASSASSINATION OF FERENCZI: JONES'S OEDIPAL STRUGGLE WITH FERENCZI

Since Ferenczi's death in 1933, the psychoanalytic community has generally accepted Jones's false and hateful version of Ferenczi's personal and clinical functioning. There have been valiant voices who have attempted to dispute Jones's claims about Ferenczi's madness (Balint 1958, Covello 1984, Fromm 1963, Lorand 1966). But the damage was done by the accusations and the veiled references to Freud as their source. Now, sixty years later, often all that is remembered about Ferenczi is Jones's accusations as fact. Analysts who have an awareness of Ferenczi can be heard to say something like, "Oh, Ferenczi. Wasn't he that wild analyst who kissed his patients?"; or "Ferenczi, he was the one who was crazy; he started off as Freud's disciple, but went crazy after a while." It is clear that the voices that have risen up over the years have not succeeded in silencing the already established, extremely negative view of Ferenczi. Therefore, I have attempted to present a detailed exposition of Jones's actual accusations and a rebuttal based on the evidence. We have now come to the point where Jones's motivation, both conscious and unconscious, needs to be examined to throw some light on this infamous deed.

In the juxtaposition of Jones's negative statements about Ferenczi with veiled references to Freud's communication with Jones, we have a very clever, albeit sinister, literary device. The reader is left to surmise that in each instance Jones was not really presenting his own opinion about Ferenczi's mental condition, but was probably expressing Freud's judgment. In the veiled references to Freud's conversations, letters, and seemingly unconscious communications to Jones, he bolstered his accusations with an appeal to the highest authority in the psychoanalytic community, its founder. Furthermore, Jones gave the impression that he was performing a noble service for Freud. By presenting Ferenczi's pathology as *his* observations, he is protecting Freud from betraying his closest friend and most beloved pupil. He would have us believe that Freud used him as his oracle because of their close and intimate relationship.

What is more likely the truth is that Jones suffered from the delusion that Freud was forming a special alliance with him for the purpose of discrediting Ferenczi. Jones (1959) by his own admission had a very special oedipal problem.

> I was deeply attached to both of my parents and regarded myself, indeed rightly so, as a bond between them. In our sitting-room I used to sit on a little cane chair between them, symbolizing both the desire to unite and, *no doubt on a deeper level, to separate them* [p. 13, italics added]

Jones, in a somewhat characteristic self-congratulatory manner, went on to describe the positive aspects of this oedipal problem, totally ignoring its deeper meaning.

It was a happy solution of the Oedipus complex that has stood me in good stead throughout my life, for it brought with it unusual capacity for double loyalties, with little tendency to divided ones. Not only was I faithful to both countries indeed, I should find it hard to say whether I have loved England or Wales more. My professional life has similarly been marked by intense devotion to both medicine and psychoanalysis, two disciplines I have always wished to be in amicable relations with each other. [p. 13]

If Jones had resolved his oedipal conflict so well, as he congratulates himself for doing, why couldn't he apply his dual loyalties theory to Ferenczi and Freud in his professional and personal life? Why did he insist on a divisive campaign to discredit Ferenczi? Why did he turn against his own analyst (in a manner unheard of in the history of psychoanalysis) and attempt to prove that Ferenczi was psychotic?

One can speculate that Jones did not resolve his oedipal conflict in the positive manner he presented, either before or during his analysis. His hidden desire to separate his parents and underlying resentment and anger were never worked through. He wanted to see Freud for analysis and did not express his resentment, rejection, and anger toward the master when he complied with the referral to Ferenczi, repressing his negative feelings. Jones had learned to repress his negative feelings toward his parents by becoming the attached son. His analysis with Ferenczi became his way of obeying Freud, currying his favor, and unconsciously sabotaging Ferenczi, the favorite son.

It must also be stated that Ferenczi bears some responsibility for Jones's unresolved negative transference to him. It is very unfortunate that the material is not available that would answer the questions about the analysis that Ferenczi was able to conduct with Jones. Lorand said that Jones had an unanalyzed negative transference to Ferenczi (see Chapter 10).

Once the analysis was officially completed, Jones became free to reconstitute the triangular relationship between himself, Ferenczi, and Freud. His unconscious aim was to separate Ferenczi from Freud and sit on the "little cane chair" between them (as he had done in his own family). Further, he wished to supplant Ferenczi in Freud's emotional life and become Freud's favorite son. Jones used every opportunity to discredit Ferenczi, but always in a veiled way. His duality of emotional functioning, left over from his oedipal struggle, produced a splitting in affective functioning. He showed positive feelings toward Ferenczi in public, but harbored negative affect to him privately. He praised Ferenczi publicly, but damned him privately. When he became aware that others were becoming critical of Ferenczi's clinical experiments, he quickly joined them, giving expression to his underlying rage. Jones was never a defender of his analyst, close friend, and member of the Society of the Rings. Certainly, one would expect loyalty and defense from someone with those kinds of emotional and professional attachments. But with Jones, judgment and emotionality were overshadowed by his need to separate Freud from Ferenczi.

Another emotional factor was the displacement of Jones's negative affect toward Freud (for rejecting him for analysis and preferring Ferenczi to Jones) onto Ferenczi. Ferenczi became the hated object instead of Freud. But because Jones split his emotional cathexis into love and hate, he could not openly express and work through his anger toward Ferenczi.

Because Ferenczi had a need for approval (in this instance from both Freud, Jones, and the psychoanalytic community), he may not have been able to confront Jones's rage toward him. He was content to deal with what seemed to be a positive manifest transference reaction. The deeper level of the ambivalence, the rage toward the rival Ferenczi for having the father Freud, was not worked through. Ferenczi was also in a pseudo-positive transference to Freud. He was not able to express any resentment or anger directly to Freud, because of his own need to gain approval and so as not to risk Freud's tendency of rejecting dissident members of the inner circle.

There were two other significant emotional traumas that Freud created for Jones that are relevant for the present discussion. Freud separated Jones from his lover, Loe Kann, after she began her analysis with him. In addition, Freud first recommended that Jones undertake an analysis and then rejected him as his analysand. These emotion-laden events also formed the basis under which Jones would suppress his anger toward Freud (the father) and project it onto Ferenczi (the sibling rival).

Jones had become acquainted with Freud through Kann, a young Dutch Jew who had sought Freud out for the morphine addiction that she developed to cope with the pain of a kidney condition. She had seldom left her bed, so in 1912 she decided to go to Vienna and place herself in Professor Freud's hands (Jones 1959).

Jones accompanied Kann to Vienna and stayed with her during her initial treatments. He came under the influence of Freud by spending several evenings talking to him. "He had taken a liking to me, and seemed to wish to open his heart to someone not of his own milieu . . . we ranged over all sorts of topics . . . above all, psychology. . . . Those were the days when I got to know Freud well (Jones 1959, p. 197).

Freud's contact with Jones may have been more important to the young Welsh physician than to the master. There were several emotional blows initiated by Freud during this early period that befell Jones and that he never acknowledged as traumatic. First, Freud separated Jones from Kann.

> [Freud] decided it would be best for Loe if Jones was not in Vienna during her analysis. (In Jones's autobiography she is discreetly described simply as Loe, whereas in his biography of Freud she is referred to as Loe Kann, a patient of Freud's and a woman of some importance in his life – with no mention of her intimate relationship with Jones). [Roazen 1975, p. 356]

Jones never mentioned any resentment about the separation or any negative feelings toward Freud. In fact, in characteristic fashion, Jones (1959) denied any anger and presented Freud's decision for them to separate as a positive experience, which enhanced their lives: "We decided to part, after which we both married happily." (p. 157).

Although it may have turned out to be a positive move for Kann and Jones to separate, at the time it was suggested it would not have been unusual for either of the couple to have resented or been unhappy about the breakup. Often, when one of a couple is being treated, the non-treated individual develops a very negative reaction to the therapist, fearing that he or she will encourage a breakup of the partnership. Jones, in both Freud's biography and his own autobiography, voiced no feelings in this regard.

If Jones felt that Freud had handpicked him to be Jung's successor because he was not Jewish and would make psychoanalysis more acceptable to the Gentile world, it would follow that Jones had great expectations to be in analysis with Freud. It is clear that Jones perceived the recommendation for analysis as a decision on Freud's part to recommend Jones as Jung's successor (Roazen 1975). Jones (1959) wrote, " . . . and this was perhaps the reason why he advised me that spring to undergo a didactic analysis" (p. 158). Furthermore, the referral for analysis would also be for didactic purposes, in order to learn the craft at the hands of the founder and master.

Freud's suggestion that Jones enter analysis seemed to come on the heels of his analysis of Kann. It is likely that Freud became intimately acquainted with Jones's personal problems though his analysis of Kann. The referral for analysis may have been directed at Jones's need to work on these personal problems. After all, Freud also recommended that Jones not remain in Vienna while Kann finished her analysis. In addition, her analysis produced a breakup in her relationship with Jones.

Jones also assumed that the recommendation for analysis would mean an analysis with Freud. Freud turned Jones down and referred him to Ferenczi. Why didn't Freud see Jones for analysis? If Jones was correct in assuming that he was being groomed as Freud's successor and that they had established such a positive contact, why wasn't he given preferential treatment?

It does not seem that Freud shared Jones's version of history. Although Freud may have enjoyed his initial contacts with Jones, he did not have plans to make Jones his successor. More likely, Freud was enjoying the company of an enthusiastic young physician who was receptive to psychoanalysis. He suggested that Jones undergo an analysis because he saw he needed help in his relationship with Loe. He was willing to embrace him as part of the psychoanalytic movement, but not turn the reins over to him. (It is clear that Freud was looking for a successor to Jung. The instant Ferenczi appeared on the scene, Freud was taken with him and gave the impression he had found his successor [Jones 1955].)

Another nagging question in this issue is why Freud chose Ferenczi as Jones's analyst. Did he feel that Ferenczi would work better with Jones than he himself would? Did he want to build up Ferenczi's practice? It is likely that Freud was aware of Jones's special feelings toward him and realized that Jones would experience a sense of disappointment, resentment, and rejection when he chose Ferenczi for analysis. Did he see something in Jones's personality that he could not tolerate?

CONFLICT BETWEEN FERENCZI AND JONES

Ferenczi was well aware of Jones's attacks on his work and person, as the following letter, dated January 6, 1930, indicates.

Letter from Ferenczi to Jones: January 6, 1930 (in German)

I don't always read your works with unmixed pleasure either. If mine are wild and fantastic, yours often give the impression of a kind of logical-sadistic violence, especially since the works, which, by the way, are equally fantastic, on child analyses have appeared. These works of your English group have not charmed me in the least.

Perhaps we should draw the lesson, from this event, that psychoanalysts in particular, more than has been the case until now, should not allow scientific and scientific-technique differences of opinion to degenerate into personal attacks. It would be useless to deny that what is really a question of scientific technique, the problem of lay analysis in America, as well as certain differences of opinion with regard to the analysis of children, has given occasion to the rise of a certain angry mood between us, old friends. As a lone worker I have used the last years, somewhat withdrawn, to attempt to go deeper into theory and technique. Perhaps by the next Congress I will be able to speak about some of these things. [Masson 1984, pp. 230–231]

Lorand, an analysand and student of Ferenczi in Budapest in the early 1920s, was the first European analyst to emigrate to the United States. He was privy to the relationship between Jones and Ferenczi before he established his analytic practice in New York City. In no uncertain terms, he has stated that Jones and Ferenczi's relationship was not good (Rachman 1977b): "There was envy and jealousy all around. He [Ferenczi] criticized Jones to me many times, weekends when I was with him" (p. 16).

There were additional factors that contributed to the conflict between Jones and Ferenczi, factors of political rivalry in the history of the psychoanalytic movement. The founding of the movement was filled with political intrigue and hateful rivalries (Roazen 1975) that continue to this day (Malcolm 1983b). Jones placed himself in the center of the personal and political controversies by virtue of his personal ambitions to play a pivotal part in the history of psychoanalysis as well as his being driven by unresolved oedipal striving. In this instance, he nurtured the secret wish to be Freud's successor.

When the First World War broke out, it concerned Freud that the center of psychoanalysis in Budapest with Ferenczi at its head would be in danger. He proposed to return the capital of psychoanalysis to England.

So he proposed to Ferenczi that he transfer me to the acting presidency of The International Association to which the Budapest

> Congress had voted him during the war. Ferenczi agreed with a good grace, but in years to come it was a source of keen regret to him that he was never called upon to function in that position and I had good reason later for thinking that he bore me an irrational grudge for having had to supplant him. [Jones 1955, p. 17]

Perhaps Jones's notion that Ferenczi bore him a grudge for supplanting him as president of the International Association showed his inability to vent any anger toward Freud, since the master did not continue to believe in him as a replacement for Ferenczi.

> Freud remarked on that occasion: "It is to be hoped we have found the right man this time," evidently expecting my position would be a lasting one. *Unfortunately, from my point of view, there were times later on when he no longer held that opinion.* [Jones 1955, p. 17, italics added]

Others have commented on the inability of Freud's followers to be directly angry at the master (Fromm 1963, Roazen 1975).

> All sorts of barriers ... prevented Freud's loyal students from competing with the master; but there was every incentive for their competing with each other for Freud's favor while he was alive, and for stature in the history of psychoanalysis after his death. Jones could be a ruthless infighter with his rivals. *All of his hostility was directed at his colleagues, instead of at Freud himself.* ... [Roazen, 1975, p. 369, italics added]

It is a matter of some fact and much speculation that Jones did not lead an exemplary personal or professional life.

> In Toronto, Jones paid a blackmailer (a former patient) five hundred dollars to prevent her from accusing him publicly as a seducer; probably innocent of the charge, Jones felt too insecure professionally not to pay the money.
>
> In London, Jones had been accused by two small children of having "behaved indecently during the speech test I had carried out with them ..."; he was actually imprisoned for a night, but the magistrate eventually dismissed the case. Later, however, a young

girl of ten whom Jones had interviewed clinically "boasted to other children in the ward that the doctor had been talking to her about sexual topics . . ."; Jones had to resign his position. His career could ill afford any more such scandal. [Roazen 1975, p. 355 n]

What is the point in dredging up some negative personal history of Jones? It is not to develop a character assassination of Jones as a way to discredit his criticisms of Ferenczi. Rather, it is to demonstrate that Jones's personal history could lead him to do inappropriate and questionable things. His personality functioning had elements of an impulse control disorder where his distorted needs interfered with his judgment. It is likely that his neurotic need to be Freud's favorite could not be harnessed and that he would stop at nothing to discredit (remove) his rival, Ferenczi. Another piece of speculative material may shed further light on this assumption. But in passing, it should be noted that there appears to be no evidence at this time that Ferenczi ever committed any unethical act in his clinical career – this, in spite of his technique of touching patients. This helps to give credence to the notion that Ferenczi's physical interaction with patients was distinguished by maternal affection, not eroticism. Ferenczi was also never accused of any unethical conduct by a patient, as far as is known. Rather, they had praise for his humanistic technique (Mrs. F. H. 1954).

But Jones's history of indiscretions continued to be an issue, as Grosskurth (1988) has suggested.

> Jones didn't welcome Ferenczi's becoming privy to the irregularities of his sexual life. These had caused Freud some alarm, particularly since he needed a gentile to replace Jung . . . and Jones was the only candidate available. "Put some stuffing in the clown," Freud advised Ferenczi, "so we can make him a king." When Jones was writing his life of Freud, he was given access to the Freud-Ferenczi correspondence, and it must have come as a shock to him to learn how much Freud had distrusted him. Consequently he omitted passages from letters he quoted, thus creating a false impression about Ferenczi.

Let us return to the speculative material that relates to Jones's personal functioning and his character assassination of Ferenczi. It is interwoven with what may have been an indiscretion by Ferenczi, who had arranged for his future step-daughter, Elma, to enter analysis with Freud at the beginning of their association.

She must have been important to him beyond being the daughter of the woman he loved. In a 1957 letter, Jones reassured Ferenczi's literary executor, Michael Balint, that the Freud biography had been most cautious in avoiding discussing Ferenczi's private life, his relation to Gizella [his wife] and *his intimacy with Elma*. Perhaps Jones was emboldened to say whatever he wanted about Ferenczi's final illness and his "mental disturbance" precisely because Balint (who had inherited Ferenczi's ring) knew that Jones was privy to unpublished information about Ferenczi's earlier years. [Roazen 1975, p. 359, italics added]

This astute speculation by Roazen might also explain why Balint's rebuttal to Jones's charges about Ferenczi seem so mild and lacking in resentment, outrage, or anger.

7

FREUD PASSES THE MANTLE TO FERENCZI: THE INTRODUCTION OF ACTIVITY INTO PSYCHOANALYSIS

FREUD REASSESSES INTERPRETATION

In traditional psychoanalysis, the analyst's primary function was to impart his or her understanding of the individual's contemporary neurotic conflicts based upon historical interaction with parental figures, as reenacted in the transferential relationship. Therefore, in the study of the technique of psychoanalysis, attention was paid to interpretation and its manifestation (e.g., timing, content, type) (Bergmann and Hartman 1976). When Freud began to realize that interpretation alone did not produce the desired effect, he began to theorize about another dimension of technique—the employment of activity by the therapist—in this way introducing the first major deviation in psychoanalytic therapy.

Freud (1919 [1918]) made it clear that psychoanalysis needed to change in order to reach different segments of society as well as to relate to changing world conditions.

> We shall then be faced by the task of adapting our technique to the new conditions. . . . the validity of our psychological assumptions will impress the uneducated too, but we shall need to find the

simplest and most natural expression for our theoretical doctrines. We shall probably discover that the poor are even less ready to part with their neuroses than the rich, because the hard life that awaits them when they recover has no attraction, and illness in them gives them more claim to social help. Often, perhaps, we may only be able to achieve anything by combining mental assistance with some material support. . . .

It is very probable, too, that the large scale application of our therapy will compel us to alloy the pure gold of analysis freely with the copper of direct suggestion; and hypnotic influence, too, might find a place in it again, as it has in the treatment of war neurosis. But whatever form this psychotherapy for the people may take . . . its most effective and most important ingredients will assuredly remain those borrowed from strict psychoanalysis. . . . [pp. 167–168]

FREUD'S EARLY INFORMAL USE OF ACTIVITY

In order to understand Freud's introduction of activity in psychoanalysis, we need to trace its early history. In the earliest period of psychoanalysis (roughly 1880 to 1900), some active measures were very much a part of its technique. Among those that Freud used were hypnosis, the application of an active, direct verbal technique; a direct physical intervention; and the pressure technique (pressure to the forehead of a patient to encourage the flow of associations) (Coltrera and Ross 1967).

Freud unwittingly introduced still another active measure in the next period of psychoanalysis when he freely offered food to patients. "In the 1890s, he went as far as to invite patients to meals with his family and, as late as . . . 1909, he would have refreshments brought on for both himself and his patients" (Coltrera and Ross 1967, p. 36).

Freud's behavior was very puzzling and disturbing to the modern analytic community. Modern analysts had great difficulty justifying the feeding of a patient as a meaningful analytic technique. What may have been for Freud a natural, human gesture, inseparable from his role as an analyst, became for some an unfathomable intervention and, what is worse, an unthinkable error in the analytic situation. After much debate and soul-searching, some analysts were able to reconcile Freud's deviation on purely humane grounds.

> (Dr. Jerome Bergler, at a seminar, called our attention to Freud's therapy notes on the Rat Man.) On one occasion his patient began his session by telling Freud that he was hungry, whereupon Freud gave him something to eat. . . . For Freud not to feed a hungry man would have been out of character. [Boyer and Giovacchini 1967, p. 323]

The publication of Freud's technical papers helped to establish a standard or classical psychoanalytic technique. Once this standard was established, one can begin to talk about the introduction of activity as a formal dimension of therapy.

By 1914, Freud had written a series of recommendations for technique that became standard procedure. In seven articles between 1912 and 1918, he formulated the general principles of psychoanalytic technique based upon fifteen years of clinical experience: (1) method of free association, (2) phenomenon of transference, (3) unfolding of unconscious motivation, (4) phenomenon of resistance, (5) removal of infantile amnesia, (6) acting out, (7) development of insight, (8) technique of interpretation, (9) working through process, (10) principle of neutrality (Freud 1911b, 1912a, 1913b, 1914b, 1915 [1914], 1919 [1918]). It is from these basic principles and techniques that we can begin to talk about deviations. Deviation traditionally meant the moving away from using interpretation as the major instrument or technical device for effecting change. It also implies that the development of insight, which is the change that interpretation is intended to foster, is also held up for reexamination.

Freud presented the technical recommendations as guidelines rather than as rules, although he did characterize the encouragement of free association as the fundamental rule. Freud's recommendations seem to be a mixture of his own personal predilection for rational thought and order, his emotional reserve, his concern for distinguishing psychoanalysis from other therapies emerging at that time (Adlerian and Jungian, in particular), and an attempt to help neophyte analysts develop appropriate behavior guidelines and to help other therapists avoid the mistakes he had made.

Freud was the first to deviate from his own formal recommendations. The need to set down rigid rules and encourage taboos of practice was to become a phenomenon after his death, particularly when psychoanalysis crossed the Atlantic to America. An often quoted joke satirizes this unfortunate development: "If Freud were alive today, he would not be a Freudian."

Gradually, Freud became aware that a negative trend toward clinical practice was developing. In 1928 he wrote to Ferenczi, who had already become the leader of deviations from classical techniques.

> . . . the "Recommendations on Technique" I wrote long ago were essentially of a negative nature. I considered the most important thing was to emphasize what one *should not* do, and to point out the temptation in directions contrary to analysis. Almost everything positive that one *should* do I have left to "tact" . . . . The result was that the docile analysts did not perceive the elasticity of the rules I had laid down, and submitted to them as if they were taboos. Sometime all that must be revised, without, it is true, doing away with the obligation I had mentioned. [Jones 1955, p. 241, italics added]

In the second decade of psychoanalysis, the seeds were planted for a revolution centered on the formal introduction of activity as a dimension of psychotherapy. Once again, Freud laid the groundwork for the change with three significant papers: "Observations on Transference Love," 1915 [1914]; "From the History of an Infantile Neurosis (The Case of the Wolf Man)," 1919 [1918]; and "Lines of Advance in Psycho-Analytic Therapy," 1919.

"Observations on Transference Love" is significant for two reasons. Freud introduced *the rule of abstinence*, which became the precursor for all experimentation with activity in psychoanalysis. Secondly, Ferenczi used the introduction of the rule of abstinence to begin a decade of clinical experiments in active therapy. In the rule of abstinence, Freud (1915 [1914]) was referring to the establishment of a particular condition. He wrote:

> The treatment must be carried out in abstinence. By this I do not mean physical abstinence alone, nor yet the deprivation of everything that the patient desires, for perhaps no sick person could tolerate this. Instead, I shall state it as a fundamental principle that the patient's need and longing should be allowed to persist in her, in order that they may serve as a force impelling her to do work and

make changes, and that we must beware of appeasing those forces by means of surrogates. And what we could offer would never be anything else than a surrogate, for the patient's condition is such that, until her repressions are removed, she is incapable of getting real satisfaction. Let us admit that this fundamental principle of the treatment being carried out in abstinence extends far beyond the single case we are considering here, and that it needs to be thoroughly discussed in order that we may define the limits of its possible application. [Freud 1915, [1914], p. 165]

In the discussion to follow, we will see how Ferenczi began his first clinical experiments in active analysis by applying the rule of abstinence to a wider range of clinical situations. For now, we should note that in the rule of abstinence Freud was outlining a guideline for behavior by the analyst that restricted the natural desire to respond in kind to a patient's overture for affection or love. Analysts were told, in essence, to "deprive" the patient of the gratification of any neurotic desire for affection, preventing an erotic transference.

Unfortunately, many analysts have interpreted the rule of abstinence as a principle of inactivity, deprivation, withholding, and rigidity. Nothing could be further from Freud's intention. In setting down his ideas on activity, he was struggling for a way to open up analytic technique to be more flexible, responsive, and helpful to patients.

We have defined our therapeutic task of consisting of two things: making conscious the repressed material and uncovering the resistances. But are we to leave it to the patient to deal alone with the resistances we have pointed out to him? Can we give him no other help in this besides the stimulus he gets from the transference? Does it not seem natural that we should help him in another way as well, by putting him into the mental situation most favourable to the solution of the conflict which is our aim? After all, what he can achieve depends, too, on the part of the analyzing physician and is unobjectionable and entirely justified too. . . . [Freud 1919 [1918], p. 162]

Furthermore, in this same classic paper Freud introduced the idea that the boundaries of meaningful activity are not limited to the principle of abstinence. He clearly wanted to open up new vistas for psychoanalytic technique:

I do not think I have exhausted the range of desirable activity on the part of the physician in saying that a condition of privation is to be kept up during the treatment . . . another quite different kind of gradually growing appreciation that the various forms of disease treated by us cannot all be dealt with by the same technique. [pp. 164–165]

FREUD'S FORMAL INTRODUCTION OF ACTIVITY: THE CASE OF THE WOLF MAN

Both the cases of the Wolf Man and the Rat Man, because of their severe psychopathology and the unusual therapy relationship, might today be designated as difficult cases. Contemporary psychoanalysis is beginning to synthesize the notion that individuals with special or difficult problems need therapy that differs from Freudian analysis for the neuroses (Gedo 1986a, Kernberg 1974, 1975, Kohut 1977, 1978b, 1984b, Masterson 1976).

The clinical interaction between Freud and the Wolf Man was challenging. It was from this difficulty that Freud blazed a new trail in psychoanalysis.

Something new can only be gained from analysis that present special difficulties, and to the overcoming of these a great deal of time has to be devoted. Only in such cases do we succeed in descending into the deepest and most primitive strata of mental development and in gaining from there solutions for the problems of the later formations. And we feel afterwards that, strictly speaking, only an analysis which has penetrated so far deserves the name. [Freud 1918, p. 10]

Whereas Freud's clinical experiments with the Rat Man helped introduce "the feeding experience" as one dimension of activity in psychotherapy, a second famous case, "The Case of The Wolf Man," became the stimulus for the formal beginnings of active technique. In 1919, Freud undertook the psychoanalysis of the Wolf Man, who had been hospitalized for various periods with a diagnosis of manic-depressive insanity.

He was in treatment for four years, from 1910 to 1914, after unsuccessful attempts at therapy by other methods. His name was derived from fact that as a child he suffered from an excessive fear of wolves. His case history dealt with a childhood phobia, although he was treated for adult problems. Freud wanted to show that "the structure of an infantile neurosis could be understood in terms of instinct theory . . . to show the force of infantile experience on a child's neurosis" (Roazen 1975, p. 281).

Four active measures were introduced by Freud in this case:

1. A cure was promised.
2. The patient was treated without a fee.
3. The therapist collected money for the individual's support.
4. A unilateral termination date was set.

The Wolf Man was a Russian nobleman who fell onto hard times as a result of the Russian Revolution. He lost his fortune after his first analysis with Freud. According to Roazen (1975), " . . . in 1919, he returned to Vienna and Freud recommended a further analysis, which lasted a few months [and] which was free of charge" (p. 155). In addition, " . . . for years he [Freud] raised annual contributions to support a favorite former patient, the Wolf-Man . . ." (p. 124). Sometimes Freud even asked his other patients for a contribution (Roazen 1975). This money helped the Wolf Man to pay his rent and medical bills, as well as to take short trips.

It is conceivable that Freud also had some guilt feelings about the loss of the Wolf Man's estate. "In the 1920's the Wolf Man blamed Freud for having advised him against returning to Russia to rescue his fortune. (Freud considered this desire to be resistance to the second analysis)" (Roazen 1975, p. 155).

The Wolf Man was not the only patient Freud treated without a fee. "Freud treated without payment Heinz Hartmann, Kata Levy, Eva Rosenfeld . . . and doubtless others" (Roazen 1975, p. 126 footnote). This deviation in technique influenced other younger analysts to become experimental. When the Wolf Man wished to return to therapy years later, Freud referred him to Ruth Mack Brunswick, who also treated him without a fee (Roazen 1975).

Freud (1918) experimented with deliberately setting a termination date for the analysis. He believed that the threat of a termination date would break the stalemate in the analysis due to the comfort and gratification the Wolf Man was receiving from their passive-dependent relationship. Although this experiment was not entirely successful, with the Wolf Man returning to analysis many times after the termination experiment (Brunswick 1929, Eissler 1953), Freud demonstrated that at times the analyst may be forced to depart from his role as the interpreter and resort to active measures (Bergmann and Hartman 1976).

An interesting comment has recently been offered as to the enduring effect of Freud's active interventions in this case. "He did progress better under Freud's care than with other therapists of the day, but can one say that in the end it was analytic insight which helped, or rather the continuing emotional support of Freud and the psychoanalytic movement?" (Roazen 1975, p. 157).

Analysts have continued to pay homage to Freud and to pay their debt to the Wolf Man's contribution to psychoanalysis. While the Wolf Man was alive, a different analyst came each year from America during the summer months to conduct daily sessions with him.

"LINES OF ADVANCE IN PSYCHOANALYTIC THERAPY": FREUD'S ACTIVE MEASURES FOR THE NEUROSIS

In his next historically significant publication, Freud extended the concept of activity even further by encouraging analysts to induce phobic and obsessional individuals to directly confront the source of their anxiety (Freud 1919 [1918]). In so doing, the analyst encouraged the individual to risk and struggle actively with change as well as to stimulate associations and memories necessary to analyze the neurosis. In other words, Freud exhorted analysts to confront first, analyze second. Furthermore, he declared that the evolution of psychoanalysis would proceed in the direction of activity.

> Developments in our therapy, therefore, will no doubt proceed along other lines; first and foremost, along the one which Ferenczi, in his paper "Technical Difficulties in an Analysis of Hysteria" (1919), has lately termed "activity" on the part of the analyst. [Freud 1919 (1918), pp. 161–162]

Freud 1919 [1918] then elaborated a new vista of activity for the treatment of phobias and obsessional neurosis. His own words make it very clear that he intended future analysts to be active, daring, and experimental.

. . . the phobias have already made it necessary for us to go beyond our former limits. One can hardly master a phobia if one waits till the patient lets the analysis influence him to give it up. He will never in that case bring into the analysis the material indispensable for a convincing resolution of the phobia. One must proceed differently. [pp. 165–166]

In the case of a severe phobic reaction (e.g., agoraphobia), Freud (1919 [1918]) recommended the most stringent of active measures.

. . . one succeeds only when one can induce them by the influence of the analysis . . . to go in the street and to struggle with their anxiety while they made the attempt. One starts, therefore, by moderating the phobia so far; and it is only when that has been achieved at the physician's demand that the association and memories come into the patient's mind which enable the phobia to be resolved. [p. 166]

With regard to active techniques for obsessional neurosis, Freud encouraged even greater use of activity.

In severe cases of obsessional acts, a passive waiting attitude seems even less indicated. . . . these cases incline to an "asymptotic" process of recovery, an interminable protraction of the treatment. Their analysis is always in danger of bringing to light a great deal and changing nothing. I think there is a little doubt that here the correct technique can only be to wait until the treatment itself has become a compulsion and then with this counter-compulsion forcibly to suppress the compulsion of the disease. [1919 (1918), p. 166]

It is important to note that Freud was advocating the use of active measures to aid the analysis. He began to realize that the analysis of a phobic reaction was enhanced by encouraging the individual to confront the fear in the natural setting in which it occurred. It is only then that the unconscious fantasy material surfaces. Ferenczi, as we shall see, further developed the use of activity in order to stimulate unconscious fantasies.

It would be a misunderstanding of Freud's writing and a sterile, parochial view of psychoanalysis to limit the idea of activity as being relevant only to the clinical material Freud discussed. In citing the use of active measures for phobias and obsessional neurosis, he was only being illustrative, not limiting. He was suggesting that through further experimentation, activity may become useful as a general tool of psychoanalysis. In departing from classical technique with both the Rat Man and the Wolf Man as well as the recommendations for phobic and obsessional neuroses, Freud was ushering in a new philosophy.

Freud insisted upon two basic humanistic principles that should guide the analyst's use of activity. First, no activity should ever compromise or interfere with an individual's own sense of ego identity.

> We refused most emphatically to turn a patient who puts himself into our hands in search of help into our private property, to decide his fate for him, to force our own ideals upon him, and with the pride of a Creator to form him in our own image and see that it is good. . . . the patient should be educated to liberate and fulfill his own nature, not to resemble ourselves. [Freud 1919 (1918), pp. 164–165]

Second, the analyst should not develop activity for the purpose of converting an analysand to a particular philosophical, social, or political point of view.

> . . . we cannot accept . . . that psycho-analysis should place itself in the service of a particular philosophical outlook on the world and should urge this upon the patient for the purpose of ennobling his mind. In my opinion, this is after all only to use violence, even though it is overlaid with the most honourable motives. [Freud 1919 (1918), p. 165]

WAS FREUD REALLY A FREUDIAN? HIS DEVIATIONS FROM TRADITIONAL TECHNIQUE

It should be remembered that Freud was a revolutionary (Sulloway 1979) and a humanist (Bettelheim 1982), although in his latter years he did show a conservative, even authoritarian bent (Fromm 1959). It is clear that Freud was attracted to Ferenczi's speculative turn of mind (Jones 1955) as well as his experimental and innovative spirit. The two men did share a revolutionary spirit; witness their collaboration on *Thalassa* (see Chapter 3), the most speculative and revolutionary application of psychoanalysis.

Freud never became an orthodox psychoanalyst. His analysis of his own daughter Anna was only one example of how unorthodox he could be. With certain patients or on special occasions, Freud was in favor of prescribed psychoanalytic techniques. But he would want to be sure that such a maneuver was really in the interest of the patient and did not merely serve the pleasure of the analyst (Roazen 1975). There is an apparent contradiction between the Spartan quality in his theory regarding doctor–patient interaction in psychoanalysis and his personal willingness and capacity to be human, generous, and active.

There was a humanistic undercurrent to psychoanalysis from its inception (Bettelheim 1982). Freud had been willing to alter his response depending upon the individual and the circumstances. We have already spoken of his humanism in actually feeding the Rat Man and raising funds for the Wolf Man. He also encouraged this humanistic attitude in younger analysts.

Roazen (1975) wrote:

> A student of Freud's was once troubled about her procedure with a patient; the analyst had given the patient money, helped her with her lessons at Radcliffe College, and commissioned a portrait . . . all the "active" things that a good analyst was supposed to avoid. Yet Freud was entirely sympathetic and said that sometimes one has to be both mother and father to a patient: "one does what one can." [p. 124]

Freud was apparently capable of greater flexibility than many present-day Freudians seem to be. A list of Freud's indulgences or parameters are as follows.

He simultaneously analyzed married couples on at least two occasions.
In the case of Jones and Alix Strachey, if one of them missed a session, then the other could have it in addition to his own, thus being analyzed for two hours that day.
According to Roazen (1975), " . . . he would tell jokes, would compliment a patient on a dress, and if he felt the need to urinate, would get up and leave the room" (p. 124).

Freud also seemed naturally drawn to active intervention.

When he thought an analysis could be helped by changes in the life of the
individual, he would intervene.

Sometimes he recommended a specific marriage choice or supported a
patient in violating a marriage bond.

He regarded certain dreams as signifying a return to health, and after
interpreting a dream could go so far as to remark: "Now you are
going to get well."

Roazen (1975) wrote: " . . . a patient was once embarrassed about something she was discussing and did not want Freud to watch her. He
got up from his chair and walked in front of the couch and looked
straight at her, saying that she had to have the courage to face him
and thereby confront her problem" (p. 124).

Being in the enviable position of leader of the psychoanalytic
movement, he could do what he wished without suffering the criticism or
rejection of colleagues. Roazen (1975) wrote:

He did what he thought best, without following his own rules. . . .
As one of Freud's patients and pupils once described it, the master's
attitude was: Do as I say, not as I do; and this dichotomy may have
been one of the sources of Freud's moralism about technique. Many
of Freud's followers mentioned the Roman maxim "Quod licet Jovi,
non licet bovi" ("What is permitted to Jove is not permitted to an
ox"). [Roazen 1975, p. 124]

In his practice, Freud broke the rules by treating the Brunswicks.

Freud had taken Ruth and Mark Brunswick into analysis simultaneously, and Mark's brother David as well. Between the three of
them they made up 60 per cent of Freud's analytic time and
income. . . . [In those days Freud carried about five analytic cases.]
Today analysts do not, however, like to treat a couple, married or
not, and it would be contraindicated by the "rules"; an analyst needs
to be able to identify with his patient, and this is made more difficult
in treating closely linked people. But Freud would violate normal
analytic procedure in the spirit of "the Rabbi may"—for the Rabbi
special exemptions were permitted. [Roazen 1975, p. 424]

There is some evidence to suggest that Freud did have some impatient, domineering personality characteristics. When the therapy didn't go his way or the patient was "unduly resistant," he may have been moved to activity to force a change, punish the patient, or act out his anger. His therapy of Dora and the Wolf Man suggests that his impatience, frustration, and anger may have played some part in the terminations. In his analysis of Hilda Doolittle, circa 1933–1934, he openly expressed his anger toward her in a moment of apparent frustration.

> He [Freud] . . . furiously pounded the back of the couch on which she was lying and said, "The trouble is, I am an old man—you do not think I was worth your while to love me" [Doolittle was forty-seven and Freud seventy-seven, at the time]. [Malcolm 1981, p. 166, n3]

Change in the time horizon for an analysis was beginning to fuel Freud's thinking. Not only was a course of therapy starting to go beyond the customary period of several months, both Freud and his disciples were seeing cases that began to last for a year or much more. Analysts were also beginning to see individuals for the second analysis if they had had either a brief or unsuccessful previous analysis. Ferenczi became known for seeing unsuccessful cases because of his creative ability to experiment and expand the techniques and process of psychoanalysis.

Freud, by his own admission, was a scientist first, a healer second.

> I . . . had only unwillingly taken up the profession of medicine, but I had at that time a strong motive for helping people suffering from nervous afflictions or at least for wishing to understand something about their states.
> . . . [nor] did I feel any particular predilection for the career of a doctor. I was moved, rather, by a sort of curiosity, which was, however, directed more towards human concerns than towards natural objects . . . . [Roazen 1975, pp. 66–67]

It was natural for him to eventually turn his full attention toward theoretical concerns, his first love (Bergmann and Hartman 1976). This became possible when Freud found a protégé whom he could totally trust not to break away from him, either personally or professionally. In Ferenczi he had his most devoted pupil and enthusiastic champion of psychoanalysis. Freud was able to turn his attention toward theory because Ferenczi was the creative technical genius that psychoanalysis needed to progress from a cognitive process into an experiential therapy. Freud showed his astuteness in sensing that in Ferenczi he had the rare blend of personal daring and clinical talent to develop psychoanalysis beyond its original boundaries.

Perhaps the most unorthodox deviation Freud ever performed was his analysis of his daughter Anna. Why he did this is very difficult to explain. Cogent and thoughtful discussions of this controversy have been presented (Roazen 1975, Young-Bruehl 1988). Freud's having analyzed his own daughter would seem to render matters of proper technique and rigid rules about psychoanalytic procedure rather open to discussion.

It is not an easy matter to conclude whether Freud's deviations from technique were solely manifestations of creativity or were personal and professional shortcomings. His active interventions with the Rat Man were clearly a humane effort. His unorthodox methods with the Wolf Man appear to be a combination of innovation and clinical dissatisfaction. Furthermore, the latest evidence suggests that Freud did do unusual things because of personal difficulties. He trained Emma Eckstein to be the first practicing psychoanalyst.

Freud was a complex, innovative, and creative individual. It does him a disservice to characterize his behavior as emanating from one psychodynamic, intellectual, or emotional source. No doubt he developed his method not only from his remarkable intellect, but also in meeting the demands of experiencing and responding to the individuals he faced in his early practice. It is also conceivable that Freud, like all analysts who came after him, was moved to make changes in his practice out of inspiration, frustration, and desperation.

FREUD'S CONTRIBUTION TO CHANGES IN PSYCHOANALYTIC TECHNIQUES

Freud's pioneering efforts in the theory and practice of technique forged the way for a host of changes in psychoanalysis and laid the groundwork for Ferenczi's clinical experiments, including

1. The introduction of deviation and evolution of psychoanalytic technique
2. The support for clinical experimentation with analytic technique

3. The introduction of activity as a therapeutic measure
4. A change in the role of the analyst from a neutral observer to an active respondent
5. The use of active measures for the treatment of obsessive-compulsive and phobic reactions
6. The introduction of several parameters into psychoanalytic therapy (feeding a patient, aiding a patient financially, unilaterally setting termination, promising a cure)
7. The encouraging of Ferenczi to develop the active dimension in psychoanalysis.

8

FERENCZI'S ACTIVE ANALYTIC METHOD

ACTIVE TECHNIQUE AND THE EVOLUTION OF FERENCZI'S CLINICAL METHOD

When Freud passed the mantle to Ferenczi in 1918 at the Budapest Congress, declaring his favorite pupil to be the leader of psychoanalysis, he ushered in the development of the role of activity in the psychoanalytic method (Freud 1919 [1918]). It was clear that Freud needed Ferenczi to develop psychoanalytic technique, because he realized that his own writings on the subject had caused a negative view.

Ferenczi's innovations in the active method were an evolutionary step toward his humanistic psychoanalysis in the following ways. They (1) established Ferenczi as the leader in technical clinical experiments, (2) developed the concept of the elasticity of the psychoanalytic situation, (3) introduced non-interpretative interventions, (4) changed the role of the analyst from neutral observer to active, caring respondent, (5) continued the evolution of psychoanalytic technique.

By focusing on the ways in which the Freudian method could be expanded, Ferenczi established his interest in the technical area of psychoanalysis and began a history of clinical experiments in the psychoanalytic method that he pursued throughout his clinical career. There has been no one since Ferenczi who viewed the psychoanalytic situation as an experiment in human relatedness. He was also willing to make changes in technique to reach an analysand and increase the effectiveness of the analytic process.

Along with an intellectual curiosity to experiment, Ferenczi had an emotional desire to expand his own functioning as well as those of his analytic colleagues. He believed that the analytic relationship was basically a healing experience predicated upon the flexibility of the healing agent. This was in contrast to the traditional view, already established by the onset of his clinical experiments, which held that the analysand's flexibility was called into question when there was difficulty in the relationship or the analysis reached an impasse. By writing and practicing "the elasticity of psychoanalytic technique," Ferenczi established the convention of the analyst's flexibility in functioning. It is also a sign of his humanistic method that the concept of elasticity of technique was suggested to him by an analysand, and he gladly responded to it by adapting it to his own techniques (Ferenczi 1928b).

Ferenczi's clinical experiments with activity introduced another innovation that predates the humanistic approach. The use of abstinence, forced fantasy, confrontation, and role-playing scenarios established the use of non-interpretative interventions. Although it was Freud who first suggested non-interpretative responses to the free-associative process, it was Ferenczi who established a variety of analytic interventions. In so doing he made it meaningful to change the free-associative process to include directed interventions initiated by the analyst. Of course, Ferenczi's aim in changing this process was to make it more flexible in order to be more effective in responding to a greater variety of therapeutic difficulties and patients.

As a consequence of introducing the active method for the analyst, Ferenczi changed the role of the analyst from a neutral observer who dared not interfere with the free associative process to an active respondent who became a partner with it. Neutrality gave way to activity that began a two-person process in psychoanalysis. Both parties were encouraged to initiate and respond in the analytic situation to encourage analytic progress and help the analysand. The issue of the analysand being the resistant individual in the process gave way to developing techniques to move beyond impasses. The analyst as interpreter of resistance was elasticized to be analyst and analysand as experimental partners. Ferenczi's identity was bound up with a healing attitude. He perceived himself as a healer, valued his capacity to work with different analysands, and enjoyed his worldwide reputation as the analyst who was successful where others had failed. With his investment in a healing identity, his clinical experiments in activity were also a caring expression of a desire to heal. He did not and would not accept that an analysand's difficulty in free-associating or inability to express affect could not be freed with the right effort and empathic attitude by the analyst. His refusal to accept clinical defeat and his invention of new activities was an expression of his desire to heal the neurotic wounds of his analysands.

Another consequence of Ferenczi's active method was that it established an evolutionary pattern for psychoanalytic technique. If any one psychoanalyst could be said to have established an ethic of clinical experimentation for psychoanalysis, it would be Ferenczi. His attempts at flexibility of technique and creative thinking established an alternative to those who believed that orthodoxy was the only standard for psychoanalysis. Ferenczi's clinical activity demonstrated that the individual analysand's needs took precedence over the continuation of a method that the analyst practiced by convention. Analysands who had had unsuccessful analysis with orthodox analysts were attracted to Ferenczi because they knew he would be flexible in his approach, as he had been with those who preceded them. But what is also significant is that he would be flexible enough to develop still newer techniques if their style of relating and the nature of their psychopathology demanded it. And, make no mistake, the difficult cases with which he worked made very dramatic demands on him. Ferenczi saw these demands or needs as an opportunity to continue the evolution of psychoanalysis toward a humanistic science.

FERENCZI'S FIRST CLINICAL EXPERIMENTS IN ACTIVE PSYCHOANALYSIS: APPLICATIONS OF THE RULE OF ABSTINENCE

Once Freud passed the mantle of technical innovation to him, Ferenczi was eager to apply Freud's new rule of psychoanalysis—the principle of abstinence. In 1919, Ferenczi reported his first clinical experiments in active techniques, which ushered in the era of active psychoanalysis and changed the face of therapy forever. Ferenczi's introduction and development of his active technique are contained in six crucial papers published from 1919–1925 (Ferenczi 1919a,b,c, 1920, 1925a) . Ferenczi paid tribute to his master when he made it clear that Freud was the inspiration for his clinical experiments (Ferenczi 1920, 1921b). Freud acknowledged this credit (Freud 1919 [1918]).

In his first paper of that year, Ferenczi (1919a) hints at his technical departures from classical analysis, and it is quite clear he is moving in a bold and new direction.

In one case I was forced, in direct contradiction to the psychoanalytic rule, to insist that the patient should always complete any sentence he had begun. For I noticed that whenever a sentence took an unpleasant turn he never completed it, but switched off in the middle with a "by the way" on to something unimportant and beside the mark. . . . [p. 181]

It was in his second paper of that year (1919b), however, that Ferenczi began to outline a system of clinical functioning based upon action. Ferenczi was in an erotic transference stalemate with a female patient whom he had seen on three different occasions for analysis of sexual dysfunction. It was not until he connected his clinical observations of her symbolic masturbatory behavior with the value of instructing her to refrain from indulging herself in such satisfaction that the full value of activity could be appreciated. Through his exceptional capacity to observe and analyze nonverbal behavior during the analytic session, Ferenczi became aware that his patient was receiving partial erotic gratification from rubbing her legs together as she was lying on the analytic couch. He reasoned that such symbolic masturbatory gratifications were siphoning off the psychic energy and motivation needed to stimulate the exploration of the unconscious fantasies underlying the patient's sexual difficulties.

He then developed the idea of prohibiting her from continuing to cross her legs while lying on the analytic couch. He applied a series of other such interventions when he saw that the first active technique moved the individual from increased anxiety to uncovering previously unexpressed unconscious material.

> The patient, to whom the customary genital discharge was forbidden, was tormented during the interviews by an almost insupportable bodily and psychic restlessness; she could no longer be at peace, but had constantly to change her position. Her phantasies resembled the deliria of fever, in which there cropped up long forgotten memory fragments that gradually grouped themselves round certain events in her childhood and permitted the discovery of most important traumatic causes for her illness. [Ferenczi 1919b, p. 191]

These interventions were the beginnings of a formal process of intervention based upon activity. Ferenczi moved his active technique beyond the couch and consultation room by prohibiting her from indulging during her daily activities as a homemaker in all the symbolic masturbatory activities she had practiced since childhood (e.g., rubbing her legs together while she swept the floor).

At no time when Ferenczi was applying these active measures did he abandon his role as a psychoanalyst. As each measure produced anxiety or an increase in or return to former symptoms, he interpreted the meaning of the anxiety and worked it through with the individual. It is also worth noting that Ferenczi was able to prohibit her from continuing her pleasurable activities because of the nature of their positive working alliance, his concern to heal the individual of her affliction, and his belief in the individual's capacity to change. At each stage in the active process, he appealed to her desire to delay gratification in order to move toward personal growth. He explained to her the benefit that the prohibitions would have on her analysis. This woman cooperated with him because of her belief in his desire to help her grow, which Ferenczi communicated in his enthusiasm, daring dedication, and motivation to cure her. (One cannot discount some influence of the erotic transference in the woman's giving herself over to her doctor, but this factor functioned to block the analysis before the active measures were employed.)

The last stage in this first reported case of active psychoanalysis was the development of a new symptom (Ferenczi 1919b): ". . . the appearance at unsensible times of a need to urinate" (p. 192). Ferenczi prohibited her from giving in to this desire, which led to a recurrence of masturbation in order to relieve the development of an intense feeling in her genitals. Through interpretation and dream analysis, Ferenczi was able to help this woman understand her psychodynamics, finally producing a breakthrough in the analysis.

> Parallel with the reconstruction of her infantile defense reaction, she achieved, after all these worries, the capacity of obtaining satisfaction in normal sexual intercourse, which . . . had hitherto been denied her. At the same time many of the as yet unsolved hysterical symptoms found their explanation in the now manifest genital phantasies and memories. [Ferenczi 1919b, p. 193]

FURTHER ELABORATION OF THE ACTIVE TECHNIQUE

Ferenczi elaborated his active technique into psychoanalysis in six papers that are crucial for this development:

1. 1919a: "On the Technique of Psycho-Analysis"
2. 1919b: "Technical Difficulties in the Analysis of a Case of Hysteria"

3. 1919c: "On Influencing of the Patient in Psycho-Analysis"
4. 1920: "The Further Development of the Active Therapy in Psycho-Analysis"
5. 1925a: "Contra-Indications to the 'Active' Psycho-Analytical Technique"
6. 1925b: "Psycho-Analysis of Sexual Habits"

An outline of the many active measures that Ferenczi introduced can be presented as follows.

1. He encouraged abstinence or the actual prohibition of the patient's symbolic sexual behavior, both in an analytic session and in everyday life. When the partial sexual satisfaction was discouraged, sexual fantasy material unfolded (Ferenczi 1919a).

2. He introduced the method of forced fantasies (Ferenczi 1924b). In order to deal therapeutically with intense resistances that threatened to hamper the effectiveness of the analysis, Ferenczi followed up the previous method of influencing the flow of associations by prohibition to directing the patient's expression of fantasies and affect. Ferenczi was never satisfied with incomplete therapeutic results. So he pushed his patients and himself until there were breakthroughs in functioning. One such example involved a patient who showed no negative affect toward Ferenczi. In order to liberate the suppressed feelings, he set a time limit to the analysis. In such an instance, he hoped the time limit would liberate negative transference feelings. When this didn't work, he would push further and encourage the analysand to produce an aggressive fantasy. Finally the patient produced a very vivid sadistic fantasy, where "he gouged out my eyes . . . [in] a sexual scene in which I played the role of a woman." There were physical changes in the fantast—e.g., "cold sweats" and a "manifest erection" (p. 72). The liberation of the sadistic fantasies enabled the therapy to progress toward the analysis of the transference and to "reconstruct the early infantile developmental history" and "the complete Oedipus complex" (Ferenczi 1924b, pp. 72–73).

3. He used confrontation with a phobic condition. Following Freud's lead, he encouraged the phobic patient to confront his fears directly both in the analytic situation and in real life (Ferenczi 1920, Freud 1919 [1918]). He realized that interpretive behavior had its limitations in helping an individual overcome his fear. The unfolding of the psychodynamics often led to an intellectual understanding and no change in the fear.

In the case of "The Female Croatian Musician," Ferenczi encouraged an opera singer who was having difficulty rehearsing because of stage fright to sing the song in the analytic session about which she was phobic (Ferenczi 1920). This was likely the first instance of a role-playing encounter in an analytic session (Rachman 1978a). When the opera singer was repeatedly encouraged to sing the song with greater emotional expression, a breakthrough occurred. The patient remembered an obscene song from childhood that was associated with an intensely negative relationship with a sibling. The emotional catharsis, coupled with an analysis of the meaning of the obscene words of the song, resolved the rehearsal phobia.

4. Ferenczi introduced active, non-interpretive intervention by the analyst. He developed role-playing or psychodramatic scenarios in his therapeutic method to heighten the level of experiencing to enable the analysand to reach the deepest levels of the emotional trauma of childhood (Ferenczi 1924b, 1931). In his last clinical phase, he referred to it as "child analysis in the analysis of adults" (Ferenczi 1931). Ferenczi (1924b) also wrote about another episode.

> . . . the patient brought me an experience of being seduced (which in all probability really happened), but with innumerable variations in order at the same time to confuse me and herself and to obscure reality. *I had again and again to constrain her to 'fabricate' such a scene*, and thus new details were established with certainty [p. 73, italics added]

Ferenczi then used the material generated by the psychodramatic experience to compare it with previous reports. The analysis helped the analysand to discontinue her obsessive behavior and, more important, helped clear away the dissociative process so prevalent in sexual abuse victims. Ferenczi (1924b) wrote: " . . . by giving expression to that idea, she had raised the certainty of the memory to the level of a direct sensory experience, and with that degree of certainty, we could both rest content" (p. 74).

ADVANTAGES OF FERENCZI'S ACTIVE METHOD

It was clear that Ferenczi's active method was an advance in psychoanalysis. There were several important ways in which this advance was significant.

1. Attention was drawn to the role of the analyst and, in particular, the inherent nature of passivity in the interpretive mode of psychoanalysis.
2. The nature of the interaction between analyst and analysand was investigated.
3. There was a focus on the analysand's behavior in the analytic situation, especially on nonverbal behavior cues. In fact, Ferenczi was the first analyst to throw light on the nature of the interaction of the therapeutic dyad and to begin the study of nonverbal communication in psychoanalysis and psychotherapy.
4. Ferenczi began the study of silent and resistant interactions.
5. Active intervention demonstrated that difficult cases can be treated successfully, if the analyst can change his or her functioning.

Even one of Ferenczi's strongest critics, Edward Glover (1955), noted the contribution that the active method made to psychoanalysis.

> . . . until Ferenczi drew our attention more closely to such details many of the previous passive analyses had erred on the side of being too passive, in the sense that many minor analytic manifestations had not been turned to legitimate advantage during treatment.
>   . . . there was no *systematic policy* of investigating continually all sorts of silent indications, attitudes, gestures, movements, facial contortions, etc., at the time when these needed systematic attention. . . . with more attention to detail in analysis coupled with more vigorous transference interpretation and on occasion employment of "forced" phantasy, we would be able to revise our estimates of difficult analyses, . . . I think that this is more than probable. [pp. 176–177]

CONTRAINDICATIONS TO THE ACTIVE PSYCHOANALYTIC TECHNIQUE

By the mid-1920s, criticisms began to mount in the analytic community regarding Ferenczi's active method (Glover 1924). However, Ferenczi was well aware of some of its shortcomings, and his discussion of them (Ferenczi 1925a) is the most meaningful.

1. Activity can increase resistance instead of reducing it.

The first and perhaps most crucial objection . . . is a theoretical one. Fundamentally it rests on a sin of omission. . . . "activity" unquestionably stimulates the resistance of the patient in so far as it seeks to increase the psychical tension by painful frustrations, injunctions, and prohibitions. . . . [pp. 218–219]

2. Active measures, if continually applied, can intensify a negative transference and encourage premature termination.

Activity as a measure of frustration acts therefore as a disturbing or destroying agent of the transference. As such it is well-nigh inevitable at the end of treatment, and if applied in untimely fashion certainly disturbs the relation between physician and analysand. If handled with unrelenting force it drives the patient from the analyst as certainly as do the inconsiderate explanations of the "wild analysts". . . . [p. 219]

3. Active measures should not be used in the initial stages of psychoanalysis, because they are ego threatening and can interfere with relationship building.

. . . the beginner should take care before he wanders from the tedious but instructive paths of the classical method to begin his career with the active technique . . . from the relation of the ego to frustration it follows that the analysis ought never to begin with active measures. [p. 219]

4. Injunctions and prohibitions, if used in an overpowering way, can encourage a negative, even mean-spirited experience. It is inappropriate to exercise your will over the patient, no matter what rationale you use to create a therapeutic effect.

Another series of difficulties arose from my putting forward certain injunctions and prohibitions far too strongly . . . ; they induce the physician forcibly to thrust his will upon the patient in an all too true repetition of the parent–child situation, or the sadistic bearing of a schoolmaster. At length I gave up altogether either ordering or forbidding my patients to do things, but now rather attempt to gain their intellectual understanding of the projected measure and only then to put it into execution. [pp. 220–221]

> 5. Realizing that rigid application of active measures, without gaining the cooperation of the patient, encouraged a negative transference reaction, where the analyst was experienced as hurtful rather than helpful, he made a 180-degree turn toward his next clinical phase, his *relaxation therapy*. This was a necessary step toward the development of his humanistic psychoanalysis.

. . . I no longer bind myself so firmly in arranging these procedures that I cannot retract them sooner or later if the difficulties are insuperable on the side of the patient. Our "active" mandates must therefore not be too rigid, . . . be of an elastic compliancy. . . . an obsessional neurotic will not fail to take the chance of making the injunctions given by the physician the subject of endless ruminations and idling away the time in over-conscientiousness in order among other things to anger the analyst.

Only when they see that the physician does not regard the strict execution of the injunction as a *conditio sine qua non* does the patient not feel himself threatened with an unyielding compulsion, and then complies with the intentions of the analyst. . . . [p. 221]

> 6. Setting of the termination date for the analysis to accelerate the analytic process is not indicated in every case.

But the most important correction which I must make . . . concerns the setting of a limit to the analysis as a device for accelerating the ending of treatment. . . . Recent experience compels me very fundamentally to restrict this generalization. . . . The dismissal works brilliantly in particular cases; in others it misfires lamentably. It shows that even the experienced analyst can be misled in his impatience prematurely to regard the patient as ready for notice. . . . I learnt from this case not only that one must be extraordinarily cautious and only leave the beaten track on rare occasions, but also that one may only take on a mandate for this as for other "activities" in agreement with the patient and with the possibility of retiring. [pp. 221–222]

Clara Thompson (1950b) a student of Ferenczi who was with him during his humanistic psychoanalytic period, has reflected on the short-comings of his active method.

> This mode of analysis certainly produced much violent emotion, and for a time he thought it was effective. Eventually he became convinced, however, that the emotion he was observing had little if anything to do with the repressed emotion he was seeking to liberate.
>
> The reactions were anger and irritability, which to a great extent were justified by the uncomfortable life situation created by the prohibitions.
>
> They [Rank and Ferenczi] were under the mistaken impression that they were thus releasing repressed emotion. If the patient was able to rant and rave against the analyst, he was supposedly freeing himself from his father or some equally important early figure. Abreaction was still considered the method of cure. Ferenczi's experiment showed that deliberate attempts to stir up anger did not produce the desired result.
>
> He relinquished his method gradually, that is, he first modi-fied it to the extent of making the undertaking of deprivation voluntary. He concluded that only if the patient was genuinely willing to undergo this kind of self-deprivation and there was no realistic resentment towards the analyst, were the emotions thus stirred up of therapeutic significance.
>
> Many patients out of fear of the analyst's disapproval agreed to the abstinence rule, which they nevertheless resented. So he aban-doned the whole method. [pp. 183–184]

FROM ACTIVE ANALYSIS TO RELAXATION THERAPY

During Ferenczi's active-analytic period, he was determined to demon-strate the efficacy of Freud's approach. Ironically, he was so intent on showing that abstinence would increase therapeutic effectiveness that he became overzealous in encouraging activity through injunctions and prohibitions. Analysands became resistant and saw Ferenczi as authori-tarian and a negative transferential figure. But, when Ferenczi's critics began to mount a campaign against his clinical extensions of the psycho-analytic method (Glover 1924, 1955), they missed the point. Ferenczi was well aware that there were limitations to the active method. Furthermore, he used his observations of the analysands' transference reactions in the psychoanalytic situation to become informed of the difficulties and changed his thinking to prepare for the next stage in the evolution of his psychoanalytic method.

His analysands expressed irritation, dissatisfaction, and resentment when he continued to apply stringent measures to create an atmosphere of abstinence. They became angry not because there was a liberation of negative affect from repressed emotion, but because they felt deprived by a negative authority or parental figure. There were two significant aspects of this negative therapeutic effect. First, Ferenczi had learned to create an ambience in the psychoanalytic situation that heightened the level of emotional experiencing. Thus, analysands were free to express their emotional reactions fully to the analyst without fear of judgment, suppression, counterattack, or loss of status. Ferenczi also learned not to rush to interpret the affect as transferential manifestations. He allowed the fuller expression of negative affect, especially toward the analyst, without the analysands having to defend or explain their negative feelings toward him. Ferenczi enhanced his capacity, thereby, to do clinical work in an experiential mode, elasticizing the analytic situation to move beyond interpretation.

A second result of Ferenczi's observing the limitations of the active method was his becoming attuned to the subjective experience of the analysand and employing an empathic stance to respond to the criticisms leveled against him. Ferenczi realized that the criticisms by analysands that he was being a negative authority or parental figure had validity. By not evoking an analysis of resistance and a transference explanation, he attuned himself to the subjective experience of the analysand and empathically responded by discontinuing the injunctions and prohibitions. This process of attuning was the embryonic stage of his next and last clinical phase—the development of relaxation therapy and the eventual evolution of his humanistic psychoanalysis.

9

FERENCZI'S INTRODUCTION OF MODERN PSYCHOANALYSIS: THE CASE OF THE FEMALE CROATIAN MUSICIAN

THE DAWN OF MODERN PSYCHOANALYSIS: FERENCZI'S PRESENTATION AT THE HAGUE

The issue of what constitutes the beginning of modern psychoanalysis makes for an interesting debate. Recently it has been suggested that Ferenczi and Rank's *Developmental Aims of Psychoanalysis*, published in 1925, is the landmark work (Haynal 1992). I concur, especially when one considers the alternative view of theory and the role of the analyst it suggested (see Chapter 10 and Chapter 11, this volume). But when one considers Ferenczi's "The Further Development of an Active Therapy in Psychoanalysis," delivered at the Sixth International Congress of Psycho-Analysis at The Hague, The Netherlands, on September 10, 1920, a case can be made for the clinical experiences and ideas contained in this paper initiating a new era in psychotherapy and psychoanalysis.

The paper focused on the avowed purpose of clarifying the integration of activity in psychoanalysis. As was often the case in Ferenczi's career, he reiterated that his ideas and methods were not a deviation from his mentor Freud, but an extension of the already established psychoanalytic technique. This tendency to avow Freud and traditional psychoanalysis must be considered a genuine effort on Ferenczi's part. He never desired to break with Freud, always wishing approval for his departures while, on the other hand, not being aware how significantly he deviated from his mentor's theoretical and clinical framework. Most likely, it was only Freud's love for his favorite pupil that allowed for Freud's continued support of Ferenczi's clinical experiments. It is also likely that Freud was genuinely connected to many of Ferenczi's innovations (see Chapter 8, this volume).

In the Conference paper, Ferenczi (1920) clarified his rationale for the use of activity:

> . . . I would emphasize at the beginning . . . [the] intention was and is to enable the patient, by means of certain *artifices*, to comply more successfully with the rule of free association and thereby to assert or hasten the exploring of the unconscious material. [p. 198]

Ferenczi introduced the concept of artifices to signify the variety of active measures he developed to encourage the flow of free associations when the analysand's capacity to associate had been curtailed. He made it clear in the introduction to the paper that artifices were only to be used " . . . [as] required in certain exceptional cases" (p. 198). He believed that in most cases the therapy can be carried out without introducing any artifices. In actuality, Ferenczi (1920) introduced a concept that was to be reintroduced in the 1950s, in Eissler's now famous "parameters" paper (see Chapter 16, this volume).

> . . . for most patients the treatment can be carried out without any special "activity" on the part of either doctor or patient, and even in those cases in which one has to proceed more actively the interference should be restricted as much as possible. As soon as the stagnation of the analysis, the only justification for and the only motive of the modification, is overcome, the expert will immediately resume the passively receptive attitude most favourable for the efficient co-operation of the doctor's unconscious. [p. 198]

No sooner did Ferenczi proclaim his allegiance to traditional psychoanalysis than he presented a case that illustrated the most far-ranging example of an active methodology that could change the face of psychoanalysis.

His innovative paper's major focus is the detailed description of the case of a young Croatian woman who suffered from a host of phobias and obsessional states. The presentation of the case material is innovative in and of itself because it is a clear exposition of the experience between analyst and analysand, as close to a verbatim account as was forthcoming during psychoanalysis's pioneering era (see also Freud 1954, for a fascinating description of the discovery of sexual seduction). With few exceptions (Freud the most noteworthy), psychoanalysts did not disclose their clinical work for scrutiny in the way Ferenczi did. Generally speaking, analysts would summarize their clinical work, rarely giving any indication of what words or experiences were actually exchanged between the participants. It was not until Carl Rogers pioneered the recording of psychotherapy sessions that analysts and psychotherapists were encouraged to be more open about their work (Rogers 1942). Ferenczi's frank and direct revelations about his work are just one aspect of this pioneering effort.

But it is Ferenczi's development of the active method of psychoanalysis that this case study and theoretical paper celebrates. By 1920, Ferenczi had practiced his active method for about five years or so, having introduced the embryonic version of it several years earlier (Ferenczi 1919a,c).

THE CASE

By the time the Female Croatian Musician was sent to Ferenczi for a second analysis, he had already developed the reputation of working successfully with the most difficult cases. Although he had extended Freud's deviations from classical technique by experimenting with the rule of abstinence and prohibition of impulses, both during and outside the analytic session (Ferenczi 1919a,b), the challenge of the Female Croatian Musician was to move Ferenczi to a moment of genius in psychoanalytic technique.

As could be predicted, the individual eventually showed the same resistance to translating her intellectual understanding into emotional experiencing and personality change as she did in her first analysis, even though Ferenczi was more active and inspiring in his behavior than her first analyst. Ferenczi was presented with a character trait that would not be changed by conventional analysis or by the influence of his personality. The situation demanded a new mode of function for the analyst.

Ferenczi's clinical material will be presented by referring to verbatim excerpts, since he was one of the first analysts to reveal his actual therapeutic behavior. The content is presented in a form that highlights the development in the analysis of a need to break with traditional technique and the daring experiments in active techniques that produced breakthroughs in the analysis of an obsessive and phobic neurosis (Ferenczi 1920).

> . . . I should like to give excerpts from some analysis calculated to substantiate . . . and to deepen to some extent our insight into the play of forces at work in "active technique." The case of a young Croatian woman, a musician, who suffered from a host of phobias and obsessional states, occurs to me at once.
>
> . . . She suffered torments of stage fright; if she was asked to play in front of others . . . she became scarlet in the face . . . she made mistakes on every occasions and had the obsessive idea that she must disgrace herself . . .
>
> . . . In the street, she believed herself constantly observed because of her too voluminous breasts, and did not know how to hold or conduct herself in order to conceal this (imagined) bodily deformity. Now she would fold her arms across her chest, now compress the breasts tightly . . . each precaution was followed by the doubt whether she were not, by these very means, attracting attention to herself . . . she was unhappy if in spite of her marked beauty no attention was paid her, but was no less disconcerted when actually spoken to by someone . . .
>
> She was afraid that she had an offensive breath and went constantly to the dentist . . . who could discover nothing. . . . [Ferenczi 1920, p. 203]

The Therapeutic Stalemate

"She came after an analysis of many months duration to me . . . and was already well initiated into her unconscious complexes; on continuing her treatment, however, I had to endorse the observation of my colleague that the progress of the cure had no relation to the depth of her theoretic insight and to the memories already laid bare" (Ferenczi 1920, p. 203).

The Encounter: "A Primal Song"

The moment of encounter is clearly described by Ferenczi:

> At one interview a street song occurred to her that her elder sister . . . was in the habit of singing. After hesitating for a long time she

repeated the very ambiguous text of the song and was silent for a long time; I extracted from her that she had thought of the melody of the song. *I did not delay in asking her to sing the song.* It took nearly two hours, however, before she could bring herself to perform the song. . . . She was so embarrassed that she broke off repeatedly in the middle of a verse, and to begin with she sang in a low uncertain voice until, encouraged by my persuasions, she began to sing louder. . . . This did not overcome the resistance; after some difficulty she confessed that her sister was in the habit of accompanying the song with expressive and indeed quite unambiguous gestures, and she made some clumsy arm movements to illustrate her sister's behaviour. *Finally I asked her to get up and repeat the song exactly as she had seen her sister do it.* [italics added]

After endless spiritless partial attempts she showed herself to be a perfect chanteuse. . . . From now on she seemed to take pleasure in these productions and began to fritter away the hours of analysis with such things. . . . I told her we knew now that she enjoyed displaying her various talents and that behind her modesty lay hidden a considerable desire to please; it was no longer a matter of dancing but of getting on with the work. [Ferenczi 1920, p. 204]

Here is illustrated a moment of scientific discovery through the process of serendipity. Ferenczi, with his unusual ability to observe nonverbal behavior while the individual was lying in the analytic position, noticed the opera singer gesticulating as she talked about a song—a very natural activity for a musician who was trained to fuse words and physical movements in the act of creating. Ferenczi translated his acute observation into a creative act. Rather than have the individual continue to only talk about her conflict, he asked her to move into action, to sing the song. The test of Ferenczi's clinical creativity was revealed in the positive result of his active clinical experiment. He reported the breakthrough.

The Initial Breakthrough

It was astonishing how favourably this little interlude affected the work . . . memories of her early childhood . . . occurred to her, memories of the time when the birth of a little brother had had a really unholy effect on her psychic development and had made of her an anxious, shy, and abnormally good child. She remembered the time when she was still "a little devil," the darling of all her family and friends, when she displayed all her talents before people and generally showed an unrestrained pleasure in muscular movement. [Ferenczi 1920, p. 204]

This was a significant moment in the history of psychoanalysis because for the first time a clinician demonstrated that action can lead to insight. Prior to this deviation, tradition demanded that verbal interaction of an objective, inquiring, but nonemotional or dramatic nature was the necessary and sufficient condition for the development of insight. But during these pioneering days, clinical experimentation was an established vehicle for the continued evolution of psychoanalytic technique. Therefore, Ferenczi was free to create new techniques in the privacy of his consultation office, reassured that he had the approval of Freud. Furthermore, Ferenczi was not, as many suggest, a wild analyst solely acting out his own need for love, but a dedicated clinician, attempting to actualize the potentiality of the analytic encounter using his rich personality as a springboard for inspiration.

When Ferenczi saw that his action was helping the Female Croatian Musician shed her defensive posture, he continued his clinical experiments and initiated a series of active measures to help her confront her fears and further develop insight into her conflicts.

Subsequent Encounters and Breakthroughs

I followed up this active measure and constrained the patient to carry out activities of which she had the greatest fear.

She *conducted in front of me (while at the same time she imitated the sounds of an orchestra)* a long phrase from a symphony; the analysis of this notion led to the discovery of the penis jealousy by which she had been tormented since the birth of her brother.

She *played to me the difficult piano piece that she had to play at the examination*; it was shown afterwards in the analysis that her fear of disgracing herself when playing the piano referred back to onanistic phantasies and onanistic disgrace (forbidden "finger exercises").

She did not dare to go to the swimming-baths on account of her idea that her breasts were disproportionately large; *only after she had overcome the resistance on my insisting* was she able to convince herself during analysis of her latent desire to exhibit.

Now that the approach to her most hidden tendencies was opened up, she acknowledged that during the analytic hour she occupied herself a great deal with her sphincter ani; sometimes she would play with the idea of passing flatus, sometimes contract the sphincter rhythmically. . . .

. . . We came upon the anal-erotic explanation of her anxiety that her mouth smelt offensively; soon after the reproduction of the associated infantile memories, while maintaining *the prohibition against anal play*, this showed marked improvement.

We owed the most marked impulse toward betterment to the patient's unconscious onanism which was rendered manifest by the help of "activity." Sitting at the piano, she experiences a voluptuous sensation of the genital parts stimulated by the movement. She had to acknowledge these sensations to herself after she had been bidden to behave, as she saw many artists do, very passionately at the piano; but as soon as she began to take pleasure in this play *she had on my advice to give it up*. As a result we were then able to take cognizance of reminiscences and reconstructions of infantile genital play, the chief source perhaps of her exaggerated sense of shame. [Ferenczi 1920, pp. 204–205, italics added]

The Meaning of Ferenczi's Experiments in the Active Psychoanalysis of the Female Croatian Musician

Ferenczi's clinical behavior in this case introduced a significant deviation from the classical psychoanalytic process and method that can be viewed as the formal beginning to a modern psychoanalytic method. The case of the Female Croatian Musician was significant for the following reasons:

1. Physical activity or action was a crucial part of the interaction. The patient was encouraged to translate ideas and feelings into some form of meaningful action associated with the neurotic conflict rather than to talk about it. She was asked to sing a song, to conduct the orchestra, to go to the baths, to stop her anal play.

2. The analyst directed the session into a particular activity or experience rather than following the associations of the individual or maintaining interaction at only a verbal level.

3. A suggestion was made that a time-extended session of a two-hour duration be employed during the first encounter. Ferenczi was able to anticipate the flexible use of time, which later came to a peak in the 1960s with the advent of encounter and marathon group therapy.

4. Heightened emotional experiencing or a cathartic breakthrough was sought. The patient was instructed to continue the action until she reached an emotional or peak experience.

5. Ferenczi relied on confrontation as a basic technique when he felt the patient was using the activity in the service of resistance.

6. Ferenczi was not a passive, neutral analyst but an active, involved one. He demonstrated caring through his willingness to both initiate activity in the analytic session and encourage the patient to face her anxieties in the real world.

7. The human, person-to-person aspects of the relationship are inherent in this case (without neglecting the analysis of the transference relationship).

8. Ferenczi demonstrated the elasticity of the analytic situation, where different modes of activity can be employed (e.g., action, prohibition, interpretation, exploration of unconscious material) until the desired therapeutic goal is reached.

9. The active method, if properly executed, doesn't interfere with the analytic process. In fact, it enhances the flow of associations, the expression of feelings, the exploration of childhood memories, and the development of insight.

10. A change in functioning—in both symptom reduction and increased mastery—and the concomitant increase in self-esteem developed as a result of the introduction of the active interventions. According to the data Ferenczi reported in this case, the active method helped in the curative process.

11. A holistic approach to the human condition and human behavior was apparent. He brought into play and reunited the emotional, intellectual, physical, and interpersonal/social parts of the individual. He understood and responded to the individual as a complex whole rather than just a series of intrapsychic conflicts.

12. The analysis was not restricted to the analytic hour, but carried out beyond the consultation session as he encouraged her to confront her fears in the real world.

13. Respect for creativity as a necessary human function is evident in Ferenczi's understanding of the psychodynamics of a musician's inhibi-

tion to perform and create; in his struggle to help her break open her constrictions; and in his flexible, daring, and innovative clinical behavior.

14. Ferenczi directed the session into a particular activity or experience, rather than only expecting the individual to unfold herself to the analyst. He was willing to give advice, develop activities, directly encourage change, and suggest avenues for potential growth.

15. The transference relationship was conceived not as encouraging regression and dependency to reach a transference neurosis, but as a living emotional experience to actively resolve and work through historical conflicts in the here and now of the analytic session and the real work.

16. The analyst took risks in the relationship. Ferenczi was willing to take a chance in suggesting actions as a means to deal with the individual's conflicts. He was willing to be wrong about the new technique and departure from tradition producing no effect or negative consequences.

17. Ferenczi took responsibility in the therapeutic relationship. It was not only the patients' responsibility to deal directly with their problems; Ferenczi was a dedicated partner in the struggle, giving of himself, not willing to rest until the desired breakthrough was achieved.

18. Ferenczi treated the opera singer with respect and believed in her capacities to face her conflicts and make the necessary changes for personal growth. By encouraging her to act, both within the session and beyond it, he was conveying to her his belief in her capacity for self-actualization.

19. A central focus was directed toward the conscious processes relevant to neurotic conflict.

20. The positive growth potential of the patient was recognized and mobilized.

THEORETICAL CONSIDERATIONS IN THE CASE OF THE FEMALE CROATIAN MUSICIAN

Besides outlining the technical parameters for the full expansion of the active method in the Case of the Female Croatian Musician, Ferenczi also summarized the theoretical issues involved in this evolution in analytic technique. The first clarification he made is that the active method is an evolutionary step in the history of psychoanalysis. In essence, he said that activity is an integral part of psychoanalysis and has always been in use.

. . . "activity" on closer inspection is found to be an old acquaintance. Not only has it played an important part already in the early history of psycho-analysis; it has in a certain sense never ceased to exist. We are dealing here, therefore, with the formulation of a conception and of a technical expression for something which, even if unexpressed, has always *de facto* been in use. [Ferenczi 1920, p. 198]

It is clear in Ferenczi's thinking that the Breuer/Freud *cathartic* method, which was the earliest technique of psychoanalysis, was an active procedure for both the analysand and the analyst.

The doctor made the greatest efforts to revive the memories relating to the symptoms and made use of every assistance that the procedure of waking or hypnotic suggestion put at his disposal. The patient, too, made every endeavour to follow the directions of his guide, and had therefore to engage in marked psychic activities, had often indeed to exercise all his intellectual faculties. [Ferenczi 1920, p. 199]

By the 1920s the cathartic method of encouraging the full expression of underlying feelings had long given way to the reliance on interpretation as the fundamental, preferred, and golden technical intervention of psychoanalysis. Traditional exponents of psychoanalysis argued that a form of passivity, rather than activity, was the proper attitude and role of the psychoanalyst. This notion of passivity meant that the analyst should not pay any particular attention to any one thought, feeling, or behavior of the analysand. Also, the analyst should not be concerned with any particular idea of understanding or curing the analysand. What was acceptable was to abandon oneself to the patient's ideas.

But Ferenczi felt there were two things wrong with this traditional notion of interpretation. First, he had already pointed out in a previous publication (Ferenczi 1919a) that interpretation was inherently a process of directing attention in a particular direction. ". . . as soon as he has been able to crystallize certain really valid opinions, he must direct his attention to them and on mature reflection must decide upon an *interpretation*" (Ferenczi 1920, p. 199).

Furthermore, Ferenczi felt that any interpretation was also an inherently active procedure.

> Communicating such an interpretation is, however, in itself an active interference with the patient's psychic activity; it turns the thoughts in a given direction and facilitates the appearance of ideas that otherwise would have been prevented by the resistance from becoming conscious. The patient must comport himself passively during this "midwifery of thought." [Ferenczi 1920, p. 200]

Ferenczi reminds us that an important distinction has to be made between the theory of psychoanalytic technique and clinical practice. On the one hand, it is clear that in psychoanalytic tradition the transference experience should not be interfered with. Ferenczi pointed out that, barring interference from the analyst, the transference will unfold in a properly conducted psychoanalysis. It is the same concept that Heinz Kohut reiterated in the elucidation of his deviation from the classical method, when he said that the "self-object transference" would naturally unfold if a properly created empathic ambience was established (Kohut 1978b). But once the transference unfolds, any attempt on the part of the analyst toward "the education of the ego"—that is, to impart some understanding of the transference process to the analysand—is an "active interference of which the doctor is capable because of the authority which has been heightened by the transference" (Ferenczi 1920, p. 200).

The reliance on the so-called passive attitude of the analyst and the intervention of interpretation became problematic when Freud and pioneers of psychoanalysis could no longer depend upon the transference of their authority as men and physicians to evoke a cure. Freud, to his credit, paved the way to reconsider this situation when he admitted that clinical psychoanalysis with anxiety hysteria, phobias, and the obsessive-compulsive disorders demanded active, non-interpretative intervention (Freud 1919 [1918]). As significant as Freud's paper "Lines of Advance" was in introducing activity as a part of psychoanalytic technique, Ferenczi's "Further Development of an Active Therapy" established the possibilities of the active method in successfully coping with the disorders that Freud outlined as needing non-interpretive intervention and also in dealing with difficult cases. It should be remembered that Freud suggested that Ferenczi pursue his clinical experiments with the active method.

Ferenczi was interested in experimenting with the so-called "dead points" in the analysis—those moments (which, of course, can grow into sessions, weeks, and months) when there is a stalemate, an impasse.

FERENCZI'S THEORY OF ACTIVITY

The accumulated clinical experience using active measures and its application in the Case of the Female Croatian Musician led Ferenczi to outline his ideas on the use of activity in psychoanalysis.

> In this case our activity may be divided into two phases. In the first, the patient [Female Croatian Musician] who guarded herself from certain activities by a phobia, had to be commanded to carry out those activities, contrary to inclination; after the hitherto repressed tendencies had become pleasurable, she had in the second place to deny herself, that is, certain activities were *forbidden*. The commands had the result of rendering *fully conscious* inclinations hitherto repressed, or only manifested as unrecognizable rudiments, and ultimately rendering them *conscious as desires*, as ideas agreeable to herself. Then when the satisfaction of the now pleasurable activity was denied her, the psychic impulse once roused found the way to long repressed material, to infantile reminiscences, or they had to be interpreted as repetitions of something infantile, and the peculiarities and conditions of the childish procedures had to be reconstructed by the analyst with the help of the other analytic material (dreams, fancies, etc.).
>
> Thus the "active therapy," hitherto regarded as a single entity, breaks up into the systematic issuing and carrying out of *commands* and of *prohibitions*, Freud's "attitude of renunciation" being constantly maintained. [Ferenczi 1920, p. 205–206]

Ferenczi's theoretical description of active therapy was an attempt to maintain his technical development as an evolutionary step in the growth of clinical psychoanalysis. As such, he outlined a theory suggesting that active intervention encouraged the free flow of associations because it helped to lift the repression barrier that was instituted to defend against the painful and forbidden pleasurable experiences of childhood. In keeping with the psychoanalytic theory of repression, the forgotten memories, once connected to the original affects and events of childhood that produced the blocking process, were liberated. But it was the analysis of the liberated material that produced the insight necessary to evoke change. Cathartic release without understanding was therapeutic, but not psychoanalytic. It was the analyst's role to use dream material, early recollections, transference material, and resistant interactions to give meaning to the liberation of repressed memories. The function of activity was to aid in retrieving the repressed memories so that the analysis could go forward.

Ferenczi demonstrated in this case that analytic theory can integrate active measures, which move clinical psychoanalysis beyond interpretative behavior. Yet, in doing so, it does not lose the capacity to help an individual develop understanding into his or her neurotic issues. In fact, what Ferenczi demonstrated was that without the active analyst the dead points, or the drying up of cases, could not be negotiated. It was the innovation of becoming active that allowed the stalemate in the analysis to be broken.

Ferenczi was aware of the relational aspect to active therapy:

> . . .when by our commands we constrain one or other patient not only to own deeply concealed impulses to himself, but *to enact them before the doctor*, and, by setting him the task, of *consciously controlling* these impulses we have probably subjected the whole process to a revision that was despatched at some other time in a purposeless fashion by means of *repression*. It is certainly no accident that just infantile *naughtinesses* are so often developed during analysis and must then be given up. [Ferenczi 1920, p. 216]

10

FERENCZI AND RANK: FELLOW DISSIDENTS

PSYCHOANALYSIS'S FIRST LAY ANALYST

Freud took Otto Rank under his wing when he first met him in 1905. The meeting was arranged by Adler, who was Rank's physician. Rank visited Freud to show him the manuscript of his book, *Der Kunstler* (*The Artist*) (Rank 1907). Rank had first come across Freud's work in 1904. He went through "almost a religious and ecstatic revelation" (Eisenstein 1966, p. 38). This kind of emotional connection to another human being was not characteristic of Rank, who wrote (Eisenstein 1966), "I have an aversion to every contact with people—I mean, to every physical contact. It costs me an effort to extend my hand to anyone . . . I first put on gloves. I couldn't kiss anyone" (p. 37).

As with all of Freud's disciples, the first contact was with the master. Then the disciples developed auxiliary relationships. Ferenczi was one of the members of the Society of Rings who was desirous of developing relationships with others than Freud. He did so with Jung, Rank, and Groddeck, the most independent thinkers of the pioneers, all of whom could not be dominated by the authority and dogmatism of Freud or the analytic community that surrounded him.

Rank became the first lay analyst and the first analyst to be groomed for psychoanalysis by Freud. Interestingly enough, Rank's path to analytic practice did not follow the usual course. Rather than training to be a physician, he trained to be a psychologist. Freud realized that his own medical education was not as helpful to him as would have been the study of man as a psychosocial being. Thus, Freud advised Rank (Gay 1988) "not to trouble with medical school for the sake of becoming a psychoanalyst" (p. 472).

The medicalization of psychoanalysis in America was a sharp contrast to the European tradition which was encouraged by Freud, both in pioneering times and beyond, when an intellectually talented and emotionally intuitive individual would be able to become an analyst in good standing in the analytic community. Ferenczi was also a champion of lay analysis (see Chapter 19, this volume). He did not want the field dominated by the medical profession, or by any one group, for that matter.

Rank's attachment to Freud was perhaps his deepest relationship with anyone, except for his mother (Taft 1958). It is clear that Rank became Freud's analytic son. Freud was so pleased with Rank's behavior — his efficiency, dependability, promptness, and faithfulness — that he wished to have "multiple copies of him" (Gay 1988, p. 471). Rank was Freud's investment, and he paid Freud handsome dividends. He was a founder and editor of *Imago*. In 1913, he also helped found the official organ of the psychoanalytic movement, the *Internationale Zeitschrift für Psychoanalyse*. Furthermore, in 1919, when Anton von Freund gave a substantial financial gift to Freud, Rank was one of the founders and directors of the Verlag, the analytic publishing house, making arrangements for a branch of the Verlag in London. In consort with Jones, the London branch included a bookstore specializing in psychoanalytic materials, a book series to publish the German sources, and, most importantly, an English-language journal, *The International Journal of Psycho-Analysis* (under Jones's editorship) (Young- Bruehl 1988).

Rank became known for his capacity to manage the affairs of psychoanalysis, verifying Freud's original faith in him as a person worthy of being an adopted analytic son. All the more difficult, then, was the fall from grace, for both Freud and Rank. A significant difference, however, existed in the differences between Freud and Rank and those that later developed between Freud and Ferenczi. Rank's differences with Freud led to a formal break in their relationship, which Rank acknowledged he wanted. On the other hand, Ferenczi never had or desired a formal break with Freud. Their differences led to Ferenczi's withdrawing from active contact with Freud and developing his dissident theories and techniques. Yet he still sought Freud's approval. Exemplifying this was Ferenczi's agonizing attempt to gain acceptance for his "Confusion of Tongues" paper, even though Freud urged him not to deliver it at the Wiesbaden Conference and also urged him not to publish it for at least one year after its delivery (see Chapter 13, this volume).

THE SOCIETY OF RINGS

In July 1912, while Freud was in Karlsbad and Jones was in Vienna, Jones had a discussion with Ferenczi about the issue of defections. Ferenczi suggested that the best strategy would be for a number of men who had been analyzed by Freud personally to be stationed in different centers or countries (Jones 1955). Since this was not a possibility at the time, Jones's counterproposal, which was more realistic, was to form an old guard around Freud. The committee was to form the function of either curtailing any further defections or, if they did occur, to at least exercise some restraint on the defector. Jones (1955) wrote:

> It would give him [Freud] the assurance that only a stable body of firm friends could, it would be a comfort in the event of further dissensions, and it should be possible for us to be of practical assistance by replying to criticisms and providing him with necessary literature, illustrations for his work drawn from our own experience, and the like. There would be only one definite obligation . . . if anyone wished to depart from any of the fundamental tenets of psychoanalytical theory, e.g., the conception of repression of the unconscious, of infantile sexuality, etc., he would promise not to do so publicly before first discussing his views with the rest. [p. 152]

After Ferenczi agreed, the idea was put to Rank. Then Jones spoke to Sachs, who was his closest friend in Vienna, and subsequently Ferenczi and Rank contacted Abraham in Berlin. In October 1919, Freud suggested Eitingon as the sixth member of the committee. Eitingon became the replacement for von Freund, whose illness and death prevented him from joining (Jones 1955).

Freud was fascinated by the idea of the committee, as it apparently hit a nerve.

> What took hold of my imagination immediately is your idea of a secret council . . . to take care of the further development of psycho-analysis and defend the cause against personalities and accidents when I am no more. . . . First of all: This committee would have to be *strictly secret* in its existence and in its actions. It could be

composed of you, Ferenczi and Rank among whom the idea was generated. Sachs, in whom my confidence is unlimited in spite of the shortness of our acquaintance—and Abraham could be called next. . . . I will not drop any utterance about the matter . . . not even to Ferenczi. . . . The future foreman of the psycho-analytic movement might come out of this small but select circle of men. . . . [Jones 1955, pp. 153–154]

Thus the Society of Rings was formed.

Jones (1955), ever ready to criticize Ferenczi, described his account of the coming together of Ferenczi, Rank, and himself as the first members of the committee.

Rank . . . was Freud's man of all work . . . devoted to him. . . . Ferenczi, he was the staunchest and most enthusiastic colleague. . . . Freud would, I feel sure, have placed no one above him in his estimation . . . when I introduced Rank to him as the latest recruit to our little group, Ferenczi eyed him . . . and put the question to him: "I suppose you will always be loyal to psychoanalysis?" I felt myself it was almost an insulting way to greet a new adherent. . . . [p. 153]

The committee first met on May 25, 1913. To seal the secrecy of the gathering and to fulfill the romantic fantasy shared by at least Freud and Jones of a coming together of "Charlemagne's paladins," Freud gave each committee member a ring that contained an antique Greek intaglio. Seven years later, Eitingon, the final member of the committee, was also given a ring that had a Greek-Roman intaglio of the head of Jupiter (Jones 1955). Ferenczi's ring was given to his successor, Balint, upon his death.

Jones ranked the committee members from most to least in Freud's affection. Jones rated Ferenczi first, himself third, and Rank fourth. Jones also rated Ferenczi and Sachs as most sensitive to any evidence of anti-Semitism; Freud was third, while Abraham and Rank were less so (Lieberman 1985). Jones (1955) also ranked the committee's intellectual and clinical abilities. "I should judge Abraham and Ferenczi to have been the best analysts. Abraham had a very sure judgment even if he lacked some of Ferenczi's intuitive penetration" (p. 161).

Rundbriefe (Circular Letters)

At the Sixth International Psychoanalytic Congress at the Hague, in September 1920, Freud proposed that the committee exchange letters, *Rundbriefe*, which would be circulated to all members. They would be written weekly, on the same day. Jones would write from London; Abraham, Eitingon, and Sachs from Berlin; Rank (after discussion with Freud) from Vienna; and Ferenczi from Budapest (Grosskurth 1991). (When Rank left Vienna in 1926 for good, he took the *Rundbriefe* with him. They were given to Columbia University by the Rank estate.) The circular letters were Freud's attempt to be informed of matters pertaining to the inner circle, as well as to maintain his authority as head of the movement. The logo of the *Rundbriefe* was Oedipus consulting the Sphinx.

The letters ranged from two to seven typewritten pages. After a number of general comments and an account of the situation in each society, the questions raised by the respective members would be answered in turn. Each member was assigned an area of psychoanalytic literature to review (Grosskurth 1991).

Ferenczi sent the first *Rundbriefe* on September 20, 1920, describing a standard form that the circular letters would take. He suggested the letters omit politics, but contain scientific matters and personal information. Furthermore, Ferenczi proposed that the various analytic institutes set common standards and that all members be consulted when a new member was to be included (Grosskurth 1991). Jones and Abraham disagreed with the proposals, beginning the differences and frictions within the committee. Grosskurth (1991) wrote:

> Complaints began to surface almost from the beginning of the circular-letter writing. Why, Rank demanded, were three signatures not to be found on the Berlin letters? In Vienna they made it a practice that Rank would write the letter on Thursday, Freud would sign it on Friday, and it was sent off the same day. Abraham replied snappishly that it was impossible to get the letters off in time if everyone signed. . . . Jones would blow up over tiny details. . . . [p. 99]

The *Rundbriefe* continued for seven years, becoming the forum for information, debate, and gossip about the committee and the psychoanalytic community. Although there seemed to be peace and unanimity on the surface, by 1924 the committee was headed for dissolution. It is generally agreed that three events occurring at that time, involving Ferenczi and Rank, encouraged its end. First, there was the reaction of the committee to the publication of Ferenczi and Rank's *Development of Psychoanalysis*. Then came their reaction to Ferenczi's *Thalassa*. Finally, the straw that broke the camel's back was Rank's (1924) *The Trauma of Birth*. Initially, Freud had positive reactions to all three works, including the blatantly dissident *Trauma of Birth*, which Rank acknowledged was his attempt to break away from the master. (For a full discussion of the committee and its vicissitudes, see Grosskurth 1991).

The Berlin Conspiracy

The Berlin group of Abraham, Sachs, and Eitingon, not willing to forgive and forget, was suspicious and ready to gather around Freud and punish the dissident Rank. Gay (1988) wrote:

> On Christmas Day [1924], the Berlin group—Eitingon, Sachs, Abraham—sent their "dear Otto" a letter welcoming him back to the fold. But the cordiality of their greeting did not conceal a certain sting; the three Berliners reminded Rank of his neurotic conduct, and strongly suggested that while he was busy revising his revisions in his return to psychoanalytic verities, he might do well to refrain from publishing. [p. 474]

Shortly after, Jones joined the Berliners in sending a similar letter to Rank. Rank saw through this faint praise and realized that his time within the charmed circle of psychoanalysis was over. But he was ready and willing to defect. Jones wrote to Rank, paraphrasing Goethe's famous line from Faust, "Am Ended is die Tot" (In the end is death) (Gay 1988).

The tradition of the *Rundbriefe* was briefly revived by Fenichel, who considered it a left-wing analytic tradition. These circular letters were a written extension of a seminar that Fenichel's political Freudian group had been part of in Berlin. His idea was to encourage analysts to discuss political issues (Jacoby 1983).

RANK BREAKS WITH FREUD

In 1924, Rank gave his first lecture in the United States to the American Academy of Medicine, introducing his trauma theory. He also gave a birth trauma lecture to the American Psychoanalytic Association. Rank's lecture appeared in the July issue of *Psychoanalytic Review* (Rank 1924). The lecture was seen as a bombshell. Significantly, Rank did not represent himself as an emissary of Freud or the committee. Rather, he stated that this was his new viewpoint. Rank thought that the birth trauma theory was a radical concept, but not a violation of Freud's instinct theory. He actually saw it as an improvement of Freudian theory. Rank did credit Freud with two fundamental concepts, which he incorporated into his birth trauma theory—that is, the primacy of birth anxiety and the usefulness of setting a termination date for the analysis.

Birth Trauma

Rank literally interpreted anxiety and trauma as the initial separation from the mother as the infant enters the world. He viewed the parting from the womb's ideal conditions of nurturance, support, and bliss and the connection to the mother in an empathy that requires no reciprocity as the fundamental anxiety and trauma of human existence that colors all subsequent experience. Furthermore, the more the separation experience was stimulated by a difficult birth, the more intense the traumatic experience and the greater the anxiety to master. Therefore, neurosis was directly related to the nature and amount of anxiety experienced in the birth trauma. Rank believed that this trauma was the imprint for all future experiences of separation. Separation was the prototype experience for neurosis.

The translation of the birth trauma theory into clinical therapeutics would mean that a successful psychotherapy would consist of a psychological rebirth. Lieberman (1985) wrote, "One gives birth to a new self, with the analyst as midwife" (p. 232). In addition, the Rankian idea is to encourage a mentor relationship between the patient and the therapist. It is through mentoring, which is close to Ferenczi's idea of the tender-mother transference and the concept of mutuality, that the individual's creativity is released. Rank and Ferenczi shared a similar humanistic/growth-oriented framework, where democratic interaction emphasizes the individual's potential and sense of self.

Rank and Freud in Conflict

Freud attributed the beginning of Rank's separation from him to psychological causes. In 1923, Rank found out from Freud's physician that Freud had a malignant disease. At the time Freud was unaware of the diagnosis. Freud maintained that the knowledge of his illness had a fatal effect on Rank. This is supported by the following passage:

> Otto Rank was the Professor's faithful Pallatine, . . . hiding his need for individuation until the Professor was deadly sick, as it was known only to Rank at first and to him alone. [Ferenczi is referred to as "the Professor's favorite Apostle, who never really saw why he could not also be the only son."] [Grotjahn 1973, p. 86]

Jessie Taft (1958) wrote about Freud:

> . . . at this bitter moment of realization of his own failing health, he expresses . . . Rank's educational lack, the absence of the scientific basis that medicine might have given, as well as his awareness of the temperamental qualities that he deplored and that Ferenczi's fundamental sweetness of disposition could have mitigated. [p. 78]

Freud, after initially showing interest and a positive response to the birth trauma theory, began to have doubts about Rank's new theory. Freud feared that Rank's *Birth Trauma* and Ferenczi and Rank's *Development of Psychoanalysis* would cause the loss of the Oedipus complex in his theory. Apparently, Freud did not see how to incorporate the birth trauma theory into his theoretical system while retaining the Oedipus complex as the cornerstone of psychoanalytic theory. Eitingon, Abraham, and Jones began to put pressure on Freud to renounce Rank (and criticize Ferenczi also) so that psychoanalysis could maintain its conservative core. The classical analysts were concerned that in Rank and Ferenczi a new heresy was beginning, in the same way Jung had created a crisis. Freud was supposed to have said to Ferenczi (Eisenstein 1966), "I don't know whether 66 percent or 33 percent of it is true, but in any case it is the most important progress since the discovery of psychoanalysis" (p. 45).

Lieberman (1985) reported that Freud admitted to Ferenczi that he had liked the book better in the beginning and that he was was moving from the 66 percent to the 33 percent. Rank later claimed that Freud had told him that anybody else would have used such a discovery to become independent (J. Jones 1960, cited in Eisenstein 1966). Abraham called the work "scientific regression." Also, Freud was willing to accept the concept of birth trauma, but was startled by Rank's attempts to develop a new psychoanalytical theory and technique around it (Eisenstein 1966).

In a letter to Ferenczi on March 26, 1924, Freud reassures Ferenczi and himself as well that

> . . . my personal feelings for you and Rank remain unchanged. I am annoyed by the weaknesses that appear in both of you, but that is no reason to forget the friendly services and collaboration of fifteen years. But I am also unable to reject the others who could bring similar claims. And a little bit more or less of wrong doing, when one is driven by emotions, give no ground for condemning people whom one likes otherwise. [Taft 1958, p. 93]

Lieberman (1985) felt that "Freud's wavering and his poor handling of conflict in the inner circle contributed as much to Rank's departure as any theoretical difference between the two men" (p. xxi).

Apparently, Rank had the same attitude that Ferenczi later displayed toward Freud and dissident views. Since they were both Freud's favorite sons, they thought they would never fall out of favor with the master, no matter how far they deviated from Freudian theory and technique.

There is a significant difference between Rank's and Ferenczi's oedipal fantasy toward Freud. Rank seemed to act out the traditional oedipal issue. He not only developed an alternative theoretical approach to Freud, but he aggressively pursued his deviations, as if to flaunt his differences, to shame or vanquish the father. Freud must have been devastated by this, since he had actually made it possible for Rank to become a psychoanalyst and a member of the elite of the pioneers through gaining membership in the committee and becoming editor of the psychoanalytic journal. Rank's unresolved aggression was acted out in the way he broke with Freud, apparently determined to cast away his mentor, as if he owed no allegiance to Freud or concern for Freud's feelings.

Esther Menaker is in a unique position to evaluate Rank's defection from Freud and has cast a new light on the subject. Having made the emotional and professional journey from Freudianism to self psychology (Menaker 1991) and having been a biographer of Rank (Menaker 1982), she has discussed Rank's departure from Freud as an expression of his own creative impulses (Menaker 1991).

[Rank's] theories, which emphasized the development of an expressive and autonomous self, led inevitably to a rift with Freud. When one considers that Freud once said to Jung, "Promise me that you will never abandon the libido theory," it is little wonder that Rank's departure from classical theory led to an acrimonious separation between the two men. [p. 76]

By 1932, Rank had clearly left the inner circle, and Freud was directly critical of his former psychoanalytic son. Toward the end of both of their lives, Freud (1937) dismissed Rank's work in a devastating statement.

[The attempt to shorten treatment] was bold and ingenious; but it did not stand the test of critical examination. Moreover, it was a child of its time, conceived under the stress of the contrast between the post-war misery of Europe and the "prosperity" of America, and designed to adapt the tempo of analytic therapy to the haste of American life. We have not heard much about what the implementation of Rank's plan has done for cases of sickness. Probably not more than if the fire-brigade, called to deal with a house that had been set on fire by an over-turned oil-lamp, contented themselves with removing the lamp from the room in which the blaze had started. . . . The theory and practice of Rank's experiment are now things of the past—no less than American "prosperity" itself. [pp. 216–217]

Freud's analogy between Rank's new therapy and America's need for therapies to match its watered-down culture is one of the most lethal criticisms he could have leveled against Rank's work. Freud's distaste for America was well known, and his linking of Rank to America was indeed his way of denigrating his former pupil and eliminating him from his physical and psychological system. However, Rank's separation from Freud was not emotionally finalized, since he displayed in his Parisian apartment a photograph of Freud (Taft 1958).

FERENCZI AND RANK'S SEPARATION

The split between Ferenczi and Rank has been dated as early as 1924 (Menaker 1982), which suggests that it occurred shortly after the publication of their joint venture *Development of Psychoanalysis*. It is curious that the split could have begun then, since both can be said to have given birth to the beginning of modern psychoanalysis (Haynal 1992). But Rank used this development to launch his separation from Freud and his followers.

There were other factors that separated Ferenczi from Rank. They developed their views on activity in very different directions after their authorship of *Development of Psychoanalysis*. Ferenczi, both in his active analytic phase and later in his relaxation therapy, explored the entire range of activity and clinical behavior in the psychoanalytic situation. According to Fay B. Karpfe (1953), Rank, on the other hand,

> limited himself to manipulation of the therapeutic situation, particularly in terms of time-setting and such auxiliary factors as the physical arrangement of the patient and therapist, which as he believed, had accidentally and arbitrarily become associated with psychoanalytic therapy. [p. 50, n3]

Ferenczi began to take issue with Rank's orientation in 1924. Specifically at issue was Rank's unusual historical point of view. On the one hand, Rank espoused a here-and-now approach in *Development of Psychoanalysis* (Ferenczi and Rank 1925), but, on the other hand, in *The Trauma of Birth* (Rank 1924), he focused on the earliest moments of the infant's psychological birth, exaggerating its importance in personality development and relevance to the psychoanalytic situation. Rank's idea was to resolve the fundamental separation anxiety from the birth trauma by reliving the well-titrated separations of the structured contact in a therapy session (Allen 1942, Taft 1962). This occurred by tolerating these regular separations as the therapist prepared the individual each session for separation. This technique placed the focus on the earliest mother–child bond (even earlier than Melanie Klein's speculations about early mother–infant interaction). Ironically, Ferenczi would go on to place similar emphasis on mother–child interaction, but he elaborated more on the nature and extent of the object relations between the original nurturing figure and the child. It was also necessary for Ferenczi to separate more fully from Freud to be able to join Rank in his more obvious and daring dissidence. Furthermore, it was not only Ferenczi's need to please and retain favor with Freud that fueled his criticisms of Rank, but a genuine difference of opinion of what constitutes the fundamental trauma.

Ferenczi was later to view seduction and emotional trauma in the object relations as fundamental.

By 1925 Ferenczi was discussing the differences with Rank regarding what he termed "the most important correction" in his active method. Ferenczi (1925a) was critical of Rank's time-limit technique, which he had first embraced.

> You know that this suggestion [setting a limit to the analysis] came from my friend Rank, and I took it over from him without reserve as a result of a few surprising successes and recommended its general application in a book written jointly with him [Development of Psychoanalysis]. Recent experience compels me very fundamentally to restrict this generalization. [p. 221]

Ferenczi outlined experience with a premature and fixed unilateral date for the termination of the analysis, suggesting it had an iatrogenic effect. He had accepted Rank's theory that a time limit encourages separation from the analyst when the therapeutic work is completed, but he found that this rule could not be applied as a general principle because some analysands had an adverse reaction to the unilateral setting of a time limit.

> . . . and so the fixed day for departure came without the patient being able to finish his treatment. There was nothing for me to do but to confess that my calculation was false, and it took me some time to dispel the bad impression of this incident under repeated hints of my ignorance. I learnt from the case not only that one must be extraordinarily cautious . . . but also that one may only take on a mandate for this as for other "activities" in agreement with the patient and with the possibility of retiring. [Ferenczi 1925a, p. 222]

Ferenczi's (1925a) criticisms of The Birth Trauma also extended to technique in an even more negative way.

> . . . Rank's views supported by his experience with giving notice have turned into a theoretical extension of the theory of the neurosis. He found in the trauma of birth the biological basis of the neurosis generally and thought that in the process of cure this trauma must, under favourable conditions, be made to repeat itself

and then be eliminated. . . . this theory . . . far exceeds what I wish to comprehend under the term "activity." As I have already explained elsewhere, the active technique . . . ought to bring about in the patient the psychical conditions under which repressed material comes forward more easily. I value the anxiety birth phantasies . . . so highly that I cannot simply regard them as a hiding-place for many painful birth and castration anxieties. *As far as I can see "activity" has in no way to accommodate itself to this particular theory.* [p. 223, italics added]

Ferenczi (1925a), at this time, firmly aligned himself with Freud, asserting that ". . .the interpretation . . . is the chief duty of analysis. So all the tendentious insinuations about a 'separatist movement' which my 'active measures' were expected to lead can be left to settle themselves. . . . 'activity' . . . implies absolutely nothing new" (p. 224).

Ferenczi (1925a) further aligned himself with Freud when he said in a startling statement that can only be understood as a neurotic need to please Freud

. . . the limits of the admissibility of the active technique allow the patient all possible modes of expression so long as the rôle of the physician does not exceed that of a friendly observer and adviser. The wish of the patient to receive signs of positive countertransference must remain unfulfilled; it is not the task of the analysis to bring happiness to the patient by tender and friendly treatment (he must be referred to the real world after the analysis to get these claims satisfied), but to repeat under favourable conditions the reactions of the patient to frustration, as it happened in childhood, and to correct the disturbance in development which can be reconstructed historically. [pp. 224–225]

Ferenczi, when he was more able to pursue his own theoretical and clinical inclinations, would reverse himself. He would later base his clinical functioning on becoming the tender mother and attempt to fulfill the real needs of the analysand in the psychoanalytic situation. But, in 1925, Ferenczi (1925a), although clearly critical of Rank, did not wish to hurt his friend and collaborator:

. . . for me and my analysis it is an advance that I take Rank's suggestion regarding the relation of patient to analyst as the cardinal point of the analytic material and regard *every* dream, *every* gesture, *every* parapraxis, *every* aggravation or improvement in the condition of the patient as above all an expression of transference and resistance. [p. 225]

FERENCZI'S FORMAL CRITICISM OF RANK

In 1927, Ferenczi reviewed the first volume of Rank's *Psychoanalytic Technique*. Ferenczi said that this publication " . . . marked the beginning of his [Rank's] new psychological views." Ferenczi also said Rank should have titled the work "The Rank Technique for the Treatment of Neurosis." He was not pleased with what Rank had written. ". . . it was with great interest that I . . . welcomed the appearance of a work from his pen upon the technique of psychoanalysis. Unfortunately, however, the feelings left by my study of this book have been almost entirely those of disappointment." (Ferenczi 1927b, p. 93). Furthermore, Ferenczi went on to be extremely critical of Rank's work. He compared Rank's technique with that of "wild analysts who neglect the historical backgrounds of the patient's personality and start off straight away upon a chase for infantile trauma" (p. 93). He was unremitting in his criticism and suggested that Rank's work did not belong in mainstream psychoanalysis.

> . . . the title of the book gives a false impression: what is discussed in it is not the technique of psychoanalysis but a modification of it which departs so widely from what has hitherto been practiced that it would have been more straightforward to have described the book as the Rank Technique (or perhaps as the "Birth Technique") for the treatment of the neurosis. The characteristic feature of the whole book is its tendency to exaggerate . . . interesting views and not infrequently to press the exaggeration ad absurdum. [p. 93]

Ferenczi clearly aligned himself with Freud and abandoned Rank as a collaborator and friend.

> . . . Freud, and all of us who follow him, leave it to the patient to repeat whatever it may have been that he was driven to . . . whereas Rank . . . actually compels his patients to repeat during the treat-

ment a kind of birth experience. But in fact the present volume completely fails to undermine the importance of historical analysis . . . a relapse into the pre-analytic way of thinking without any scientific basis . . . Rank simplifies his task too much by insisting that the only place where a symptom . . . can be acquired in the womb and that the only time at which it can be acquired is the moment of birth. . . . [pp. 93–95]

Ferenczi does not spare Rank any criticism, becoming sarcastic and comparing him to those who were no longer considered part of the analytic circle.

This task of interpretation may sometimes seem a hopeless one, but . . . Rank can achieve it, though only by being arbitrary to an unparalleled degree in his method of interpretation, which in its one-sidedness surpasses the efforts of Jung and Adler. Such one-sidedness is the logical consequence of Rank's . . . conviction that . . . birth shock has said the last word on the neurosis; he is thus relieved of the trouble and duty of examining each fresh case . . . with an unprejudiced . . . eye. . . . What he seeks and, of course, what he finds is only the confirmation of what he already knows. [p. 94]

Ferenczi continued his diatribe against Rank, comparing him to Stekel, who was asked to resign from the movement because of his fabricated case histories:

. . . Rank was fooled by his patient into taking her ironically exaggerated agreement seriously, and into actually using it as a support for his birth theory. Proceeding from this technical innovation, Rank then goes on to throw over his earlier views. . . . [Ferenczi castigates Rank's view as "an almost complete neglect of the associative material"] It is hard to say whether Stekel's loose interpretations of symbols is not preferable to such rigid dogmatism as this . . . equivalent to renouncing all the valuable knowledge Freud has given us in his theory of dreams. [Ferenczi 1927b, pp. 95–96]

Ferenczi did not spare Rank any criticism when he discussed the new elaboration of the birth-trauma theory.

The latest addition to the birth-trauma theory is perplexing in the highest degree. It looks upon weaning and learning to walk as completions of the shock of birth. Why, however, should we stop there and refuse to recognize the significance of the last . . . event of separation, that which follows the break-up of the Oedipus complex? Rank is on particularly dangerous ground when he bases his arguments upon therapeutic success. . . . After all it is possible to "cure" people by every kind of technique . . . but there is no kind of treatment which would give us a magical security against therapeutic failure . . . according to Rank's view at the deepest instinctual level the biological attachment to the mother regularly dominates the analytic situation whereas . . . Freud assigns to the analyst . . . the part of the father. This view of Rank's, which had . . . been put forward previously by other writers . . . becomes worthless when it is carried to such violent extremes. I became convinced that explanations based upon birth-anxiety are willingly accepted precisely on account of their lack of current significance and are in fact taken over by the patient as a means of protection against the much more terrible castration-anxiety. [pp. 97–98]

Ferenczi, in one of his more positive comments, which were sparse, separates his method from Rank's without rancor.

I myself was one of the first to argue that increased importance should be assigned to the factor of experience . . . it was possible and desirable to intensify the emotional character of analysis by setting the patient certain tasks alongside the requirement of free association (i.e., by what is known as "activity"). But all such experiencing during an analysis was . . . no more than a means for arriving rather more rapidly or more deeply at the roots of the symptoms, and this latter part of the work—the real guarantee against a relapse—was always thought of as something intellectual, the raising of an unconscious process to the preconscious level. [p. 94]

Ferenczi continued the process of separation from Rank by emphasizing his version of the curative process.

The essential agent is not intellectual insight into the historical origin . . . but emotional displacement (transference) of the instinctual impulses which are inhibited in the current conflict on to the infantile conflict, and its representation in the analytical situation. [p. 95]

Ferenczi had tried Rank's new technique, but abandoned it when he found that patients willingly accepted interpretations about birth trauma and mother transference and then used it as a defense against castration anxiety (Eisenstein 1966). For example, he discussed the use of a time limit, which Freud himself had introduced in his pioneering treatment of The Wolf Man (see Chapter 7, this volume). Ferenczi wrote, "As regards the question of imposing a time limit in every treatment, I was originally of his opinion, but increased experience has led me to put a drastic limit upon my agreement with him" (p. 97).

In this regard, Ferenczi did not agree with Rank's reinterpretation of "the dream of wolves" in Freud's "History of an Infantile Neurosis" (Freud 1909).

> I will only mention a few points which will throw into relief the recklessness and even frivolity of Rank's method of interpretation . . . the data, however, which Professor Freud has now put at my disposal completely demolish Rank's hypothesis. . . . Rank's interpretation is a pure invention. . . . Rank has evinced a degree of superficiality—indeed of recklessness—that can only be the result of a complete infatuation . . . and has shattered our confidence in the author's judgement to psycho-analytic theory and technique. [Ferenczi 1927b, pp. 99–100]

Ferenczi was very critical of Rank's concentration on early trauma. At this time he was trying to pay allegiance to the master and join the committee and the larger analytic community in cutting Rank off from mainstream psychoanalysis. Not only was this unfortunate, unkind, and unfriendly, it was also ironic. Ferenczi was himself by 1927 moving toward a trauma theory of neurosis (see Chapter 16, this volume). Whatever shortcomings Rank's theory may have had, it was an interesting and meaningful conceptualization of trauma at the beginning of human psychological existence. Ferenczi could have incorporated the notion of trauma in the early parent–child experience without doing damage to Freud's oedipal theory, since he later went on to conceptualize the actual components in the parental–child object relationship as traumatogenic of neurosis (Ferenczi 1932c). Ferenczi's devotion and attachment to Freud blinded him to integrating Rank's contribution.

FERENCZI AND RANK GO THEIR SEPARATE WAYS

Taft's (1958) view of the rift between Ferenczi and Rank was stated as follows.

> For Ferenczi, the actual helping of patients was always a major concern . . . what more natural than he should have followed Rank's lead with enthusiasm at first? It was only much later, after Freud's final rejection of *The Trauma of Birth*, that he saw the threat to his relation to Freud, and withdrew his name and contribution from their joint work. [p. 74]

Lieberman (1985) believed that "in late September, Ferenczi renounced Rank, under pressure from Freud and persuaded by Rank's intemperate stance" (p. 246).

By 1926, Ferenczi and Rank's association was apparently over. Both were interested in emigrating to America, where Rank saw a fertile ground for his dissident views. Rank went there hoping to establish himself so that he could soon leave Europe. Ferenczi also was beginning to have a following in America as his innovative work with difficult cases spread across the Atlantic, both through his publications and the reports of his analysands. He also needed the money the trip could provide.

Rank's reception in traditional analytic circles in the United States was less than enthusiastic (Taft 1958):

> Although Freud gave him [Rank] letters of introduction to . . . analysts in New York, his lecturing about his new view did not make for a favorable climate during his trip. *He was particularly pained by his encounter with Ferenczi in Pennsylvania Station, when, according to Rank, Ferenczi pretended not to see him.* [Taft 1958, p. xvi, italics added]

Furthermore, Taft (1958) quoted Rank as having said, "He was my best friend and he refused to speak to me" (p. xvi). Apparently, Ferenczi's neurotic need to please Freud clouded his judgment, encouraging him to turn his back on his friend and collaborator. Ironically, Ferenczi was to suffer the same fate, when, during their last meeting, Freud would refuse to shake his hand and walk away from him (see Chapter 13, this volume).

According to Lieberman (1985), at that time "Ferenczi's alienation from Rank was complete, as evidenced by both his harsh review of the *Technique* and, even more hurtfully, by what happened . . . in Pennsylvania Station" (p. 267). Taft (1958) also spoke of Rank's hurt as he told it to her, although she did not indicate when it was that he revealed it to her:

> At this time, I had no idea of Rank's growing difference from Ferenczi or of his alienation from the Vienna group. . . . I combined with my daily hour a weekly evening lecture given by Rank for the New York School of Social Work, another by Ferenczi for the New School of Social Research. . . . Never did I sense on Rank's part the bitterness or resentment that he might well have been feeling at a time, when Ferenczi . . . was refusing to speak to him. I did not try to account for the look of pain and constraint that characterized his appearance at the evening lecture. [pp. xi–xii]

Rank was apparently milder in his criticisms of Ferenczi. Most of his citations accentuate his points of departure from Freud. In 1932, there is a neutral footnote in *Art and Artist* (Rank 1932), mentioning Ferenczi and his contributions: "One stage of gesture-language in the development of the child is dealt with also by S. Ferenczi in his 'Entsicklungsstufen des Wirklischkeitssine' " (*Internationale Zeitschrifte für Psychoanalyse* I, 1913). One citation to Ferenczi in *Will Therapy* was:

> I soon realized that all the active measures which could not be entirely avoided even by Freud and whose specific use as prohibitions by Ferenczi naturally could only lead to an increase of the resistance, at bottom mean nothing except challenges of will, and that it would make no difference therefore, whether one forbade to the patient smoking or sex activity or certain foods. [Rank 1945, p. 14]

In the translator's introduction, Taft (1945) quotes Rank:

The analyst must keep before his eyes the task which is to allow the patient to experience and to understand something quite definite in the treatment. Thus the analytic treatment gets not only a quite precise, sharply defined form and content, but also a definite period of time. . . . the turning of my technical viewpoint into therapeutic power might perhaps be called "activity," if one does not understand the giving of prohibitions and commands to the patient (in Ferenczi's sense) which is a course I have never taken systematically. I mean only a courageous application of our knowledge especially that of the deepest psychical layers to which access by the patient is forever closed. [pp. xv–xvi]

In a footnote on page 82, Karpfe (1953) says that

> Rank had commented on Ferenczi's active procedures by stating that "all therapy, by nature, is 'active,' that is it purposes an effect through volitional influence and a change resulting from it." The passivity of psychoanalysis, according to him, is a virtue in the investigator, not in the therapist, who "must proceed 'actively' . . . if he aims at attaining any therapeutic effect worthy of the name." He then explained that the reason that psychoanalysis has failed to recognize this is that in the classical analytic situation "the person of the therapist stood in the center," so that the patient must adjust to the therapist rather than the other way around, when "the patient himself as the chief actor" is placed in the center of the therapeutic situation and his reactions are utilized constructively as opportunities for assistance in the strengthening of his personality. [source given as *The Trauma of Birth*, p. 203, and *Will Therapy*, pp. 9–10, 21] [p. 82n]

RANK'S LEGACY

There are many areas where Rank's legacy can be felt. Rank's emphasis on the role of the mother and the mother–infant interaction would definitely be welcome in contemporary psychoanalytic circles, especially those that have welcomed Ferenczi's relational emphasis (e.g., the interpersonal, object relations, and self psychology perspectives). The modern concepts of good and bad mother, primal love, return-to-the-womb fantasies, and fusion with the mother may owe their origins in part to Rank (Eisenstein 1966).

Rank's work helped introduce the active technique into clinical psychoanalysis, such as in the structure of an analytic session to deal with the issue of separation and the time limit of an analysis (Taft 1962). The application of Rank's ideas of separation and role of mother–infant and the relationship between early experience and later behavior have encouraged working on dependency in the analysis (Eisenstein 1966).

One of the most unique aspects of Rank's ideas that is beginning to be appreciated is the concept of self and will.

> Except in the work of Rank, the uniqueness of the self has been insufficiently appreciated in psychoanalytic theory and practice. . . . And according to him it is the will which implements the individual's creative growth. Currently it is in the work of Kohut (1977), with its emphasis on introspective-empathic stance which enables the psychological observer to regard the individual self as a center of initiative, that we find opposition to the deterministic viewpoint of classical psychoanalysis which cannot account for the phenomena of choice, decision, and free-will. [Menaker 1983, p. 464]

Rank's thinking is more in the realm of an existential/humanistic orientation and is concerned with the processes by which individuals separate and individuate by mastering anxiety, depression, and mortality (Menaker 1982).

RANK AND FERENCZI: POSTMORTEM REUNIFICATION

Jones (1957) reunited Rank and Ferenczi through shared vilification: "Rank in a dramatic fashion . . . and Ferenczi more gradually . . . developed psychotic manifestations that revealed themselves in, among other ways, a turning away from Freud and his doctrines" (p. 471).

Jones vilified Rank because he dared to break away from Freud. Furthermore, he took it upon himself to declare Rank and Ferenczi psychotic because dissidence from Freud is only comprehensible as a deviation in personal functioning. The supposition is clearly made that if one were emotionally stable, one could see in Freud and his ideas everything that is necessary in order to function successfully as a clinician and theorist. Jones's character assassination of Rank and Ferenczi and the analytic community's silence regarding this mean-spirited behavior did much to remove their work from mainstream psychoanalysis. Contemporary psychoanalysis, which is freeing itself from the politics and divisions of the past, is discovering the merits of Rank and Ferenczi not simply as dissidents, but as important figures in the history of psychoanalysis who can contribute significant ideas and methods for contemporary psychoanalysis.

11

THE DEVELOPMENT OF PSYCHOANALYSIS

THE EVOLUTION OF PSYCHOANALYTIC TECHNIQUE

Entwicklungsziele der Psychoanalyse (*The Development of Psychoanalysis*) (Ferenczi and Rank 1925) appeared in December 1923, attracting a great deal of attention. The monograph was written in the summer of 1922 and then was modified somewhat by the events of the International Psychoanalytical Congress, held in Berlin (Newton 1925). The book revisions were completed in 1923.

The critical part of the book was written by Ferenczi and the chapter "The Analytical Situation" by Rank. They then jointly then jointly revised the work (Newton 1925). The English version was published in 1925.

The Development of Psychoanalysis was written to fill the void of "technical recommendations" that Freud had abandoned since his Budapest Congress paper in 1918 (Freud 1919 [1918]) (see Chapter 7, this volume). Although there had been rapid growth in development of theory, there was, according to Ferenczi and Rank (1925), a serious neglect of " . . . the technical and therapeutic factor, which was originally the heart of the matter and the actual stimulus to every important advance in the theory. . . " (p. 2). Furthermore, Ferenczi and Rank noted that there was an even more serious issue regarding technical advances in psychoanalysis: "[Freud] has always been, as is well known, extremely reserved . . . on the issue of technical developments . . . to such an extent, indeed, that it is almost ten years since he has published any work on the subject . . ." (p. 2).

Freud would later admit to Ferenczi that

. . . the "Recommendations on Technique" I wrote long ago were essentially of a negative nature. I considered the most important thing was to emphasize what one should *not* do, and to point out the temptation in directions contrary to analysis. Almost everything positive that one *should* do I have left to "tact" . . . . The result was that the docile analysts did not perceive the elasticity of the rules I had laid down, and submitted to them as if they were taboos. Sometime all that must be revised, without, it is true, doing away with the obligation I had mentioned. [Jones 1955, p. 241]

Subsequently, Ferenczi and Rank felt that a false impression had been created, that no technical developments had occurred during the last ten-year period.

In the critical and historical sections, Ferenczi and Rank specified the errors that might result from Freud's analytic technique and indicated how to avoid them. *The Development of Psychoanalysis* also provides a comprehensive survey of the abundant but previously unsummarized material acquired in the preceding years of psychoanalytic investigation.

The Development of Psychoanalysis was reviewed in great detail by Franz Alexander in 1925. He pointed out that the book – a synthesis and survey of the fundamental problems of psychoanalytic therapy from systemic, critical, and historical viewpoints – filled a great general need: "The rich store of the experience acquired during an investigation carried on for thirty years needs to be worked through into general theoretical principles in order to open up new paths for further research" (p. 485).

The problem of the evolution of psychoanalytic technique had a fundamental difficulty connected to the hero worship of Freud. Analysts had become too dependent upon Freud's technical articles. The articles had become " . . . for analysts who had not themselves undergone an analysis, the only correct indication for their technical activity" (Ferenczi and Rank 1925, p. 2). Freud, to his credit, never felt his recommendations were the last word or "the only correct indication for . . . technical activity" (p. 2). Freud felt they were incomplete, but Ferenczi and Rank felt these technical recommendations were "antiquated and seem to need modification" (p. 2). This dependence upon Freud for the last word on technique had not only caused a stagnation in technical advance, but explained the reluctance of the analysts to integrate Ferenczi's advances in active intervention (see Chapters 8 and 9, this volume).

One can therefore understand why the majority of those analysts who were dependent upon the study of the literature adhered too rigidly to these technical rules, and could not find the connection to the stages of progress which the science of analysis had made in the meantime. [p. 2]

It may have been true that Freud and other analysts of this period were not developing or reporting technical advances, but Ferenczi was clearly in the forefront of active intervention.

One explanation for Ferenczi's active analytic method not taking hold was that analysts were frozen in their experience and dependent on Freud for technical advice, though Freud had clearly endorsed Ferenczi's experiments. The dependency was due not only to the enormous shadow that Freud cast, but also to most analysts not having undergone a therapeutic analysis. Thus, not having experienced the emotional reliving of their personal issues, they consequently were either not mature enough or insufficiently trained to understand and relate to the technical developments of active analysis.

Ferenczi, in his clinical experimentation with the Freudian method, had demonstrated that active intervention could lead to a reassessment of the analyst's role and function, as well as the nature of the analytic process in therapy.

Gedo (1986b) wrote on the significance of *The Development of Psychoanalysis*, assessing the contributions of the Ferenczi and Rank monograph as a classic in psychoanalysis.

Ferenczi's major contribution in this monograph on technique was his novel stress on the crucial importance of affective experience in the here and now of the analytic transference. . . . [previous theory] laid exclusive emphasis on the effects of genetic interpretations. . . . Ferenczi demonstrated his understanding of the revolutionary significance of the new model of the mind Freud had proposed (1923b). He also understood that the next task consisted in the translation of this general theory into specific improvements in technique. He gave a beautiful exposition of the reciprocal influence of analytic theory and practice—the improvement of technique that follows advances in theory and simultaneously retests them. He was the first to enunciate that if confusion resulting from its manifold details is to be avoided, analysis must be understood as a *process*. . . . [and that] "symptom-analysis" and "complex analysis" had become outdated.

An adequate analytic process must promote affective reliving and the working through of the infantile neurosis by means of repetition as a transference neurosis. This aim, Ferenczi explained, can be attained only by overcoming the resistance of the ego, certainly never by the naïve attempts to fill gaps in the patient's knowledge that characterized psychoanalysis before 1920. Hence resistances . . . must not be treated as undesirable or worse, sinful. [p. 44]

Furthermore, Gedo (in press) in his reassessment of the significance of the Ferenczi/Rank classic, has noted the issue of authoritarianism in psychoanalysis addressed in 1925 and the continued relevance of this idea in contemporary psychoanalysis.

[Ferenczi's] critique of analytic authoritarianism was well founded. Some traces of these undesirable attitudes continued to linger in our procedures until quite recently. . . . even today one may read current accounts of recent analytic encounters terminated on the *analyst's* initiative, as recommended in . . . the 1924 monograph. . . . The authors [criticized] the propensity of analysts to try to force acceptance of certain interpretations. . . . Alert to the significance of Freud's then recent revisions of basic theory, Ferenczi came back several times to the danger of persevering on theories that had already become superannuated. [pp. 6–7]

A CRITIQUE OF THE PSYCHOANALYTIC METHOD

Ferenczi and Rank surveyed the established psychoanalytic method as it had developed over the period of analytic practice in the generation between Freud's initial therapeutic efforts and the creation of "The Ego and the Id" (Gedo in press). The list of critical comments encompasses many aspects of the traditional Freudian method, especially a focus on the cognitive/intellectual interpretive behavior calculated to produce insight.

Collecting Associations

The tendency to compulsively collect associations had become an end in itself, as if associations themselves were the key to unlocking the process.

> . . . the collecting of associations . . . in themselves [became] the essential thing, and not . . . showing us where or perhaps what depth under the surface, the active affects were concealed, and particularly what motives drove the patient in a given case to use the ways of association which he seemed to prefer. [Ferenczi and Rank 1925, p. 29]

Ferenczi's preoccupation with stimulating affect is revealed, as well as Ferenczi and Rank's focus on the underlying experience.

Fanaticism of Interpreting

By 1924, interpretation had become the golden behavior of psychoanalysts. Ferenczi and Rank (1925) pointed out that the preoccupation with interpretation led to a dogmatic, ritualistic form of analytic behavior.

> . . . the fanaticism of interpreting, which resulted in overlooking, in a cut and dried translation according to the dictionary, the fact that the technique of interpretation is but one of the means of help in understanding the unconscious mental condition of the patient, and not the aim, or certainly not the chief aim, of the analysis. . . . [p. 29]

By questioning the overutilized reliance on interpretation, Ferenczi and Rank opened up for examination the primary mode of analyst intervention in the Freudian system and created the atmosphere for considering non-interpretative behavior as a significant alternative to interpretation.

Analysis of Symptoms

It was another shortcoming of psychoanalytic method in the post-pioneering era to focus on the analysis of symptoms, rather than, as Ferenczi and Rank (1925) suggested, to develop a holistic focus.

> Another faulty method was holding fast to the already overcome phase of the analysis of the symptoms. . . . It is, indeed, not even a matter of getting the symptoms to disappear . . . but rather preventing their return, which means making the ego of the patient more capable of resistance. For this purpose an analysis of the whole personality is necessary. [p. 30]

Direct Questions

The use of questions as the primary means to encourage interaction was wisely considered as a deterrent to free association. In fact, the reliance on series of direct questions was to take on the emotional aura of a detached investigator, much like a courtroom lawyer or prosecutor: "Direct questions merely succeeded in turning the attention of the patient towards . . . the many 'interpretations' which one symptom can have in a particular case . . . establishing his resistances at this point . . ." (Ferenczi and Rank 1925, p. 31).

The concern for the cool and detached ambience that the direct questioning of the analysand created was part of the questioning of the ambience of a traditional psychoanalysis that both authors pioneered. Ferenczi would go on to create a very significant alternative to direct questions and the analyst as investigator when he introduced the empathic method as part of his relaxation therapy (Ferenczi 1928b, 1930b, 1931, 1932c, 1933).

Nonverbal Communication

Ferenczi and Rank point to the importance of nonverbal communication in the psychoanalytic situation, which Ferenczi had pioneered in his earliest clinical work with the active method (see Chapters 7, 8, and 9, this volume): "In an analysis fine details, apparent incidentals such as voice, gesture, expression, are so important" (1925, p. 29).

The Analysis of Complexes

Ferenczi and Rank had very strong feelings that the analysis of complexes was seriously retarding the evolution of psychoanalytic technique. The concentration on complexes actually prevented the uncovering of unconscious material. This they believed held true for the analysis of the castration complex.

> . . . [do] away entirely with the now useless rudiment of an earlier time, and to have given up the terminology . . . the analysis [was] carried out with the object of "analyzing out" one complex after the other, or the attempt was made of treating the whole personality as

a sum total . . . of complexes. . . . The analysis of complexes easily misleads the patient into being pleasing to his analyst, by bringing him "complex material" as long as he likes, without giving up any of his really unconscious secrets. . . . [pp. 31–32]

Dogmatic Sexual Interpretations

Analysts of the era had seized upon Freud's theory of sexual development and repeatedly applied the interpretations in a ritualistic and rigid way. Such interpretations actually overlooked important underlying material. It was not necessary to uncover every single detail of a neurosis to have a successful analysis. Ferenczi and Rank (1925) wrote, "In this searching for the constructive elements of the theory . . . the actual analytic task was neglected. . . . still less should the uncovering of all theoretically established details and gradations be used as a principle of healing in the neuroses" (p. 34).

A Contribution to the Psychoanalytic Method

The second level of critique that Ferenczi and Rank discussed was a reevaluation and reformulation of the purpose of psychoanalysis. Theoretical knowledge, especially the contributions of Freud, had advanced far beyond the contributions of method. Clinicians were attempting to perform an analysis primarily on theoretical grounds, which led to the abuses that have been outlined in the previous section.

Ferenczi and Rank wished to accomplish several important things with their discussion. Psychoanalysis needed to consider returning to its origins and viewing itself as a method of therapy. It needed to realize that new advances had to come from a reconsideration of method and technique instead of rigid adherence to Freud's theoretical advances and a blind attempt to apply the theory to technique. Freud's two devoted disciples were attempting to contribute their clinical expertise and innovative thinking to the evolution of psychoanalysis.

Several traditional technical issues were reconsidered and formed the basis for a new direction for psychoanalysis. Although the authors did not outline a step-by-step technical program (Gedo in press), this monograph can be viewed as a turning point, especially for Ferenczi. If we take his 1920 paper, "The Further Advance," we have him applying activity in a more emphatic manner, leaving behind prohibitions and the aggressive style of the earlier applications of the rule of abstinence. The more relaxed and tender he became in his clinical approach, the greater the analysand's positive response to his interventions. The "Female Croatian Musician" case demonstrated non-interpretive intervention in an emotionally heightened atmosphere, where the active role of the analyst is reflected through an empathic stance (Ferenczi 1920).

The *Development of Psychoanalysis* was the theoretical result of the further experimentation with the Freudian method that Ferenczi had executed in the "Female Croatian Musician" case. It became clear for Ferenczi that the interpretive period of the analysis must be preceded by a period of empathy, relationship, and activity.

Ferenczi and Rank did not wish to create the same impression that Freud had made in his recommendations for technical behavior by emphasizing what one should not do. Rather, they wished to outline positive recommendations for therapeutic activity so that analysts would not continue to function under the repressive atmosphere of taboos.

It was a valiant and necessary attempt to provide an alternate voice to the judgmental injunction that was used to discourage deviation from tradition—the famous phrase, "This is not analysis." Phrases that had been attributed to Freud, like this one, had become the rallying cry for unduly conservative analysts who were threatened by change. Ferenczi and Rank, two clinical innovators, were attempting to express their creative spirit in that conservative atmosphere. Freud realized he had a conservative side and encouraged his two star pupils to express his own revolutionary spirit.

The technical advances that Ferenczi and Rank outlined were rooted in early Freudian theory and technique. In fact, Ferenczi's future developments in theory and technique would bring him back to the earliest period in Freud's work, a trend that Freud could not understand and thought was a regressive step. It never dawned on Freud that Ferenczi realized that his teacher's original work was still valid, at least to the extent that they both were treating a similar population with similar issues. In essence, Ferenczi had verified that Freud had gotten it right the first time (Masson 1984). In the present attempt, six areas were discussed that could lead to a modification in analytic technique: subjective factors in the analyst; remembering, repeating, and working through; full expression of the negative reaction to the analyst; negative transferences (resistances); energetic activity; and affective experience.

1. Subjective Factors in the Analyst

This monograph highlighted a rarely mentioned issue in the analytic process, namely the relationship between analyst and analysand and the personal equation of the analyst in this relationship. Ferenczi, of course, had been moving in this direction for years, since his modifications in analytic technique encouraged a more direct and active role for the analyst. With this move away from neutrality, detachment, observation, and interpretation, the possibilities of analyst countertransference and personal reaction grew. Both Ferenczi and Rank (1925) were experimenting with a change in the role and attitude in the psychoanalytic situation. They pointed out some of the personal and subjective issues.

> . . . an important rule of psycho-analytic technique must be mentioned in regard to the personal relation between the analyst and the patient. The theoretic requirement of avoiding all personal contact outside of the analysis mostly led to an unnatural elimination of all human factors in the analysis, and thus again to a theorizing of the analytic experience. . . . Some practitioners all too readily failed to attribute that importance to a change in the person of the analyst. . . . A change of analysts may be unavoidable for other reasons in rare, exceptional cases. . . . [pp. 40–41]

2. Remembering, Repeating, and Working Through

Ferenczi and Rank made clear that *The Development of Psychoanalysis* was directly connected to Freud's technical paper "Remembering, Repeating and Working Through" (Freud 1914b). In Freud's paper, *remembering* was elevated to the actual aim of psychoanalytical work. But the *desire to repeat* was regarded as a symptom of resistance. Suppression of the tendency to repeat in the analytic situation was recommended, particularly in the privation of sexual and relationship issues.

Ferenczi and Rank introduced a modification in technique based upon their extension of Freud's "Remembering and Repeating" and then connected their modifications of emphasizing remembering to repetition. They based the repetition issue on another of Freud's papers, "Beyond the Pleasure Principle" (Freud 1920), suggesting that repetition is necessary and useful: " . . . certain resistances . . . oppose themselves to the repetition compulsion, particularly the feeling of anxiety and of guilt which we can only overcome by active intervention, that is by requiring the repetition (Ferenczi and Rank 1925, p. 4).

From this modification of repetition instead of remembering, they emphasize two basic issues.

> From the technical point of view we undoubtedly emphasize greater "activity," by which we mean absolutely requiring the tendency to reproduce. . . . From the theoretic side, we lay stress on the adequate recognition in the neurosis also of the overwhelming importance of the repetition compulsion. . . . It is really the insight gained from understanding the repetition compulsion which first makes the results of "active therapy" comprehensible and gives the theoretic reason for its necessity. [pp. 4–5]

Ferenczi and Rank's development of elevating repeating to a significant place in psychoanalytic technique ushered in the focus on the experiential dimension in the analytic process and the reenactments of the trauma derivatives in the psychoanalytic situation. Rank was later to highlight the dimension of time limits and birth trauma in his version of improving psychoanalytic technique (Rank 1924, Taft 1962). Ferenczi's focus remained truer to the outlines of change first suggested in *The Development of Psychoanalysis*. He went on to develop the heightened emotional experience and the reliving of trauma in the psychoanalytic situation.

Issues in repeating also ring loud in contemporary psychotherapy in the area that Ferenczi pioneered – the analysis of the incest trauma (Rachman 1993a). The recovery from the incest trauma is conceptualized as a clinical process of recall, retrieval, and reliving in the psychoanalytic situation. Among the technical issues is the reliability of childhood memories of seduction, which are especially contaminated if influenced by an overly intrusive or suggestive technical inquiry (Loftus and Ketcham 1991, Tavris 1993).

3. Full Expression of Negative Transference to the Analyst

The narcissism of the analyst was also discussed as a source of countertransference reactions, as well as limiting the encouragement of full expression of negative transferences.

. . . The narcissism of the analyst seems suited to create a particularly fruitful source of mistakes, among others the development of a kind of narcissistic countertransference which provokes the person being analyzed into pushing into the foreground certain things which flatter the analyst and, on the other hand, into suppressing remarks and associations of an unpleasant nature in relation to him. [Ferenczi and Rank 1925, p. 41]

Ferenczi was to develop his idea of encouraging the full expression of the negative transference, which will be practiced to its fullest as reported in his *Clinical Diary* (Ferenczi 1932c), the beginnings of which appear in this monograph.

The analyst [has] the necessity of noticing the delicate indications of criticisms, which mostly only venture forth hesitantly, and helping the patient to express them plainly or to abreact them. The anxiety and the sense of guilt of the patient can never be overcome without this self-criticism, requiring indeed a certain overcoming of himself on the part of the analyst; and yet these two emotional factors are the most essential for bringing about and maintaining the repression. [Ferenczi and Rank 1925, p. 42]

4. Negative Transferences (Resistances)

Were Freud to utter an injunction regarding a technical intervention, it was clear it became not only the folklore of analytic therapy, but a rule of behavior.

At times, one heard . . . that this or that analysis failed on account of "too great resistances" or a too "violent transference." . . . Because Freud once uttered the sentence "Everything which impedes the analytic work is resistance," one should not, every time the analysis comes to a standstill, simply say, "This is a resistance." This resulted . . . in creating an analytic atmosphere in which they, so to speak, were fearful of making the "faux pas" of having a resistance, and the analyst found himself in a helpless situation. [p. 40]

Ferenczi, in particular, was so keen an observer of the clinical process and had several personal qualities (empathy, emotional fortitude or resilience, tolerance for intense affect, self-scrutiny, and lack of defensiveness) that it allowed him to understand the therapeutic meaning of negative transference.

> The negative transference . . . cannot express itself otherwise than as "resistance" and the analysis of which is the most important task of the therapeutic activity. One need, of course, not be afraid of the negative reactions of the patient for they constitute, with iron necessity, a part of every analysis. [p. 40]

Being able to tolerate the emotional outburst and barrage of borderline patients when they criticize, condemn, or insult the therapist's capacities, would become one of the hallmarks of Ferenczi's therapeutic interaction. By being able to tolerate such negative transferences and, further, respond empathically rather than defensively (interpretations of transference or resistance that "blame the patient"), Ferenczi was able to understand that the negative transferences were the necessary "reliving in the transference" of the childhood trauma, to use his terminology, or, in the Freudian system, the natural manifestations of the resistances and the neurotic adaptation that is compromised by therapeutic intervention.

Ferenczi and Rank also talked about strong positive transference as resistance and a need to unmask the unconscious desires behind their manifestation (p. 40). Ferenczi would later deviate from this position and view the positive transference as a vehicle for the empathic bond, the so-called tender-mother transference so important in his clinical work with trauma. As Ferenczi would discover in his work with R. N. (Elizabeth Severn – see Chapter 19, this volume), the occurrence of an intense positive transference may also be seen as a sign that the patient is displaying signs of childhood sexual trauma.

5. Energetic Activity

Ferenczi's pioneering introduction of activity into psychoanalytic method was met with criticism by some (Glover 1924) and overzealous acceptance by others. By 1925 he had reevaluated his original enthusiasm, as well as his overcritical attitude, toward his innovations. Now he placed activity in perspective, as a dimension of the affective subjective analytic method (Ferenczi and Rank 1925):

> . . . "activity" resulted in some analysts . . . overwhelming the patient with commands and prohibitions, which one might characterize as a kind of "wild activity." This, however, must be looked

upon as a reaction to the other extreme, to holding too fast to an over-rigid "passivity" in the matter of technique. . . . This easily leads to sparing the patient the pain of necessary intervention, and to allowing him too much initiative in his associations as well as in the interpretation of his ideas.

The moderate, but, when necessary, energetic activity in the analysis consists in the analyst taking on, and, to a certain extent, really carrying out those rôles which the unconscious of the patient and his tendency to flight prescribe. By doing this the tendency to the repetition of earlier traumatic experiences is given an impetus, naturally with the goal of finally overcoming this tendency by revealing its content. [p. 44]

6. Affective Experience

The nature of reconstruction in analytic therapy was reconsidered because an emphasis was being placed on the intellectual/cognitive side. To have meaning and depth and contribute to genuine change, the unfolding and reconstructive process needed to be embedded in affective experiences. Ferenczi and Rank felt that Freud's method had intended to emphasize affects: " . . . Freud has never departed in his technique from the fundamental conception that the affective factor of experience is the essential factor of the cure" (p. 59).

RECOMMENDATIONS FOR THE FUTURE OF PSYCHOANALYSIS

This monograph also grappled with some far-reaching issues that psychoanalysts would debate into the modern era. Ferenczi and Rank lent their cogent, creative, and nondogmatic thinking to the issues of a therapeutic, or didactic, analysis, the question of lay analysis, and the education of the layman in psychoanalysis.

Therapeutic Analysis

Ferenczi and Rank made a strong and clearly correct argument for a therapeutic analysis as a necessary part of all analysts' training. In particular, they were concerned that the training of analysts was emphasizing a didactic analysis, a therapeutic experience focused on learning the method of analysis from a complete understanding of theory. They wished analysts to have an emotionally focused experience, as was being given to patients. In this way, analysts were prepared to know themselves sufficiently to work with trauma. Furthermore, given the elaborations of his trauma theory in later years, Ferenczi was also suggesting that the analysts must work through their own traumatic childhoods through reexperiencing and emotionally working through to what he later termed *rock-bottom* (Ferenczi 1933) (see also Chapter 16, this volume). In this way, analysts would be as well analyzed as the analysands, and only clinicians who had been through an emotional struggle to confront and work through their demons could take part in the psychoanalytic dialogue of unconsciousnesses (Ferenczi 1932c). Ferenczi and Rank (1925) wrote:

> It was a fatal mistake to believe that no one was completely analyzed who had not also been theoretically familiarized with all the separate details of his own abnormality. . . . The fact that the desire to learn and to teach creates an unfavorable mental attitude for the analysis is well known but should receive much more serious attention . . . our therapeutic analyses have not up to now often been too "didactic," whereas the so-called didactic analyses taught less analysis than the theory, which should only have been acquired separately later on. We could formulate our standpoint in these questions. . . . : *too much knowledge on the part of the patient should be replaced by more knowledge on the part of the analyst.* [pp. 39, 60–61]

Ferenczi and Rank could not make a stronger recommendation for a therapeutic analysis than the following statement: "But just as in the therapeutic analysis the mere imparting of academic knowledge belongs, as it were, to the pediatrics of this subject, . . . the correct didactic analysis is one that does not in the least differ from the curative treatment" (p. 60).

The German school (Abraham, Eitingon, Simmel) were adamant that a control analysis be an integral part of the Berlin Institute (Grosskurth 1986). So the differences in the committee, especially between Ferenczi and others, were heightened by this monograph.

Laymen as Analysts

Some of the nuggets of wisdom in *The Development of Psychoanalysis* are still not matched in contemporary thinking. Witness this cogent idea about the nature of lay analysis.

> In the future, not only will psycho-analytic knowledge be the common property of all physicians, . . . but there will, of course, be specially trained therapists who . . . need not necessarily be doctors since education as well as care of mental life, are really psychotherapeutic or prophylactic tasks. This settles the somewhat elaborate questioning of certain specialists as to whether "laymen," that is, nonmedical people, shall analyze at all. As the situation stands to-day, physicians limited by their one-sided training in the natural sciences are actually laymen in psychological matters. [Ferenczi and Rank 1925, p. 66]

Education of the Layman to Prevent Neurosis

As psychoanalysis became better known beyond the confines of its adherents, it would be influenced by interaction with the lay public. Psychoanalysis would need to change its technique. It would also shift its focus to include not only treating neurosis but also preventing it: " . . . to change our technique and must force us to adjust it to the increasing enlightenment of society as to the cause and nature of the neurosis" (pp. 62–63).

The optimism of those pioneering times, when psychoanalysis would cure the world, has not been realized. "According to Freud the spread of psychoanalytic knowledge will, in time, automatically bring about the disappearance of those forms of neurosis that we have known up to now" (p. 63).

FREUD'S REACTION TO *THE DEVELOPMENT OF PSYCHOANALYSIS*

Apparently, Ferenczi and Rank broke the agreement between the members of the Society of Rings and did not consult with any one of them before publishing the monograph (Marthe 1966). This was a serious breach of protocol, since the idea behind the committee was twofold: to form a support group around Freud and to be able to review any manuscript before publication so that controversies could be averted and a unified front regarding Freud's psychoanalysis could be presented. It is clear, then, that there was some statement of emancipation from the committee in publishing the book, but not as clearly a move away from Freud. Rank did use *The Development of Psychoanalysis* as his emancipation proclamation, but Ferenczi did not. Rank dated his deviation from Freud to the publication of this book (Taft 1958).

> This [book] was my first parting, not from Freud, but from his whole ideology, which is erected on the fundamental importance of intellectual understanding as a curative factor. [Taft 1958, p. 150, from Rank's remarks to the First International Congress on Mental Hygiene, Washington, D.C., May 8, 1930]

Freud saw the manuscript in 1922. When he was consulted about the book's publication, he had no objections. However, the committee did have unfavorable thoughts about the ideas that Ferenczi and Rank were outlining. In fact, there was great concern that the seeds had been planted for a new dissident movement. Jones and the Berlin analysts reminded Freud that, exactly ten years earlier, Jung had rebelled and left the movement as a result of following the same course (Marthe 1966). Freud apparently disagreed with this in a letter to Ferenczi:

> . . . I know that I am not very accessible and find it hard to assimilate alien thoughts that do not quite lie in my path. It takes quite a time before I can form a judgment about them, so that in the interval I have to suspend judgment. . . . that you or Rank should in your independent flights ever leave the ground of psycho-analysis seems to me out of the question. Why shouldn't you therefore have the right to try if things won't work in another way from that I had thought? If you go astray in so doing you will find that out yourself some time or other. Or, I will take the liberty of pointing it out to you as soon as I am myself sure about it. [Jones 1957, pp. 57–58]

Freud's reserved criticisms were mildly expressed because of his affection for his two close disciples. The other members of the committee, who were more conservative in their approach, were more openly critical and, ironically, correct in their perception that there were seeds of dissidence in the manuscript. Rank was clearly in opposition to Freud's interpretive view and saw himself as developing an alternative framework. Ferenczi was the perfect collaborator, since he was on a voyage away from Freud himself, although neither Ferenczi nor Freud wished to acknowledge this. They both tried, in vain, to believe in the fantasy that Ferenczi would come back into the fold. Furthermore, Freud tried to believe that Ferenczi's deviations were only momentary and that he would see the error of his ways.

The orthodox within the committee were not as gentle in their concerns as was Freud and began to voice serious doubts about Ferenczi's and Rank's faithfulness to the cause. In particular, they were uneasy about certain important shifts in theory and technique: the emphasis on the mother's role in the development of psychopathology, the de-emphasis on the use of interpretation; the focus on a more active and shortened analysis, and the issue of the centrality of trauma in the origin of neurosis. Realizing that the dissention in the committee needed to be addressed, Freud sent a *Rundbriefe* to all members (Marthe 1966).

> Liebe Freunde, I have heard . . . that the recent publications of our Ferenczi and Rank . . . have evoked considerable disagreeable and agitated discussion. . . . please do not think I am obtruding. I should myself prefer to keep as much as possible in the background and let each of you follow his own way.
>
> When Sachs was here recently I exchanged some comments on the Birth Trauma with him; hence perhaps the impression that I discern an antagonistic tendency in the publication of that work or that I absolutely disagree with its contents. I should have thought, however, that the very circumstance of my accepting the dedication should invalidate this idea.
>
> The fact of the matter is this: neither the harmony among us nor the respect you have so often shown me should hinder any of you in the free employment of his productivity. . . . Complete agreement in all scientific details and on all fresh themes is quite impossible among half a dozen men with different temperaments. . . . The sole condition for our working together fruitfully is that none of us abandons the common ground of psychoanalytical premises. . . . I do not find it easy to feel my way into alien modes of thought, and I have as a rule to wait until I have found some

connection with any meandering ways. So if you wanted to wait with every new idea until I can endorse it you would run the risk of getting pretty old. [pp. 46–47, from Circular Letter of February 15, 1924, pp. 59–60. *Rundbriefe*. Rare Book and Manuscript Library, Columbia University]

CONTEMPORARY ISSUES RAISED BY THE DEVELOPMENT OF PSYCHOANALYSIS

The issues that were raised in *The Development of Psychoanalysis* have reverberated throughout the history of psychoanalysis and began a debate on such issues as the emphasis on emotional experiencing in the psychoanalytic situation, focus on the here and now in the interaction, the notion of transference interpretations, the ambience of the psychoanalytic situation, use of interpretation to develop insight, therapeutic value of non-interpretative behavior, and what is curative in the psychoanalytic experience.

A cognitive, or didactic, analysis had become the vogue as Ferenczi and Rank were writing their monograph. The growing popularity of psychoanalysis beyond the initial circle of pioneering analysts and analysands encouraged young physicians and intellectuals to become analyzed. Ferenczi and Rank realized that such analyses were sterile intellectual investigation. Instead they advised the introduction of heightened emotional intensity in a session, which was, in a sense, a link with psychoanalysis's past, in the Breuer-Freud cathartic method period.

The emphasis on the here and now in contemporary analysis as well as the early interpretation of transference (Gill 1979a,b, Stone 1981a) have their origins in Ferenczi and Rank's early work.

Gill (1979a,b) recommends searching out the day residues in the transference reaction, noting the reality of the analysand's response. The assumption in this approach, which was first stressed in Ferenczi and Rank's monograph, is echoed in Gill's thinking—that the psychoanalytic situation is a two-person psychology. The analytic drama is played out between two adults in the here and now.

In the classical tradition, Stone introduced a more flexible view of transference. Rather than interpret transference only when it became a manifest resistance, he recognized it as a propulsive force (Stone 1981a). In this regard, he said

> . . . There has developed over the years with increasing momentum . . . the affirmative active address to the transference, i.e., to the analysis—or sometimes the active interpretive by-passing—of the "resistance to the awareness of transference." While this has occasionally become a travesty . . . the tendency—in rational form and proportions—must be regarded as an important component of progressively evolving psychoanalytic method. [p. 724]

Stone's own view assumes the transferences in the analytic situation " . . . to be, at least latently, directed ultimately toward the analyst (as against other important persons in the environment)" (p. 725).

The interpretation of transference only as resistance is no longer the exclusive precept in classical analysis. Stone believes that active interpretation is advisable in early transference emergencies, as in regressive transference manifestation of borderline patients and erotic or hostile transference reactions in neurotic patients. However, barring these kinds of special circumstances, Stone (1981a), speaking in the classical tradition, applies an old principle of Freud's for all interpretive interventions: " . . . unconscious elements be interpreted only when the patient evidences a secure positive attachment to the analyst" (p. 726).

The issue of interpretation versus dramatization was also raised by *The Development of Psychoanalysis*. Ferenczi would go on to emphasize the dramatization of a psychoanalytic session (Ferenczi 1928b, 1930b). Ferenczi and Rank argued for an exploitation of the transference resistance, especially in the sense of intense emotional expression and discharge. Their emphasis was on the issue of the affective experience as the essential dimension of the analytic process—the living through or the heightened experience of the transferences. All therapeutic approaches that emphasize the affective experience owe their debt to this monograph.

During pioneering times and from orthodox technique, the intensity of the transference interpretations comes from silence of the analyst. This form of deprivation was a misapplication of Freud's rule of abstinence (see Chapter 7, this volume). There developed a stinginess of response, a withholding attitude, a deprivation mode as the correct theoretical and clinical way of being in the psychoanalytic situation.

Stone (1981a) noted that a more intense focus on the transference relationship and the here and now does not indicate that Ferenczi and Rank repudiated a genetic reconstructive emphasis. Actually, Stone realized that heightening the emotional experience in the here and now encouraged the retrieval of repressed memories, which are essential to a meaningful reconstruction of genetic issues. Emotional intensity helps lift the repression barrier to childhood memories. When trauma occurred, the experience was repressed to cope with pain and to aid self-cohesion.

Ferenczi and Rank's ideas are more acceptable to Stone because they are in the Freudian tradition of respecting the past—reconstructing genetic material to develop insight into neurotic conflict. Stone is critical of Gill because the intense and early focus on transference increases resistance and actually obscures transferences that emerge in a more gradually unfolding approach. In this view, the more active the approach, the more it intrudes into the natural unfolding of the analytic process (Stone 1981a).

12

THE RULE OF EMPATHY: INTRODUCTION OF THE EMPATHIC METHOD INTO PSYCHOANALYSIS

THE LEGACY OF EMPATHY

The legacy Ferenczi contributed to the empathic method is formidable. It was a combination of his lively intellect, remarkable clinical skill, and personal capacities that allowed him to introduce empathy as a concept and a clinical tool in psychoanalysis. These advances were not only extraordinary for their time, 1924 to 1933, but still require special emotional and analytic skill. They are just beginning to be part of psychoanalytic thinking and practice today. In order to gain the necessary perspective on the theory, technique, and personal capacities involved, one should consult the three major figures in the history of psychotherapy regarding empathic functioning, namely Ferenczi, Heinz Kohut (1959, 1971, 1978a,b), and Carl Rogers (1951, 1959a,b, 1967, 1975, 1986). Despite familiarity with Kohut's and Rogers's contributions to empathy, most psychotherapists and psychoanalysts remain unfamiliar with Ferenczi's advancements.

FERENCZI'S PERSONAL QUALITIES OF EMPATHY

Several distinct issues emerged from Ferenczi's family experience (see Chapter 1, this volume) that were relevant to his empathic capacities. He used his own traumatic childhood as a gift to his patients by developing his personal empathy into clinical empathy, thereby empathizing with their sense of deprivation. It is clear that Ferenczi had a special awareness of the importance of maternal–child relations.

Thompson (1964b), through her experiences with Ferenczi as an analysand, student, and colleague, described his empathic qualities.

> Ferenczi's personality as well as his intelligence was especially well suited to the use of his method of treatment. . . .
>
> Possessed of a genuine sympathy for all human suffering, he approached each new day with an enthusiastic belief in his ability to help and in the "worthwhileness" of a patient.
>
> His efforts were tireless and his patience inexhaustible. He was never willing to admit that some mental diseases were incurable, but always said, "Perhaps it is simply that we have not yet discovered the right method." Conseqently, he tried more and more to apply psychoanalysis to very difficult cases. . . .
>
> His simplicity and absence of all pretense was another invaluable trait in his therapeutic approach. He completely lacked the pompous, important air and authoritative manner so common to many physicians. He won the confidence of his patients by making them feel that they have found a friend who would use all of his intelligence to help them. His simplicity encouraged them to lay aside their sick pretenses. [p. 66]

CLINICAL EXAMPLES OF FERENCZI'S EMPATHIC METHOD

There are several published sources for examples of Ferenczi's empathic functioning as an analyst, including Ferenczi's first case of psychoanalytic therapy (Ferenczi 1930b); "The Case of the Female Croatian Musician" (Ferenczi 1920, Rachman 1978a); the "Grandpa Encounter" in Ferenczi's discovery of the language of empathy (Ferenczi 1931); and Thompson's report of "The Case of the Slovenly Soldier" (Thompson 1964b). Thompson reported the following incident as an indication of Ferenczi's brilliant intuition and empathic capacity. She said his special intuitive ability enabled him to guess at the patient's thoughts almost before the patient himself knew them.

During the war, a soldier . . . was being disciplined for some serious misdemeanor. Under the strain of the disgrace, the man developed an acute mental illness in which he became very slovenly, neglecting all care of his body. On hearing of this, Ferenczi hastened to the man and . . . embraced him in genuine concern. Intuitively, without a word from the man, he had seen his need of being reassured that a friend could like him no matter how great his disgrace. The man's recovery began in that hour. [Thompson 1964b, p. 66]

THE INTRODUCTION OF THE CONCEPT OF EMPATHY: THE ELASTICITY OF PSYCHOANALYTIC TECHNIQUE (1928)

Stage 1: The Issue of Tact

Ferenczi's interest in empathy began with his technical recommendations for changing the emotional atmosphere of an analytic session. His keen powers of clinical observation had been demonstrated in many clinical cases where he was the first analyst to employ nonverbal cues to interpret unconscious processes (Ferenczi 1919a, 1920, 1924b, 1925b). At this point in time, he began to observe and concern himself with the nature of resistances to the analyst's interventions. As a participant observer, he was emotionally attuned to the impact of his interpretations on the analysand. Furthermore, he was a model of the elasticity of technique that he theorized about.

Ferenczi (1928b) wrote about his emotional attunement and elasticity of technique in the following example.

I recall, for instance, an uneducated, apparently quite simple patient who brought forward objections to an interpretation of mine, which it was my immediate impulse to reject; but on reflection, *not I, but the patient, turned out to be right,* and the result of his intervention was a much better general understanding of the matter we were dealing with. [p. 94]

From empathic interchanges like the one just illustrated, Ferenczi reached the following conclusion, which ushered the use of tact, or empathy, into psychoanalytic practice: "I have come to the conclusion that it is above all a question of psychological tact whether one should tell the patient some particular thing. But what is 'tact'? It is the capacity for empathy" (p. 89).

Ferenczi's observations led to the clinical recommendation that, in order to reduce the resistances, one should present any interpretation in a tactful manner. What he was suggesting was an empathic focus in relating and responding to an analysand.

Ferenczi's new method was also a call to analysts to be more empathic and flexible about accepting patients for analysis. In his growing experience as the analyst of difficult cases, he used his new method to work successfully with patients whom other analysts had either terminated prematurely or found unanalyzable or whose problems persisted after years of Freudian therapy. He urged analysts to follow the rule of empathy for patients who act out their feelings of rejection by being "bad patients." If an analyst has an excessive degree of antipathy, he or she should strive for empathic understanding of such patients. Ferenczi (1928b) said that individuals who trigger such negative feelings in an analyst do so "because the unconscious aim of intolerable behavior is often to be sent away. Also, . . . dropping the patient . . . would be merely leaving him in the lurch. . ." (p. 95). He felt that the empathic method he was proposing was crucial for understanding the clinical work of psychoanalysis: "One gradually becomes aware how immensely complicated the mental work demanded from the analyst is. . . . One might say that his mind swings continuously between empathy, self-observation and making judgements" (p. 96).

In Ferenczi's use of the concept of tact to begin his discussion of empathy, he once again indicated his close intellectual ties to Freud. It was Freud who introduced the concept of tact into psychoanalysis (Levy 1985), although it had appeared in German in the late nineteenth century (Chessick 1985a). The earliest references in Freud with regard to empathy concerned the analytic mode of listening (Levy 1985). Freud (1912b) described the experience of attuning to the unconscious of the analysand—how the analyst listens to the patient with "evenly-suspended attention" (p. 111) and how the analyst "must turn his own unconscious like a receptive organ toward the transmitting unconscious of the patient" (p. 115). He was referring to two aspects of the empathic process: creating an atmosphere of free association where the analysand is free to express all thoughts and feelings, and attuning to the unconscious of the analysand. Freud's (1921) much later references to empathy (Einfühlung) referred to "the mechanism by means of which we are enabled to take up any attitude at all towards another" (p. 110 n2) and "the process . . . which plays the largest part in our understanding of what is inherently foreign to our ego in other people" (p. 108).

Ferenczi was indebted to Freud for his views on the clinical use of tact and the beginnings of a theoretical understanding of empathy as a factor in the analytic situation. Ferenczi built his empathic method on this foundation.

FREUD'S RESPONSE TO FERENCZI'S INTRODUCTION OF EMPATHY INTO PSYCHOANALYSIS

Freud's response to Ferenczi's introduction of empathy into psychoanalytic technique was extremely positive and congratulatory. In a letter dated January 4, 1928, Freud said

> Your accompanying production ["Elasticity of Psychoanalytic Technique"] displays that judicious maturity you have acquired of late years, in respect of which no one approaches you. The title is excellent and deserves a wider provenance. . . . There is no doubt that you have much more to say on similar lines, and it would be very beneficial to have it. [Jones 1953, p. 241]

Freud realized that he needed Ferenczi's clinical genius to further develop the technique of psychoanalysis. His own attempts at technical recommendations produced a negative atmosphere for psychoanalysts, who felt constrained not to experiment or to modify Freudian methods. By 1928 analytic behavior was guided by taboos rather than flexible guidelines. Freud admitted this in this same letter when he said

> . . . the "Recommendations on Technique" I wrote long ago were essentially of a negative nature. . . . the most important thing was to emphasize what one should not do, and to point out the temptations in directions contrary to analysis. Almost everything positive that one should do I have left to "tact," . . . The result was that the docile analysts did not perceive the elasticity of the rules I had laid down, and submitted to them as if they were taboos. Some time all that must be revised, without, it is true, doing away with the obligations I had mentioned. [Jones 1953, p. 241]

Toward the end of this congratulatory letter, Freud could not resist expressing his reservations about the subjective approach (empathic method) that Ferenczi was introducing. Freud had cause to be concerned, but not for the reasons he offered. Consciously, Freud was expressing, as he had done in the past, his concern that psychoanalysis would lose its intellectual character and succumb to a mystical factor. He may also have been indicating his personal anxiety over an emotional expressive method that made demands on the analyst for vulnerability and responsiveness that he was not willing to assume. At still another level, Freud may have sensed in Ferenczi's subjective method a deviation that would change the nature of their professional and personal interests and lives. So the master gave the student a gentle reproach, in order to stem the growing sense of separation and individuation of his favorite pupil.

> All that you say about "tact" is assuredly true enough, but I have some misgivings about the manner in which you make those concessions. All those who have no tact will see in what you write a justification for arbitrariness, i.e., subjectivity, the influence of their own unmastered complexes. What we encounter in reality is a delicate balancing for the most part on the preconscious level of the various reactions we expect from our interventions. The issue depends, above all, on a quantitative estimate of the dynamic factors in the situation. One naturally cannot give rules for measuring this; the experience and the normality of the analyst have to form a decision. But with beginners, one therefore has to rob the idea of "tact" of its mystical character. [Jones 1953, p. 241]

Freud was also expressing his discomfort with a more experiential approach, which encouraged the analyst to be more human in the relationship. As he grew older, he became comfortable with a more intellectual, emotionally reserved role.

Unfortunately, as always, Freud's "gentle" reproaches caused Ferenczi to feel rebuked and rejected. However, whatever his personal vulnerability to Freud's criticisms, Ferenczi's need to follow his own clinical course prevailed. With the publication of "The Elasticity of Psychoanalytic Technique" paper in 1928 and the introduction of empathy into psychoanalytic technique, Ferenczi took a major step forward in developing an alternative to the Freudian method of psychoanalysis. His humanistic psychoanalysis paved the way for all modern dissidents, including Kohut (Gedo 1986a).

THE FURTHER DEVELOPMENT OF FERENCZI'S EMPATHIC METHOD

After the publication of the "Elasticity" paper, Ferenczi devoted the rest of his clinical career to the development of his empathic method of psychoanalysis. From 1928 until his death, he immersed himself in his alternative view to the Freudian method.

The empathic method was noted in a series of papers, brief notes, a clinical diary, and correspondence. Among these papers were "The Principle of Relaxation and Neo-Catharsis" (1930b), "Child Analysis in the Analysis of Adults" (1931), and "The Confusion of Tongues Between Adults and the Child: The Language of Tenderness and Passion" (1933).

"The Confusion of Tongues" paper and the *Clinical Diary* were so controversial that they were not published until many years after Ferenczi's death. (The "Confusion of Tongues" controversy is treated in depth in Chapter 13.) Ferenczi's *Clinical Diary* contains his clinical notes on therapy cases during the last year of his practice, 1932 (Ferenczi 1932c). At this late period, Ferenczi was practicing his empathic method to the fullest and only shared his work with his closest and most trusted colleagues, like Balint, De Forest, and Thompson, fearing Freud's criticisms and ostracism from the psychoanalytic community.

The Analytic Session: The Precursor for Empathic Functioning: "The Principle of Relaxation and Neo-Catharsis" (1930)

All analysts who believe in empathy as a basic means of interaction in the psychoanalytic method owe a considerable debt to Ferenczi. Beginning with the introduction of his ideas about the nature of a psychoanalytic session in 1924 (Ferenczi and Rank 1925) and elaborated in this humanistic psychoanalysis of his final clinical period, from 1927 to 1933, Ferenczi changed the nature of an analytic session. These changes were first discussed in his paper "The Principle of Relaxation and Neo-Catharsis" (1930b). The designation of relaxation therapy is an important reference to the ambience of the analytic session, which was characterized by an austere, somewhat authoritarian climate. It was not a situation of relaxation or friendly contact. This term was prophetic, and it now has a place in contemporary psychoanalysis (Kohut 1984a).

Ferenczi was trying to establish the emotional climate for empathic functioning. He wanted the analyst to be attuned to the analysand in a particular manner and for the analysand to feel free to express his or her deepest feelings about his or her internal phenomenological self. As early as the 1920s, he believed that the traditional analytic session had become a place where open and deep emotional expressions were being stifled. Both he and Rank made an impassioned plea for the continued attention to emotional reliving as a basic component in an analytic experience (Ferenczi and Rank 1925). Originally they felt such emotional reliving was an opportunity to shorten the time frame of an analysis. Ferenczi broke with Rank over the time issue, and Rank went on to develop the issue of time-limited therapy on his own (Rank 1926). Ferenczi developed his ideas of emotional experiencing as a means of deepening the analysis in order to bring it to what he described as rock bottom. He was interested in encouraging the deepest level of emotional functioning humanly possible in an analytic session. In order to accomplish this depth of feeling, a particular emotional atmosphere needed to be created.

Prior to Ferenczi's recommendations regarding relaxation therapy, psychoanalytic sessions were characterized by an austere, somewhat somber, perhaps authoritarian quality (Roazen 1975, Thompson 1964b). The prevailing model was that of a physician, a strong father figure, possessing the necessary diagnostic and treatment skills to effect a cure. The analysand was perceived as a patient suffering from an illness, inferior to the analyst, in a subordinate position, who, although treated with compassion and kindness, was not an equal (Roazen 1975, Thompson 1964b).

These attitudes, which were second nature to the analysts of the time, often produced an intimidating, tense, and compliant atmosphere. When the interaction was as its best, the passive, compliant analysand ascribed great healing power to the physician and the analyst dispensed treatment in the form of intellectually oriented interpretations regarding the unconscious strivings of the patient. By becoming consciously aware of these unconscious determinants, the analysand was afforded insight (usually of a cognitive nature) into his or her neurotic symptoms and functioning. The issues of the analysand's receptivity, the analyst's attitude, the emotional relationship, and the humanistic component of the interaction were not significant aspects of an analytic session.

Ferenczi realized that these factors were a crucial part of the process of an analysis. If one wanted to develop psychoanalysis so that it tapped the deepest levels of human feeling and awareness, an atmosphere of empathy needed to be created. By a process of mutuality, Ferenczi transformed the analytic session into a democratic, humanistic experience. The analyst became a responsive, giving, warm, and empathic partner in the process.

Ferenczi's Developmental Theory of Empathy

Although Ferenczi's previous clinical papers hinted at a developmental theory of empathy in the early mother–child paradigm, he was not able to elaborate these notions until the very end of his clinical career. Between 1927 and 1933, he began to work and think in a separate clinical, social, and intellectual atmosphere from Freud. Vienna and Budapest had become worlds apart as the relationship between the two men began to strain and unravel.

Ferenczi continued to follow his own course, surrounded by a small group of devoted followers and friends. Freud was openly displeased with his once favorite disciple's desire to pursue his own alternate method. Actually, Ferenczi kept many of his thoughts and clinical practices secret for fear of further alienating Freud. He noted them in his *Clinical Diary* (Ferenczi 1932c).

In his last two clinical papers, he did elaborate on the technical and theoretical issues in empathic functioning. "Child Analysis in the Analysis of Adults" (Ferenczi 1931) presents his technical discovery of the language of empathy – the mode of communicating with an adult to retrieve the childhood traumas or developmental arrests. In "The Confusion of Tongues Between Adults and Children: The Language of Tenderness and Passion" (Ferenczi 1933), he outlined a theory of neurosis that relied on disturbances in the early childhood experience of empathic failure rather than on oedipal conflicts. Furthermore, he argued that children who became disturbed adults had real abusive experiences with parenting figures, not imagined erotic fantasies. This departure from the Freudian theory of the oedipal conflict as central to the development of neurosis was his final dissenting view.

Ferenczi was the first analyst to report that there were patients whose pathology could not be explained, at least in its entirety, in terms of the vicissitudes of the oedipal conflict. Furthermore, these individuals' problems did not respond to interpretation. Actually, Freud was the first analyst who recommended changes in analytic use of interpretation and suggested active measures for the phobic and obsessional neurosis (Freud 1919 [1918]; see Chapter 7, this volume).

First Ferenczi and then Winnicott and Kohut have helped us to understand why this was so. Michael Basch (1984) wrote, "Patients like those described by Ferenczi do not develop problems because of overstimulation and premature sexual excitement, but, rather, because they were emotionally neglected and/or misunderstood." (p. 10). In other words, Ferenczi became the first dissident in psychoanalysis to offered an alternative to the Oedipus complex.

Ferenczi's reformulation of the seduction theory focuses on the original empathic relationship between mother and child. These patients "have as children been understimulated rather than overstimulated and, instead of defending themselves against an instinctual overload, are struggling with an inability to deal appropriately with their emotional needs" (Basch 1984, p. 10). Thus, they have been deprived. "For these patients it is not the unconscious thought of forbidden erotic love that generates anxiety, but the anticipation of reexperiencing the devastating, potentially disintegrating disappointment of early empathic failures if they dare once again to reach for emotional fulfillment" (Basch 1984, p. 10).

Ferenczi, in the "Confusion of Tongues" paper, described what he listed as experiential data from his clinical practice of actual sexual abuse of children by parental figures. Recently, Masson (1984) has argued that reports of child abuse were readily available to clinicians of Freud's time. Both Freud and the analytic community were not prepared or willing to overturn the cherished concept of the oedipal complex as the central organizing theory of psychoanalysis (Malcolm 1983b, Masson 1984). By 1933, when Ferenczi attempted to return to Freud's original seduction theory, Freud and his followers were so heavily invested in the Oedipus complex that they closed ranks and were successful in censoring Ferenczi's ideas.

The Language of Empathy: "Child Analysis in the Analysis of Adults" (1931)

"Child Analysis in the Analysis of Adults," presented before the Child Psychoanalytic Society of Vienna in 1931, allowed Ferenczi to outline his discovery of the language of empathic communication—i.e., the capacity for the analyst to talk child-to-child with the adult patient (Ferenczi 1931). As he encouraged his analysands to take full advantage of his relaxation therapy, he noticed that there were significant changes in the process of free association. The more relaxed they became, "the more naive (one might say, the more childish) did the patient become in his speech and his other modes of expressing himself" (Ferenczi 1931, pp. 128–129). Apparently, the more empathic and less interpretive the interchanges were, the more traumatic were the childhood experiences uncovered.

There were many moments in Ferenczi's clinical career when he took risks that led to profound changes in technical and clinical functioning. One such incident was his discovery of the empathic language of reaching the child in the adult. The description of the "Grandpapa Encounter" (Ferenczi 1931) was one such incident:

> . . . a patient, in the prime of life, resolved . . . to revive in his mind incidents from his earliest childhood. . . . I was aware that in the scene revived by him, he was identifying me with his grandfather. Suddenly . . . he threw his arms around my neck and whispered in my ear: "I say, Grandpapa, I am afraid I am going to have a baby!" Thereupon I had what seems to me a happy inspiration: I said nothing to him for the moment about transference, etc., but retorted, in a similar whisper: "Well, but what makes you think so." [p. 129]

The use of this kind of empathic language helped to fulfill Ferenczi's (1931) demanding goal of psychoanalysis:

> " . . . that one has no right to be satisfied with any analysis until it has led to the actual reproduction of the traumatic occurrences associated with the primal repression, upon which character and symptom are ultimately based" (p. 131).

Ferenczi was then the first analyst to use the analytic session to revive the childhood trauma by heightening the emotional experience of the moment. His indulgent, relaxed, empathic attitude and the communication directed at the child-in-the-adult created an atmosphere where trust, vulnerability, and self-disclosure were fostered. In addition, he was also creating a tender maternal transference, which also contributed to an intense emotional reaction and a feeling of being nurtured, thereby lowering defensiveness. He demonstrated that empathy (not solely the use of interpretation) could foster uncovering.

The Contribution of the Analyst to the Treatment Situation

Ferenczi's contribution to the development of an empathic method for psychoanalysis places heavy emphasis on the contribution that the analyst makes to the treatment process. His first contribution was to encourage Freud to require that all analytic candidates undergo a personal analysis (Thompson 1950b).

As his clinical experiments in active and humanistic psychoanalysis flourished, it became evident that the analyst's functioning was a potent factor. The further he deviated from the passive observer role, the more his own personality, style, and countertransference reactions became evident. Rather than revert to the traditional methods of transference analysis or interpretation of resistance, he developed a new method of humanistic factors that emphasized mutual analysis, positive use of countertransference reactions, encouragement of the expression of negative affect toward the analyst, and self-disclosure by the analyst.

Mutual Analysis

Ferenczi's process of mutual analysis fostered a democratic attitude toward the analysand. The individual is seen as a therapeutic partner in the analytic process. There is open, frank, and direct discussion of the relationship. The analyst examines his or her contribution to the treatment process, countertransference reactions, and relationship difficulties. The analyst does not immediately resort to transference or resistance interpretations, but accepts the analysand's statements as carrying an essential truth about the analyst's behavior and the interaction.

Ferenczi's humility, unending optimism about finding a cure, and respect for the individual combined to form an empathic bond with the analysand. He was someone who did not hide behind his professional role or clinical facade. He could admit his mistakes and be a vulnerable partner in the struggle toward understanding. In a far-reaching clinical experiment, he carried mutuality to its limits (Ferenczi 1932c). The analyst was analyzed by the analysand, a forerunner of Harold Searles's (1979b) concept of the patient as therapist to the analyst.

Countertransference Analysis

Ferenczi advanced the study of the analyst's contribution to the treatment process in a way that few analysts have done since. In Freud's time the analyst's main focus was on the transference portion of the transference/ countertransference relationship. As such, the emotional focus was on the patient. The concern was to encourage the patient to express freely what he or she felt about the analyst. Such a focus encouraged the authority/ subordinate vector of the relationship. Analysts of that time, therefore, emphasized one aspect of the relationship: it was clearly a one-person psychology. In this they followed the master, since Freud was decidedly more comfortable with the patient emoting than dealing with his own emotional reactions to patients (Bergmann and Hartman 1976, Roazen 1975).

Besides Freud's personal difficulties with patients' emotional reactions to him (as witnessed by his self-confessed introduction of the face-away position of the couch), he also had theoretically introduced the concept of countertransference as a negative occurrence (Freud 1910a, 1912b). Freud's notion was that countertransference was a necessary evil in the analytic process, to be eradicated as soon as possible. Once countertransference was eliminated, the analysis could go forward. The Freudian notion of countertransference was extremely influential and has survived into modern times (Reich 1951, 1966).

Ferenczi was the first analyst to depart from the tradition of countertransference as a negative occurrence. He combined his emotional and intellectual gifts into a new version of countertransference analysis that was based upon empathic understanding.

De Forest (1954) summarized Ferenczi's theory of countertransference.

> 1. His theory of therapy also brought to the fore the significance of the countertransference. It stressed the fact that it is the most essential tool of the therapist: one that must arise from his innate temperament, and one that is solely concerned with the patient's recovery of emotional health. . . .
> 2. The essential character of countertransference is one of tenderness. It is the analyst's responsibility to offer . . . a setting of security and warmth, in which the patient by means of his varying expressions in transference exposes the unsolved problems of his infancy.
> 3. The context of the countertransference changes with the improving health of the patient: (1) From the careful and sympathetic study and observation at the beginning of treatment, (2) to the

more matter-of-fact, meticulous and empathic examination of the patient's phantasies and behavior in a later period, (3) it progresses to the final "give and take" with the patient, as a person of equal emotional vigor. [pp. 122–123]

Encouragement of Criticism and Negative Affect toward the Analyst

Since Ferenczi encouraged an attitude of mutuality, analysands were free to be openly critical of him. Because he did not react with defensiveness, they eventually could trust him to empathize with their feelings. They could vent their negative transference feelings, using him as the container of their childhood rage. He would not retaliate, distance himself, or become unresponsive. The empathic bond would be put to its most difficult test as he struggled to accept, understand, and respond to the criticism and negative affect. Ferenczi laid the groundwork for the object relations orientation to countertransference (Winnicott 1949).

Analyst Self-Disclosure

Ferenczi's notion of the elasticity of the analytic situation also introduced the controversial practice of the analyst becoming a human partner in the clinical interchange. Thompson (1944), who experienced both the traditional role of the analyst as well as Ferenczi's, described the difference. In order to maintain neutrality, "the ideal taught by Freud was of the passive non-reacting analyst who was only a mirror in which the patient's reactions are reflected. Attempting to achieve this ideal, an attitude of cold, stiff aloofness, was assumed by many analysts" (Thompson 1944, p. 248).

On the other hand, Ferenczi discouraged the power, control, and status of the analyst. "Ferenczi stressed that the real personality of the analyst was important in the therapeutic situation . . . if he can admit his mistakes to the patient, the unfavorable situation can be made therapeutically valuable . . . the analyst . . . will be sincere with the patient" (Thompson 1944, p. 249).

Ferenczi (1928b) called for analysts to practice emotional courage, and they would do well to use him as an empathic role model as portrayed in his prophetic words.

One must never be ashamed unreservedly to confess one's own mistakes. It must never be forgotten that analysis is no suggestive process, primarily dependent on the physician's reputation and infallibility. All that is called for is confidence in the physician's frankness and honesty, which does not suffer from the frank confession of mistakes. [p. 95]

Ferenczi's (1931) description of his personal struggle to own his countertransference reactions and enter into a mutual analysis with an analysand are instructive. When he gave what he considered a learned scientific interpretation, and was met with rebuffs, he had to deal with his personal reaction. "I need hardly tell you that my first reaction to such incidents was a feeling of outraged authority. For a moment I felt injured at the suggestion that my patient or pupil could know better than I did" (Ferenczi 1931, p. 130). His profound understanding of the function of empathy in therapeutic interaction led him to recognize his countertransference reaction and develop an innovative response: "Fortunately, however, there immediately occurred to me the further thought that he really must at bottom know more about himself than I could with my guesses" (p. 130). Ferenczi's attunement to the internal frame of reference of the other enabled him to respond in a self-disclosing way: "I therefore admitted that possibly I had made a mistake, and the result was not that I lost my authority, but that his confidence in me was increased" (p. 130).

FERENCZI'S INFLUENCE ON CONTEMPORARY EMPATHIC METHODS

Recently, several authors have discovered parallels in the work of Kohut and Rogers, since they both place a heavy emphasis on empathic functioning (E. Kahn 1985, Stolorow 1976). It seems fitting at this point to introduce some comparison between Rogers, Ferenczi, and Kohut, since they all based their method on the bedrock of empathy.

Ferenczi and Rogers

Rogers, writing within the humanistic psychotherapy tradition, pioneered the introduction of empathy as one of the essential conditions for psychotherapy (Rogers 1951, 1959a, 1967, 1975, 1986). He was influenced by Ferenczi's analytic tradition through a contact with a Rankian social worker who was influenced by Ferenczi and Rank's joint focus on the experiential component in therapeutic interaction (Ferenczi and Rank 1925), helped Rogers orient his thinking and functioning to the underlying feelings in a client's manifest communication (Rogers 1975). This reflection of feelings response that characterized Rogers's client-centered psychotherapy evolved into the focus on the use of empathy as a necessary and sufficient condition of the therapy (Rogers 1959a).

Rogers's work built on the foundation of Ferenczi and Rank's formulations for a focus on the emotional experiential (rather than cognitive) component in psychotherapy. It also adhered to Ferenczi's belief that the analysand's communication contains an essential truth. Rogers's theory and method elaborated Ferenczi's introduction of the empathic method in the following ways.

1. A focus on the subjective experience of the client is the major source of information to be used by the therapist.
2. Attention is paid to the manifest level of communication as providing essential truth about the individual.
3. The task of the therapist is to help create order and meaning within the individual's subjective experience.
4. The phenomenological method is used to study the subjective experience of the individual.
5. Empathy is the major force for conveying a sense of understanding of the individual's subjective world.
6. Empathy by the therapist is the vehicle for the individual's "feeling understood" by the therapist. Feeling understood is the basis of trust, emotional connectedness, and communication.
7. Empathy is the means by which the therapist maintains a focus on the client's subjective experience, anchoring and maintaining the therapist in the frame of reference of the other.

Ferenczi and Kohut

There are areas in which Ferenczi's and Kohut's work have parallels. They were both concerned with the quality of relatedness between parent and child. They argued that feeling unloved, unappreciated, and misunderstood interfered with normal personality development, especially with the development of a secure sense of self and self-worth. They were also both concerned about the danger of re-traumatizing the patient in the analytic situation by withholding an empathic, concerned, and sincere appreciation of the analysand.

They both felt the need to provide a better therapeutic version of the love, understanding, and security that the patient missed in the childhood relationship with his or her parents. Finally, they were both aware of the patient's unconscious reactions to the analyst's manner of relating to them and how this affected the analysand's transference and associated resistances.

In this regard, both Ferenczi and Kohut view the relationship as a mutually influencing interpersonal system, or a two-person psychology, rather than the patient endowing the neutral analyst with archaic transference projections and striving.

There is an irony in contemporary psychoanalysis. As Kohut's work becomes better known, it paves the way for a rediscovery of Ferenczi. Although Kohut was unfortunately uninterested in his empathic forerunner, Ferenczi laid the groundwork for Kohut's work (Rachman 1989b). He courageously insisted, in the face of severe criticism, personal hostility, ostracism, and censorship, that there were analysands who suffered from emotional deprivation and that empathy was the corrective emotional experience for this childhood trauma. Let us hope that Kohut's acceptance will create a climate for the appreciation of Ferenczi's brilliant and inspiring contributions to psychoanalysis. Such an occurrence would reestablish the necessary empathic bond between Ferenczi and the analytic community and begin to heal the wounds of past empathic failures (Rachman 1994a).

13

CONFUSION OF TONGUES THEORY

FERENCZI'S LAST CLINICAL PRESENTATION[1]

"The Confusion of Tongues Between Adults and the Child: The Language of Tenderness and of Passion"[2,3] (Ferenczi 1933) was Ferenczi's most controversial and most profound paper. Controversy surrounded this paper before it was written, when it was presented, and after it was delivered.

---

1. It was generally thought that the Confusion of Tongues paper was Ferenczi's last paper (Ferenczi, 1933). Recent evidence has pinpointed that it was his last presentation (12th International Psychoanalytic Congress, Wiesbaden, Germany, September 4, 1932). But his last paper was actually entitled "Trauma in Psychoanalysis," published first in the Hungarian medical journal Gyógyászat, 74:20, 1934a, under the title "Trauma and Psychoanalysis." It was printed in Hungarian and German. The first English translation was in the Indian Journal of Psychology, 9:29–38, 1934. It was delivered posthumously by Dr. Fanny Hann and translated by Dr. I. Hermann.

2. First published in German in the Internationale Zeitschrift für Psychoanalyse, 19:5–15, 1933, under the title "The Passions of Adults and Their Influence on the Sexual and Character Development of Children," then subsequently in Bausteine zur Psychoanalyse, vol. III, Berne, 1939.

3. The English translation first appeared in "Sándor Ferenczi Number," M. Balint (Ed.), International Journal of Psycho-Analysis, 30: Whole No. 4, 1949; reprinted in Final Contributions to the Problems and Methods of Psychoanalysis: vol. 3, M. Balint (Ed.). New York: Basic Books, pp. 156–167, 1955; a new translation made by Jeffrey M. Masson and Marianne Loring, in Masson, J. M., The Assault on Truth: Freud's Suppression of the Seduction Theory. New York: Farrar, Straus and Giroux, Appendix C, pp. 283–295, 1984.

Ferenczi's was the first paper presented on Sunday, September 4, 1932. Freud, suffering from cancer of the mouth, was too sick to attend, but many of the leading analysts of the time were there. Their response to the paper was uniformly negative. These senior analysts, "the bearers of the ring," were of the opinion that views such as those expressed in the paper should not be circulated more widely than was absolutely necessary, that the dissemination of such views constituted a danger to society (Masson 1984).

The "Confusion of Tongues" paper raised enormous issues of a professional, personal, and social nature for psychoanalysis, Ferenczi, and the psychoanalytic community. It signaled the development of a new method of psychoanalysis, the reintroduction of the seduction hypothesis, a professional focus on the acceptance of sexual abuse in children, and the emotional demands on the analyst in treating difficult cases, as well as the final disruption in the Freud/Ferenczi relationship and Ferenczi's break with the analytic community.

THE THEORY

Ferenczi outlined his confusion of tongues theory to explain the pathological effect that childhood seduction has on the child's development and its subsequent pathological outcome for the adult:

1. The child is confused (traumatized) by the adult (parent or parent surrogate) when the adult seduces the child sexually (or emotionally).

2. The child wants tenderness, not sexual passion.

3. The adult is not really showing love or tenderness to the child, but is aggressing against the child, intruding his or her sexual needs onto the innocent longings of a child for love and maternal tenderness.

4. The child is tongue-tied, confusing sexuality for love, but cannot speak of the confusion.

5. The child cannot refuse the sexual advances of the adult because he or she feels helpless, paralyzed by fear and needing tenderness.

6. The child uses a pathogenic defense mechanism to identify with the aggressor (Ferenczi 1933), which Ferenczi was the first to name (Masson 1984).

7. Besides identification with the aggressor, a host of pathological defenses can develop to cope with the seduction experience (e.g., denial, dissociation, splitting, depression, schizoid withdrawal, blunted affect).

8. Ferenczi (1933) wrote, "These children feel physically and morally helpless, their personalities are not sufficiently consolidated in order to be able to protest, even if only in thought, for the overpowering force and authority of the adult makes them dumb and can rob them of their senses" (p. 162).

This variable that Ferenczi is explicating forms the basis for understanding the psychodynamics of victimization. A child who has been abused by an adult internalizes a sense of victimization by virtue of his or her greater physical and emotional helplessness. If this dynamic is not worked through in childhood and adolescence, the individual enters adulthood programmed, as it were, to repeat a victimized reaction to perceived abuse.

9. Ferenczi (1933) wrote, "The same anxiety, however, if it reaches a certain maximum, compels them to subordinate themselves like *automata* to the will of the aggressor, to divine each one of his desires . . ." (p. 162).

10. The guilt of the parental abuser is denied: "The most important change produced in the mind of the child by the anxiety-fear-ridden identification with the adult partner, is *the introjection of the guilt feelings of the adult* which makes hitherto harmless play appear as a punishable offence" (Ferenczi 1933, p. 162).

11. The parental abuser, in denial, threatens the child with physical harm, if she/he reveals the evil secret. An emotional connection between sex and violence is then solidified. The child's view of sexuality and love is altered.

Although Ferenczi's focus was on the victimization of the child by the adult, it is clear from his formulation that the adult perpetrator is also emotionally altered by the sexual seduction. The molestation is only a momentary satisfaction of narcissistic needs that will need continual satisfaction by a less powerful object.

12. To cope with the anxiety, and to maintain the illusion of parental tenderness, the child sinks into "a dream-like state as is the traumatic trance to the primary process . . . the attack as a rigid, external reality ceases to exist and in the traumatic trance the child succeds in maintaining the previous situation of tenderness" (Ferenczi 1933, p. 162).

13. The childhood pathology lays the groundwork for adult perversions, disturbed object relations, lack of trust, special need for empathy,

and the establishment of a narcissistic or borderline adaptation. Ferenczi was suggesting that sexual abuse in childhood plays a significant role in the development of severe narcissistic and borderline conditions.

The second version of the confusion of tongues that Ferenczi first identified is between the individual and his analyst. Ferenczi describes the confusion of tongues that a patient, seduced in childhood, can reexperience in analysis with an analyst who maintains the stance of a cold, detached, neutral, or nonparticipant observer. By being removed from the emotional experience of the analysis and evoking the concept of resistance when the patient expresses negative feelings toward him or her, the analyst unwittingly re-creates the childhood trauma. The analyst confuses the analysand by this communication and interaction. The analysand is speaking in genuine emotional terms about feelings of coolness and detachment. The analyst responds with additional coolness and detachment by evoking the notion of resistance rather than examining his or her feelings.

Ferenczi argues for a more genuine emotional encounter in which the analyst examines his or her countertransference to rock bottom in order to create a corrective emotional experience that will help uncover the childhood trauma of sexual seduction and emotional abuse.

The concept of the confusion of tongues, because it describes in a parsimonious and meaningful way a particular universal psychological phenomenon, can be extended beyond Ferenczi's formulations to include these five related experiences:

1. The individual and his or her family
2. The individual and his or her analyst
3. The individual and his or her mentor (role model)
4. The individual and his or her peer group
5. The individual and society

There are several issues related to the "Confusion of Tongues" paper and its implications that will also be discussed. Recent evidence has suggested that Ferenczi himself may have suffered in his own childhood both a sexual seduction and emotional trauma.

Although not mentioned directly by Ferenczi in this paper, there was, as a background to the controversy surrounding the presentation of this paper, a confusion of tongues between Ferenczi and Freud, who disapproved of this paper. He did not want Ferenczi to present it at Wiesbaden. Ferenczi, for personal and political reasons, did not make his feelings known at the time, although he wrote of his dissatisfaction in his secret *Clinical Diary* (see Chapter 18, this volume). The administrators of the Freud archives apparently suppressed the materials that would fully illuminate the controversy (Malcolm 1983a, Masson 1984). The French materials and the recently available English translations of the *Clinical Diary* can begin to illuminate the confusion of tongues controversy between Freud and Ferenczi (Dupont 1985, Sabourin 1985, Sylwan 1984; see also Rachman 1989a, 1991d, 1992c, 1993a,b, 1994a).

Finally, there was also a confusion of tongues between Ferenczi and the analytic community. The oedipal rivalry between Jones and Ferenczi for Freud's love produced a professional and personal trauma for Ferenczi (Rachman 1989a, Roazen 1975).

THE CONFUSION OF TONGUES BETWEEN ADULTS AND THE CHILD: THE LANGUAGE OF TENDERNESS AND PASSION (FERENCZI 1933)

The Seduction Hypothesis

At the Wiesbaden conference, Ferenczi focused on a theoretical and clinical issue that had lain dormant in psychoanalysis for many years. Ever since Freud abandoned the seduction hypothesis and introduced the Oedipus complex as an alternate explanation for the report of childhood sexual experiences, psychoanalysis shifted its focus from interpersonal to intrapsychic issues of sexuality. Furthermore, the actual incidence of sexual experiences between children and parents (or other adults) became neglected.

During the founding of psychoanalysis, Freud was interested in the traumatic effect of childhood sexual seduction on the adult patient and believed it was a causal factor in the development of neurosis (Freud 1954). In the now famous letter from Freud to Fliess, dated September 21, 1897, Freud said that he was mistaken in believing the reports of sexual seduction. Specifically, he could not believe that all the reports of father–daughter incest were true (Freud 1954). Freud's letters to Fliess also "hint at the theoretical revolution which was soon to come, with the abandonment of the seduction theory for a conception that saw in the myth of Oedipus a universal archetype" (McGrath 1986, p. 197).

The cause of Freud's abandonment of the seduction hypothesis has been the subject of much debate within psychoanalysis. Jones (1953) saw the event as an intellectual advance and suggested that Freud's self-analysis was the decisive factor. Others have both concurred with this view and elaborated upon it (Anzieu 1975, Schur 1972, Sulloway 1979). Masson (1984) attacks the established view, suggesting that the shift from seduction to oedipal fantasy was a loss of courage for Freud in the face of professional opposition. Krüll (1986) also views the shift as a retrogressive step and emphasizes its personal importance as a creative solution to Freud's ambivalent feelings for his father.

Although tradition wears well in psychoanalysis, some current discussions encourage a reexamination of the seduction hypothesis in order to explain pathological behavior and to define treatment (see especially Kohut 1971, 1977, 1978b, 1984a). Ferenczi attempted to main-tain a tradition within psychoanalysis to preserve the seduction hypoth-esis that Freud actually began. Ferenczi delineated theoretical formulations and clinical observations regarding childhood seduction, emotional trauma, and the etiology of severe psychological disorders during the latter part of his clinical career in a series of monographs and papers (Ferenczi 1928a,b, 1930b, 1931, 1932c, 1933; Ferenczi and Rank 1925). At the time, Ferenczi wished these ideas to be integrated into Freudian psychoanalysis (Gedo 1976, 1986a). He was always ambivalent about his deviations from Freud and never seemed to realize how far he had separated or the extent to which he was founding an alternate view (Rachman 1984a,b, Thompson 1944). At the present time, there is new evidence that clarifies Ferenczi's later clinical behavior and his own thinking as being different from Freud's (Dupont 1988a,b, Ferenczi 1932c, 1933, Sabourin 1985, Sylwan 1984).

Ferenczi's theory has other implications of which he was aware but could not follow up due to his premature death in 1933.

1. Emotional trauma, due to unempathic parenting, is also concep-tualized as an etiological factor in psychological disorder. This idea was more fully developed by Balint and integrated into an object relations framework (Balint 1968a, Rachman in press).

2. Relational psychodynamics in the family are identified as a central issue in the development of psychopathology.

Identification with the Aggressor

As discussed, identification with the aggressor is one step in the process that Ferenczi outlined. Controversy surrounds this discovery as well.

The term *identification with the aggressor* appears for the first time in the original German version of "The Confusion of Tongues." On page 11, Ferenczi wrote of an identification and introjection based on fear, "ängstlicher Identifizierung und Introjekzion . . ." In the *Clinical Diary* Ferenczi uses the term and the concept repeatedly (Ferenczi 1932c).

Ferenczi wished to explain the psychodynamics that occur after the child has been molested by the adult and continues to have a relationship with the abuser. The parental seducer is able to continue the molestation because the child's ego is not fully developed and can be submerged by the force and authority of the adult (Ferenczi 1933). Furthermore, as the child's anxiety reaches maximum proportion, the defense mechanism identification with the aggressor (IWA) sets in.

Identification with the aggressor has been attributed to Anna Freud, supposedly introduced in her book, *The Ego and the Mechanisms of Defense.* A summary of Anna Freud's 1936 presentation of this concept is as follows.

> Child introjects some characteristic of an anxiety object and so assimilates an anxiety experience which he has just undergone. Here the mechanism of identification and introjection is combined with a second important mechanism. By impersonating the aggressor, assuming his attributes, or utilizing his aggression, the child transforms himself from the person threatened into the person who makes the threat. [p. 113]

The chronology of discovery favors Ferenczi. Not only was "The Confusion of Tongues" published three years before Anna Freud's *The Ego and the Mechanisms of Defense,* Ferenczi's paper was delivered in September 1932, four years before the book. Furthermore, Anna Freud not only attended the conference but was the recording secretary, detailing the event in the *International Journal* (A. Freud 1933). The paper was not available in English until 1949, when Balint, Ferenczi's literary executor, lifted its suppression of this material (Balint 1949).

Because of the paper's unavailability to English-speaking analysts for fourteen years, it is understandable that Ferenczi's use of the concept was not recognized. However, since German was the mother tongue for Anna Freud and the Freudian circle, it is plausible that they were aware of Ferenczi's discovery. It is likely that this discovery of identification with the aggressor was lost on the German-speaking analysts because the focus on "The Confusion of Tongues" presentation was on the sexual trauma theory as the etiology of neurosis and the recommendations for deviations in technique. The paper and its discoveries were not considered a part of mainstream psychoanalysis and therefore were not studied.

Ferenczi's IWA concept helps explain the incidence of abused children acting out the sexual abuse with someone else. A child abused by a father then molests a sibling or friend. There is an inherent communicative function or effort in IWA. An individual wishes to convey his or her internal state to another person. In a way, it is an attempt to force others to feel what you feel, which is contained in the idea of projective identification (putting your own internal state into the other person and acting with him or her in such a way as to induce in the other person what you are feeling—they know your experience on a visceral level).

Ferenczi's difficult cases and the seduced child struggling with IWA illustrate not just the wish to be powerful or to inflict harm on others or solely to master anxiety, but to somehow alert the other person to what they are feeling, to signal their distress about the trauma by causing the other person to feel it. IWA, therefore, is not just an interpersonal manifestation of an intrapsychic process, but has a relational function. The individual wants his or her distress to be understood and ameliorated by a significant other.

EMPATHIC FAILURE AS TRAUMA

Perhaps no analyst has ever spoken so empathically on behalf of abused children and their adult traumatized selves as has Ferenczi. It would be comforting to dismiss these conclusions about sexual seduction of children as a function of a different era, when puritanical values forced covert sexual activity within families. But the evidence mounts regarding the incidence of sexual abuse of children in contemporary society (Burgess et al. 1978, Groth and Birnbaum 1979, James and Nasjleti 1983, Rush 1980).

Ferenczi also opened the door for psychoanalysts to consider emotional abuse as trauma. Although he focused on sexual seduction as the etiology of adult psychopathology, he had been developing the notion of empathic failure in the early mother–child relationship as a primary source of emotional disturbance (Ferenczi 1928b, 1930b, 1931, 1932c, Rachman 1988a). In the "Confusion of Tongues" paper, Ferenczi developed these ideas to the fullest by suggesting that sexual seduction of children was the result of adults' intrusion of their sexual needs onto the needs of children.

Interestingly enough, a traditionalist, Kurt Eissler, influenced by Ferenczi's paper, added another voice to the concept of emotional trauma. Eissler (1965) actually suggested that the trauma-of-childhood hypothesis can be applied to all individuals, from the neurotic to the so-called normal population. He believes that childhood is trauma—basically an unhappy period of life under the best of circumstances:

> Adults often remember from their childhood incidents or even periods of sadness, frustration, and grief, which no adult unhappiness can match. . . . it very often turns out that these incidents of suffering actually occurred more frequently than had been originally recalled, and that childhood took place under a general sign of sadness, only occasionally interrupted by episodes of incomparable joy. This [is] why almost every adult harbors (manifestly or latently) excessive reproaches against his parents or their substitutes. [p. 212]

In contemporary psychoanalysis, the British object relations orientation (Balint 1968b, Guntrip 1961, 1969, 1971, Khan 1969, 1974, Little 1951, 1960, Winnicott 1958, 1960a,b, 1965a,b) and the self psychology framework (Basch 1984, Kohut 1984a, Stolorow and Lachmann 1980) describe trauma as empathic failures in the parent–child relationship, extending Ferenczi's original findings with the same patient population (narcissistic, schizoid, borderline, and psychotic cases).

The Confusion of Tongues between Analyst and Analysand

It is not difficult to imagine Freud and his followers being angered by Ferenczi's statements regarding sexual seduction as the etiology of neurosis, the confusion of tongues between parent and child. After all, this idea brought into question the oedipal theory of neurosis and challenged, albeit in a nonconfrontational way, Freud's authority. There was also a third, darker issue that struck a chord in the unconscious of these elder statesmen of psychoanalysis. By implication, what Ferenczi (1933) reported in the following dramatic statement (although it echoed Freud's observations of 1889, when he first formulated the seduction theory [Freud 1954]), pointed a finger at the upper-middle-class father as seducer of his female children. Freud and his followers were very much a part of this class of society. They did not want to hear that they were child seducers, as Ferenczi implied.

> I obtained . . . new corroborative evidence for my supposition that the trauma, especially the sexual trauma, as the pathogenic factor cannot be valued highly enough. Even children of very respectable, sincerely puritanical families fall victim to real violence or rape much more often than one had dared to suppose. Either it is the parents who try to find a substitute gratification in this pathological way for their frustration, or it is people thought to be trustworthy such as relatives . . . governesses or servants, who misuse the ignorance and the innocence of the child. [Ferenczi 1933, p. 161]

The second area of confusion of tongues that Ferenczi identified was between the analyst and the analysand. No doubt this angered Freud and the analytic community still further, since the implication was that the analyst was involved in an emotional and interpersonal seduction of his analysand. To suggest that Freud, through his behavior in the psychoanalytic session, might actually have been causing the individual to repeat the trauma of his childhood, however unknowingly, was an outrage. Now Ferenczi was calling analysts not only potential private seducers of their children, but also seducers of their patients. With this contention, Ferenczi alienated the entire analytic community.

Ferenczi (1933) introduced the concept of professional hypocrisy to describe another version of a confusion of tongues.

> We greet the patient with politeness when he enters our room, ask him to start with his associations and promise him faithfully that we will listen attentively to him, give our undivided interest to his well-being and to the work needed for it. In reality, however, it may happen that we can only with difficulty tolerate certain external or internal features of the patient, or perhaps we feel unpleasantly disturbed in some professional or personal affair by the analytic session. [Ferenczi 1933, p. 159]

Ferenczi was identifying a confusion of tongues in the psychoanalytic situation, characterized by the analysand experiencing the analyst as unempathic. The analysand cannot speak of the experience. Ferenczi (1933) wrote, "Something had been left unsaid in the relation between physician and patient, *something insincere* . . ." (p. 159, italics added). Ferenczi was identifying the relational dimension in the psychoanalytic situation, where the analyst is not willing to create a democratic, mutual, and emotionally sincere relationship with the analysand. The analyst hides behind the tradition of interpretation of transference and resistance when faced with negative feelings being expressed by the analysand. Such a tradition does not incorporate, as Ferenczi recommended, an ongoing analysis of the countertransference, or a stance that encourages the analyst to examine his or her contribution to the analytic process.

Ferenczi (1933) urged analysts to renounce professional hypocrisy in order to distinguish the analysis from the "unbearable traumatogenic past" (p. 160). He argued that all analysts commit blunders. As Kohut pointed out forty years later, unempathic interventions and omissions are an inevitable part of an analysis. But Ferenczi made another daring suggestion: a curative element is introduced if the analyst is sincere with the analysand. He wrote

> . . . the admission of the analyst's error produced confidence in his patient. . . . the restrained coolness, the professional hypocrisy, . . . a dislike of the patient . . . such a situation was not essentially different from that which in his childhood has led to the illness. . . . we created a situation that was indeed unbearable. . . . Small wonder that our effort produced no better results than the original trauma. The setting free of his critical feelings, the willingness on our part to admit our mistakes and the honest endeavor to avoid them in future, all these go to create a confidence in the analyst. *It is this confidence that establishes the contrast between the present and the unbearable traumatogenic past.* [Ferenczi 1933, p. 160]

Ferenczi's Personal Sexual Trauma

If we can accept the relational perspective as part of the issue of the concept of identification with the aggressor, then we can attempt to apply it to Ferenczi's functioning as well. There is some suggestive evidence that Ferenczi himself may have suffered a childhood seduction and emotional trauma.

There are several passages in his *Clinical Diary* (Ferenczi 1932c) that suggest he was the victim of a childhood sexual seduction.

1. "The analyst's associations in fact move in the direction of an episode in his infancy the 'Száraz dajka' ("nurse," in Hungarian) affair, at the age of one year" (p. 13).
2. ". . . The identity between the analyst and the analysand: both had been forced to do more and endure more sexually than they had in fact wanted to" (p. 15).
3. "While telling the 'analyst' about this, I submerged myself deeply in the reproduction of infantile experiences; the most evocative image was the vague appearance of female figures; . . . then the image of a corpse, whose abdomen I was opening up, presumably in the dissecting room; linked to this the mad fantasy that I was being pressed into this wound in the corpse. Interpretation: the after-effect of passionate scenes, which presumably did take place, in the course of which a housemaid probably allowed me to play with her breasts, but then pressed my head between her legs, so that I became frightened and felt I was suffocating. This is the source of my hatred of females: I want to dissect them for it, that is, to kill them." [pp. 60–61]

Sexual trauma in childhood has been a factor in the lives of other psychoanalytic pioneers such as Freud (Krüll 1986), Jung (McGuire 1974), and Rank (Goldwert 1986).

If Ferenczi were to communicate to Freud about the difficulties in their relationship, symbolized by the "Confusion of Tongues" paper, he might have said the following:

I know about the experience of sexual and emotional trauma firsthand. That is why I can acknowledge it in my analysands, that is why I can listen to them when they tell me they have been abused.

I want you to listen to the idea of sexual and emotional trauma in my COT paper because you have always had difficulty with this idea. Originally you believed in trauma, but ever since you abandoned your clinical studies and focused on your oedipal theory you have been closed to this idea.

Early in my relationship with you, on your Sicily trip, I tried to get you to deal with the emotional components in our relationship, but you felt it was my problem (see Chapter 3, this volume).

Then in my analysis with you I tried to go deeper into our relationship and tell you of the trauma, but once again, you could not listen.

My COT presentation is my final attempt to convince you that I, like my analysands, have been traumatized by childhood experiences. What is more, I have also realized that I can repeat the analysand's trauma in the analysis when I behave in a detached, cool, clinical way, interpreting their needs as resistances. It was only when I liberated myself from the taboos of psychoanalytic technique and softened my analytic superego that I could respond to them in a human, healing way. This is the kind of response I want from you.

Why can't you give it to me? Why do you insist that I am trying to undermine your theories? Why do you condemn me for my clinical observations? Don't you see my pain? I am traumatized by your way of relating to me. You treat me like a bad child, who has disobeyed the parent.

You make me feel I am crazy because I have these ideas about trauma. . . . I know you can't deal with these issues in a direct, open way. You are too wedded to your theory and to being the father of psychoanalysis to hear me. But I know that my trauma, my analysands' trauma, and the trauma I am experiencing with you have similar elements. This is what I am trying to convey in my COT paper.

The confusion of tongues between Ferenczi and Freud can be viewed as follows:

1. Ferenczi's attempt to gain tenderness and affection from Freud.

2. Ferenczi's desire to communicate his childhood sexual trauma to Freud.

3. Freud's attack (psychological rape) on Ferenczi, misinterpreting the "Confusion of Tongues" paper as an attack on his theory, position, and leadership.

4. Ferenczi could not speak of the feeling of attack and condemnation openly, directly, to Freud. He needed Freud's approval, tenderness, and affection.

5. Confusion, suppression, condemnation, and trauma developed out of the experience.

6. Freud was traumatized by his feeling that his favorite son turned away from him, but he couldn't speak of the trauma in relational terms. He could not see it as a two-person psychology (an emotional and interpersonal experience between them, with both contributing to the experience and both needing to examine their contribution and arrive at a resolution in a mutual way).

7. Freud aggressed against Ferenczi still further by trying to suppress his presentation and then suppressing the publication of the "Confusion of Tongues" paper in English. When Ferenczi tried to gain some last minute tenderness from Freud in their last meeting, Freud turned his back on him. The confusion of tongues trauma was complete. Ferenczi spent his last days physically traumatized from his bout with pernicious anemia and emotionally traumatized by Freud's rejection and aggression against him.

Confusion of Tongues between Ferenczi and Society

The public announcement of Ferenczi's (1933) idea that " . . . children of very respectable, sincerely puritanical families fall victim to real violence or rape much more often than one had dared to suppose . . ." (p. 161), made at the Wiesbaden Conference, clearly suggested that Hungarian, Viennese, and Eastern European society contained professional, business, and political leaders who were involved in sexually abusing their daughters. Respectable fathers were sexually seducing their mostly female children. But he also suggested that women were also seducing young men (e.g., governesses, nursemaids, tutors, family relatives, and friends).

Eastern European society preferred to remain in denial about child molestation. The reluctance of society in Ferenczi's time to acknowledge childhood seduction paralleled the analytic community's wish to deny. Ferenczi was saying that fathers were seducing their daughters and that analysts were seducing their patients; both ideas were unacceptable.

Creation of a Corrective Emotional Experience through Empathy, Mutuality, Responsiveness, and Tenderness

In order to create a nontraumatic experience for an analysand who had suffered sexual seduction or emotional abuse as a child, Ferenczi argued for a revision of the traditional analytic situation to include a more interpersonal encounter based upon a democratic partnership where empathy was an essential ingredient in the intervention process.

The analyst creates a responsive emotional atmosphere when the analysand's feelings, especially feelings of anger derived from the child-hood abuse, are transferred onto the analyst and responded to with empathy. What is particularly important is that the analyst does not assume a coolness and evoke an interpretation of resistance to the critical and angry comments by the analysand. In this new method of psycho-analysis, the analyst accepts rather than interprets. He or she empathizes with the analysand's traumatic past that gave rise to suppressed rage. The analyst also searches his or her own functioning to detect the reality of the analysand's criticisms and rage. Ferenczi was able, like no other analyst of his era, to examine his own functioning to see what contribution he made to the re-creation of the trauma within the analytic situation. He practiced self-criticism, perhaps putting himself at emotional risk in order to empathize with these difficult cases (Gedo 1986a). Ferenczi (1933) wrote

> However, as the state of the patient, even after a considerable time, did not change in essentials, I had to give free rein to self-criticism. I started to listen to my patients when, in their attacks, they called me insensitive, cold, even hard and cruel, when they reproached me with being selfish, heartless, conceited. . . . Then I began to test my conscience in order to discover whether, despite all my conscious good intentions, there might after all be some truth within these accusations. [p. 157]

When he realized that his patients were inhibited in their criticism of him, Ferenczi encouraged them not to spare him in any way. Even with such encouragement, he found his patients reluctant to be open in their expression of dissatisfaction with their analyst's behavior.

Ferenczi believed that his concept of identification with the aggressor explained the reluctance of analysands to express their negative feelings to their analyst because they identify with him or her.

> . . . the patients have an exceedingly refined sensitivity for the wishes, tendencies, whims, sympathies, and antipathies of their analyst, even if the analyst is completely unaware of this sensitivity.
>   Instead of contradicting the analyst or accusing him of errors and blindness, the patients *identify themselves with him* . . . normally they do not allow themselves to criticize us. [p. 158]

Curative Factors for the Confusion of Tongues Syndrome

Ferenczi's recommendations for therapeutic cure of the confusion of tongues syndrome was also revolutionary. He suggested several important deviations in traditional technique.

The rule of empathy (Ferenczi 1928b) was introduced to give the analyst the capacity to respond to the subjective experience of the analysand, rather than solely to evoke a resistance or transference interpretation. Ferenczi found that the more he attuned to the subjective experience of difficult analysands and did not offer interpretations, the less resistant and open they became (a finding that Kohut verified forty years later). The use of empathy, or tact, as it was originally termed, was particularly necessary for individuals who were survivors of trauma.

Ferenczi actually introduced the concept of therapeutic empathy into psychoanalysis in his 1928 "Elasticity" paper (Rachman 1988a) and elaborated on it in a series of other publications during the latter part of his clinical career (Ferenczi 1930b, 1931, 1932c, 1933; see also Chapter 12, this volume).

The rule of empathy was also introduced to create an empathic and democratic atmosphere in the psychoanalytic situation. It must be remembered that the ambience of a psychoanalytic session was not considered a factor until Ferenczi began his clinical experiments, first with his active methodology and, then, his humanistic techniques. His deviations in technique were intended to explore the optimal responsiveness that would encourage a continued flow of associations, allow uncovering of unconscious material, and enhance the working-through process. The "Confusion of Tongues" paper addressed the issue of changes in the psychoanalytic situation from the vantage point of Ferenczi's clinical experience from roughly 1924, when he wrote the groundbreaking monograph with Rank, *Developmental Aims of Psychoanalysis* (Ferenczi and Rank 1925), through 1932, when he was empathically attuned to the relational dynamics of his clinical work with sexually and emotionally traumatized analysands. In a rare combination of intellectual and emotional response, he became aware that a more open, honest, and democratic interaction was needed in the analysis of difficult cases. To this end he pioneered several humanistic dimensions of the psychoanalytic situation.

Ferenczi developed five basic techniques to encourage his new humanistic psychoanalysis. He was the first analyst to seriously develop Freud's discovery of the countertransference reaction and apply it to understanding the therapeutic process. Prior to Ferenczi's explorations in humanistic psychoanalysis, the Freudian method linked countertransference to temporary stalemates in the analysis due to blind spots (Freud 1910b, 1915, 1931, 1937). Ferenczi extended the concept of countertransference to include the analyst's emotional reactions as an indication of the truthfulness of the analysand's feelings about the interaction and the relationship with the analyst (see Chapter 14, this volume). This revolutionary attitude paved the way for the interpersonal and humanistic view of countertransference (Balint 1933, 1949, Balint and Balint 1939, Little 1951, 1960, Searles 1979a, Winnicott 1949).

Ferenczi became excruciatingly aware of his countertransference and the need to be empathic as a result of his work with adults who were sexually abused as children. Their abusive experiences left a traumatic legacy that seriously affected their relationship with all other adults. In the analysis, the effects were clearly visible in their inability to form a positive transference to an analyst who practiced in the traditional manner (the detached observer).

Ferenczi (1933) was critical of himself as well as of Freud and the analytic community: "Small wonder that our effort produced no better results than the original trauma" (p. 160). But Ferenczi was not being critical to be mean-spirited. His purpose was the further development of the empathic method. He was actually following in the footsteps of his mentor. Freud had discovered his analytic method by analyzing his own dreams. Ferenczi was discovering his empathic method by analyzing his countertransference reactions.

The self-criticism was aimed at detecting the countertransference so that the analysis would not re-create the traumatic past.

> The setting free of his critical feelings, the willingness on our part to admit our mistakes, and the honest endeavor to avoid them in future all go to create in the patient a confidence in the analyst. *It is this confidence that established the contrast between the present and the unbearable traumatogenic past*, the contrast which is absolutely necessary for the patient in order to enable him to re-experience the past no longer as hallucinatory reproduction but as an objective memory. [Ferenczi 1933, p. 160]

The change from the Freudian technique to the empathic method was Ferenczi's creation of a successful second analysis from a failed first attempt, rediscovered by Kohut (1979) over forty years later in the "Two Analyses of Mr. Z."

As mentioned, Ferenczi encouraged the analyst to renounce professional hypocrisy. His empathic method was developed to the fullest when he recognized that genuine sincerity and emotional attunement were the only techniques to reach a traumatized individual.

> I may remind you that patients do not react to theatrical phrases, but only to real sincere sympathy. Whether they recognize the truth by the intonation or colour of our voice or by the words we use or in some other way, I cannot tell. In any case, they show a remarkable, almost clairvoyant knowledge about the thoughts and emotions that go on in their analyst's mind. To deceive a patient in this respect seems to be hardly possible and . . . it leads only to bad consequences. [Ferenczi 1933, p. 161]

Honest emotional communication and expression are the means by which empathic contact is maintained. He introduced the technique of analyst self-disclosure.

> . . . perhaps we feel unpleasantly disturbed in some professional or personal affair by the analytic session. . . . I cannot see any other way out than to make the source of the disturbance in us fully conscious and to discuss it with the patient, admitting it . . . as a fact. [pp. 158-159]

Ferenczi believed that therapist's self-disclosure would not harm the analytic process. In fact, he suggested that it would improve matters: "It is remarkable that such renunciation of the 'professional hypocrisy'—a hypocrisy hitherto regarded as unavoidable—instead of hurting the patient, led to a marked easing off in his condition" (p. 159).

Ferenczi said that the result of therapist honesty is a positive change in patient functioning. It reduces the possibility of reproducing the trauma in the analysis: "The traumatic-hysterical attack, even if it recurred, became considerably milder, tragic events of the past could be reproduced in *thought* without creating again a loss of mental balance; in fact the level of the patient's personality seemed to have been considerably raised" (p. 159).

Ferenczi was a leader in stating that a training analysis is a fundamental requirement for the development of an analyst. In the "Confusion of Tongues" paper, he extends this idea in his notion of the analysis of the analyst. He argued against a didactic analysis, which originally lasted from a few months to one and a half years. Ferenczi's own analysis with Freud was conducted over a several-week duration on two occasions. He was not only dissatisfied with the duration but also with the lack of depth, criticizing Freud for his unwillingness to explore the negative transference (Ferenczi 1932c). Ferenczi wanted the analyst-in-training to have a therapeutic experience that lasted as long and was as deep as the ones that analysts were providing for patients. If analytic candidates were not well analyzed, down to rock bottom, it could lead to an impossible situation, in which our patients become better analyzed than the analysts. Such an inequity in the emotional capacity of the analyst vis-à-vis the analysand would produce a confusion of tongues in analyses conducted by analysts who have been improperly analyzed. What would happen in such an instance is that, as Ferenczi (1932c) wrote, " . . . although they may show signs of such superiority [been better analyzed], they are unable to express it in words; indeed, they deteriorate into an extreme submissiveness obviously because of this inability or because of a fear of occasioning displeasure in us by their criticism" (p. 158).

In order to ensure an empathic, nontraumatic interaction in the analysis, the final recommendation was for the analyst to have a thorough training. Ferenczi had always advocated a personal analysis for the analyst. When he entered analysis with Freud in 1917 he was the first to do so for training purposes. Jones (1959) therefore was incorrect in asserting that he himself was the first to undergo a training analysis.

On the basis of his soul-searching work with the trauma cases of childhood seduction, Ferenczi became aware, as never before, that the analyst's personality was a crucial factor in the analysis. The final note to such soul-searching training analysis is that the analytic situation can retraumatize the patient if the analyst's personal vulnerabilities are now known to him. " . . . we must discern not only the painful events of their past from their associations, but also—and much more often than hitherto supposed—their repressed or suppressed criticism of us" (Ferenczi 1933, p. 158).

After his clinical experiments with the role of activity in psychoanalysis, Ferenczi realized that he had gone too far in implementing Freud's rule of abstinence. The activity had in some instances encouraged resistances as Ferenczi became perceived as an authoritarian parental figure.

Realizing the negative effect that such activity was having, he introduced a new role for the analyst—all changes in technique should occur from the principle of relaxation (Ferenczi 1930b). The psychological atmosphere in the psychoanalytic situation should be characterized as relaxed, free, affective, warm, responsive, empathic, and sincere, not cool, objective, intellectual, and reserved. Furthermore, that ambience should be of tenderness and affection.

These ideas about a relaxed ambience found their way into self psychology many years later when Kohut (1984a) talked about the empathic stance of the analyst.

In "The Confusion of Tongues," Ferenczi further developed the principle of relaxation as a curative element in the analysis of the incest trauma, which was also being chronicled in his *Clinical Diary*, written at the same time (Ferenczi 1932c).

Mutual analysis.   Ferenczi's concept of mutual analysis was gradually developed over the course of his final clinical period (1928–1933), but most dramatically reported in his *Clinical Diary* (1932c). It should be seen as an experimental procedure, in that he explored the limits of the therapist's contribution to the treatment process by inviting the analysand to become the source of therapeutic information. The analysand's perceptions, feelings, and conceptual ideas about the analyst's behavior and the nature of the relationship and the method of interaction became the focus of the analysis. Ferenczi was aware that he was taking a risk in encouraging this revolutionary process, as is witnessed in this entry in his *Clinical Diary*.

Thus I would be confronted with the possibility that people who are complete strangers to me will come into full possession of my most intimate, most personal emotions, sins, etc. Consequently, I either have to learn to accept the impossibility, even madness of this whole idea and technique, or I must go on with this daring enterprise and come around to the idea that it really does not matter if a small group of people is formed whose members know everything about one another. This could even facilitate relations . . . in contrast . . . [to] mutual secrecy, suspicion . . . (Ferenczi 1932c, p. 74).

This attuning to the analysand's view of the therapeutic process, as well as the belief that the analysand's view was as significant as the analyst's, was truly revolutionary. It challenged the traditional medical model of therapy in which the analyst is the physician who administers the cure to the patient. It also challenged traditional analytic concepts of resistance and transference interpretation. The analyst, in a Ferenczian analysis, would first search his or her own functioning to see whether the criticism of the analysand had validity before considering it a resistance or evoking a transference interpretation.

The issue of granting the analysand a mutual contribution to the therapeutic process was an essential part of the humanistic psychotherapy of Rogers (1961, 1967, 1980, 1986) and was reintroduced into psychoanalysis by Kohut (1971, 1977, 1978b, 1984a).

Freud's Confusion of Tongues with Ferenczi

With the publication of Ferenczi and Rank's 1925 essay on the shortcomings of Freudian psychoanalysis, the relationship between Freud and Ferenczi began slowly to deteriorate. The book was the first within the analytic community to be openly critical of Freud's theories and methods. Although Freud did not react angrily at the time, his followers were alarmed at the dissidence and warned him of a potential heresy (Roazen 1975). What is also important is that the essay marked the start of a hidden separation and individuation process for Ferenczi, during which he began to develop his own ideas more fully. As Fromm (1959) has pointed out, Freud had great difficultly throughout his life with disciples who began to show signs of separate thought and functioning. However, it is Fromm's contention that Freud mistreated Ferenczi in a particularly mean-spirited way.

In one of the darkest moments in the history of psychoanalysis, a plan developed to suppress the ideas and techniques that Ferenczi outlined in "The Confusion of Tongues." The suppression caused a trauma for Ferenczi, Freud, and the analytic community that has taken many years to heal (Balint 1968a). The major players in the suppression of Ferenczi were Freud and Jones. Freud's role centered around preventing Ferenczi from reading his paper at the Wiesbaden Conference. As was the custom when Freud was alive, all the psychoanalysts who were the original members of the Society of Rings would show their scientific papers on psychoanalysis to Freud for his comments before presenting them at a conference. This served two basic functions. One was to have the benefit of the master's comments, thinking, and criticisms on their ideas of theory and technique. A paper would be better with the benefit of Freud's brilliant mind scrutinizing the material. But there was an additional, darker function not usually acknowledged. Freud's approval apparently was based upon the extent to which the analyst's ideas, both theoretical and clinical, adhered to the tradition of psychoanalysis he had established.

Freud's Suppression of Ferenczi's "Confusion of Tongues" Presentation

The suppression of Ferenczi's confusion of tongues ideas occurred in two phases. First was the suppression of the paper at the Wiesbaden Conference. There is a series of letters, not yet published in English, that detail this process of suppression. (At present, the first volume of the Freud/ Ferenczi correspondence has been published in English [see Brabant et al. 1993a]. Volumes 2 and 3 are being prepared. The translations cited here are from volume 3, as yet unavailable in English. These materials are translations of some of the French citations. The author is grateful to Sylvie Teicher Kamens for help with these translations.)

A very significant interchange is contained in several letters between Freud and Eitingon, which chronicled the attempt at suppression. First, Freud mobilized the Society of Rings to back his move against Ferenczi. Freud wrote to Eitingon on August 29, 1932, "He must be prevented from reading his essay. Either he will present another one, or none at all. . . " (Sylwan, 1984, p. 10).

Next Freud sent a telegram to Eitingon on September 2, 1932 (Sylwan 1984). "Ferenczi read me his paper. Harmless. Stupid. Another way [for Ferenczi] to be unreachable" (p. 109).

Ferenczi had the courage to persist in his desire to present his clinical findings over the objections of Freud and the members of the Society of Rings. On September 27, 1932, after the infamous last meeting between Freud and Ferenczi and before the Wiesbaden Conference and the "Confusion of Tongues" presentation at the 12th International Congress, Ferenczi wrote to Freud to regain some semblance of a cordial relationship (Sylwan 1984). "The other unpleasant surprise is your insistence that I abstain from publishing. To this day, I cannot admit what I say can harm me, or harm the cause" (p. 107). Ferenczi realized that their last meeting was a trauma for both of them, that he maintained fond memories of past meetings and he admitted he lacked the courage to disclose his deviations in theory and technique to Freud.

Freud responded on October 2, 1932, to Ferenczi's attempt at reconciliation, but it was clear from these two letters that he was traumatized by the whole affair and the feeling that, in giving the "Confusion of Tongues" presentation, Ferenczi had irrevocably moved away from Freud and the Freudian tradition (Sylwan 1984). ". . . you have been asked to renounce publishing . . . for a year . . . a demand made primarily in your interest . . . [that] you would recognize yourself the technical errors of your technique and the limited validity of your results" (p. 111). Freud then rescinded his prohibition on Ferenczi publishing the COT paper. But Freud goes on to accuse Ferenczi of turning against him and wanting to defect, being unable to accept Freud's criticisms of his new techniques.

Freud wrote to Ferenczi again on January 11, 1933 (Sylwan 1984). Freud had hardened himself to any reconciliation with Ferenczi, believing his student was beyond help and that he was not responsible for the problem: ". . . and my consolation is the certitude that my own contribution to this change has been minimal. There is in you the work of some psychological fatality" (p. 112).

The Final Wound: Freud's Rejection of Ferenczi

To understand the trauma Ferenczi suffered over the "Confusion of Tongues" presentation, one only needs to focus on these words that Ferenczi told to De Forest about his last meeting with Freud, when he visited Freud before the Wiesbaden Conference to gain his approval for his ideas.

> When I visited the Professor I told him of my latest technical ideas. I have tried to discover from my patients their association of ideas, the way they behave, especially toward me, the frustrations which arouse their anger or depression, and . . . the manner in which they suffered rejection at the hands of their mothers or their parents or surrogates. I have also endeavored through empathy to imagine what kind of loving care . . . the patient really needed at that early age . . . which would have allowed his self-confidence, his self-enjoyment, to develop wholesomely. Each patient needs a different experience of tender, supporting care. . . . It is possible to sense when I am on the right track; for the patient immediately uncon-

sciously gives the signal by a number of slight changes in mood and behavior. Even his dreams show a response to the new and beneficent treatment. This should be confided to the patient. . . . Whenever mistakes are made by the analyst, the patient again gives the signal by becoming angry or despondent. And his dreams make clear the analyst's errors. . . . The analyst must then continue his search for the beneficent treatment, so deeply needed by his patient. This process is one of trial and error with eventual success, and must be pursued by the analyst with all skill and tact and loving-kindness, and fearlessly. It must be absolutely honest and genuine.

The Professor listened to my exposition with increasing impatience and finally warned me that I was treading on dangerous ground and was departing fundamentally from the traditional actions and techniques of Psychoanalysis. Such yielding to the patient's longings and desires . . . would increase his dependence on the analyst. Such dependence can only be destroyed by the emotional withdrawal of the analyst. In the hands of unskilled analysts my method, the Professor said, might easily lead to sexual indulgence rather than be an expression of parental devotion.

This warning ended the interview. *I held out my hand in affectionate adieu. The Professor turned his back on me and walked out of his room.* [Fromm 1959, p. 65 n3, italics added]

Jones's Suppression of the Publication of "The Confusion of Tongues" Paper

Jones shared Freud's view that the "Confusion of Tongues" should not be presented or published. Originally, Jones, as editor of the *International Journal of Psycho-Analysis*, promised his former analyst that he would publish the paper. After Ferenczi died, Jones began his plans to suppress the publication of the paper. (The issue of Jones's animosity to his analyst has been the subject of much discussion among Ferenczi historians — Covello 1984, Dupont 1988a, Rachman 1989a, Roazen 1975, Sylwan 1984.)

As in 1925, when Ferenczi and Rank's "Development of Psychoanalysis" had become public, Jones saw the "Confusion of Tongues" paper as heretical. He apparently shared the negative opinion of other senior analysts regarding Ferenczi's talk.

Jones lied to Ferenczi when he told him he would publish the paper (Masson 1984). Ferenczi wrote to him on March 22, 1933 (Masson 1984):

"I thank you for wanting to publish my Congress paper in the English Journal" (pp. 151-152). Jones did not have the courage to tell Ferenczi his true feelings (Masson 1984), and Ferenczi never learned of Jones's insincerity.

After Ferenczi died, Jones found the courage to express his views on the "Confusion of Tongues" openly to Freud in a letter on June 3, 1933 (Masson 1984).

> Eitingon did not wish to allow it [the paper] to be read at the Congress, but I persuaded him. I thought at the time of asking you about its publication in the *Zeitschrift*. I felt he would be offended if it were not translated into English and so asked his permission for this. He seemed gratified, and we have not only translated it but set it up in type as the first chapter in the July number. Since his death I have been thinking over the removal of the personal reasons for publishing it. Others also have suggested that it now be withdrawn and I quote the following passage from a letter of Mrs. Riviere's with which I agree: "Now that Ferenczi has died, I wondered whether you will not reconsider publishing his last paper. It seems to me it can only be damaging to him and a discredit . . . no good purpose could be served by it. Its scientific contentions and its statements about analytic practice are just a tissue of delusions, which can only discredit psychoanalysis and give credit to its opponents. It cannot be supposed that all *Journal* readers will appreciate the mental condition of the writer, and in this respect one has to think of posterity, too!" [Masson 1984, p. 152 (letter, Jones to Freud, June 3, 1933)]

As yet, Freud's response to Jones's desire to suppress the "Confusion of Tongues" has not been revealed. But there is a clue that Freud agreed with the suppression: in a letter to A. A. Brill on June 20, 1933, Jones wrote (Masson 1984), "To please [Ferenczi] I had already printed his Congress paper, which appeared in the *Zeitschrift* . . . but now, after consultation with Freud, I have decided not to publish it" (pp. 152-153).

Brill became another conspirator when he wrote to Jones on August 11, 1933 (Masson 1984): "I fully agree with you about the publication of his paper. The less said about this whole matter, the better" (p. 153).

It took sixteen years (1933-1949) for the paper to appear in English. In 1949, Balint translated the paper from the German (the English original proofs had been destroyed) and finally fulfilled Ferenczi's wish to have the paper published in English (Balint 1949).

Contemporary Applications of the Confusion of Tongues Theory

The confusion of tongues theory was one of the first unitary theories in psychoanalysis (Haynal in press). Its capacity to elucidate complex phenomena in a parsimonious way is one of its enduring qualities. Furthermore, it has the capacity to observe and analyze the emotional components in an authority/subordinate relationship where the authority figure is exercising power over the other individual.

As has been discussed, the importance of the "Confusion of Tongues" paper and its ideas was lost to several generations of analysts owing to the suppression of its publication in English. Even Ferenczi's celebrated students, like Balint, De Forest, Lorand, and Thompson, rarely referred to it, either in their descriptions of Ferenczi's work or their own elaborations on his clinical ideas and techniques. Apparently, they were influenced by the trauma that accompanied the presentation of the paper and its aftermath. A variety of explanations can be put forth to explain this neglect: they did not want to encourage a further breach in the analytic community, they did not want Ferenczi's reputation to be further maligned, they shared Freud's and the early psychoanalytic pioneers' negative assessment of the ideas and techniques in the paper.

It must be pointed out that certain historians and scholars of psychoanalysis, such as Dupont, Fromm, Masson, and Roazen, were exceptions to the condemnation and neglect of "The Confusion of Tongues" (Dupont 1988a, Fromm 1959, Masson 1984, Roazen 1975). This author has also been adding his voice to a new appreciation of the meaning and significance of the confusion of tongues theory (Rachman 1989a, 1991d, 1992a,b,c,e,f, 1993a,b, 1994b, 1996).

As an illustration of the application of the confusion of tongues theory to a new understanding of psychological issues, Freud's Case of Dora will be discussed from a Ferenczian framework (Rachman and Mattick 1994).

Freud's Confusion of Tongues with Dora

In Freud's (1905a) Case of Dora, he said the following in referring to their unsatisfactory relationship and her leaving analysis with him.

> Might I perhaps have kept the girl under my treatment if I myself had acted a part . . . and had shown *a warm personal interest in her—*

a course which . . . would have been tantamount to providing her with a substitute for *the affection she longed for*? I do not know. [p. 109, italics added]

It is clear that Freud could not imagine giving Dora any form of affection. Furthermore, he couldn't conceive of any relationship with her, other than a sexual one. Is this not a confusion of tongues, in that Freud interprets the demand for affection as a demand for sex? He also refers to Dora's homosexual love for Frau K. Freud never relates this to the fact that Dora has no functional relationship to her mother and that she might be expressing the need for tenderness and affection, not passion — the Ferenczian interpretation of such a demand. Freud insisted that she wanted passion, that she was conflicted about it and could not admit it. She broke off the therapy because, according to Freud, she could not admit that she wanted passion from her analyst. Freud had a confusion of tongues with Dora, misinterpreting tenderness for passion. His failure was in not encouraging her to discuss her mother, dismissing the mother as insignificant.

There were two issues in the psychoanalytic situation with Dora that have recently come under examination (Decker 1990). Freud's difficulty, if not failure, with Dora had to do with his lack of experience; he had not yet fully formulated the issues of transference and countertransference. He did not realize that during the treatment Dora had come to identify him with her father and Herr K., and he therefore did not understand the ways in which she perceived him as a threat. Second, Decker concluded that Freud failed to come to grips with his own emotions concerning Dora. She believed that Freud harbored erotic feelings toward his patient and that those feelings were accompanied by hostility and resentment. Such an argument certainly bolsters the idea of a confusion of tongues, since it suggests that Freud sexualized the relationship and then became angry. Rather than relate to Dora's need for tenderness, he was focused on the erotic components in the material, both from a personal and theoretical preoccupation. Freud's treatment of the Dora case may have been influenced by his need, at the time, to buttress the development of his ideas on the oedipal theory of neurosis, dream analysis, infantile sexuality, masturbation, bisexuality, and somatic illness.

The Emotional Meaning of the "Confusion of Tongues" Paper

The "Confusion of Tongues" paper is such an eloquent and phenomenologically revealing description of the world of a child who has been abused by a parent that it can be therapeutic to an individual who reads it. Such a reading can provide an affirmation of and help develop insight into the shared experience of sexual and emotional trauma. Analysands who are also mental health professionals have found the paper particularly helpful as an emotional statement of their struggles, so that reading it was a form of bibliotherapy.

Two analysands who are incest survivors and mental health professionals described their experience of reading the "Confusion of Tongues" paper. In the words of the first:

> This is the most realistic view of relations between adults and children that I have read. I applaud Ferenczi's ability to look at himself in relation to his patients. I also believe that the other theories should have been thrown out, and his followed.
>
> Actually, I feel like a child reading this, and like I am truly understood.

The other analysand's experience reading the paper is related as follows:

> A woman I know . . . recently handed me an article she was assigned to read for class. The article authoritatively described the existence of "repressed memory therapy" and the "lies of the mind" it is producing with devastating consequences on patients and families. I read this twisted piece of journalism as I was preparing to write down my thoughts for this article, and I remembered how deeply grateful I felt the first time I read Ferenczi's "Confusion of Tongues" paper.
>
> I am first and foremost grateful for Ferenczi. He was a man of not only compassion and empathy, but courage. As a woman who suffered through years of sexual abuse from my father beginning at age three, and who managed to repress all of these memories until age thirty-four, when I had stopped using alcohol and drugs, I am daily confronted with media articles about how my current knowledge of myself is incorrect. The dynamics of incest are such that, often, I want to believe these stories and say, yes, I made all this up. But to what end? Here is where I get stuck, because my memories serve no one but myself and in the end I am the one who suffers if I don't believe my truth. When I read Ferenczi, his words sear through my psyche like Excalibur, and I know I can have faith that at least one person understands the trauma and dynamics of incest.

Ferenczi was the first to describe to me the scene of the crime and the dynamics of seduction.

He says:

> A typical way in which incestuous seductions may occur is this: an adult and a child love each other, the child nursing the playful fantasy of taking the role of (husband or wife) to the adult. This play may assume erotic forms but remains, nevertheless, on the level of tenderness. . . . Adults . . . may mistake the play of children to the desires of a sexually mature person or allow themselves to be carried away [Ferenczi, 1933, p. 161].

Susan Sgroi, David Finkelhor, and others have described these dynamics since Ferenczi first presented this paper sixty years ago. These theorists describe in a scientific way the progression of the engagement between victim and perpetrator. But Ferenczi, with compassion and human words, describes the horrifying confusion of this interaction.

He describes why the children do not react, why they do not fight back. They are physically and morally helpless. The authority of the adult makes them dumb. According to Ferenczi, this same anxiety, if it reaches a certain maximum,

> compels them to subordinate themselves like automata to the will of the aggressor, to divine each of his desires, completely oblivious of themselves. As a result, in future events, the weak and undeveloped personality reacts to sudden *unpleasure* not by defence, but by anxiety-ridden identification and by introjection of the menacing person or aggressor (Ferenczi 1933, p. 162).

Ferenczi stated that his patients refused to react to unjust or unkind treatment of pain with hatred and defence. He says his patients arrive at the assumption of a mind which consists only of the id and super-ego, and which, therefore, lacks the ability to maintain itself with stability in the face of unpleasure. . . . Ferenczi suggests that the capacity for object-love must be preceded by a stage of identification, a stage of passive object-love or tenderness. These are some of the maladaptions which may occur when love, passion, and guilt are laden on an immature, guiltless, needy child. . . .

Not surprisingly, the first description that jumped out at me from Ferenczi's writing concerned why the adult acted as he did. He was confused. He was confusing tenderness for passion. When I went to my father for tender touches of affection, he thought I wanted to be sexual with him. This lets everyone off the hook! What a relief! I thought I could forgive my father and go on, never to have to deal with the effects of sexual abuse again. I did not know at this time how pervasive the emotional effects of this confusion were. As I first failed to see, the confusion not only affected my father, but also me.

I have lived a great part of my relational life completely confused. Although I am tall, very smart, educated, and well-spoken, in the face of abuse, I became tongue-tied. For the past twenty years I have been in a series of abusive relationships where I felt unable to talk back and say no or stop. My friends were always aghast at my reactions to public berating by a boyfriend who often was smaller and much less powerful than I. . . . Ferenczi spoke the words for me in his paper. I was reliving a trauma where my abuser was completely unconnected to my feelings, leaving me confused, feeling morally and physically helpless, and unable to speak the truth. My life question was, "Why are you hurting me?" This phenomenon would always occur in the face of interpersonal pain. I had no threshold for the normal scrapes and psychic bruises that often occur in love relationships. Nor surprisingly, I began using drugs and alcohol at an early age to avoid feeling this pain and to re-create the dangerous, but compelling, restful state of dissociation.

In my path of recovery I have had to first stop, or actively try to stop, using substances that keep me numb. These included alcohol, drugs, including cigarettes, overwork, abusive relationships, oversleep, and sugar. I had to come to believe that I would not die from my feelings and I could contain them within my adult body. One way I accomplished this was to imagine myself as a vessel for my feelings, a sort of alchemical container with a lid. Sometimes the feelings needed to be kept in to cook and change into something else and sometimes they needed to be let out. My goal was to be purposeful in my expression, not reactive. I was a beautiful, ancient, intricate, but hardy vessel, not a pressure cooker. Therapy and twelve-step programs are pivotal to my success in this endeavor.

Concurrently, I needed to stop focusing on the feelings of the aggressor. To this day I am still worried if I have hurt the feelings of someone who has treated me horribly! It is not a natural reaction for me to say, "That is enough, I won't take any more." I have needed to develop an understanding of what enough pain is. I was not able to integrate this growing up in a family where I had to experience unbearable trauma from a young age. I needed to stop concentrating on why someone was hurting me and start to practice saying, "Stop hurting me." This was an amazing transition for me.

I had never realized how paralyzing it is to focus on why someone else is acting the way he is. I had always prided myself on being psychic, and being able to figure out the other person's desires and needs. What a trap! My own need for control was being acted out through trying to second-guess the other person's desires and fulfilling them, rather than asking myself what I wanted. When I finally asked myself this question, I realized I did not have an answer at first. Interestingly enough, this answer has progressed from answers such as a child would have . . . to my present desires to become myself in partnership with other whole adults.

Ferenczi's focus on the confusion of passion and tenderness developed into a research project for me around the issues of intimacy and seduction. Here I found the personal and political arenas to explain the widespread occurrence of sexual abuse. All one needs to do it to look at the papers every day to see how confused we all are about this issue. We live in a culture where we think seduction is a positive thing! I soon realized that the one common component in all my abusive relationships, whether in business or love, was the seductive nature of the engagement. In the beginning all these relationships were too good to be true. And, they were; so, in the end, I always ended up feeling betrayed–the perfect scenario to reenact my relationship with my father and mother.

I became vigilant in my search to find out the difference between seductive and intimate relationships. I thought, if only I can find out this clue I can protect myself from abuse for the rest of my life! I interviewed people in abusive relationships and healthy relationships. This is what I thought I found. Seduction is fast, quick, and powerful. Intimacy is slow, equal, and tender.

I have at least now learned to say no, to know the feeling of confusion is now, and may always be, a big trigger for me, and if someone wants to carry me away to a desert island, don't go. I look for the answer to "why" less often, and do not let myself get paralysed by this question. Many spiritual programs say there is no answer to the question of why. . . . Many religions suggest a trust in God that is not possible for us without relinquishing the question of why. We have had to personally come to terms with one of the most difficult spiritual considerations: How can there be a God if there is such indiscriminate evil? But as Rilke says, by living the question and not expecting an answer we can go on and become richer in our lives and hopefully will never again ask the question, why are you hurting me.

The "Confusion of Tongues" paper can also have great meaning for individuals who are struggling with emotional trauma. A female psychologist delineates the universal appeal of the confusion of tongues theory.

Ferenczi's "Confusion of Tongues" paper (1933) catalogues the severest psychopathological adaptations materializing out of a complex matrix of caretaker dysfunctions. However, this paper is a psychoanalytic classic because it goes beyond its target population and offers an empathic bridge which spans the difference between the sexually abused and the non–sexually abused adult. Everyone staggers through a childhood fraught with wounding experiences of some sort with caretakers. Thus, a confusion of tongues becomes a maturational legacy, a conduit for the uneasy remembrance of our past naivete, gullibility, and ignorance in comparision with these adults, who towered over us like gods.

The "Confusion of Tongues" paper poignantly reevokes the inevitable denouement to childhood: adults are not always wise, truthful, and honest protectors, immune from the vagaries of vanity and folly. . . . The triumphant resurgence of his "Confusion of Tongues" paper and the reparative potential of his suggestions on how to stop the confusions is analogous to a fairytale ending. Ferenczi seems similar to the youngest child in the fairy tales, scorned by all as a simpleton or a dolt, but ultimately the only family member who can save the kingdom, confront his detractors, and then forgive them.

Personally, I read Ferenczi's paper during a difficult year characterized by strained relations with my antediluvian, authoritarian, and hierarchical analytic institute. The "Confusion of

Tongues" paper resuscitated my original belief that psychoanalytic training need not be discordant with my feminist ideology, or with practicing a multi-modal psychotherapy that included patient-informed and phenomenologically framed dimensions. He returned to me some measure of hope—in my past, I had found kindred spirits to unite with, and though I was now alone, I had not been "abandoned in my great distress" (Ferenczi, 1933) . I might yet again find another congenial coterie.

Healing Ferenczi's Confusion of Tongues Trauma

The negative reaction by Freud and the analytic community to the "Confusion of Tongues" paper created a trauma for Ferenczi. To this day, Ferenczi's reputation suffers because of these events. In an effort to redeem his reputation, it is necessary to add other voices to those who originally suppressed and censored this material.

Fromm (1959) had the following reaction to the paper: " . . . it is a paper of extraordinary profundity and brilliance—one of the most valuable papers in the whole psychoanalytic literature; it contains, however, certain important though subtle deviations from Freud's thought" (p. 165).

John Gedo (1986a) provides a final word of healing:

> . . . [Ferenczi's] "deviation" did not lead to a secession from psycho-analysis . . . his activities amounted to the formation of one of the psychoanalytic schools of his day. . . . Adherents of those schools believe themselves to be the true inheritors of the Freudian tradi-tion, albeit each school may define the essence of that tradition in a different manner.
>
> In contrast, former members of the psychoanalytic commu-nity who initiate anti-psychoanalytic movements . . . explicitly dis-avow sharing any premises with the Freudian heritage. Unlike such secessionists, Ferenczi continued to follow prevailing psychoanalytic observations and theories, except for matters about which he indi-cated explicitly that he disagreed with accepted views. [p. 39]

There is a need to heal the wounds of the Confusion of Tongues syndrome that traumatized Ferenczi's personal and professional life. By viewing his personal functioning and professional career with an empathic attitude, one can accept his daring and dissidence as part of the evolution of psychoanalysis. A new assessment of his work is beginning to reveal that he anticipated contemporary developments in psychoanalysis by fifty years (Basch 1984, Cremerius 1983, Gedo 1986b, Rachman 1978a, 1988a, 1989a).

14

COUNTERTRANSFERENCE ANALYSIS

FREUD'S INTRODUCTION OF COUNTERTRANSFERENCE

The term countertransference was first used by Freud (1910a) in a now famous statement:

> We have become aware of the "counter-transference," which arises in him [the psychoanalyst] as a result of the patient's influence on his unconscious feelings, and we are almost inclined to insist that he shall recognize this counter-transference in himself and overcome it ... no psychoanalyst goes further than his own complexes and internal resistances permit. [pp. 141–142]

In subsequent papers, shortly after the introduction of the concept of a countertransference reaction, Freud elaborated the importance of this new phenomenon. He initially considered countertransference as a hindrance, warning analysts not to reveal themselves in the process. "The doctor should be opaque to his patients, and, like a mirror, should show them nothing but what is shown to him ... (1912b, pp. 118).

Freud saw countertransference in this original formulation as an obstruction to the freedom of the analyst's understanding of the patient. In this manner, he regarded the analyst's mind as an instrument, being negatively affected in the analytic situation by countertransference (Freud 1913b).

Finally, Freud repeatedly stressed the analyst's psychological blind spots, indicated by the countertransference reactions (Freud 1912b, 1915, 1931, 1937). He first advocated a training analysis (Freud 1912b) and then later a reanalysis about every five years (Freud 1937) to reduce the influence of countertransference reactions in the analysis.

FERENCZI'S FOCUS ON COUNTERTRANSFERENCE

Like in many other discoveries of Freud, Ferenczi enthusiastically took up the banner and began to add his own special blend of technical, intellectual, and personal touches to the study and application of countertransference. Ferenczi became the first psychoanalyst to employ his countertransference reactions as a significant tool for understanding the analytic process and to contribute to the curative process, a point that Freud finally reached during his latter years (Freud 1937).

Freud clearly credits Ferenczi with making a significant contribution to our understanding of what constitutes a successful analysis and its natural endpoint. Apparently, both Ferenczi's thinking and his analysis with Freud strongly influenced the material in "Analysis Terminable and Interminable" (Gedo 1986a). The discussion has relevance for an understanding of countertransference.

Freud referred to Ferenczi's paper on the "Termination of Analysis" (Ferenczi 1927a). In it, he concluded that "analysis is by no means an interminable process" (p. 86). Freud felt that Ferenczi's warning, based on his years of experimenting with setting a time limit for the analysis, was well worth heeding. It became a watchword for psychoanalysis thereafter, as Freud (1937) summarized the idea: "The paper as a whole, however, seems to me to be in the nature of a warning not to aim at shortening analysis but at deepening it" (p. 247). The deepening of the analysis, to which Ferenczi turned his attention in the final phase of his clinical work, rests on his ideas about the participation of the analyst in the deepening process.

Freud, writing in 1937, made some remarkable statements regarding his concordance with the humanistic views that Ferenczi developed shortly before his death and that contributed to the near fatal conflict between them. Evidently, Freud had time to analyze his anger and his desire to censure Ferenczi and began to appreciate the focus on the analyst's contribution to the treatment process that his once favorite pupil had initiated. Freud stated his belief in this new focus for psychoanalysis.

Ferenczi makes the further important point that success depends very largely on the analyst's having learnt sufficiently from his own "errors and mistakes" and having got the better of "the weak points in his own personality." This provides an important supplement to our theme. Among the factors which influence the prospects of analytic treatment and add to its difficulties in the same manner as the resistances, must be reckoned not only the nature of the patient's ego but the individuality of the analyst. [Freud 1937, p. 249]

In the conclusions reached in Freud's famous paper on termination, it is difficult to discern his thinking from Ferenczi's. The ideas seemed fused. It is a fitting tribute to their twenty-five-year relationship, with all its difficulties, that in the years after Ferenczi's death Freud contributed to Ferenczi's ideas of the central role of the analyst's contribution to the treatment process. Note the ring of Ferenczi's thinking in Freud's discussion of the analyst's personal characteristics.

> . . . whereas the special conditions of analytic work do actually cause the analyst's own defects to interfere with his making a correct assessment of the state of things in his patient and reacting to them in a useful way. It is therefore reasonable to expect of an analyst, as a part of his qualifications, a considerable degree of mental normality and correctness. In addition, he must possess some kind of superiority, so that in certain analytic situations he can act as a model for his patient and in others as a teacher. And finally we must not forget that the analytic relationship is based on a love of truth — that is, on a recognition of reality — and that it precludes any kind of sham or deceit. [Freud 1937, p. 248]

Ferenczi's theory of psychopathology, which rests on the trauma theory and childhood seduction (De Forest 1942, Ferenczi 1933), and his technique of analysis, which centers on the empathic method (Ferenczi 1928b, 1930b, 1932c, 1933, Rachman 1988a, 1989a), focus on countertransference analysis to maintain the analytic process. His work with difficult cases (narcissistic, borderline, and psychotic disorders) was used to develop these ideas. The clinical work with difficult cases, which he was the first to undertake, necessitated the introduction of a two-person psychology, as Kohut was to do almost fifty years later (Rachman 1989a). It was natural to become aware of the analyst's personal reactions because difficult cases stimulate intense feelings. Rather than conceptualize these reactions as pathology or hindrances to the analytic process, Ferenczi considered the analyst's reaction to be an opportunity to promote greater understanding, warmth, and empathy with the analysand. He broke with tradition when he did not interpret the analysand's expressions of hostility or criticism as resistance in the transference. Rather, he took the outbursts as having some essential truth about the analysis. He examined himself for the contribution he had made to the feelings of the analysand. For example, he would say, "Perhaps that issue you raise is a problem of mine . . ." (Ferenczi 1928b, p. 24).

Ferenczi's concept of maintaining constant good will toward the patient in response to intense negative behavior by the analysand is another factor in the countertransference analysis. He spoke of how the analysand had the capacity to stimulate negative reactions in the analyst.

> One might actually speak of the patient's unconscious attempt consistently . . . to test the analyst's patience in this respect, and to test it, not just once, but over and over again. Patients sharply observe the physician's reaction, whether it takes the form of speech, silence, or gesture, and they often analyze it with great perspicacity. They detect the slightest sign of unconscious impulse in the latter, who has to submit to these attempts at analysis with inexhaustible patience. [Ferenczi 1928b, p. 93]

BALINT CONTINUES FERENCZI'S IDEAS ON COUNTERTRANSFERENCE

The development of a modern view of countertransference was influenced by Ferenczi through some of his students and their influence in the development of the British object relations approach to psychoanalysis. The Balints were among the first to develop Ferenczi's humanistic approach to countertransference. In their paper (Balint and Balint 1939), they questioned the now established Freudian notion of countertransference. By the late 1930s, Freud's early ideas about countertransference became solidified as the orthodox analytic position. This position has many elements to it.

1. It is a grave mistake to contaminate the transference situation by any means other than interpretations.
2. The task of the analyst is not to transfer any of his or her feelings onto the patient.
3. The analyst is to act on the basis of Freud's often quoted simile: "The analyst must behave like the surface of a well-polished mirror."
4. Analysis is comparable to a surgical operation and the behavior of the analyst with the sterility of the surgeon.

5. Transference is a one-sided process—it develops without any assistance from another person.
6. A certain passivity on the part of the analyst is also required, so as to maintain the role of a nonintrusive object and to maintain the sterility of the transference situation.

Michael Balint, in collaboration with his first wife, Alice, carried on Ferenczi's courageous deviations from the Freudian system with the publication of their 1939 paper. Ferenczi had deviated from the Freudian view of countertransference significantly by the 1930s, as he devoted his entire clinical energies to working with narcissistic, borderline, and psychotic conditions. In the papers on his emerging humanistic method, written in the 1930s, Ferenczi became immersed in the empathic method, attempting to develop a two-person psychology (Ferenczi 1928b, 1930b, 1931, 1932c). His *Clinical Diary* details even further the use of the analyst's reactions as a significant part of the analytic process (Ferenczi 1932c).

The Balints (1939) attempted to develop their discussion so as not to be critical of Freud and to create a climate for the acceptance of Ferenczi's ideas at the same time.

Returning to Freud's metaphor, we see that the analyst must really become a well-polished mirror—not, however, by behaving passively . . . but by reflecting without distortion the whole of his patient. The more clearly the patient can see himself in the reflection, the better our technique; and if this has been achieved, it does not matter greatly how much of the analyst's personality has been revealed by his activity or passivity, his severity or lenience, his methods of interpretation, etc. [p. 229]

What must be kept in mind is that the analytic community, just prior to and shortly after Ferenczi's death, was suffering from the traumatic effects of the Freud/Ferenczi conflict. The Balints were was very careful not to add to the trauma. But it is also very clear that Ferenczi's alternate view of psychoanalysis and countertransference is reflected in the Balints (1939) discussion.

1. Passivity and sterility are not desirable ingredients in the analytic process.
2. There are many personal elements in the process that are unavoidable.

3. Personal elements and the personality of the analyst are discussed privately, and even with interest, but scarcely, if ever, publicly.
4. There are differences in the analytical atmosphere that are brought about by the analyst.
5. There are significant differences in the style and manner in which different analysts conduct the therapy (e.g., the decorations in the office, how the hour is ended, how an interpretation is handled).
6. There are differences in the way analysts treat different patients (e.g., children, psychotics).
7. The different analytic atmospheres created by the analyst's personality influence the actual transference situation and, consequently, the therapeutic results.

FERENCZI'S DEVELOPMENT OF COUNTERTRANSFERENCE ANALYSIS

It is interesting to note that of all of Freud's original followers, Ferenczi was the only one who was impressed with the idea of a countertransference reaction and developed it into a significant new tool for psychoanalysis. There were some very meaningful reasons for this development.

1. Freud concentrated his efforts on the issue of transference, not only because it appealed to him theoretically, but because it maintained the focus on the patient and not the analyst.
2. Freud was more comfortable in the role of a theoretician than of a clinician; the shift to countertransference as a central issue in the analytic process would mean a greater focus on his own emotional contribution to the treatment situation.
3. The majority of the early pioneers who followed Freud looked to him as a role model for their own theoretical and clinical behavior. If he concentrated on transference as the focal issue in an analysis, so did they. There were only two followers of the original circle of seven (Freud, Abraham, Eitingon, Ferenczi, Jones, Rank, Sachs)—namely Rank and Ferenczi—who were developing their own ideas and methods.

4. Ferenczi's concern for empathy, his work with difficult cases, his emotional openness, and his dedication to healing and cure combined to move him in the direction of believing that countertransference analysis was a central aspect of the analytic cure. The concern for empathy meant that the focus was on a two-person psychology, where the analyst's interventions were examined in order to understand the analysand's negative reaction in the transference. The change from a resistance explanation to empathic understanding marked a significant shift in analytic focus.

Ferenczi was the first analyst to work with difficult cases for an extended period of time. His initial observations about narcissistic, borderline, and psychotic conditions have been verified by modern analysts (Kernberg 1974, Kohut 1968, Searles 1979a, Spotnitz 1979, Winnicott 1960b). The point is that working continuously and intensively with difficult cases, the analyst's own emotional reactions are being stimulated and become a constant part of the interactive process of the analysis. The question then arises as to what to do with the analyst's emotional reactions to the negative, erotic, dependent, and other feelings that are aroused. Ferenczi addressed this issue and experimented with a daring technique.

It is clear that Ferenczi's personality contained a significant degree of comfort and desire for openness and sharing. He brought these personal qualities to his analytic work. This led to a natural focus on the analyst's emotional participation in the process.

Ferenczi's dedication to healing was well known. He believed that there was no reason for abandoning a patient if he or she was willing to continue coming for analysis. He believed in working on the analyst's stance and emotional reaction in order to effect an analytic cure. This idea was prophetic, since it has now been established that effective work with non-neurotic individuals is dependent upon the analyst's capacity to confront his or her own subjective experiences in the analytic process (Balint and Balint 1939, Kohut 1984a, Little 1957, Racker 1968, Searles 1979a, Winnicott 1949).

With these considerations in mind, it is necessary to point out further that Ferenczi took the idea of a countertransference reaction and began to develop the notion of a countertransference analysis. A countertransference analysis not only acknowledges an emotional reaction in the analyst as part of the analytic process, but encourages the analyst to explore that reaction as part of his or her contribution to the treatment process. Ferenczi made many contributions to the analysis of counter-transference. This idea was to be even more fully developed in modern times by a student of Kleinian theory, Heinrich Racker. (It should be noted that Melanie Klein's first analyst was Ferenczi [Grosskurth 1986].) Racker's formulations centered on the essential contribution of the countertransference to the analytic process and the necessity for the analyst to examine his or her own sense of self in this process (Racker 1953). It is not a coincidence that a student of Klein's would extend Ferenczi's original contribution on countertransference analysis.

There are four basic areas in which Ferenczi contributed to the development of a countertransference analysis: becoming the analytic tool of countertransference analysis, a positive view of countertransference reactions, encouraging the patient's negative affect, and the analyst's self-disclosure and mutual analysis.

POSITIVE VIEWS OF COUNTERTRANSFERENCE REACTIONS

The Freudian system from the onset had incorporated a negative view of countertransference (Epstein and Feiner 1979, Gorkin 1987, Slakter 1987, Wolstein 1959). Ferenczi was the first psychoanalyst to criticize the Freudian view of countertransference, offering the view that far from being a hindrance, the countertransference was a significant part of the analysis.

De Forest (1954) best described this theory of countertransference.

1. It stressed the fact that it is the most essential tool of the therapist: one that must arise from his innate temperament, and one that is solely concerned with the patient's recovery of emotional health . . .

2. The essential character of countertransference is one of tenderness. It is the analyst's responsibility to offer . . . a setting of security and warmth, in which the patient, by means of his varying expressions in transference, exposes the unsolved problems of his infancy.

3. The context of the countertransference changes with the improving health of the patient:

a. From the careful and sympathetic study and observation at the beginning of treatment,

b. to the more matter-of-fact, meticulous and empathic examination of the patient's phantasies and behavior in a later period,

c. it progresses to the final "give and take" with the patient, as a person of equal emotional vigor. [pp. 122–123]

Ferenczi's positive view of countertransference emerged over a period of fifteen years or so, beginning with the period when he introduced his active method (Ferenczi 1919a,b, 1920, 1924b, 1925a,b). The active method began a change in the analyst's role from a neutral observer to an active respondent. The more active the analyst became in the analytic situation, the greater the possibility for a countertransference reaction. The traditional analytic stance had protected the analyst from intense emotional reactions because this clinical stance encouraged a more authoritative, distant, and one-sided interaction. Ferenczi initiated an interactive, open, and two-person stance in the analytic situation. During the last decade of his career, when he devoted himself exclusively to difficult cases (Ferenczi 1928b, 1930b, 1931, 1932c, 1933), the elaboration of the countertransference became the central pathway to the maintenance of his empathic method (Rachman 1989a) and the analysis of the psychopathology of childhood seduction and emotional trauma (Rachman 1989b).

Ferenczi's amplification and extension of the theory and method of countertransference laid the foundation for a modern view of the field. Ferenczi in Europe and Harry Stack Sullivan in the United States both challenged the negative view of countertransference. Balint became the conduit of the modern European view, echoing Ferenczi and providing a continuation of these views for the British object relations school. Sullivan, who greatly respected Ferenczi, sent Thompson to him for her second analysis. She became the conduit for the American expansion of countertransference.

ENCOURAGEMENT OF CRITICISM AND NEGATIVE AFFECT TOWARD THE ANALYST

The positive view of countertransference also encourages the analysand to freely express all feelings toward the analyst, including negative feelings, which are among the most difficult that can arise in the therapeutic interaction. No analyst before Ferenczi and few since have encouraged analysands to be so openly critical of them. Because Ferenczi did not react with distance, silence, retaliation, or defensiveness, the difficult analysand could use him as the container for his or her childhood rage toward parental figures. The empathic bond was put to its most difficult test as the analyst struggled to accept, understand, and therapeutically respond to the hostility, criticism, ridicule, or anger. In so doing, Ferenczi laid the groundwork for the object relations orientation to countertransference (Heimann 1950, 1960, Little 1951, 1957, 1960, Racker 1953, 1957, 1968, Winnicott 1949, 1960a).

Ferenczi urged analysts to take verbal attacks as serious statements about the emotional state of the therapeutic relationship and, most importantly, *not as inherent resistances* to the transference relationship. In his typical empathic manner, he wrote the following as a guide to future analysts to develop the capacity to therapeutically deal with negative reactions to the analyst:

> I started to listen to my patients when . . . they called me insensitive, cold, even hard and cruel, when they shouted at me: "Help! Quick! Don't let me perish helplessly!" Then I began to test my conscience in order to discover whether . . . there might after all be some truth in these accusations. [Ferenczi 1933, p. 157]

The notion that the accusations against the analyst contained kernels of truth was a remarkable shift in thinking and produced a new avenue for clinical function regarding countertransference. Ferenczi, when faced with a critical, hostile, or downright insulting analysand, began to search for the nature of the interaction as well as his own clinical and personal functioning, in order to listen to the subjective experience of the angry or hurt analysand. Freudian analysis had established the tradition that such outbursts of negative feeling were indications that the analysand was defending against aggressive or sexual drives and resisting the exploration of the transference. In this paradigm, the analyst does not search for kernels of truth in the interaction, which may have contributed to the angry outbursts, but interprets the analysand's psychodynamics as it pertains to transference. It is a one-person rather than a two-person psychology. To suggest that the patient could be expressing a righteous anger toward the analyst for untherapeutic behavior, which he or she could not discern on his or her own, was an outrageous and dissident point of view. Ferenczi was siding with his patients, not with Freud and the analytic community.

Ferenczi had the daring to depart from the established view of transference interpretations when a patient became angry or insulting and had the emotional courage to examine his own functioning to discern what contribution he had made to the interaction. The process he was initiating was twofold. By accepting the analysand's view of the defects of the therapeutic interaction, he was further establishing an empathic methodology. When analysts are faced with negative statements about the therapy, they are to search their method and soul for the truthfulness of the accusations. The mandate is to empathize with the underlying feelings of the angry and disgruntled patient. Secondly, analysts should establish countertransference analysis. They need to search out their own feelings about the patient and the nature of the interaction. Once analysts accept that their feelings contributed to the interaction, they must explore those feelings, both as they exist in the here and now and in their past history. The analysts then face a change in feeling and behavior in order to alleviate the negative experience of the analysand. Both the empathic method and countertransference analysis were essential aspects to a Ferenczian analysis because they acknowledged the essential sexual and emotional traumas of childhood as the source of the anger, ridicule, hostility, and dissatisfaction and helped to create a corrective emotional experience in the analytic situation.

ANALYST'S SELF-DISCLOSURE

As part of Ferenczi's work with his countertransference reactions, he took another daring and courageous step that helped establish a humanism in his analytic method. In a paper that inaugurated the empathic method in psychoanalysis (Ferenczi 1928b, Rachman 1988a), Ferenczi also took another step toward defining the analyst's role in the countertransference. By 1928, the Freudian notion that the analyst needed to maintain neutrality by remaining a mirror had been firmly established. Ferenczi introduced the notion that the analytic situation should possess a certain elasticity, a flexibility in functioning that allows for nontraditional behavior.

He became aware that the infallible authoritarian position of the traditional approach would not open up the analysis of countertransference. Furthermore, in order to make the analytic situation a more democratic and emotionally open experience, a greater frankness on the point of the analyst needed to be forthcoming. The analytic community may not have been prepared for Ferenczi's recommendation, although Freud did not seem to be against it (see Chapter 12, this volume).

Ferenczi called for analysts to open up the countertransference reaction to include the analyst's practicing self-disclosure. He took one of his boldest steps by suggesting that the analyst reveal his or her feelings in order to maintain the empathic relationship and to correct the therapeutic lapse that the countertransference reaction had initiated.

> One must never be ashamed unreservedly to confess one's own mistakes. It must never be forgotten that analysis is no suggested process, primarily dependent on the physician's reputation and infallibility. All that is called for is confidence in the physician's frankness and honesty, which does not suffer from the frank confession of mistakes. [Ferenczi 1928b, p. 95]

The benefit of admitting a therapeutic error not only earns the confidence of the analysand, but also contributes significantly to the healing of the original trauma of childhood. Ferenczi compared the attitude of hypocrisy or dislike for the patient to those attitudes in the patient's history and relationship to parents that originally led to the psychological illness, and he urged that the analyst confess those attitudes to the patient, to help create a new and sincere relationship (De Forest 1954).

The key to therapeutic success was a continual empathic relationship through the monitoring of the countertransference reaction. And the key to working through the countertransference reaction was the willingness to admit that the analyst had emotional reactions to the patient, that these feelings could be positive or, more important, intensely negative, that these negative reactions could be discerned by the patient, even at times when the analyst was not aware of them, and that the analysis would benefit from the analyst admitting these negative reactions to the patient, especially when the patient confronted him or her with them. The theoretical rationale for the analyst's confession of mistakes rests once again on Ferenczi's (1933) theory of trauma.

> The setting free of his [the patient's] critical feelings, the willingness on our part to admit our mistakes and the honest endeavor to avoid

them in the future, all these go to create in the patient a confidence in the analyst. *It is this confidence that establishes the contrast between the present and the unbearable traumatogenic past*, the contrast which is absolutely necessary for the patient in order to enable him to re-experience the past no longer as hallucinatory reproduction but as an objective memory. [p. 160]

The capacity to confess one's mistakes as an analyst directly to the analysand was no easy matter for Ferenczi. It involved several important factors. He needed to transcend his Freudian training, which put a premium on the analyst as an unrevealing object in the analytic situation. It was also necessary to move beyond the prescribed authority role for the physician that was so prevalent in European society in the early twentieth century. Of course, there were professional and personal issues to overcome. Ferenczi risked being viewed as a wild analyst and madman by telling patients that he was angry, bored, or frustrated with them. It is to his credit that he entered into this struggle.

When he gave what he considered to be a learned scientific interpretation and was met with rebuffs, Ferenczi had to deal with his personal reaction. He wrote, "I need hardly tell you that my first reaction to such incidents was a feeling of outraged authority. For a moment I felt injured at the suggestion that my patient or pupil could know better than I did." (Ferenczi 1931, p. 130). His profound understanding of the function of empathy in therapeutic interaction led him to recognize his countertransference reaction and to develop an innovative response: "Fortunately, however, there occurred to me the further thought that he really must at bottom know more about himself than I could with my guesses" (p. 130).

Ferenczi's attunement to the internal frame of reference of the other enabled him to respond in a self-disclosing way "I therefore admitted that possibly I had made a mistake, and the result was not that I lost my authority, but that his confidence in me was increased" (Ferenczi 1931, p. 130). Contemporary psychoanalysis is just beginning to view the benefits of analyst self-disclosure as a meaningful part of the analytic process (Gorkin 1987, Rachman 1990a).

MUTUAL ANALYSIS

Ferenczi's clinical experiments with mutual analysis were his most controversial technical innovations and the most misunderstood. Because he preserved this innovation in secrecy, without consulting Freud or any other colleagues, much of this discovery is shrouded in mystery. Ferenczi's clinical papers do not seem to refer to the technique of mutual analysis. There are two sources of information regarding this technique. One is the analysis of Severn (1920, 1934), and the other is Ferenczi's *Clinical Diary* (Ferenczi 1932c). Apparently, Severn had a profound influence on Ferenczi and may be credited with encouraging him to use mutual analysis (Masson 1984). It is clear from both Dupont's introduction and an examination of the *Clinical Diary* that, during Ferenczi's last year of clinical practice, 1932–1933, he experimented with the use of mutual analysis.

The technique of mutual analysis is based on the idea that the analyst can offer the analysand something of value at moments when he or she is unable to provide a correct interpretation or an empathic response. The least the analyst can do under such circumstances is be genuine about his or her inadequacy. It is assumed that all analysts have blind spots, countertransference weaknesses that they cannot control. The analyst actually needs analysands to tell about these weaknesses, since no one possesses total self-awareness or is in total control of his or her behavior at all moments of the analysis.

Basically, mutual analysis is the analyst trading places with the analysand, allowing the patient to analyze the behavior of the doctor. In other words, by creation of an empathic ambience, the analyst encourages the analysand to say what he or she may think or feel the analyst's problem is in the relationship or in his or her ability to respond.

Mutual analysis can become a lifetime process of personal and professional growth for the analyst because it provides a mirror through which the analyst can view his or her behavior. The mirror is the analysand and his or her reactions to the analyst's behavior. In order for this type of mirror response to produce personal growth in the analyst, several factors need to be present. The analyst must be willing to maintain a humble and inquisitive attitude that allows for a questioning of his or her theoretical assumptions, method, and techniques of therapeutic intervention, and personal contribution to the treatment process. Additionally, what is needed for this difficult task of mutual analysis is the desire and capacity for self-scrutiny. The analyst must be willing and intellectually and emotionally able to examine his or her own functioning as it is being reflected in the reactions of the analysand. Often, after one's training analysis has been completed, a certain closing off of feelings and self-exploration takes place naturally. It is as if the mind wishes to heal the emotional wounds stimulated by the opening up of conflicts and trauma. But to work regularly with difficult cases means to be willing to open up the wounds, inadequacies, conflicts, and uncertainties of our personal functioning and keep them open. It is a choice that many analysts are not willing to make.

Ferenczi was an emotional astronaut in his willingness to remain vulnerable and explore the deepest recesses of his own functioning in order to discern his contribution to the treatment process. There are those who feel he risked his own emotional well-being in practicing his humanistic method (Gedo 1986a). It must be understood that Ferenczi developed mutual analysis from his experiences with the most difficult of cases. It was an experiment of last resort (Dupont 1988b). What he realized was an essential truth in the analysis of difficult cases (narcissistic, borderline, and psychotic conditions). Individuals who have been severely traumatized develop a sixth emotional sense—the capacity to attune to the emotional unconscious of the other. Searles, building on this notion, developed the concept that the patient can help the analyst treat the patient (Searles 1979a).

The idea for mutual analysis occurred in the analysis of a particular case, R.N., reported in Ferenczi's *Clinical Diary* (Ferenczi 1932c). It is fitting that mutual analysis was actually the invention of the analysand, since mutual analysis stretches the notion of empathy to the limit. It is the analyst's attempt to respond to the expressed need of the analysand. So, if the analysand indicates that the only way he or she will be able to respond to the therapy being offered is a reversal of roles, it is a profound test of an empathic method to fulfill the need. Ferenczi's clinical genius was that he realized that the idea of mutual analysis needed to be responded to, as well as analyzed.

Ferenczi had been seeing R.N. for two years. During the first period of analysis, Ferenczi was aware that he had negative feelings about her. Instead of dealing directly with these feelings, he overcompensated and practiced his concept of indulgence and relaxation therapy (Dupont 1988b). An eroticized transference developed, where the indulgences led the analysand to believe she had found an ideal lover. Ferenczi retreated from his relaxation therapy and *returned to his active therapy technique* of confronting the analysand about her unexpressed negative feelings toward him. What happened next was a testimony to both the patient and Ferenczi. R.N. had the sense of self to respond to Ferenczi's intervention by offering him a mutual interpretation that suggested that *he had angry feelings toward her.* Ferenczi practiced analyst self-disclosure and conceded that R.N.'s interpretation had validity. This was another moment in psychotherapy history that Ferenczi had created. He had encouraged R.N. to freely express her feelings toward him, and, when she suggested that *he* was causing the therapeutic impasse, he did not counter with a resistance or transference interpretation. What he did do was to accept her interpretation of his behavior. Ferenczi became the patient, and R.N. was, for that moment, the analyst. The mutual analysis had very significant results. Ferenczi reported that the analysis made progress after a two-year stalemate, and he felt less anxious and more liberated (Dupont 1988b). With this initial success, Ferenczi initiated a formal experiment in mutual analysis, where sessions were alternated for the analyst and the analysand.

Ferenczi did not undertake the clinical experiments with mutual analysis without being aware of the difficulties and dangers involved. He was keenly aware that by putting himself in the hands of a patient, he was taking a risk: "This would not have been enough, however, had I, myself, not submitted to the unusual sacrifice of risking an experiment in which I, the doctor, put myself into the hands of a not undangerous patient" (Ferenczi 1932c, pp. 99–100). This quote clearly indicates Ferenczi's willingness to risk his own emotional safety in order to maintain an empathic connection. There are those who could see this as a sign of Ferenczi's instability; however, it can be viewed in a positive way. His dedication to healing, willingness to experiment, and desire to elasticize psychoanalysis so that it could become effective in difficult cases were special qualities that made him an exceptional clinician and a pioneer of psychoanalysis. He was willing to offer his personal gifts as a sacrifice to psychoanalysis and to his analysands. Furthermore, like all great explorers, he was willing to take a dangerous journey that others could not and would not make; exploring inner space—that dark, hazy, and vulnerable space in human contact, where two people attempt to negotiate the level of basic fault in order to discover their true selves.

Ferenczi was well aware of the difficulties and complications that mutual analysis presented. In three separate entries in his *Clinical Diary* in 1932, he discusses the dilemma and limitations of mutual analysis:

1. The risk of seeing the patient deflect attention from him or her self and search for complexes in the analyst in a paranoid way,

2. The impossibility of letting oneself be analyzed by every patient,

3. The imperative need to respect the patient's sensibilities, and
4. The problem posed by the discretion owed to other patients, whose secrets the analyst would in principle be obliged to reveal to the patient-analyst.

Ferenczi thus became aware that a mutual analysis guided only by the needs of one party (either analyst or analysand) is limited. In the case of R.N., it became clear to him that as a result of the experiment, the analysand was seriously distorting the interaction. Actually, what happened was that the therapeutic technique of mutual analysis itself became a resistance and an impasse. She developed ideas bordering on delusion that their collaboration was allowing Ferenczi to maintain his therapeutic skills. Looked upon from R.N.'s subjective frame of reference, there is truth in this observation. The mutual analysis did allow R. N. to become, at least temporarily, a therapist to her analyst and to help cure him of the neurotic difficulties he was having with her (Searles 1975, 1979b). For mutual analysis to be more effective, it needs to meet the needs of both the analyst and the analysand.

Ferenczi decided to terminate the experiment of mutual analysis with R.N. after he was convinced she had reached a period of near delusion about their collaboration. He reported that after a period of hostility and disarray, R.N. decided to carry on with the analysis in the usual manner and made substantial progress (Ferenczi 1932c).

On the basis of his clinical experiments with the technique of mutual analysis with R.N., Ferenczi reached the following conclusions, which he noted in a June 3, 1932, diary entry:

No special training analysis!

1. Analysts should be analyzed *better, not* worse, than patients. [Is Ferenczi referring to his limited analysis with Freud, where the master failed to deal with the transference/countertransference issues?]
2. At present, they are analyzed worse.
   a. time limit
   b. no relaxation (patient's expression)
   [Ferenczi was pointing out the difficulty of inadequate(ly) analyzed analysts analyzing difficult analysands. In their formal analysis, analysts were not benefiting from the relaxation therapy that Ferenczi provided to his analysands. Ferenczi's analysis with

Freud suffered from the formal, authoritative, and definitive manner in which such early training analyses were conducted (Wolstein 1990)].

3. If six to eight years required, impossible in practice. But should be corrected to repeated supplementary analysis. But even so, not quite satisfactory. [Ferenczi became aware in the course of this experiment that the length of analysis can be related to the difficulty of the countertransference. Training analysis, at this early pioneering time in psychoanalysis, did not yet include countertransference analysis as an integral phase of the analysis.]

4. A special group of truly analyzed persons—who have the ambition to know more than analyzed patients. [Ferenczi was calling for training analysis to go down to what he had termed *rock bottom*—that is, to work through the vicissitudes of the transference and countertransference in the manner he was attempting to do in the mutual analysis of R. N. But what analyst of his day would allow a democratic, vulnerable, and mutual relationship to flourish?]

5. Mutual analysis: only a last resort! Proper analysis by a stranger, without any obligation, would be better. [The experiment with R. N. had limited success, but it cannot be considered a failure, since, when Ferenczi returned to a conventional analysis, significant progress was made, presumably through the new technique. Furthermore, the experiment pioneered a change in process and function of psychoanalysis. The issues of analysts's blind spots, empathic failure, countertransference interpretations, and analyst self-disclosure are still the darker corners of psychoanalysis that bear continued illumination.]

6. The best analyst is a patient who had been cured. Other pupils must be first made ill, then cured and made aware. [Once again, Ferenczi is aiming his criticisms at the inadequate therapy in training analyses. The didactic analysis conducted primarily for training does not encourage a sufficient emotional experience of vulnerability. Analysts need to be patients when they are being analyzed, in the way he wished to be when he was in analysis with Freud. Considerations of frequency setting and availability influenced the course of the training analysis. But, in their analysis, Freud and Ferenczi failed to go rock bottom, because of Freud's need to be the master and Ferenczi's idealization of him.]

7. Doubts about *supervised analyses:* last resorts: recognition and admission of one's own difficulties and weaknesses. Strictly supervised by the patients! No attempts to defend oneself. [The experience with mutual analyses convinced Ferenczi that a patient had the special capacity to ascertain the empathic failures of the analyst. In some ways, one could suggest that the patient is in an excellent position to experience the empathic failure of the analyst as long as two conditions are met: (1) the patient has to be in a nonpsychotic transference; (2) the analyst is willing to be emotionally open to receive the information.] [Ferencezi 1932c, pp. 10–13]

It is essential not to lose the special significance of Ferenczi's daring and pioneering clinical experiment in mutual analysis, especially in the light of his own criticisms of it and of the incredible furor that was created (Ferenczi 1932c). Dupont (1988b), in her excellent introduction to *The Clinical Diary,* cautions us not to throw the baby out with the bathwater.

Indeed, perhaps all experimentation with mutual analysis is essentially the consequence of training analyses as they were practiced at the time, . . . rapid, fitful analyses, often undertaken abroad, in a foreign language, during walks or travel together or visits to the home of analyst or patient. . . . the questions raised by mutual analysis remain relevant, . . . How can the analyst successfully deal with weaknesses and blindness? [p. xxii]

Ferenczi's remarkable discovery of mutual analysis should not be lost or seen as a historical curiosity. He had the foresight and emotional courage to grapple with the issue of empathic failure in therapeutic stalemates. His pioneering use of countertransference as a two-person psychology naturally moved in the direction of mutual analysis. When R. N. pushed him further than others had done, he responded with an empathic response, not a resistance interpretation. Searching for the far reaches of empathic attunement was one of the essential elements of mutual analysis. He was attempting to search for a way of responding to the analysand, at a moment of therapeutic crisis, that did not blame the analysand for the stalemate and that encouraged a sense of understanding and emotional communion. This was what Ferenczi was trying to cure in the analysis he conducted and in the one Freud conducted with him. Mutual analysis is an attempt to use the analysand's awareness of empathic failures to help the analyst conduct a better analysis (Searles 1979b, Winnicott 1949).

It should be remembered that in relinquishing control in the analytic situation by developing the practice of mutual analysis, Ferenczi was showing a tender and loving attitude. Furthermore, he was empowering the individual in a two-person therapy. He was not afraid that there would be a negative effect in the analysis to grant the same power to the analysand as was granted to the analyst. There is embedded in the concept of mutual analysis, therefore, a humanistic assumption—that is, a belief in the capacity of the individual to use empowerment to grow, to trust the perception, thoughts, and feelings of an analysand as containing basic truths, and the healing and curative aspect of an emotionally vulnerable and mutual relationship between two human beings.

15

FERENCZI'S RELAXATION THERAPY AND HUMANISTIC METHOD

STAGES OF FERENCZI'S CLINICAL CAREER

If we trace Ferenczi's clinical journey, highlighted by two cases—Rosa K. in 1902 (see Chapter 2, this volume) and Elizabeth Severn in 1932 (see Chapter 17, this volume)—it is clear that a consistent humanistic technique is evident in his version of psychotherapy and psychoanalysis.

Ferenczi's technique of psychoanalysis developed over almost a thirty-year period, roughly from 1902 to 1932. His humanistic psychoanalytic method of his latter clinical period (1924–1932) was different from his initial work as a psychiatrist in his pre-Freudian period, yet the seeds for some of his humanistic method were evident in his earliest work. His clinical work can be divided into four phases:

I. Pre-Freudian Humanistic Psychotherapy: 1902–1908

This period was characterized by Ferenczi's clinical work with disadvantaged patients, such as the poor, criminals, prostitutes, and homosexuals. It was characterized by the humane treatment of such patients, which was contrary to the attitudes of many in the psychiatric and lay communities. He also began his clinical experimentation, developing innovative techniques. Ferenczi began the active involvement of the psychotherapist by directly demonstrating compassion and concern for patients and becoming involved in the medical and lay communities on behalf of patients.

II. An Enlivened Traditional Analysis: 1909–1912

During this period, Ferenczi became a Freudian analyst, but began to enliven this method. He encouraged a focus on the uncovering of childhood trauma, experimented with the transference relationship through the clinical experimentation of Freud's "rule of abstinence" (Freud 1915 [1914]) and introduced the integration of the personality of the analyst with the analytic process.

III. Active Psychoanalysis: 1913–1923

Ferenczi's clinical experimentation with the analytic method reached an intense level. He introduced the role of activity into analytic method. These innovations were characterized by (1) dramatic interaction, (2) encouragement of patient activity, (3) active participation of the analyst, (4) heightened emotional atmosphere, (5) use of prohibitions to delay gratification, (6) time limit for the analysis, and (7) active analysis of phobias, obsessions and compulsions, and sexual disorders.

IV. Humanistic Psychoanalysis: 1924–1933

In his last clinical period, Ferenczi began to break away from the orthodox Freudian theory and method. During this period, he introduced his confusion of tongues theory, the analysis of the incest trauma, a two-person psychology, the relationship as curative, and the necessity of the tender mother transference. Clinically, he developed relaxation therapy and the relaxation principle, empathic interventions, countertransference analysis, dramatic enactments, reliving and reexperiencing childhood trauma, analyst self-disclosure, and mutual analysis.

Ferenczi began his clinical career developing nontraditional techniques to meet the needs of his difficult cases and ended his career doing the same thing. It must be noted, however, that during his Freudian period (stage 2), when he was under the greatest emotional influence of Freud, there was a temporary suspension of clinical experimentation. But that quickly changed when Freud realized that in Ferenczi, psychoanalysis had its greatest innovator.

There are many factors that contributed to the perception that

Ferenczi did not develop an alternate method of psychoanalysis. Because Ferenczi became an alter ego of Freud, the psychoanalytic community did not see him as having ideas and methods different from Freud's. Ferenczi, as Fromm (1959) and Thompson (1944, 1950c) pointed out, was someone whose personality favored following a strong leader, rather than becoming that strong leader himself. He definitely had the charisma of a leader, but he did not exercise these natural talents to encourage people to join him in a new direction. It is clear that Ferenczi was a secret rebel (Thompson 1944) who was too concerned about receiving Freud's blessing for every clinical innovation he developed, no matter how serious a deviation it was from the Freudian method. Thompson (1944) commented on her mentor's difficulties in breaking away from his mentor, Freud: "During the period of active technique, Ferenczi was still following closely in the footsteps of Freud. Only the extreme lengths to which he carried the ideas might be interpreted as indications of his ambivalence and his real doubt as to the correctness of the method" (p. 248).

Thompson was with Ferenczi during the development of his humanistic method. She chronicled his deviations as well as the formal expression of his own ideas and methods.

> Ferenczi began to be aware that he differed in important ways from Freud's thinking; and he devoted the last six or seven years of his life to the development of his own ideas of the analytic situation.
>
> . . . I believe that here *at last* Ferenczi was seeking to express his own convictions—not Freud's—for the theory of his relaxation technique was based on his ideas of the child–parent relation. [p. 248, italics added]

Ferenczi's humanistic technique as it reached its peak can be found in the papers of his latter period of clinical practice (Ferenczi 1928b, 1930b, 1931, 1932c, 1933). In these publications, as well as in letters he may have written to Freud during the latter part of his clinical career (unpublished in English), he is clearly deviating from traditional Freudian psychology and definitely developing a new technology for psychoanalysis.

There is a long-standing tradition within psychoanalysis to acknowledge Freud's thinking and work as the precursor for any new development, no matter how clearly it is at odds with the prevailing idea of mainstream psychoanalysis. A second trend in this regard is to actually try to demonstrate that you are not deviating from Freudian thinking, but that your new idea or technique is actually inherent in orthodox thinking and practice. In essence, if you feel obligated to gain the favor of the traditional analytic community, you are compelled to demonstrate that you are not really deviating from mainstream psychoanalysis and that the development was stated in some work by Freud. Therefore, your innovation is merely a clarification of Freud's original thinking.

Ferenczi, as many authors have demonstrated, was a victim not only of the jealousy and conservatism of Freud's inner circle, but also of his own need to have Freud be his father substitute (Balint 1968b, Cremerius 1983, Haynal 1989, Roazen 1975, Thompson 1944). Ferenczi's need to please Freud while still wanting his approval for his daring deviations from Freudian theory and technique produced an intolerable situation that neither analytic giant could resolve. I would speculate that if Ferenczi were to have lived beyond his premature death due to pernicious anemia and survived the Holocaust, he would have been forced to break away from Freud. It is clear from his humanistic analytic period that as a secret rebel he had deviated so far afield from Freud that it would be preposterous to expect his mentor to acknowledge his deviations as remaining within conservative psychoanalysis.

Ferenczi's boyish enthusiasm for his ideas and his need to have Freud respond to his daring, as if he were his revolutionary-spirited father, created a dilemma for Freud, who although a revolutionary himself in his earlier years, became increasingly more concerned about protecting psychoanalysis from outside attack. He consequently surrounded himself with adherents who would not only protect him from attack, but also adhere closely to the rules he developed for theoretical and technical behavior. By and large, they were company men (Fromm 1959) who were delighted to be in the presence of genius and be part of a revolution. The followers who were daring, innovative, and free minded, like Jung, Adler, and Rank, had to leave the Freudian-based analytic community to find their own identity as analysts and individuals. Because these analysts were able to separate emotionally from Freud, they were able to become open and direct about their disagreement with their mentor. They were able to gather their own adherents who agreed with their own view of psychoanalysis. This allowed their ideas and technical innovations to evolve and flourish. Furthermore, institutes espousing the new vision of psychoanalysis were established to create and nourish alternative schools of psychoanalytic thought. One of the most damaging aspects of traditional psychoanalytic thinking is the attitude that there is only one correct psychoanalysis—that of the Freudian orientation. This attitude has stifled creativity, caused a great deal of emotional pain, and hampered the evolution of psychoanalysis and its contributions to society.

There are many Ferenczi scholars who firmly believe that the only way to be true to the spirit and intent of his thinking and contributions is to see his work as an extension of the Freudian system (Balint 1968a, Dupont 1988a,b, Gedo 1986a, Grünburger 1980, Haynal 1989, Hoffer 1985). There are some authors who view his work as being a serious departure (Basch 1984, Cremerius 1983, De Forest 1954, Fromm 1959, Rachman 1989a,b, 1990a, Roazen 1975, Thompson 1944). But no one has discussed Ferenczi's work as being the conduit for a new school of psychoanalysis. With all due respect to Ferenczi's desire to remain within the Freudian system of psychoanalysis (Gedo 1986a), his work is a departure not only from the Freudian school, but also from other alternative views of psychoanalysis, thus constituting a separate system. Thompson (1944), who was an eyewitness to as well as a participant in Ferenczi's humanistic clinical experiments, came closest of all psychoanalysts to believing that he was developing a new orientation. This did not mean she agreed with his deviations, because she was critical of some of them (Thompson 1942). Balint (1949), who was also a witness to Ferenczi's humanistic analytic work, never discussed his teacher's work as being the beginning of a new school.

Contemporary analysts usually place Ferenczi as the precursor for interpersonal psychoanalysis (Bacciagaluppi 1989, 1992, Fromm 1959, 1964, 1970, Thompson 1950a,b, Wolstein 1989, 1990) or object relations (Aron 1990, 1992) or self psychology (Bacal 1987, Bacal and Newman 1990, Basch 1984, Rachman 1989b). While one can make a meaningful case for his making a significant contribution to all three developments in psychoanalysis, his contributions constitute a separate designation of humanistic psychoanalysis, based upon the following criteria.

1. There is a theoretical departure that espouses the real experiences in the relationship between parent and child as the causal factors in psychological disorder.

2. Real-life trauma, rather than the internal conflicts of fantasy, are central to human behavior.

3. Conscious factors play a significant role in human motivation.

4. Sexual seduction in childhood is a significant real-life trauma occurring much more frequently than imagined. Furthermore, childhood sexual molestation is one of the most significant factors in the develop-

ment of psychological disorders, including neurotic, borderline, and psychotic disorders.

5. The nature of the relationship between the child and his or her parental figure is the most fundamental causative factor in human experience and personality development.

6. A confusion of tongues conceptualization explains the specific nature of psychological adaptation to trauma and continued emotional stress. In fact, this theory establishes an object relations psychoanalytic view of human development. Furthermore, it also concentrates on the nature of the issues of power, control, and status in analytic and general human relationships.

7. There is fundamental change in the theory of the oedipal complex, from biological drives of sex and aggression to disturbed object relations. The fundamental determinants of human behavior are to be found in the nature of the object relations in the family.

8. There is a new concern for the technical aspects of the analytic situation in order to create an empathic, democratic, responsive, and loving attitude. This includes a spirit of daring, innovation, elasticity, and creativity, in order to meet the needs of individual analysands.

9. The integration of active and humanistic measures guarantees the continuation of an empathic ambience as well as responding to the needs of the analysand.

10. There is a focus on the personality and functioning of the analyst in the development of a two-person psychology.

FUNDAMENTALS OF FERENCZI'S RELAXATION THEORY AND NEOCATHARTIC METHOD

Ferenczi (1930b) can be viewed as initiating a 180-degree turn in his method when he de-emphasized the active technique and developed the principle of relaxation and neocatharsis." He reflected on the difference. "Subsequent reflection has convinced me that my explanation of the way in which the active technique worked was really a very forced one: I attributed everything that happened to frustration, i.e., to a 'heightening of tension' " (Ferenczi 1930b, p. 115). He became aware that in encouraging an analysand to change his or her behavior, he was really encouraging him or her to relax: "It is much more honest to confess that here I was making use of a totally different method which, in contrast to the heightening of tensions, may safely be called relaxation" (p. 115).

The relaxation principle involved reducing the tension and frustration in the analytic situation by (1) empathic intervention rather than interpretation; (2) demonstration of actual caring, affection, and love; (3) use of relaxation measures when necessary; (4) sincerity and honesty on the part of the analyst; (5) emotional reliving and dramatic interactions; (6) reduction of need for power and control in the relationship; and (7) mutuality in interaction when necessary.

Ferenczi (1930b) began to find that, as he employed empathy rather than active confrontation of resistances, "it became possible for physician and patient to join forces in a less disrupted analysis of the repressed material . . . to tackle the objective resistances" (p. 117). He realized that the active method, continually employed, was creating new problems (see Chapter 8, this volume). In reducing tension rather than heightening it, Ferenczi did not mean to imply that one should conduct an analysis by attempting to remove all instances of anxiety, tension, frustration, or deprivation. He clarified his idea of the ambience in relaxation therapy by introducing a new concept (Ferenczi 1930b):

> Now, I do not deny that every neurotic must inevitably suffer during analysis; theoretically it is self-evident that the patient must learn to endure the suffering which originally led to repression. The only question is whether sometimes we do not make him suffer more than is absolutely necessary.
>
> I decided on the phrase "economy of suffering" to express what I have realized and am trying to convey. . . . [p. 118]

Neocatharsis

Ferenczi's relaxation method produced some very significant results: created a heightened emotional atmosphere, altered the analysand's conscious state by reviving traumatic memories, and reached core emotional trauma. He wrote (Ferenczi 1930b)

> Without any such intention on my part and without my making the least attempt to induce a condition of this sort, unusual states of consciousness manifested themselves . . . trances . . . auto-hypnotic.

... *neocatharsis* ... like many dreams, only a confirmation from the unconscious, a sign that our toilsome analytical construction, our technique of dealing with resistance and transference, have finally succeeded in drawing near to the aetiological reality. [p. 119]

Trauma

The relaxation method deepened the analysis, as Ferenczi noted: "The recollections that neocatharsis evoked or corroborated lent an added significance to the original traumatic factor in our aetiological equations. Accordingly, no analysis can be regarded (at any rate in theory) as complete unless we have succeeded in penetrating to the traumatic material" (Ferenczi 1930b, p. 120).

Relaxation therapy was not only a change in the conceptualization of the activity between analyst and analysand, but a focus on the contribution of the analyst to the treatment process. It highlighted the idea of a two-person psychology; the analyst's functioning, style of interaction, personality, and skill were introduced as a dual focus, alongside the functioning of the analysand. Sincerity and honesty were essential to create an empathic ambience where the analyst acknowledges both the analysand's criticisms and evaluations of the interaction, as well as admitting his or her contribution to any difficulties in the relationship. Ferenczi considered sincerity and honesty of the analyst among the most crucial of factors in the analytic process. He was aware that only through open, direct, and emotionally vulnerable communication could the analyst ensure that he or she did not engage in any double-bind interactions with the analysand. If an analysand challenged him by saying that he was involved in a negative interaction, Ferenczi wanted to acknowledge his contribution so as to retard a repetition of the childhood trauma in parental interaction. Thompson (1944) wrote:

Under sincerity in the analytic relationship, Ferenczi stressed the fact that ... all shortcomings or blind spots in the analyst are recognized as therapeutic hazards; but, if the analyst does not feel he must deny these, if he can admit his mistakes to the patient, the unfavorable situation can be made therapeutically valuable in that it may [project] the feeling that the analyst is unafraid to face himself and well be sincere with the patient. This will help the patient in knowing reality and create a different situation from that of the childhood where . . . attitudes of infallibility and false protestations of love rising from parents' guilt feelings often left the child in a state of confusion as to what was real and what was false. . . . [p. 249]

There are two other aspects to relaxation therapy that are very closely related to each other. The willingness of the analyst to create a democratic and mutual atmosphere and interchange in the analytic situation helps reduce the detrimental effects of issues of power and control, which are inherent in the authority role of the psychoanalyst. In instances where the analysand has serious issues of power, control, domination, manipulation, or intrusion, the analyst is willing to relinquish sole authority in the analytic relationship, allowing the analysand to share the authority. However, at no time does the analyst relinquish the role of the psychoanalyst whose mandate is to focus the analysis on healing the analysand. So at no time is the mutuality intended to supersede the analysis of the analysand.

Psychopathology of Difficult Cases: Regression

It bears repeating that Ferenczi's humanistic techniques arose as a result of a lifetime of clinical experiences with difficult cases, not as a result of his personal psychopathology, as Jones asserted in the Freud biography and as Freud himself began to believe (Freud 1933c). Ferenczi advocated his alternative to the Freudian approach because he was convinced that non-neurotic individuals suffered from real, not imagined, childhood traumas that left them with serious emotional problems in the area of object relations. His first efforts were to use the classical method of Freud, but it did not satisfy the needs of preoedipal traumatized individuals who asked for and needed a two-person experience. It was an indication of his foresight that he realized the necessity to heal trauma victims through empathic responsive object-related interaction.

CORRECTIVE EMOTIONAL EXPERIENCE

Ferenczi believed that the fundamental curative factors in the analytic situation were the empathic ambience created and the tender and caring attitude of the analyst who, instead of being a neutral mirror, attempts to reduce anxiety and tension. The emotional and interpersonal attitude of tenderness is actively established by the analyst, which is also in contrast to the restrained or even aloof position of the orthodox analyst. Ferenczi was aware that restraint, neutrality, and aloofness, although theoretically correct in the Freudian system, were actually anti-therapeutic when working with traumatized individuals. He observed this difference as follows.

> On analyzing the patient's former obstinance and comparing it with the readiness to give way, which resulted from the method of relaxation, we found that the rigid and cool aloofness on the analyst's part was experienced by the patient as a continuation of his infantile struggle with the grown-ups' authority and made him repeat the same reactions in character and in symptoms as formed the basis of the real neurosis. [1930b, p. 118]

The analyst creates a responsive emotional ambience where the personal caring, honesty toward the analysand, and expressive and dramatic reliving in the transference create a corrective emotional experience. With this attitude, one says in effect (Thompson 1964a), "I am interested in you not only as an adult patient, but I am interested in and have sympathy for the child part of you also. In the childish attachment you have formed for me, I will continue to be your interested friend" (p. 67).

Also fundamental to the corrective experience was the notion that the analyst must accept and love the analysand, in order to undo the childhood trauma. The reasoning behind the loving empathic acceptance is related to childhood emotional trauma. Since the individual has had unloving, unempathic, emotionally damaging experiences with parents, the traumatized individual must find a loving, empathic parent in the analyst. The new experience with a parent (analyst) who makes a special effort to meet the needs of the individual allows the traumatized individual to find hope. In the tender, loving analyst, the analysand will find the parent for whom he or she has yearned. The analyst, by virtue of a humanistic theory, method, and attitude, strives to respond to these yearnings and needs of the traumatized individual.

Ferenczi's corrective experience in the psychoanalytic situation is also predicated on the observation (interestingly enough, first made by Freud) that interpretations in adult language do not always reach the patient and provide the necessary insight that produces change (Freud

1919 [1918]). In addition, interpretation was developed with a conflict model of human behavior in mind (Cremerius 1983).

Conflict psychology strives to interpret resistance and transference. Ferenczi sought to create an existential experience, in the here and now of the psychoanalytic situation, where something new could happen to soothe and cure the wounds of childhood trauma. Ferenczi in his corrective experience was willing to go into the regressive world of the traumatized child-in-the-adult. The analyst has to be willing to deal with the regressed individual at the level of developmental arrest, in a language and response that reaches the core trauma or level of basic fault.

Ferenczi's humanistic concept of the experience with the analyst in the psychoanalytic situation as curative has been accepted by several succeeding generations of analysts (Balint 1968a, Cremerius 1983, Fromm-Reichmann 1950, Khan 1969, Sullivan 1940, 1953, 1954, Winnicott 1951, 1958, 1960a, Yalom 1975), although the term *corrective emotional experience* has been credited to Franz Alexander. In 1946, Alexander and colleagues described psychoanalytic cure.

> The principal curative powers of this treatment, however, lie in the fact that he can express his aggressiveness toward the therapist without being censured. This actual experience is needed before the patient gains the emotional perception that he is no longer a child facing an omnipotent father. This . . . we call "corrective emotional experience" and we consider it the most important factor in all uncovering types of therapy. [p. 22]

Alexander (1965) emphasized the emotional aspect of the experience and suggested that the analyst may have to be an actor and play a role in order to create the desired emotional atmosphere (Alexander 1965). His idea about a corrective experience, although influenced by Ferenczi (Alexander 1935), implies a manipulative element. Ferenczi's concept was to be sincere and honest. The analyst's response is an attitude of empathy and acceptance geared to fulfilling the expressed needs of the analysand, not the analyst's theoretical conception of creating a particular therapeutic effect. Alexander has the thought, but not the spirit, of Ferenczi's corrective emotional experience.

The criticism of the concept and practice of the corrective emotional experience has been severe, even condemnatory. Orthodox psychoanalysis has condemned it as an acting out in the transference an indication of the analyst's psychopathology and a misunderstanding of what constitutes psychoanalytic therapy. Even self psychology originally conceptualized the therapeutic relationship as being involved in interpreting the need for a self object, but not providing a selfobject experience (Kohut 1977, 1984, Kohut and Wolf 1978). However, Kohut (1984a) himself began to accept the idea that his clinical work could be described as a corrective emotional experience. Contemporary self psychology is clearly moving in the direction that Ferenczi first indicated by introducing the notion of a "corrective selfobject" (Bacal 1990b).

One of the most meaningful and thoughtful discussions of the issues involved in the corrective emotional experience described by Ferenczi was by Balint (1968a), who raised several important concerns and shortcomings of his mentor's approach. He felt that Ferenczi confused primary object with good mothering. "To offer oneself as 'primary object' is not the same as giving 'primary love.' Also the mother does not give the child primary love but acts as a primary object, that is she lets herself become the primary object of primary love" (p. 218).

Balint also believed that the analyst is not obliged to provide the analysand that which he or she has been deprived of. He did not believe that the analyst has to give the analysand the care, love, and affection that the parents had not given. He did believe that the analyst should give the analysand

> . . . time and a place to discover himself, to experience his own way to the objects. The analyst should also be an object that recognizes needs, as well as satisfies them in a certain way, be utmost an object that understands needs, that is furthermore able to communicate this understanding with the patient. [p. 219]

Balint believed that Ferenczi's tender loving care was nontherapeutic because it shifted the dynamics between analyst and analysand. The analyst can be experienced as too powerful, where dependency needs are repeated, not relinquished and worked through: He believed the analyst should avoid being omnipotent and powerful. "To spoil someone always takes place on different levels of power" (p. 211).

According to Balint, Ferenczi's corrective emotional experience was most meaningful for cases where benign regression is necessary, but not for oedipal cases.

Recently, one of Europe's Ferenczi scholars has added some additional thoughtful comments about the debate on the corrective emotional experience. Johannes Cremerius (1983), a German analyst, reviewed Ferenczi's ideas and clinical work as it was reflected in "The Confusion of Tongues," and arrived at the following conclusions.

> The analyst leaves the as if role, becomes the object. He concedes not to interpret, but to indulge. . . . Now everything is in danger to become simple reality. . . . Is the work on the level of regression sufficient to help a patient? Does one need to move onto the level of oedipal conflict? . . . daily practice of our work sets a limit to how far we can join the patient. It would put us under a strain that we could barely handle. In a practice where we have patients every hour, how could we manage to go into deep regression with one patient and 10 minutes later be emotionally stable and protected enough that we can cope with destructive assaults of an anal sadistic patient in a technical rational way? [p. 1013]

There is also research to bolster Ferenczi's idea that the fundamental curative factor is the emotional relationship. In a study of twenty successful group psychotherapy patients, Irvin Yalom (1975) inquired as to the "single critical incident in therapy which seemed to be a turning point, or which was the most helpful single event in therapy" (p. 26). The results revealed that the events that were turning points were not moments of insight developed by interpretation given by the analyst, but emotionally laden interactions between group members, where strong feelings were expressed and self-disclosure led to greater involvement with the group.

TENDER-MOTHER TRANSFERENCE

The tender-mother transference of Ferenczi's humanistic method is as significant an advance as Kohut's selfobject transference (Rachman 1989b). Ferenczi discovered the efficacy of encouraging a motherly nurturing transference in the psychoanalysis of difficult cases just as Kohut realized that the selfobject transference naturally unfolds in the analysis of narcissistic and borderline conditions (Kohut 1977).

Recently, the eventual estrangement between Freud and Ferenczi was blamed on Ferenczi's development of the tender-mother transference

(Cremerius 1983). The mother tenderness, as Freud called it (Jones 1957), was provided in the transference because the traumatized analysands had lacked it as children. In the "kissing letter" (Jones 1957), Freud expressed his dissatisfaction with Ferenczi's method. In a letter to Eitingon on December 4, 1932, he said the following (Jones 1957): " . . . [Ferenczi] is offended because one is not enchanted that he plays mother and child with his patients" (p. 206). As mentioned, Freud attempted to deal with the conflict over the tender-mother transference by attempting to get Ferenczi more involved in the political organization of the International Society. Freud reasoned that Ferenczi's deviations, especially his physical contact with analysands, was a result of his isolation from the greater analytic community. By the 1920s, Ferenczi devoted himself exclusively to difficult cases and his evolving humanistic psychoanalytic method. His professional contacts were limited to his Hungarian colleagues in Budapest and his most devoted students and analysands. Ferenczi was well aware that his deviations from Freudian methods did not meet the approval of Freud or the orthodox circle that surrounded the master. Ferenczi's awareness of the disapproval of Freud and his conservative followers indicated that he was in good contact with reality.

It is a matter of opinion as to whether Freud's attempt to bring Ferenczi back into the fold was an act of affection and concern for his once favorite son or a supreme manipulation of his vulnerable follower. Freud suggested that Ferenczi run for the president of the International Psychoanalytic Association. After much soul-searching, Ferenczi turned down the offer. It was a remarkable act of courage and honesty, as Ferenczi knew it would antagonize Freud to refuse the honor of the presidency. He risked further alienation from the master because he wanted to be true to his own ideas and the groundbreaking work that he was doing with difficult cases. Therefore, he told Freud that his new ideas and methods were contrary to the accepted principles of psychoanalysis. Ferenczi felt it would not be honest to represent psychoanalysis in an official position. Freud may have also tried to use his influence and status in the analytic community to force Ferenczi to abandon his humanistic deviations by making him part of the political organization of psychoanalysis, thereby undermining his independent thinking and functioning.

Ferenczi gives two descriptions of the tender-mother transference. It has the characteristics of what Winnicott was later, under the influence of Ferenczi's work as well as his students, to call *good enough mothering* (Winnicott 1958, 1960a). Ferenczi (1931) wrote

It is important for the analysis that the analyst should be able to meet the patient as far as possible with almost inexhaustible patience, understanding, goodwill, and kindliness. . . . The patient will then feel the contrast between our behaviour and that which he experienced in his real family and knowing himself safe from the repetition of such situations. . . . [p. 132]

The analyst's behaviour is thus rather like that of an affectionate mother, who will not go to bed at night until she has talked over with the child all his current troubles, large and small, fears, bad intentions, and scruples of conscience, and has set them at rest. [p. 137]

The difference between Ferenczi's and the classical position regarding transference is that activity and action can aid interpretation. A tender-mother transference is encouraged by the activity of the analyst who acts in a motherly way toward the analysand. It is not an as-if situation, but a real situation where motherly behavior is offered directly to satisfy the individual needs.

Ferenczi's approach to transference predates Kohut's selfobject transference by almost fifty years. Kohut's approach, generally speaking, is closer to the classical model, since interpretation is seen as the standard (Goldberg 1978). However, Kohut was moving toward a more liberalized view of the analytic situation (Kohut 1984a, Rachman 1989b). I think this foreshadows a developing trend in psychoanalysis toward a contemporary version of humanistic practice.

The tender-mother transference was developed out of a basic theory of technique. It was Ferenczi's contention that the analyst's mandate was to develop techniques that allow the analysis to continue. Ferenczi (1931) wrote

It is thus only with the utmost reluctance that I . . . give up even the most obstinate case. . . . I have refused to accept such verdicts as that a patient's resistance was unconquerable, or that his narcissism prevented our penetrating any further, or the sheer fatalistic acquiescence in the so-called "drying-up" of a case. I have told myself that, as long as a patient continues to come at all, the last thread of hope has not snapped. [p. 128]

With Ferenczi's optimism regarding the eventual breakthrough in a difficult case, he searched for techniques that could alleviate the impasses. He combined his own creative impulses with an empathic capacity to attune to the phenomenology of the analytic experience. He listened and responded to the manifest content of the analysand's experience in the analytic situation. Of course, he had created an emotional atmosphere where the analysand felt free to give voice to dissatisfactions as well as needs. Ferenczi (1931) wrote, "But it was a very long time before the first suggestions of how to do this came to me, and, once more, they came from the patients themselves" (p. 129). Ferenczi's theory of technique found a contemporary voice in Rapaport (1959), who agreed "to choose the therapy that fits the patient and not the patient that is fit for the therapy" (p. 115).

Ferenczi believed that he could enhance the positive working relationship by adapting a flexible attitude toward interpretation. An individual who has been traumatized and is in a state of regression may not be able to be reached with words, particularly by an analyst who presents his or her interpretations in a neutral, objective, and distant manner. Interpretations in traditional analysis are addressed to the intellect, to the ability to make genetic connections in order to gain insight. But there are those analysands whose childhood traumas may predate verbal usage and who need not only a tender-mother transference, where communication is on a preverbal level, but also the introduction of a variety of parameters in order to heal the wounds of childhood trauma (Rachman 1981a, 1982, 1988b, 1991a). This kind of humanistic approach suggests that insight and working through have to be replaced at times with living through an emotional/transference experience.

Ferenczi felt that the anxiety in the analytic situation can be reduced when the analyst openly shows his or her feelings and thoughts toward the analysand. By so doing, the analyst behaves in a non-traumatizing manner, in contrast to the traumatization of the childhood family. The tender-mother transference thus builds up a positive emotional relationship and a sense of trust. Both factors allow the analysand to enter into a regression that is necessary for the uncovering and analysis of the basic trauma.

Ferenczi's humanistic approach did maintain strong ties to psychoanalytic procedure. The employment of a tender-mother transference does not eliminate the analysis of appropriate material. On the contrary, the analysis follows the active expression of feelings and behavior. Ferenczi (1931) wrote

> But I never let an analytic hour pass without thoroughly analyzing the material provided by the acting out, of course making full use of all that we know (and have to bring to the patient's consciousness) about transference and resistance and the metapsychology of symptom-formation. [p. 132]

Ferenczi was aware of the difficulties of a tender-mother transference, and he reiterated his devotion to the analytic method.

> It might justly be said of my method with my patients that it is like "spoiling" a child. In following it, one gives up all consideration of one's own convenience and indulges the patient's wishes and impulses as far as is in any way possible. The analytic session is prolonged till the emotions roused by the material are composed. The patient is not left to himself until the inevitable conflicts in the analytic situation have been solved in a reconciliatory way by removing misunderstandings and by tracing the conflicts back to infantile experiences. [p. 137]

FLEXIBILITY, *NACHGIEBIGKEIT* (INDULGENCE), AND THE RELAXATION PRINCIPLE

Ferenczi experimented with Freud's rule of abstinence and initiated a series of clinical experiments where he prohibited the symbolic expression of sexual impulses within the session as well as in everyday life (Ferenczi 1919a) and the expression of associations and directed it toward specific affects (Ferenczi 1924b). This active period gave way to a reevaluation of the theory and technique of activity. Ferenczi became aware that the active technique was based upon forcing the patient to perform a certain activity. He also realized that he had attributed the changes in behavior that developed to frustration, or a heightening of tension (Ferenczi 1930b, p. 115).

> When I told a patient . . . that she must not [cross her legs], I was actually creating a situation of libidinal frustration, which induced a heightening of tension and the mobilization of psychic material hitherto repressed. But when I suggested . . . that she should give up the noticeably stiff posture of all her muscles and allow herself more freedom and mobility, I was really not justified in speaking of a heightening of tension, simply because she found it difficult to relax from her rigid attitude. [p. 115]

The relaxation principle was a 180-degree turn in theory and technique from the rule of abstinence. Ferenczi (1930b) traced this development from his earliest pre-analytic cathartic successes to Freudian psychoanalysis through activity then finally to relaxation.

> I could describe many other "cathartic successes." . . . But I soon discovered that . . . the results were but transitory . . . I tried by means of a deeper study of Freud's work . . . to master the technique of association, resistance, and transference. I followed as exactly as possible the technical hints that he published during this period. . . . As I followed these technical rules, there was a steady decrease in the striking and rapid results I achieved. The earlier, cathartic therapy was gradually transformed into a kind of analytical re-education of the patient. . . . I tried to think out means for shortening the period of analysis and producing more visible therapeutic results.
> By a greater generalization and emphasizing of the principle of frustration . . . and with the aid of artificially produced accentuations of tensions ("active therapy"), I tried to induce a freer repetition of early traumatic experiences and to lead up to a better solution of them through analysis. . . . The worst of these was the measure suggested by Rank and, for a time, accepted by myself—the setting of a term to the analysis. I had sufficient insight to utter a timely warning against these exaggerations, and I threw myself into the analysis of the ego and of character-development.
> . . . The somewhat one-sided ego-analysis, in which too little attention was paid to the libido . . . the distribution of energy between the patient's id, ego, and super-ego being exactly traced out . . . the relation between physician and patient was becoming far too much like that between teacher and pupil. I also became convinced that my patients were profoundly dissatisfied with me, though they

did not dare to rebel openly against this didactic and pedantic attitude of the analyst.

. . . I encouraged my colleagues to train their patients to a greater liberty and a freer expression in behaviour of their aggressive feelings toward the physician. . . . I urged analysts to be more humble-minded in their attitude to their patients and to admit the mistakes they made, and I pleaded for a greater elasticity in technique, even if it meant the sacrifice of some of our theories. . . .

So you must not be too surprised if, once more, I have to tell you of fresh steps forward . . . that I have followed. . . . I, for one, have learnt humility through the many vicissitudes which I have just sketched. So I would not represent what I am about to say as in any way final. [pp. 112–113]

Nachgiebigkeit (Indulgence)

Ferenczi's ten-year period of clinical experiments with Freudian psychoanalysis finally gave way to a new rule, the relaxation principle, which Ferenczi wished to include as a complementary rule alongside the principle of abstinence (Ferenczi 1930b). The term he used to designate this principle was Nachgiebigkeit. The translation of this term presents somewhat of a problem. It is found in Eric Mosbacher's translation of "The Principle of Relaxation and Neocatharsis" (Ferenczi 1930b). It is translated as "indulgence," which has been the accepted designation for this concept since the publication of Volume II of Ferenczi's Collected Works in 1950. "Indulgence," however, seems negative, unsatisfactory, and inaccurate, with regard to Ferenczi's technique of elasticity. It has a negative therapeutic connotation—that is to say, a giving in to the neurotic desires of a manipulative analysand. The analyst, in this negative connotation, indulges the wishes of an analysand.

My discussions with several German-speaking colleagues in the United States and Europe suggested that there was some room to challenge the traditional translation to Ferenczi's concept of Nachgiebigkeit. I believe a new translation of the concept should be considered that replaces "indulgence" with flexibility. Based on the usage of the term in Ferenczi's time as well as in modern times, Nachgiebigkeit is derived from the German verb nachgeben, which means to yield, to be pliable or flexible. It refers to a willingness to give to the other person (Hoffer 1994, Larivière 1994a, Mattick 1994, Menaker 1994b).

As a final attempt to unravel this difficulty, I consulted the English translator of the Freud/Ferenczi correspondence. Peter Hoffer (1994) said that he would translate *Nachgiebigkeit* to mean compliance, pliability, or a willingness to concede.

Integrating these opinions, it seems that *Nachgiebigkeit* was Ferenczi's later formulation of the elasticity concept first introduced in his earlier paper (Ferenczi 1928a). He used the German term *Die Elastitizität der psychoanalytischen Technik* to introduce the idea that the psychoanalytic method needed to evolve in the direction of becoming elasticized, flexible, or responsive to the needs of the analysand. This concept of elasticity (the English translation of the German *Elastitizität*) was actually suggested to Ferenczi by an analysand (Ferenczi 1928a).

> A patient of mine spoke of the "elasticity of analytic technique," a phrase which I fully accept. The analyst, like an elastic band, must yield to the patient's pull, but without ceasing to pull in his own direction, so long as one position or the other has not been conclusively demonstrated to be untenable. [p. 25]

Ferenczi is referring to an example of relaxation – a permission, so to speak, to relax, but definitely not a giving in. He encouraged the person to reduce tension. Indulgence is inappropriate here, since Ferenczi is not indulging her in a wish or need. He is helping her to do something that she is having trouble doing by herself. Ferenczi (1930b) further elaborates on the connection between *Nachgiebigkeit* and elasticity/relaxation as follows.

> I am speaking of cases in which I myself, with the one-sided technique of frustration, had failed to get any further but, on making a fresh attempt and allowing more relaxation, I had not nearly so long-drawn-out a struggle with interminable personal resistances, and it became possible for physician and patient to join forces in a less disrupted analysis of the repressed material. . . . On analyzing the patient's former obstinacy and comparing it with the readiness to give way, which resulted from the method of relaxation, we found that the rigid and cool aloofness on the analyst's part was experienced by the patient as a continuation of his infantile struggle with grown-up's authority, and made him repeat the same reaction

in character and in symptoms as formed the basis of the real neurosis. [pp. 117–118]

In the original German publication of "Relaxationsprinzip und Neokatharsis" (Ferenczi 1930a), we find the following: *"Ich bin mis natürlich auch der gesteigerten anforderungen bewusst, die diese doppelte Einstellung der Versagung und Gewährung an die Kontrolle der Gegenübertragung und des Gengenwiderstandes an den Analytiker selbst stellt"* (p. 163). The Mosbacher translation (Ferenczi 1930b) is "I am of course conscious that the twofold method of frustration and indulgence requires from the analyst himself an even greater control than before of counter-transference and counter-resistance" (p. 124). Therefore, the official translation has rendered *Gewährung* as "indulgence." *Gewährung* in a modern German–English dictionary is translated as "granting, giving, affording" (Collins 1981). Giving is not synonymous with indulgence.

The third sentence of this paragraph refers to the danger of the analyst's use of the principle of frustration for the indulgence of his sadistic needs (Ferenczi 1930a):

Nichts ist leichter, als unter dem Deckmantel der Versagungsforderung, en am Patienten und Kinder den eigenen uneingestandenen sadistischen Neigungen zu frönen, aber auch Übertrieben Formen und Quantitäten der Zärtlichkeit Kindern und Patienten gegenÜber magmehr den eigenen, vielleicht unbewussten libidinösen strebungen als dem wahle des Pflege-begohlenen zugrite kommen.

Nothing is easier than to use the principle of frustration in one's relation with patients and children as a cloak for indulgence in one's own unconfessed sadistic inclinations. [p. 124]

Here the translator has rendered what in the German is actually a verb, *frönen*, which does mean "to indulge in." This is the one place where "indulgence" seems to capture the sense of the original – but here Ferenczi is not recommending a technique; rather, he is warning against a danger (Mattick 1994).

The spirit of *Nachgiebigkeit* is the capacity of the analyst to be flexible without giving up his or her own point of view of what is transpiring in the encounter. The analyst does not impose this view, but leaves a space for the analysand's feelings, thoughts, and differences of opinion. This psychological space for the other is the democratic form of psychoanalysis that Ferenczi pioneered. Resorting to a transference or resistance interpretation can be seen as a countertransference reaction. That is to say, the analyst is involved in a power struggle. Countertransferentially, he or she must win, rather than allow the analysand to have a difference of opinion. Furthermore, the relaxation principle may also signal the possibility of finding new ways to function with an analysand (non-interpretive behaviors), so as to reduce the issues of power, control, status, and intrusion in the analytic relationship.

Non-interpretive Behavior

Ferenczi, therefore, espoused the use of non-interpretive behavior by the psychoanalyst. The psychoanalyst permits, encourages, and introduces flexibility in behavior, feelings, or thoughts that are responsive to needs or that help the analysand feel less frustrated in his or her own functioning. Depending upon the extent and nature of the trauma, the expressed desires of the analysand, the analyst's judgment as to the need for benign regression, and his or her capacity to tolerate and empathically respond to the analysand, non-interpretive intervention may take many forms. Ferenczi (1930b) described some that he permitted.

> In some cases I was even obliged to let patients stay in bed for days and weeks and to relieve them of the effort of coming to my house.
> The sudden breaking-off of the analysis at the end of the hour very often had the effect of a shock, and I would be forced to prolong the treatment until the reaction had spent itself; . . . often if I would not or could not do this, my inflexibility produced a resistance which I felt to be excessive and a too literal repetition of traumatic incidents in the patient's childhood; it would then take a long time even partly to overcome the bad effects of this unconscious identification of his.
> . . . My attempt to adhere to the principle that patients must be in a lying position during analysis would at times be thwarted by their uncontrollable impulse to get up and walk about the room or speak to me face to face.
> . . . Difficulties in the real situation, and often the unconscious machinations of the patient, would leave me with no alternative but

either to break off the analysis or to depart from the general rule and carry it on without remuneration. [p. 114]

Thompson (1964a), who studied with Ferenczi during this period, also described various non-interpretive behaviors.

The giving of five or ten minutes extra and in extreme cases even longer—at times when an interaction had been extremely powerful and prostrating. . . . a patient who was always very punctual. Her first lateness, due unmistakably to resistance, was accompanied by great anxiety and fear of disapproval. In order to express understanding of her true state of mind, the lost time was given her at the end of the hour as a present with an explanation of the meaning of the gift. . . . Ferenczi even went so far in a few cases . . . that he conducted the analysis for a time in the patient's home. His feeling was, however, that the patient must be practically psychotic to require this. . . . A case . . . of a woman who had grown up in an intolerant small-town community where childhood sexual activities . . . brought her open disgrace and ostracism. . . . At the start of the analysis, it was apparent that she wished to make her body unattractive and avoided, to an extreme degree, all physical contact. A time came in the analysis when not only did it seem important to talk of whether her body was repulsive to the analyst, but to test it. To this end she was encouraged to try a natural expression of her feelings. It seemed necessary for her to kiss the analyst not only once but many times. . . .

Thompson also developed her own non-interpretive behavior:

A young man, suffering from severe narcissistic neurosis, was making no headway lying on the couch. . . . in childhood he was accustomed to confide in his mother while kneeling beside her with his head in her lap. He obviously wished to repeat this, and although it seemed clear that he wished to gain some gratification this way, I suggested that also there might be something which he could say better in that position than lying on the couch.

The scene was enacted not once but many times, the analyst assuming the mother role natural in the situation—that of stroking his head. The situation brought clear to consciousness the incest interest, as well as his sexual interest in the analyst; but what is more important . . . is that after this process had continued for two or three weeks the reason for his difficulties in the prone position became conscious. It appeared that a deeply repressed very pleasurable fantasy was that of lying defenseless and have a woman sit astride him. During analysis he had been unconsciously thinking daily the fulfillment of this wish, and he had more reason for resistance to insight into this situation than into the more informal supposedly more stimulating situation of kneeling by the analyst. And by being adaptable to the child's ways of thinking and setting aside the formal rules when it seems indicated, we learn that formal technique at times actually functions to the patient's mind as adult morality to the child's mind. That is, the formal technique actually confuses all the more because it has nothing to do with the moral problem which is puzzling the patient at the time. [pp. 67–69]

During my supervisory sessions with Bruno Bettelheim, while I was a graduate student in clinical psychology at the University of Chicago, he told me of an experience that he had with a patient that also illustrates the use of non-interpretive behavior. At the time, which was in the 1960s, I was very surprised to hear this story from an avowed Freudian (Bettelheim 1962). We had been talking about the issue of empathy in client-centered psychotherapy, as compared to Freudian analysis. He illustrated the role of empathy in analysis by citing a male patient who would bend down on his knees and pray to God when he felt especially upset during a session. At first, Bettelheim watched the patient go through this ritual, responding verbally in an empathic and nonjudgmental way (although he did not practice any religious belief and did not believe in prayer as a vehicle for salvation). But Bettelheim realized that the verbal empathy, although meaningful, did not create the kind of emotional communion that this individual wanted and needed. So the next time the patient went down on his knees to pray, Bettelheim left his chair and knelt down with the patient. Bettelheim felt this flexibility was necessary to improve the empathic connection. The patient was very grateful, felt understood and accepted, and felt genuine affection from his analyst.

Bettelheim, I remember, presented this as a meaningful example of analytic behavior. He was able to transcend the clinical taboos that haunted many of the Freudians of his generation. His clinical work with autistic children, of which he was a pioneer, demonstrated his capacity to be creative; like Ferenczi, he believed in the elasticity of the psychoanalytic situation. Furthermore, it was to his credit that he mentioned Rogers as the foremost exponent of empathy (as has been mentioned, this was in the 1960s, before Kohut developed self psychology).

Of course, Ferenczi's relaxation principle raises the problem of fulfilling a need as it affects the analytic process. In this humanistic method, the analyst abandons the as-if role and becomes the object that gratifies. The analyst deliberately decides not to use interpretation as a means to identify the need, to empathize with it, or to develop insight into it. The analyst's behavior is not tranferential, but real. Ferenczi (1930b) was well aware of the pitfalls of his departure.

> What motive will patients have to turn away from analysis to the hard reality of life if they can enjoy with the analyst the irresponsible freedom of childhood in a measure which is assuredly denied them in actuality?
>
> My answer is that even in analysis by the method of relaxation, as in child-analysis, conditions are such that performance does not outrun discretion. [p. 123]

Ferenczi introduced the concept of *teratoma* to explain the traumatized individual's capacity to cope with childhood abuse. The individual has developed a dual ego in order to cope with the trauma. There is what Ferenczi (1930b) called " . . . a double malformation, something like the so-called *teratoma* which harbours in a hidden part of its body fragments of a twin-being which has never developed" (p. 123). This is not unlike the theory of dual ego recently proposed by Alexander Wolf and Irwin L. Kutash (1991). It was Ferenczi's notion that through the practice of relaxation and the tender-mother transference, the split in the individual's functioning would be healed. Relaxation and flexibility in functioning would reach the underdeveloped portion of the ego, yearning for nurturance, kindness, free expression, and acceptance.

Parameters

The issue of Ferenczi's relaxation principle was a problem for classical psychoanalysis until Eissler introduced the notion of parameters in his now famous 1953 paper. Eissler's definition of a parameter is " . . . the deviation, both quantitative and qualitative, from the basic model technique . . . which requires interpretation as the exclusive tool" (p. 110). In traditional analysis, there was no use of parameters during any period of the treatment. However, Eissler discussed the necessity of the use of parameters in the treatment of phobias. "A point is reached when it becomes evident that interpretation does not suffice as a therapeutic tool, and [the] pathogenic material is warded off despite the analysis of all those resistances which become clinically visible" (Eissler 1953, p. 109).

In addition to the phobias, Eissler (1953) recommends that parameters can be employed in the schizophrenias and delinquencies, because free association cannot be applied in either of those groups. He reasoned that free association does not work in the treatment of schizophrenia because the patient is "incapable of co-operating; moreover the technique might precipitate regressions. In the delinquencies the basic rule is inapplicable because of the patient's intentional and adamant refusal to follow it" (pp. 113–114).

Eissler (1953) formulated four general principles that must be fulfilled if a parameter is to be employed in psychoanalysis:

1. A parameter must be introduced only when . . . the basic model technique does not suffice.
2. The parameter must never transgress the unavoidable minimum.
3. A parameter is to be used only when it . . . leads to its self-elimination; . . . the final phase of the treatment must always proceed with a parameter of zero.
4. The effect of the parameter on the transference relationship must never be such that it cannot be abolished by interpretation.

Eissler cautioned that the use of parameters could encourage a resistance, which would be eliminated but not analyzed, as well as cover up the analyst's inability to properly employ the interpretation-technique.

Eissler's concept of parameters was intended to apply Ferenczi's relaxation principle to specific diagnostic categories and to ensure that the traditional approach was separated from Ferenczi's dissident method. But what is also important is that Eissler (1953) confirmed that Ferenczi's introduction of flexibility was a necessary condition for the successful treatment of non-neurotic conditions, or the so-called difficult cases.

The parameters necessary in the psychoanalysis of schizophrenia will be most extensive and numerous.

. . . in some phases of the treatment of the schizophrenic, transference must be produced by action, gesture, or words. [p. 134]

[In the delinquencies] . . . the main tool of interpretation is thrown out of gear, and insight cannot be conveyed to these patients by verbal interpretation—at least not in the initial phase of treatment. [p. 114]

Widening Scope of Psychoanalysis

In a still further discussion of the concept of parameters, Leo Stone (1954) widened the scope for the use of parameters in psychoanalysis. Although he generally accepted the guidelines that Eissler had laid down, he was more willing to accept that Ferenczi's original conceptualization was based upon the reality of clinical work with seriously disturbed individuals. Stone, therefore, did not accept that any parameter introduced must terminate before the end of the analysis. He reasoned that

[t]here are very sick personalities who, to the very end of analytic experience, may require occasional and subtle or minimal emotional or technical concessions from the analyst, in the same sense that they will carry with them into their outside lives, vestiges of ego defects or modifications, which, while not completely undone, are— let us say—vastly improved. [p. 576]

Stone realized that there were very special considerations in the treatment of borderline conditions. Echoing Ferenczi's original ideas, he said that

the decisive factor is the ability to stand the emotional strains of the powerful tormenter and tormenting transference and potential counter-transference situations which such cases are liable to present over long periods, without giving up hope, or sometimes, alternatively, the severe "acting out" which borderline patients may exhibit as the other alternative to intercurrent clinical psychosis. [p. 587]

As if Ferenczi were talking, Stone spoke about the personal equation of the analyst.

> Another consideration in our field is the analyst himself. . . .
> a therapist must be able to love a psychotic or a delinquent and be
> at least warmly interested in the "borderline" patient . . . for op-
> timum results. . . . their "transferences" require new objects, the
> only ones having been destroyed or permanently repudiated. . . .
> [pp. 592–593]

Stone's contemporary theory has a kinship with British object relations clinicians, such as Balint, Khan, Little, and Winnicott, self psychology clinicians, such as Bacal, Basch, Kohut, Lachmann, and Stolorow, interpersonal psychoanalysts, such as Fromm, Thompson, and Wolstein, and representatives of American psychotherapy and psychoanalysis, such as Coleman-Nelson, Rogers, and Searles.

PHYSICAL ACTIVITY BETWEEN ANALYST AND ANALYSAND

A myth has been developed in the history of psychotherapy surrounding Ferenczi's recommendations for the use of physical contact between analyst and analysand as well as the conduct of his own behavior with his analysands (Kaplan 1975). The most serious charge is that he advocated sexual contact between analyst and analysand.

On the basis of my research over the last ten years on Ferenczi's clinical writings and his behavior described by analysands, colleagues, and friends, there is no evidence to even hint at any recommendation toward direct sexual contact between analyst and analysand. What is more, the only evidence for physical contact between Ferenczi and analysands was touching via an affectionate embrace or kiss (Rachman 1993a).

Basically, what Ferenczi suggested was that some physical contact between analyst and analysand was permissible within the very defined limits of affectionate, not sexual, contact for individuals who, by virtue of their intense need for demonstrations of empathic attunement, required nonverbal means of communication and contact. The use of physical contact, which was never a primary modality in his therapeutic technique, developed out of his work with difficult cases. It has been well established since Ferenczi's time that nonverbal contact with the more emotionally disturbed patient population is a meaningful form of communication and healing (Rachman 1993a).

Let us never forget that Ferenczi's teacher, Freud himself, pioneered the use of parameters in psychoanalysis in both the cases of the Rat Man and the Wolf Man, which allowed a more providing, need-satisfying role for the analyst (see Chapter 7, this volume). During one session Freud touched the hand of an analysand (Cremerius 1983). He freed himself to respond to the particular needs of an analysand as well as to express his own individuality as an analyst. It wasn't as if Freud was deliberately breaking the rules of behavior that he had created for analysts. He was doing what all creative therapists need to do once they learn the fundamentals of clinical practice—express their own individual emotional, social, and intellectual version of psychoanalysis. Ferenczi had witnessed this as a student of Freud's, both in their discussions of analytic theory and technique and in his training analysis. Ferenczi, then, in discussing the permissibility of touching in psychoanalytic technique, was both following the lessons of flexibility he had learned from the master as well as giving expression to his own creative urges.

It must be remembered that Ferenczi's active method influenced the nature of the interaction between himself and an analysand. He had no compunction about being very direct when it came to matters of sexuality. In one such instance, a man suffered from persecutory ideas that every man who approached him was an enemy who wanted to ridicule and poison him. He also had anxiety attacks that he would die due to an anal fistula. At the onset of the persecutory ideas, intercourse with his wife had ceased because he had "other things on his mind" (Ferenczi 1911). With the hypothesis that paranoia can be a symptom of homosexuality (Freud 1911a, Ferenczi 1912a), he confronted the analysand (Ferenczi 1911).

> I asked the patient straight out whether in his boyhood he had not done forbidden things with other boys. . . . there was a long pause before he answered, and confessed rather shamefacedly that at the age of five or six he had played a remarkable game with another boy of the same age who was now one of his greatest enemies. This boy used to challenge him to play "cock and hen." . . . The other boy used to insert his erect penis or his finger into his rectum. [p. 297]

But what did Ferenczi actually advocate regarding physical contact as indicated in his published writings? There are several instances where

Ferenczi deals with both the erotic longings of the analysand for the analyst and the issue of physical expression between the two parties. In an early paper he states that he is aware of the possibility that a patient can be sexually aroused by the analyst's behavior (Ferenczi 1909). But he makes it quite clear that the analyst's behavior should be "used as a bridge to the transference of conscious feelings of sympathy and unconscious erotic phantasies" (p. 41).

Ferenczi is recommending in this instance, from standard analytic practice, that the analyst employ the conscious erotic feelings as a vehicle for understanding and working through the transference. What is different in Ferenczi's case would have been his comfort and acceptance of the erotic feelings by an analysand. By welcoming erotic feelings and feeling comfortable with them, one can give the impression of being sexual. For his time, Ferenczi was far ahead of his master and colleagues in his capacity to create an atmosphere where sexual feelings could be comfortably expressed and accepted, without the analysand experiencing them as seductive. Ferenczi's warmth, friendliness, and lively, enthusiastic manner, as well as his tender parental attitude, probably evoked strong erotic feelings in his female analysands, who were used to dealing with reserved, authoritative males characteristic of the time.

Ferenczi was also clear about the interaction when the analysand initiates a sexual overture toward the analyst. He described two such incidents in his active technical period (Ferenczi 1919a). "Thus one patient at certain exciting moments in the analysis jumped up suddenly off the sofa, walked up and down the room and ejaculated abusive words" (p. 181). Ferenczi, allowing the physical outburst, was not angered by it and did not interpret it as resistance, but accepted the patient's need for the physical movement: "In rare cases, patients are overwhelmed by an impulse, so that instead of continuing to associate they begin to *act* their psychic content" (p. 181).

Inherent in his comment is an empathic attunement to the analysand's needs based on an understanding of the individual's psychodynamics. Ferenczi used this empathic understanding as the basis for the need phase of the therapy: "The historical basis for the movements as well as for the abusive words was then revealed by the analysis" (p. 181).

A second example involved a direct attempt by an analysand to seduce Ferenczi.

An hysterical patient of the infantile type surprised me after I had succeeded in weaning her temporarily of her childish seduction artifices (constant imploring contemplation of the doctor, striking or exhibitionist apparel) by an unexpected direct attack; she jumped up, demanded to be kissed, and finally came actually to grips. [p. 182]

Ferenczi's response to the attempted seduction can be used as his basic rule for sexual contact between analyst and analysand. What must be noted, once again, is that Ferenczi's rules of conduct are based upon empathy, understanding, compassion, and a comfort with sexual expression, both verbal and physical. But the prohibition on sexual contact is clearly stated (Ferenczi 1919a).

. . . the doctor must not lose his attitude of benevolent patience even in the face of such occurrences. He must point out . . . the transference nature of such actions, toward which he must conduct himself quite passively. An indignant moral rebuff is as out of place in such cases as would be the agreement to any of the demands. Such a reception, it will be found, rapidly exhausts the patient's inclination for assault, and *the disturbance—that is to be interpreted psychoanalytically* in any case—soon settles itself. [p. 182, italics added]

Ferenczi's capacity to be empathic and humanistic in the face of a sexual overture by his analysand should not be taken to mean he condoned sexual contact between analysts and analysands. What he said was that the disturbance is to be interpreted psychoanalytically. He also wrote (Ferenczi 1930b), "However great the relaxation, the analysis will not gratify the patient's actively aggressive and sexual wishes or many of their other exaggerated demands" (p. 123).

Ferenczi (1919c) reported that he encouraged a patient to have intercourse. "At the beginning of a communication by Sadger, on the other hand, the behaviour of a patient is described after he 'in consequence of my (the author's) advice, had performed coitus for the first time' " (p. 236).

This intervention was justified as part of his active method. In cases of anxiety hysteria and hysterical impotence, Ferenczi (1919c) reported that the analysis reached an impasse when the analysand's associative process became blocked. He then turned to his teacher for advice.

In this predicament some verbal advice of Prof. Freud's came to my assistance. He explained to me that after a certain time one must call upon anxiety hysterics to give up their phobically strengthened inhibitions and to attempt to do just what they are most afraid of, . . . [This] brings to the surface untouched psycho-analytic material that without this shaking up could only have been obtained much later or not at all. [pp. 236–237]

Ferenczi's openness to sexual content and behavior has been criticized. It has been suggested that Ferenczi's use of physical contact, as well as his willingness to respond to the real relationship (Greenson 1965), may have placed an inordinate demand on both patient and analyst (Kaplan 1975).

Ferenczi's reputation as a proponent of extramural contact between analyst and patient was probably gained by a combination of his own open, active, humanistic method and several historical factors. Ferenczi's relationships with both Freud and Jones may have contributed to the myth of his condoning sexual contact. Freud and Ferenczi's relationship began to change when Ferenczi's clinical experiments with difficult cases began to include affectionate physical contact as a nurturing dimension. Although Freud was in total agreement with Ferenczi's clinical experiments in the active method and initial innovations during his humanistic method, he did not approve of the physical contact dimension, as is seen in the kissing letter. Ferenczi allowed analysands who had traumatic backgrounds (incidences of sexual abuse and emotional neglect) to satisfy their hunger for affection in their interaction of the analytic situation. It was part of his clinical experiments with his humanistic method. He was not encouraging this kind of contact with neurotic individuals. Freud's concern was that Ferenczi was not only deviating from standard analytic procedure, but that he was encouraging the next generation of young analysts to follow his example.

As discussed elsewhere (Rachman 1993a), Ferenczi is clear that he did not believe in satisfying sexual needs of patients (Ferenczi 1930b):

However great the relaxation, the analysis will not gratify the patient's actively aggressive and sexual wishes or many of their exaggerated demands. There will be abundant opportunity to learn renunciation and adaptation.

Our friendly and benevolent attitude may indeed satisfy that childlike part of the personality which hungers for tenderness, but not the part of the personality which has succeeded in escaping from the inhibitions in its development and becoming adult. [p. 123]

16

THE TRAUMA THEORY
OF NEUROSIS

FREUD'S SEDUCTION THEORY

Psychoanalysis has had a love/hate relationship with the seduction theory and the treatment of the incest trauma. In point of fact, the origins of psychoanalysis are based upon Freud's discovery that neurosis (hysteria) was caused by the sexual seduction of mostly female patients by their fathers (and secondarily by surrogate father figures). This was a remarkable discovery and established psychoanalysis on a phenomenological basis – that is to say, the data for the analysis was generated from the subjective report of the patient.

Psychoanalysis eventually became not only unreceptive but unfriendly to the idea of real sexual experiences in childhood as causal factors in neurosis and other psychological disturbances. It is a matter of continuing debate as to what factors contributed to Freud's abandoning the seduction theory of neurosis. Much focus has been concentrated on the development of the oedipal theory as an intellectual tour de force for Freud. It became the cornerstone of psychoanalytic theory, and the idea of fantasy replaced real experiences as the etiology of neurosis.

On the basis of his work with difficult cases, Ferenczi verified Freud's original seduction theory and emphasized a return to the original findings.

There is an additional issue that has not been given sufficient attention that may also have some significance in the history of the seduction theory, namely, Freud's analysis of his daughter Anna. Both Freud's vehement reaction to "The Confusion of Tongues" and his "blindness" in analyzing his daughter suggest personal factors in the abandonment of the seduction theory.

Psychoanalysis and Child Seduction

Freud's monumental discovery of the seduction theory was chronicled in his correspondence to Wilhelm Fliess (Freud 1954). During the founding of psychoanalysis, Freud was intellectually interested in the traumatic effect of childhood sexual seduction. His theory of childhood seduction emphasized that repressed memories could produce hysterical symptoms or neurosis.

Freud's attention was clearly diverted from the seduction theory as dramatically as it was focused on it. The oedipal theory, which supplanted the idea of real sexual seduction and abuse of children, not only became his lifetime preoccupation, but was embraced by the psychoanalytic community as the cornerstone of their theoretical formulation for the development of emotional disorders.

Now there is an extensive literature in psychoanalysis and in the intellectual community at large regarding the reasons for Freud's change in emphasis. Recently, there has been a trend to examine personal factors in this change (Grosskurth 1986, Krüll 1986, Masson 1984, Rachman 1991a, 1993a, Roazen 1975).

Freud also had personal issues in not identifying men and fathers as the abusers of female children. He may have been protecting himself and the male members of the analytic community. Recently I have suggested that Freud's psychoanalysis of his daughter Anna can be viewed as an indication of psychological seduction (Rachman 1991d).

Freud did lay the foundation for an understanding of the profound effects that overstimulation and parental narcissism can have in the etiology of psychological disorder. Freud, however, did not linger, theoretically or clinically, on the analysis of the incest trauma. The theory of the oedipal conflict, which supplanted the seduction theory, emphasized the wish for seduction. As a result, psychoanalysis emphasized fantasy over real seduction.

Freud's final emphasis was on *the sexuality of the child*, and, as such, it deterred an understanding and focus on *the sexuality of the parent*. Ferenczi established a focus on adult sexuality, aggression, and abuse of children. In addition, parental psychopathology—narcissism, rage, empathic failure, sadism, perversion—are considered the locus for trauma (not the child's internal process of oedipal fantasy). As Freud pointed out and Ferenczi verified, the perpetrators of sexual seduction are family members, not strangers.

History of Freud's Seduction Hypothesis

Freud had entertained the seduction theory as early as 1892, when he said that sexual traumas occurring before the age of understanding (that is, before the child understood that he or she was being sexually misused) might be the cause of hysteria (neurosis) (Freud 1954).

The first hint of the role of sexual seduction in the etiology is found in a letter of Fliess on May 30, 1893 (Freud 1954): "I see quite a possibility of filling another gap in the sexual aetiology of the neurosis. I believe I understand the anxiety neurosis of young people who must be regarded as virgins with no history of sexual abuse" (p. 73).

In a series of letters in October 1895, Freud (1954) continued to chronicle his growing confidence in his sexual seduction hypothesis:

> Note that among other things I suspect the following: that hysteria is conditioned by a primary sexual experience (before puberty) accomplished by revulsion and fright; and that obsessional neurosis is conditioned by the same accompanied by pleasure. [p. 126–letter of October 15, 1895]

> Have I revealed the great clinical secret to you either in writing or by word of mouth? Hysteria is the consequence of a presexual *sexual shock*. . . .
> "Presexual" means before puberty, before the production of the sexual substance; the relevant events become effective only as *memories*. [p. 127–letter of October 15, 1895]

> I am practically sure I have solved the riddle of hysteria and obsessional neurosis with the formulation of infantile sexual shock and sexual pleasure, and I am just as sure that both neuroses are radically curable now–not just the individual symptoms *but* the neurotic disposition itself. [p. 128–letter of October 16, 1895]

Freud was thrilled with his discovery and shared his enthusiasm with his confidant and friend, Fliess: "Confirmation from neurotic material keeps pouring in on me. The thing is really true and sound" (p. 130).

By the end of the year, Freud was able to add a significant discovery of sexual seduction in a male patient, in a letter of November 2, 1895:

> To-day I am able to add that one of the two cases has given me what I was waiting for (sexual shock, i.e., infantile abuse in a case of male hysteria!) and . . . further working through the doubtful material has strengthened my confidence in the correctness of my psychological assumptions. I am enjoying a moment of real satisfaction. [p. 132]

On April 21, 1896, Freud delivered a talk before the Viennese Society for Psychiatry and Neurology. There he eloquently presented his seduction theory in its full formulation. He claimed that the aetiological precondition for hysteria, obsessional neurosis, chronic paranoia, and hallucinatory psychosis was to be found in sexual abuse of infants and prepubescent children by adults or by older children who themselves had been sexually misused by adults. These molesters, he said, were nursemaids, governesses, servants, teachers, and brothers and sisters.

Freud did conclude that a sexual seduction was the cause of hysteria or neurosis (Freud 1896a,b). This original formulation was not really a theory of the immediate effects of the trauma or childhood personality development. He believed that the effects and memories connected to the trauma were repressed in the child's psyche. Freud did not formulate any affective or behavioral consequences for the child as a result of the seduction.

It is at the onset of puberty that the sexual trauma now becomes of consequence in Freud's original seduction theory. The activation of sexual feelings, a normal development in adolescence, transforms the repressed experience into a trauma (Freud 1896a): " . . . it is not the experiences themselves which act traumatically but their revival as a memory after the subject has entered on sexual maturity" (p. 164).

As much as Freud's original seduction hypothesis was a valiant but preliminary formulation (Levine 1990), it was also a pioneering attempt both to bring into scientific study anecdotal reports of sexual abuse and to listen and respond empathically to his mostly female patients, who were indicating that they were suffering from real events of childhood. In so doing, Freud was laying the foundation for an understanding of the profound effects that overstimulation and parental narcissism can have in the etiology of psychological disorder. Freud, however, did not linger theoretically on the importance of the object relations paradigm as central to human development, although it can be said that he pointed the way (Klein 1981).

The Abandonment of the Seduction Theory

Freud's interest in the seduction theory seemed to come to an end when he wrote an important letter to Fliess on September 21, 1897. This is a crucial letter in terms of its historical, emotional, and theoretical importance for psychoanalysis.

Freud said, "I no longer believe in my *neurotica*," his sexual theory of neurosis (Freud 1954, p. 215). He gave four reasons for the abandonment of the seduction theory:

1. The premature termination of the very patients he thought would prove the theory;
2. His incredulity that these patients always named their fathers as the perpetrators of the incestuous acts;
3. His increasingly difficulty in distinguishing between objective reality and hysterical fantasy;
4. His inability to reach the bedrock of the unconscious due to resistance.

Although Freud was disappointed, he was proud of his intellectual prowess. He began to develop his metapsychology and eventually, his oedipal complex theory to replace the seduction theory.

Jones's (1953) account of the Freud/Fliess letter is very significant:

> Up to the spring of 1897 Freud still held firmly to his conviction of the reality of childhood traumas, so strong was Charcot's teaching on traumatic experiences and so surely did the analysis of the patients' association reproduce them. At that time, doubts began to creep in although he made no mention of them in the records of his progress. . . . Then quite suddenly, he decided to confide to him "the great secret of something that in the past few months has gradually dawned on me." It was the awful truth that most—not all—of the seductions in childhood which his patients had revealed, and about which he had built his whole theory of hysteria, had never occurred. [pp. 265–266]

There is more to the renunciation of the seduction theory as chronicled by Jones:

> Freud at first accepted his patient's stories of their parents' sexual overtures towards them when they were children, but came to realize that the stories were simply fantasies derived from his patients' own childhood. [p. 5]

> Less astonishing . . . was the credulous acceptance of his patients' stories of paternal seduction which he narrated in his earlier publications on psychopathology. When I commented to my friend James Strachey on Freud's strain of credulity he very sagely remarked: "It was lucky for us that he had it." Most investigators would have simply disbelieved the patients' stories on the ground of their inherent improbability—at least on such a large scale—and have dismissed the matter as one more example of the untrustworthiness of hysterics. [p. 430]

Freud (1933d) verified Jones's version of his abandonment of the seduction theory: "Almost all my women patients told me that they had been seduced by their father. I was driven to recognize in the end that these reports were untrue and so came to understand that the hysterical symptoms are derived from phantasies and not from real occurrences" (p. 120).

Jung (1912), interestingly enough, came to Freud's defense regarding his change in thinking about childhood seduction:

> You may perhaps be inclined to share the suspicion of the critics that the results of Freud's analytical researches were therefore based on suggestion. . . . But anyone who had read Freud's works of that period [when Freud had the seduction theory] with attention, and has tried to penetrate into the psychology of the patients as Freud had done, will know how unjust it would be to attribute to an intellect like Freud's the crude mistakes of a beginner. [p. 95]

Jung's thoughtful and affectionate comment toward his master puts the shift from seduction to fantasy in perspective. It does not do justice to Freud's genius, both as an intellect and the clinical originator of psychoanalysis, to assume the change in theoretical viewpoint was a mistake. His original discovery of seduction was an indication of brilliant clinical and theoretical capacities. The change, therefore, points all the more to a series of complex issues as an explanation. In the discussions to follow, the notion of some personal issues not fully considered will be elaborated upon.

Jung attempted, as other analysts had done during psychoanalysis's pioneering period, to adjust to Freud's shifting theoretical ideas. He suggested that the seduction theory had, in essence, been proven true in principle, meaning that fantasies can be just as traumatic as real trauma (Jung 1912). This view of interpreting the oedipal fantasy as having a traumatic effect became part of the traditional approach to viewing sexual trauma, which greatly influenced psychoanalytic thinking and clinical practice up until recently. A contemporary view of the analysis of the incest trauma focuses on the necessity to acknowledge, both theoretically and clinically, the actual occurrence of childhood seduction.

Although Freud considered Ferenczi his favorite son and collaborated with him in many ways (new introductory lectures; activity in psychoanalytic technique; *Thalassa*, theory of bioanalysis), he could not follow his clinical alter ego in considering the object relations implications of his original theory of neurosis. In the 1930s, Ferenczi attempted to demonstrate to Freud and the analytic community that the seduction theory continued to have meaning. Freud was adamant about rejecting Ferenczi's "Confusion of Tongues" theory, which could have ushered in a modern version of the seduction theory and moved psychoanalysis toward the evolution of an object relations framework. Although Ferenczi's work should be seen as laying the foundation for an object relations focus, it took psychoanalysis several decades to integrate Ferenczi's ideas into the mainstream, particularly through his pupil Balint and his contributions to the Independent Group of the British Psycho-Analytic Society.

Freud's difficulty, or blindness, as Milton Klein has called it (Klein and Tribich 1982), in accepting Ferenczi's view of the damaging influence of parents on children, was apparent before Ferenczi was on the scene. In all of Freud's major case histories (Little Hans, Dora, the Rat Man, Schreiber, and the Wolf Man), he actually presented evidence that destructive parental behavior was the cause of the psychopathology that he was seeing in these individuals. Klein and David Tribich (1982) wrote, "Many of the parents in these case studies were disturbed. Yet, Freud did not see in their behavior a cause of his patients' neurosis.

Without fail, in each case, he traced the problem to the child's own nature and the vicissitudes of the child's inborn Oedipus 'Complex.' "

It is puzzling that Freud became so closed to the mistreatment of children and its effects on the development of neurosis, since his original thinking was an empathic and humane response to the sexual abuse that his female patients suffered at the hands of their parents.

Development of the Oedipal Theory

William J. McGrath (1986) wrote that Freud's letters to Fliess also "hint at the theoretical revolution which was soon to come, with the abandonment of the seduction theory for a conception that saw in the myth of Oedipus a universal archetype" (p. 197). McGrath pinpoints the central intellectual issue in the shift from seduction to oedipal theory: "The central importance of this intellectual event lies less in the issue of 'seduction' per se than in the implied shift in theoretical focus from neurotic abnormality to the general human condition" (p. 197).

Both McGrath (1986) and Lewis (1984) clarify that Freud did not abandon the seduction hypothesis – that is to say, he continued to believe in the actuality of sexual trauma. But Freud did abandon the idea of sexual seduction as the frequent source of neurotic symptoms (Lewis 1984). In addition, childhood fantasy played a more significant role in child development than he had realized (McGrath): "This realization that repressed phantasy could acquire a driving force strong enough to mold psychic reality, a realization which he experienced directly in his own case, allowed him to unify his exploration of a whole range of phenomena, both normal and abnormal" (p. 197).

It must be noted that the cause of Freud's abandonment of the seduction hypothesis has been the subject of much debate within psychoanalysis and in the intellectual community at large. In his influential book on Freud, Frank Sulloway (1979) dates the abandonment of the seduction theory to the fall of 1897 and sees it as an intellectual triumph for Freud as well as for psychoanalysis. Jones (1953) also sees the event as an intellectual advance and suggested that Freud's self-analysis was the decisive factor. Other scholars both concur with this view and elaborate upon it (Anzieu 1975, Schur 1972). Masson (1984) attacks the established view, suggesting that the shift from seduction to oedipal fantasy was a loss of courage in the face of professional opposition. Marianne Krüll (1979) also views the shift as a retrogressive step and emphasizes its personal importance as a creative solution to Freud's ambivalent feelings for his father. Richard Karpe (1956) associates the reversal with Freud's mourning for his father, but sees it as an intellectual advance. Finally, McGrath (1986) also sees it as an intellectual advance, accepting that there were personal motives, but emphasizing the role of political forces in the process. Furthermore, he feels that previous scholars did not recognize the importance of Freud's Hannibal fantasy while on his trip to Italy in the summer of 1897. McGrath (1986) believes that "in conjunction with his mourning, this key self-analytic success brought about the collapse of the seduction theory immediately after his return from that trip" (p. 198).

The controversy regarding the reasons for Freud's abandonment of the seduction theory do not diminish the significance of the impact that this event had on the history of psychoanalysis. According to Freud's (1954) account, he abandoned the seduction hypothesis because, as he wrote to Fliess, he discovered "love for my mother and jealousy of my father" (p. 223). In a dream, he realized he wanted to get rid of his father and possess his mother. He generalized these personal feelings to suggest that "each of us was once a budding Oedipus" (pp. 223–224). Finally, Freud said to Fliess that he couldn't remember being actually seduced by his mother; therefore, it must have been *his wish* to have his mother.

Freud generalized from these personal insights to develop the oedipal conflict theory to replace the seduction hypothesis. The oedipal theory switches the issue of seduction from the actual to the fantasy level. The conflict is thought to be a wish for seduction in each individual (to be seduced or to seduce) and to murder the rival. The oedipal fantasy is the corollary of the wish. What we think once may have happened (e.g., sexual trauma)—the seduction by the mother and fear of castration or, if you're a girl, the opposite—is really a projection of what the individual wishes to do to the other. The neurosis is really an elaborate way of defending against and retreating from those fantasies and wishes.

Freud believed that the Oedipus complex was the nucleus of the neurosis because a decisive shift or change takes place in the mind of the child during this period. This shift takes place universally. Whether the parent(s) are seductive or not, the boy child develops incestuous desires for the mother and hate for the father; this causes tremendous conflict. The mother is also hated because she is having sex with the father, which the child experiences as rejection. It is also a natural tendency to identify and be like the father. For female children the process is somewhat more complicated. The female must exchange her first love object for the father. The switch is fueled by the child's disappointment over her lack of a penis, which is blamed on the mother, and her valuing of the father for his possession of a penis. For the female child, the oedipal conflict is resolved through modification of values. She must accept her lack of a penis, and her wish to have her own will aid her in giving up her desire for her father.

As a result of the analyst's skepticism toward reminiscences of childhood experiences, how did this come across to the patient (nonverbally)? Did it affect the patient that he or she was believed? What effect did it have in the emotional atmosphere in the analytic situation? It is not farfetched to assume that an analysand would feel that his or her recall of childhood seduction was, in fact, a fantasy if it was being treated as a fantasy. Furthermore, in instances of actual sexual seduction, such an attitude of skepticism encourages the dissociative process. Unwittingly, the analyst conspires to reinforce the splitting off and repression of the analysand's sexual trauma and any other traumas suffered during childhood. This would lead to what Winnicott (1965a) called *false self analysis*. Kohut talked about an analysis that didn't get into the narcissistic core: early narcissistic needs get split off and don't get analyzed. Ferenczi talked about an analysis that gets down to rock bottom.

Several significant intellectual conclusions developed as a result of the switch to the oedipal conflict theory:

1. Real sexual seduction was diminished in importance as a causal explanation for neurosis and psychological disorder.
2. The wish or fantasy of seduction replaced the acceptance of actual sexual seduction.
3. If the conflict (wish, fantasy) of seduction is universal, there is no need to search out the actual behavior of a seducer.
4. The recognition of real seduction and its negative consequences is not a concern.
5. Any focus on real seduction, the actual interpersonal experience of seduction, and the need to recover from seduction would be a resistance to uncovering the unconscious oedipal wish that is the core of the neurosis.

The child's capacity for hysterical lying is another issue that was a consequence of the shift from seduction to oedipal theory. Florence Rush (1980) wrote

> Freud's claim that children who reported sexual abuse by adults had imagined or fantasized the experience is highly questionable. Chil-

dren perceive the difference between reality and fantasy . . . and sexual advances are in fact made to children in the course of everyday life. To insist that these advances are imagined is to underestimate a child's perceptive capacity, create doubt and confusion, undermine self-confidence, and provide the food upon which nightmares are nourished. [p. 80]

Sigmund Freud's Analysis of His Daughter Anna: Implications for the Seduction Theory

Freud's analysis of his daughter Anna has, until recently, been one of the most obscure and taboo topics in psychoanalysis (Roazen 1969, 1975). It is one of the most intriguing and unusual issues in the life and clinical work of these two major figures of psychoanalysis. What does it say of psychoanalysis and its teachings if we cannot acknowledge this issue and examine the implication of the special relationship between Sigmund and Anna Freud? Is there any one of us who hasn't wondered about this relationship, the analysis that was conducted with Anna, and the implications for psychoanalytic theory and technique? Most distressing for those of us who struggle to understand this issue is the veil of denial, secrecy, and splitting that prevents both research and psychoanalytic discussion. What's more, there has been an implied threat of criticism and condemnation if the taboo were to be broken.

There are many puzzling issues involved in Freud's analysis of Anna. Roazen (1969) wrote

> Perhaps the most extraordinary illustration of Freud's allowing himself privileges he might have condemned in any other analyst was his analyzing his youngest child, Anna. . . . In letters Freud was quite open about this analysis, and it became a public secret to a small group of his inner circle. [Note: according to Kata Levy, her own analysis with Freud began at the time of the Budapest Congress (1918), and Anna was already in analysis with her father then. When Oliver Freud visited home in 1921 his sister Anna was then in analysis with their father. Mrs. Edward Hitschmann, Dr. Anny Katan, Dr. Edith Jackson, Dr. Herman Nunberg, Dr. Irmarita Putnam, and Dr. Sandor Rado have all confirmed that Freud did indeed analyze Anna.] [pp. 100, 215]

From Freud's point of view there were probably some good reasons for doing what he did. But considering all the discussion in later years about what constitutes proper psychoanalytic technique, Freud's liberty in analyzing his own child make one skeptical of ritualism in therapy or training. [p. 100]

There is no direct evidence regarding Anna's analysis. There are no process notes, and Freud did not devote a clinical case study to Anna's therapy. The main documents for considering the course of Anna's psychoanalysis are those she wrote herself: her poems and her own paper, "Beating Fantasies and Daydreams. . . ." for which she used Freud's "A Child Is Being Beaten" as her starting point (Young-Bruehl 1988).

There is no documentation as to how the analysis was arranged. We do not know who proposed the arrangement, whether it was Freud or Anna. Rumors that Lou Andreas-Salomé was her analyst persisted because, as Elisabeth Young-Bruehl (1988) wrote, "people were scandalized by the thought that her father had filled that role" (p. 112).

Anna started her analysis with her father in the fall of 1918, and it apparently continued into 1922 (Young-Bruehl, 1988). In 1924, after a two-year pause, they resumed their analytic work. She had written to Andreas-Salomé on May 5, 1924, that

[t]he reason for continuing . . . was the not entirely orderly behavior of my honorable inner life: occasional unseemly intrusions of the daydreams combined with an increasing intolerance—sometimes physical as well as mental—of the beating fantasies and of their consequences [i.e., masturbation] which I could not do without. [Young-Bruehl 1988, p. 122]

As Anna's first analysis became part of Freud's "A Child Is Being Beaten," it is suggested that her second analysis became part of a 1925 paper, "Some Physical Consequences of the Anatomical Distinction Between the Sexes." In this paper, many of the themes of Anna's inner life are discussed (Young-Bruehl 1988).

. . . her envy of her brothers and her father, her anger at her mother, who was fonder of Sophie; the early-awakened genital sensations related to masturbation; her jealousy of her mother and Tante

Minna as objects of her father's love; and her identification with her father. [Young-Bruehl 1988, p. 126]

In her second analysis with her father, she focused on being overly good and coming to terms with the harshness of people and events and not escaping into saintly hopefulness that all would turn out well in the end (Young-Bruehl 1988). She later discussed this trait under the concept of altruistic surrender. In *The Ego and the Mechanisms of Defense* (1936), she understood altruistic surrender as a projection of forbidden or dangerous wishes onto other people. Young-Bruehl (1988) wrote, "The chief example of altruistic surrender in *The Ego and the Mechanisms of Defense* is a governess who has lived an uneventful life entirely dedicated to other people's needs" (p. 128).

During the pioneering period of Anna's analysis (1918 through the 1920s) and well into the 1930s, the psychoanalytic community had not yet adopted the rule of dual relationships, which discourages an analyst from analyzing a family member, friend, or associate (anyone with whom a relationship had already been established prior to the onset of the analysis). There were no formal recommendations for crossing boundaries of family and friendship when one wished to analyze someone in one's life (Young-Bruehl 1988).

Freud . . . analyzed both of his friend Oscar Rie's daughters, Margarethe and Marianne, his friend Sándor Ferenczi's future stepdaughter [Ferenczi was also involved in analyzing his future stepdaughter . . . and his friend Anton von Freund's sister Kata Levy.

Before the first World War, both Carl Jung and Karl Abraham had worked analytically with their young daughters and written essays on their observations. [Young-Bruehl 1988, p. 114]

A gender issue was perhaps the most important theoretical consideration in Freud's decision to analyze his daughter. Freud felt there were fewer psychological difficulties in analyzing a daughter than a son. Young-Bruehl (1988) wrote that "Freud's assumption at the time of his daughter's analysis was that boys would—like 'Little Hans'—feel hostile and rivalrous towards a father-analyst but girls, who were not in competition for the mother, would not" (p. 114).

In a 1935 letter written to Edoardo Weiss, who had asked Freud to comment on his desire to analyze his own son, Freud answered (Young-Bruehl 1988), "that is certainly a ticklish business. With a young, promising brother it might be done more easily. With [my] own daughter I succeeded well. There are special difficulties and doubts with a son" (p. 114). With this assumption that the oedipal drama is not as intense and difficult for a daughter, Freud apparently felt that the transference would not test his capacities to negotiate hostile feelings or deal with regression, both issues with which he was known to have great difficulty (Balint 1968b, Ferenczi 1932c). The consideration of an oedipal romance as an issue in a transference relationship with a daughter in analysis did not seem to hinder Freud's willingness to see the analysis to the end.

Freud and Emotional Seduction

In analyzing his daughter, Freud was myopic to the emotional seduction involved in such an emotionally complicated enterprise. In analyzing his daughter's oedipal conflict, it is reasonable to assume that he would discuss her sexual feelings and fantasies about him, both past and present. Contemporary analysts specializing in the treatment of incest survivors would say that such discussions constitute a form of psychological incest—incestuously tinged seduction that would be overstimulating to both parties and would violate the generational boundaries between parent and child. It is what Ferenczi originally pointed to as retraumatizations in the psychoanalytic situation.

Freud's blindness to the possible psychological seduction of his daughter is particularly puzzling, since he later condemned Ferenczi's behavior when he viewed it as sexually seductive. In a letter to Ferenczi on October 10, 1918, he was not concerned with the potential seduction when he said (Young-Bruehl 1988), "Anna's analysis will be very elegant" (p. 116). Young-Bruehl also wrote, "But, Freud was certainly aware that his daughter's adoration of him was not an unproblematic affair. He knew the extent of her idealization of him and revealed it—sometimes in jest and sometimes somberly—in his letters" (p. 116).

If Freud would not acknowledge the difficult transference situation, his daughter could. She was aware of the difficulties in her analysis. Young-Bruehl (1988), quoting a letter that Anna wrote to Andreas-Salomé on May 24, 1924, wrote

> She acknowledged "the absence of the third person, the one onto whom the transference advances and with whom one acts out and

finishes off the conflicts. . . ." the analyst who was supposed to be a neutral party, a "blank screen," was, in the nature of the case, missing. And, further, she understood clearly that what she called her "extra-analytic closeness" to her father produced "difficulties and temptations to untruthfulness" in the analysis. [p. 123]

Anna (1967), working on the theme of altruistic surrender both in her analysis and in her clinical work, may have described the situation with her father in her own writings:

> . . . displaced her ambitious fantasies onto her men friends [Anna's work with analytic community] and her libidinal wishes onto her women friends [Andreas-Salomé and Dorothy Burlingham]. The former succeeded to her affection for her father and her big brother, both of whom had been the object of her penis envy, while the latter represented the sister upon whom . . . the envy was displaced in the form of her beauty. The patient felt the fact that she was not even a pretty enough girl really to be attractive to men. In her disappointment with herself she displaced her wishes onto objects who she felt were better qualified to fulfill them. [A. Freud 1967, vol. 2, p. 131]

To Freud's personal difficulties with a maternal transference we need to add two other matters of sexuality to help explain his accusatory and repressive attitude toward Ferenczi. Krüll has recently written a well-researched and scholarly book, *Freud and His Father* (Krüll 1986). Krüll's main thesis is that Freud was led to abandon his seduction theory in deference to his father, who had died a year earlier and who had given him a covert but urgent dream message not to delve into the family's history. Holding on to the seduction theory might have meant breaking his father's taboo. She also suggested that Freud may have been a victim of sexual abuse with a nursemaid, Resi Wittek. These experiences, she reasoned, were primary and had a fundamental influence on his personality.

Freud's moralizing about Ferenczi's "sexual" behavior, when it was clearly a matter of executing the tender-mother transference in order to cure childhood trauma, is in keeping with his assumed role of a stern father, feeling the need to control a rebellious and free-spirited child. Such a parental and punitive role is one that he assumed easily, not only with Ferenczi, but with other disciples. It was also a role that Ferenczi contributed to as he secretly practiced his humanistic method, rather than openly declare his alternate theory and technique. Also, he was too concerned about his relationship with Freud to break away and form his own dissident movement (Thompson 1944). It is tempting to speculate, in view of those ideas, about Freud's own conflicts about his own early unintegrated sexuality, which led him to project this onto Ferenczi and distort the actual nature of Ferenczi's interventions. He then punished Ferenczi for something that he hadn't resolved in himself.

As a footnote to this discussion of seduction, I offer the observation of an incest survivor when she gave me the Anna Freud biography by Young-Bruehl (1988) as a gift. On the cover of this book is a photograph of Freud and his daughter, obviously having a midday meal or a drink at a Viennese sidewalk cafe. Anna is a young woman, perhaps in her twenties. She is looking away from her father, staring into the distance. Freud is staring straight ahead, having just taken a puff on one of his famous cigars. The analysand, who prides herself on her intuitive capacities, thought she identified the theme of incest in the faces of his photograph. She said, "The photograph on the cover looks like a man and his lover. Her face is turned. She is caught in his orbit."

Then she exclaimed that it was her opinion that Anna Freud was the victim of incest. This declaration by an incest survivor is typical. Because of her wounds from childhood seduction, she, like many other traumatized individuals, has a special sensitivity to detecting the same psychological wounds in others. Of course, this kind of psychic wisdom based on trauma can also lead to an exaggerated view, which distorts the presence of pathology. Given my interest in the seduction theory and the analysis of incest, her reaction to Freud's "seduction of his daughter" encouraged a desire to test out her hypothesis. (Young-Bruehl's Anna Freud biography makes no mention of sexual seduction as a variable in the relationship with her father.)

In order to see if this incest survivor's seduction hypothesis could have any validity beyond her own sensitivity, I conducted an informal survey using the Freud picture. The reactions of several analysands, some of whom were incest survivors and some who were not, produced some interesting responses:

1. "Dirty old man with a young woman" (incest survivor).
2. "Woman . . . looks angry, failed to make any connection with him. Look of despair, as if he just said something very hurtful to her."

3. "A bad marriage between two people of disparate ages. She takes the back seat *and he ruined her life.* He used her for himself. He used her as a wife. She never married; maybe she was homosexual."

Without attributing any undue significance to these anecdotal findings, it is clear that the picture generates thought and feelings about a romance between Freud and Anna, whether it was in spontaneous remarks or recall of the folklore of psychoanalysis.

Freud's analysis of his daughter Anna had implications for both his oedipal theory and Ferenczi's attempt to revive the seduction hypothesis. No doubt, in her analysis, Anna had oedipal fantasies. In Freud's theory of therapy, such fantasy material naturally unfolds as the resistance and transference are analyzed. Also, it is logical to assume that during the period of Anna's analysis, roughly 1918 to 1925, Freud was practicing his analytic technique while being guided by the principle that the oedipal complex was at the heart of neurotic personality functioning. Furthermore, Freud knew that any manifestation of oedipal material was not a result of an actual childhood seduction of his daughter, since there is no evidence to suggest that she was the victim of sexual abuse at the hands of her father. Since the oedipal material was not a product of sexual trauma, in Freud's mind it gave him verification of the theory that such fantasies are innate, the product of drive. This upheld his theory that sexual trauma in the etiology of neurosis is a function of fantasy, not a real-life event.

Apparently, Freud did not connect the oedipal fantasies that his daughter was reporting in her analysis to any quality in the object relationship he was having with her, either in their daily life together, where she clearly idolized him, or in the analytic situation of her analysis with him. Freud was behaving as if his emotional impact on his daughter did not have any significance for her analysis and, what is more, as if there were no real event issues to consider. He did not see the associations and the material that he received in her analysis as being colored by their current interpersonal situation or that the very act of analyzing his daughter seriously influenced the analysis.

Freud's condemnation of Ferenczi, exemplified in his attempt to censor the reintroduction of the seduction theory, is also puzzling. He failed to see in Ferenczi's theory and clinical behavior a pioneering attempt to treat patients, mostly women, suffering from the trauma of incest at the hands of their fathers (and other parental figures). Ferenczi's emphasis of empathy and non-interpretative clinical interaction was aimed at creating safety, nonintrusiveness, honesty, and caring.

Freud was unnecessarily concerned with Ferenczi's sexuality, since there is no evidence to suggest that, during his twenty-four-year career as a psychoanalyst, Ferenczi ever had sexual contact with a patient (Rachman 1993a). He may have read into Ferenczi's behavior his own unresolved and unconscious incestuous feelings for his daughter, which influenced his decision to suppress the "Confusion of Tongues" paper. Ferenczi's attempt to revive the seduction theory may have triggered anxiety in Freud regarding his unresolved notion that fathers could not perform perverted acts against children (Freud 1954).

These thoughts are by way of trying to understand why Freud continued to neglect and then oppose the reintroduction of the seduction hypothesis. After all, Ferenczi was Freud's favorite student and collaborator and was presenting evidence that verified Freud's original ideas. It was also clear that Ferenczi was working with difficult cases, which we would now characterize as narcissistic, borderline, or psychotic disorders. He was prophetic, as it now turns out, in his observations that actual sexual seduction is often an etiological factor in these disorders and that modifications of traditional technique need to be considered.

THE FREUD/FERENCZI CONFLICT ABOUT TRAUMA THEORY

It has been suggested by the French analysts that the Freud/Ferenczi conflict was related to their disagreement about Ferenczi's notions of trauma theory (Sabourin 1985, Sylwan 1984). Apparently the issue of differences regarding trauma as a causal factor in neurosis predated "The "Confusion of Tongues" (Ferenczi 1933), dating back to 1929. Ferenczi at that time was caught in an emotional turmoil: trying to be true to his own work and ideas while trying to please Freud and fend off the criticisms of the analytic community (Sylwan 1984). Freud considered Ferenczi to be in emotional difficulty and social isolation. Vienna and Budapest, which were still united only ten years before, had become worlds apart by 1929. In order to cure Ferenczi of his "illness," Freud proposed that Ferenczi run for president of the International Psychoanalytic Association. The plan was to divert Ferenczi's interest in his trauma theory and funnel his energy into the presidency. Ferenczi's clinical immersion with difficult cases, with individuals traumatized by sexual molestation, was his disease, and the presidency was shock treatment (*gewaltier*) (Sylwan 1984). Masson (1984) wrote, "In a letter to Ferenczi, Freud made these feelings clear: But you will have to leave this dream island where you are camping with imaginary children to join again the men's struggle" (Freud to Ferenczi, May 12, 1932; p. 167). Ferenczi withdrew his candidacy for the presidency of the IPA ten days before the Wiesbaden Congress, citing differences in theoretical and clinical outlook.

Ferenczi did not protect his own narcissism, the narcissism of an analytic method that accuses the patient of resistance rather than change its method to empathize with the analysand. Sylwan wrote

> Free associations are not free when expressed in an icy atmosphere or in a climate of fear. Only a climate of trust can allow the patient to enact the initial trauma. . . . Ferenczi espouses the mood of the patient . . . lets himself be guided by the patient. . . . When he denounces the confusion of tongues, he is also denouncing the analyst's attitude which can be hypocritical, double and fraudulent. The patient is no more fooled by the analyst's insecurity than he was by the parent's. But Ferenczi also knows. . . that the Oedipus conflict according to Freud is only a child's fantasy, that it does not correspond to any real desire. [p. 107]

Freud had his difficulties in dealing with trauma, which may explain the difficulty he had accepting Ferenczi's capacity to deal directly with trauma. For example, Freud refused to acknowledge the impending catastrophe of the enveloping Holocaust during the 1930s. Jones (1957) characterized Ferenczi's attempt to warn Freud of the impending trauma as if it was the voice of a hysterical person. Ferenczi tried to convince Freud to leave Austria in 1933, when Freud would have easily escaped, reducing the trauma, but Freud had difficulty facing the reality of the Holocaust and left Austria very late. During the year he left, 1938, he suffered the trauma of having his daughter Anna detained by the Nazis and wondering whether he would see her again.

Ferenczi believed in the reality of trauma, acknowledging it in his own history with his mother (see Chapter 1). He also realized the presence of trauma in his analysands and helped them confront it in their histories. Furthermore, Ferenczi realized that trauma can also occur in the psychoanalytic situation. He also confronted the possibility that he was a traumatizing agent in his work with difficult cases. He developed humanistic techniques to cope with this kind of trauma (see Chapter 15).

Freud abandoned his belief in trauma early in his career when he felt that his patients were lying about their traumatic childhoods. After that he invested his energies into the intellectual notion of the fantasy version of childhood trauma. He erected an intellectual edifice in his formulation of the oedipal complex that did not allow for the reality of trauma. The oedipal complex may have served as a protective shield for Freud that made the reality of trauma intellectually remote and emotionally distant. He convinced the remaining members of The Society of Rings and the analytic community that there was no room for trauma in psychoanalysis. They didn't have the independence of thought or the emotional fortitude to deviate. Fearing ostracism, which Ferenczi was beginning to experience, they closed ranks behind Freud. Such myopia did a disservice to Freud and psychoanalysis. As Kohut (1984a) and the British object relations theorists were to demonstrate several generations later, psychoanalysis can accommodate trauma (Balint 1932, 1959, 1968a, Fairbairn 1954, Guntrip 1971, Khan 1974, Winnicott 1958, 1965a). Freud's difficulty in dealing with trauma may have its origin in his childhood. Krüll (1979) as mentioned, demonstrated that there was a family prohibition on delving into the past. Furthermore, Freud's childhood experience of sexual seduction may have been influenced by the family prohibition on recalling and confronting trauma.

There are two curious aspects to the issue of trauma in the history of psychoanalysis (i.e., the Freud/Ferenczi conflict and Ferenczi's analysis of Jones). Freud was not particularly responsive to the trauma that evolved in their relationship. Ferenczi repeatedly tried to communicate to Freud that he was unhappy, hurt, disappointed, and devastated as a result of their relationship. But Freud never understood that his behavior was a causal factor in Ferenczi's trauma. Freud did not believe in a two-person psychology or in the reality of trauma in an object relationship. So he would attribute any difficulty in their relationship as a sign of Ferenczi's immaturity and humanistic deviations in his clinical practice as a sign of a deterioration in Ferenczi's personality. The conflict that arose over the "Confusion of Tongues" paper was illustrative of Freud's capacity to contribute to a trauma, but not to understand the necessity of tender-mother transference. Witness the statements that Freud makes to Ferenczi regarding their relationship during troubled times (Jones 1957):

You speak of many years of good understanding between us. . . . it was more than that, rather a close sharing of our life, emotions, and interests. When today I have to conjure all this from my memory, the sole consolation is the certainty that I contributed remarkably little to the transformation. Some psychological fate has brought it about in you. At all events we are glad to hear of the restoration of your health, a precious piece of the more beautiful past. [Freud to Ferenczi, January 11, 1933; p. 177]

Jones did not have any insight into the trauma he created for Ferenczi. Any student of the history of psychoanalysis is struck with the mean-spirited attack on Ferenczi by Jones (see Chapter 6). As suggested, there is the likelihood that Ferenczi left unresolved the negative transference reaction by Jones to him. The analysis was only a two-month experience, which was standard for those pioneering days. Ferenczi was in the beginning of his active technique period during 1913, so he would have heightened the negative transference if he needed to encourage the analytic process. More research is needed in this area.

FERENCZI'S METAPSYCHOLOGY

By the time Ferenczi introduced his humanistic psychoanalysis, he was aware that the analyst's functioning was a central key. He outlined this aspect of his metapsychology in the first part of the new psychology, the "Elasticity" paper (Ferenczi 1928b).

I should like to mention, as a problem that has not been considered, that of the metapsychology of the analyst's mental processes during analysis. [By metapsychology we mean, of course, the sum-total of the ideas about the structure and dynamics of the psychical apparatus which our psychoanalytic experiences have caused us to adopt. See Freud's papers on metapsychology in his *Collected Papers*, Vol. IV.] His cathexes oscillate between identification (analytic object-love) on the one hand and self-control or intellectual activity on the other. . . . he can never allow himself the pleasure of giving his narcissism and egoism free play in reality, and he can give free play to them in his fantasy only for brief moments. A strain of this kind scarcely occurs otherwise in life, and . . . sooner or later it will call for the creation of a special hygiene for the analyst.

Unanalysed ("wild") analysts and incompletely cured patients are easily recognizable by the kind of "compulsive analysing" from which they suffer; in contrast to the unhampered mobility of the libido which is the result of a complete analysis, which makes it possible to exercise analytic self-knowledge and self-control when necessary, but in no way hampers free enjoyment of life. The ideal result of a completed analysis is precisely that elasticity which analytic technique demands of the mental therapist. This one more argument for the necessity of the second fundamental rule of psycho-analysis. [pp. 98–99]

Ferenczi's metapsychology has several aspects:

1. There is a shift away from the biological drives of sex and aggression as the fundamental motivation for human behavior and a move toward the nature of the object relations in the parent–child experience.
2. The development of psychopathology is based in the interpersonal experience of the child and the parent(s).
3. The development of neurosis (and other more serious disorders) resides in the nature of the emotional relationship between parent and child.
4. Trauma is central to the development of neurosis; the trauma is a real event of childhood, sexual or emotional in origin.
5. The confusion of tongues theory explains the individual's method of coping with trauma.
6. A teratoma, or underdeveloped double self, is part of the personality of a traumatized individual.
7. A regression can take place in the object-relationship, which is an acting out or reenactment of the primal trauma.
8. A tender-mother transference that emphasizes empathy, loving, indulgences, and mutuality is the creative experience for the regression to the basic fault.

Ferenczi (1930b) declared his growing theoretical independence, moving away from the oedipal conflict explanation: "To-day I am returning to the view that, beside the great importance of the Oedipus complex in children, a deep significance must also be attached to the *repressed incestuous affection of adults, which masquerades as tenderness"* (p. 121).

In a letter to Freud on May 22, 1932, Ferenczi said (Sylwan 1984), ". . . in our group, castration complex and penis envy in women are the subject of heated discussions. I have to confess that, in my practice, this complex doesn't hold such an important place in comparison as it could be from the theory. What is your experience?" (p. 101).

This letter is of enormous importance in Ferenczi's relationship to Freud as well as a statement of Ferenczi's move toward a trauma theory of neurosis. In the first instance, Ferenczi boldly states that the Hungarian school of psychoanalysis, which he founded, was involved in a heated debate regarding the clinical work with difficult cases, the incest survivor cases to which Ferenczi devoted his full attention. It seems like a naïve question that he frames for Freud when he asks him if he is also dissatisfied with the oedipal explanation. Such talk only fueled the controversy between them just prior to the enormous difficulty that would break out in the "Confusion of Tongues" paper. In fact, the letter can be seen as an elaboration of the "Confusion of Tongues," since that material introduced Ferenczi's alternate theory to Freud's oedipal theory.

The development of Ferenczi's metapsychology of the analyst is linked to several important developments. When involved in clinical work with difficult cases, he was thrown back on an awareness of his own functioning in the psychoanalytic situation. Rather than resort to the traditional intervention, when an analysand is in so-called "resistance"–a psychoanalytic euphemism for not behaving according to the prescribed manner, Ferenczi would enter into a two-person dialogue and examine his functioning.

Ferenczi's clinical experiments, from active analysis to relaxation therapy, moved him to consider the nature and process of the psychoanalytic situation. Its first formal examination, as well as the advent of modern psychoanalytic thinking, was marked by Ferenczi and Rank's *The Development of Psychoanalysis*. As Ferenczi modified his clinical experiments with active intervention, he began to realize that it was not the prohibition of impulses or the command or encouragement to respond that was the key element in unblocking associations, but the creation of an empathic, democratic, tender, and responsive atmosphere. In *The Development of Psychoanalysis*, he and Rank emphasized the experience between the analyst and analysand not from a traditional intellectual/cognitive/insight framework, but as an emotional experience occurring in the here and now of the analytic process. Ferenczi was to develop and refine the nature of the emotional experience between the therapeutic dyad, which reached the height of clinical experimentation in the mutual analysis of R.N. (Elizabeth Severn), as reported in the *Clinical Diary*.

Ferenczi's relationships with Rank and Groddeck must also be mentioned as influences in the development of his metapsychology of the psychoanalyst. Rank was his collaborator in the study of a psychoanalytic session and the way the experience impacted upon the analyst. Groddeck, after Rank and Ferenczi separated, became both a confidant and an analytic peer, inspiring him to mutual analysis. The experiences with Rank and Groddeck gave Ferenczi important self objects that accepted and valued his daring and creative spirit. Their encouragement, acceptance, and ideas helped Ferenczi have an island of acceptance in the analytic community so that he could pursue his studies of the analyst's role and response.

Ferenczi's dissatisfactions with his relationship and personal analysis with Freud also fueled his desire to understand the analyst's experience in the analytic field of study. Ferenczi had unrealistic expectations for his relationship with his mentor. It was clear from the history of Freud's relationships (Fliess, Jung, Adler) that he could not enter into an emotionally vibrant, intimate peer relationship where mutuality would prevail. Everyone in the analytic community seemed to accept this, whether they were consciously aware of the compromise or not. But Ferenczi needed and wanted more than a traditional relationship. Freud's continued frustration of this need for mutuality drove Ferenczi toward experiencing firsthand the frustrations of an analysand longing for a more empathic and responsive contact with his or her analyst.

It is conceivable that the frustration that Ferenczi experienced with Freud contributed to his willingness to enter into a mutual analysis with R.N. Ferenczi, on the urging of Severn, was willing to take the part of the analysand in order to break the difficulties in their relationship. The limitations of his clinical experiment with the analysand are not as important as Ferenczi's willingness to participate in such a study of the analytic process, akin to being a cultural anthropologist who is studying a phenomenon in human behavior in its natural surroundings. The experience of the analyst in this role reversal advanced the understanding of the phenomenology of the analyst's functioning. The concentration on the active, changing role of the analyst moved Ferenczi toward pioneering the practice of countertransference analysis.

Ferenczi's clinical research naturally led to a conceptualization of the intersubjective field (Haynal in press, Stolorow et al. 1983). It was inevitable that Ferenczi would focus on the phenomenology of the analyst's experience, since he was never satisfied, theoretically, with a one-person psychology and, clinically, he strove toward mutuality. It is axiomatic in considering Ferenczi's functioning to say that clinical practice gave birth to theoretical ideas. With this consideration, we can examine his clinical functioning from his earliest period to his last phase and easily see that he was always experimenting, elasticizing the role of the analyst in response to the clinical experience with an analysand. Comparing Ferenczi's early clinical functioning in the Case of Rosa K. (Ferenczi 1902) to his experience with Severn in the late 1920s (Ferenczi 1932c), we see a never-ending response of the analyst to the experience of being with the analysand. Whether it was his clinical experiments with activity (Ferenczi 1919a,b,c, 1920, 1924b, 1925a,b), the heightening of the emotional dimensions of the psychoanalytic situation (Ferenczi and Rank 1925), the introduction of empathic understanding (Ferenczi 1928b), or the final development, relaxation therapy (Ferenczi 1930b, 1931, 1932c, 1933), the psychoanalysis was informed by both the analysand's and the analyst's experience. Of course, the analyst's experience meant that Ferenczi was willing to examine his countertransference reactions as an integral part of the analytic process. In fact, he pioneered the analyst's focus on analyzing countertransferences, not to get rid of them (as Freud had originally recommended), but to encourage a mutual experience as the growth factor in the analysis (see Chapter 14). This focus on the positive function of countertransference—the analyst's emotional, interpersonal, and intellectual reactions to the analysand—was the beginning of what André Haynal (in press) calls a "metapsychology of the analyst's mental processes during the analysis."

FERENCZI'S VIEW OF TRAUMA

Freud and Ferenczi differed in how they saw the traumatized child. According to one of the members of Le Coq-Héron, the Ferenczi study group, the difference can be characterized as follows (Sylwan 1984).

Freud's child swallows his tears, his rage, his pain. A severe adult refuses to grant him the "expected compassion" when he has "bit his tongue" or "let his finger be caught": instead, he is asked to answer the question "why did you do this?" [p. 106]

For Ferenczi, it meant the following (Sylwan 1984).

It is a child who has been engulfed in a catastrophe who has split himself from this catastrophe to build a new equilibrium elsewhere, outside of himself, on the grave of his self, erecting an untouchable monument. . . . Ferenczi can recognize the child whose self has spun out secret shames and humiliations, when he is accused of being responsible for his own fall, when he has cut off a part of his self during or after a traumatic experience. [p. 106]

What Is "Trauma"?

Ferenczi described trauma as an "unbearable" external (object related) or internal (intrapsychic) stimulus that impinges on the individual, so that the self of the individual is modified. The effect of the trauma so modifies the ego that a process of disintegration occurs where splitting is predominant. How much disintegration takes place depends on the relative strength of the unbearable excitation. Changes in ego functioning include:

1. Change in consciousness (trance, dream state);
2. Loss of consciousness;
3. Syncope ("a partial or complete temporary suspension of respiration and circulation due to cerebral ischemia and characterized by sudden pallor, coldness of the skin, and partial or complete unconsciousness; faint, swoon" [Webster 1981, p. 2318]);
4. Death.

Changes in consciousness, from denial to death, are the individual's attempt to cope with trauma by removing the ego from observation, titrating anxiety, and reducing the pain. This form of intrapsychic functioning allows some part of the functioning ego to remain intact. That portion of the ego that remains intact is better able to recover from the trauma. When the individual regains enough homeostasis to recover from the dissociative state and return to reality, a gap in functioning occurs.

There are, Ferenczi (1932c) wrote, "gaps in remembering or in the certainty-of-remembering in relation to the events, while in shock." If the traumatic conditions continue or if the ego is not able to develop additional strengths, the individual is threatened with disintegration and reconstruction (pp. 181–182).

Ferenczi's Challenge to the Oedipal Theory

Ferenczi presented his alternate view to the oedipal theory (1930b):

> To-day I am returning to the view that, beside the great importance of the Oedipus complex in children, a deep significance must also be attached to the *repressed incestuous affection of adults, which masquerades as tenderness.*
>
> On the other hand, I am bound to confess that children themselves manifest a readiness to engage in genital eroticism more vehemently and far earlier than we used to suppose.
>
> Many of the perversions children practice probably indicate not simply fixation to a pregenital level but regression from an *early genital level.*
>
> But, the premature forcing of genital sensations has a no less terrifying effect on children; what they really want, even in their sexual life, is simply play and tenderness, not the violent ebullition of passion.
>
> *The first reaction to a shock seems to be always a transitory psychosis,* i.e., a turning away from reality.
>
> Sometimes this takes the form of negative hallucination (hysterical loss of consciousness—fainting or vertigo), often of an immediate positive hallucinatory compensation, which makes itself felt as an illusory pleasure.
>
> . . . it seems likely that a *psychotic splitting off* of a part of the personality occurs under the influence of shock. The dissociated part, however, lives on hidden, ceaselessly endeavouring to make itself felt, without finding any outlet except in neurotic symptoms. [pp. 121–122]

Child sexuality, as viewed in the oedipal theory of trauma, focused on the child as a sexual being, an advance that Freud had pioneered from his "Studies on Hysteria." As great an intellectual accomplishment as it was that Freud demonstrated the developmental pattern of child sexuality, orthodox psychoanalysis subsequently concentrated its thinking on the child as seducer. Ferenczi in 1929 accepted Freud's pioneering observation on the child as having sexual feelings and thoughts. But he began a different understanding of childhood sexuality. When perversions exist in childhood, it is not a sign of pregenital regression, but an indication of precocious sexuality due to earlier trauma. Ferenczi is suggesting that early childhood sexual behavior is not developmentally normal, but fueled by child abuse by an adult (or older child). The child's so-called flirting behavior is what Erik Erikson would later term "psychosocial play." It is a child's developmental need to experiment with the family romance and sexuality at a fantasy level of functioning. The role of the parent is to accept the flirting and to value and mirror it (as in the self psychology perspective), hold it and contain it, be the container (as in the object relations perspective), and accept and prize it (humanistic person-centered perspective) for the child's developmentally appropriate sexuality. But under *no circumstances* should the parent either respond to or initiate any sexual activity with the child. Any sexual physical touching or seductive emotional behavior by the adult is traumatic. The child's flirting, seductive behavior is to be maintained at a developmentally appropriate level of a fantasy romance. The parent should not encourage a real romance.

Children who are involved in psychosocial sexual play want tenderness, *not sexual passion*. Tenderness mirrors values and accepts the child. Sexual passion traumatizes the child. In this first theoretical explanation of a trauma theory, Ferenczi began his confusion of tongues concept. Sexual seduction of the child by the parent leads to trauma shock. The child who has been traumatized by sexual seduction becomes temporarily psychotic in order to cope with the trauma. The psychosis involves the mechanisms of denial, dissociation, detachment, confusion, and splitting off of the personality, so that the child loses a firm grasp on reality. Ferenczi, in the "Confusion of Tongues" paper, described the phenomenon of the child entering a psychological twilight zone. The child becomes what Ferenczi described as an automaton (Ferenczi 1933), a psychological robot. In the most dramatic form of dissociation and splitting, multiple personality disorder is the result.

Ferenczi's emerging trauma theory has a very interesting reference. He credited Severn with a collaborative effort in the development of these ideas. Severn, herself a therapist, was in analysis with Ferenczi for many years (see Chapter 17, this volume). She was an incest survivor who pushed Ferenczi technically to develop the grand experiment and mutual analysis. He used his clinical experience with R.N. (as she was referred to in the *Clinical Diary*) to inform both his intellectual understanding and his clinical functioning.

Oedipal Theory and the Role of Trauma

With all the previous discussions as to what really divided Freud and Ferenczi (Balint 1968b, Dupont 1988a, Gedo 1986a, Grünberger 1980, Haynal 1989, Jones 1957), contemporary developments in theory and clinical practice point out that the very significant issue of Ferenczi's fundamental departure may have been his revision of the oedipal theory of neurosis and the role of trauma as the foundation of psychoanalysis. Ferenczi, for all his innocence and desire to please Freud, deviated significantly from the mainstream of psychoanalysis in the 1930s and, for that matter, psychoanalysis until the 1960s and 1970s. With the advent of interpersonal object relations orientations to psychoanalysis in the 1940s and 1950s, and the development of self psychology in the 1970s, the mainstream of psychoanalysis is no longer being defined as Freudian psychology. In the 1990s we are finally catching up to Ferenczi's ideas, especially that of an alternative to the oedipal theory.

Ferenczi (1932c), in his *Clinical Diary*, noted another possibility: "Is the *Oedipus Complex* also a consequence of adult activity–passionate behavior? Thus: no fixation through pleasure but fixation through *anxiety*: Man and woman will *kill me, if I don't love them* (do not identify with their wishes)" (p. 173).

The crucial difference between Freud and Ferenczi was that Ferenczi began to question the efficacy of the oedipal theory and changed analytic therapy away from the analysis of oedipal conflicts (Cremerius 1983). He proposed a change in theory, a trauma theory of behavior based on sexual seduction and disturbed emotional interaction in the parent–child relationship (Ferenczi 1930b, 1931, 1932c, 1933).

Emotional Trauma

Ferenczi, in the "Notes and Fragments" of August 31, 1930, spoke about the issue of "Maternal Hatred or the Lack of Affection." Clearly, he spoke of the emotional trauma rooted in primary object relations, especially in the preoedipal relation with the mother (Ferenczi 1930b, 1949).

Ferenczi cited the childhood experience of his analysand, Dm. as an example of his attempt to outline the psychodynamics of emotional trauma rooted in disturbances in child–mother relations. He discussed the issues of maternal coldness, hatred, cruelty, and overpowering love (see Chapter 17 this volume).

> Dm. has always had the compulsion to seduce men and to be thrown into disaster by them. In fact she has done so only to escape from the loneliness which was *brought upon her by her mother's coldness*. Even in the overpassionate ruthless expressions of love by her mother, she felt her mother's hatred was a disturbing element. . . .
>
> S. had to be brought up by the father because of his mother's aggressiveness. The father died when the child was eighteen months old, then he was delivered over to the cruelty of the mother and the grandfather. *These traumata have led to disturbance of all object relations.* Secondary narcissism.
>
> The relation between the strong heterosexual trauma (father) and the defective mother fixation must remain problematic for the time being. Further experience needed. [Ferenczi 1930c, p. 233]

Trauma and Memory

As Ferenczi fully described in "The Confusion of Tongues" (Ferenczi 1933, Rachman 1989a, 1992a,c,e, 1993a; also see Chapter 14), the sexual trauma produces a profound alteration in the state of consciousness and level of reality testing for the child, as well as the child-in-the-adult. The alterations in functioning are related to the child's developing personality as well as to the real nature of the object relations to the parental figures (both abusing and enabling parents) (Rachman 1993b). The continuation and intensification of the trauma circumstances, the implied or real threats by the abuser and enabler, and the progression of the dissociative process can result in an overwhelming shock, seriously inhibiting, as Ferenczi (1930c) wrote, "every kind of mental activity and thereby provoking a state of complete passivity devoid of any resistance" (p. 239). When the overwhelming shock intrudes into the psychological state of the individual, profound changes occur.

> The absolute paralysis of motility includes also the inhibition of perception and [with it] of thinking. The shutting off of perception

results in the complete defenselessness of the ego. An impression which is not perceived cannot be warded off. The results of this complete paralysis are:

1. the course of sensory paralysis becomes and remains permanently interrupted;
2. while the sensory paralysis lasts every mechanical and mental impression is taken up without any resistance;
3. no memory traces of such impressions remain, even in the unconscious, and thus the causes of the trauma cannot be recalled from memory traces. [p. 240]

Ferenczi suggested that such a profound state of psychological alteration makes it difficult, if not impossible, to retrieve the memory trace of the trauma:

If, in spite of it, one wants to reach them, which logically appears to be almost impossible, then one must repeat the trauma itself and under more favourable conditions one must bring it *for the first time* to perception and to motor discharge. [Ferenczi 1930c, p. 240]

Dissociated Self

Ferenczi's confusion of tongues theory relies heavily on the notions of dissociation and splitting. This is also a difference in the theoretical formulations between Ferenczi and Freud. After Freud focused on the oedipal complex as the central dynamic, he lost interest in the construct of dissociation and became more interested in the concept of repression. The distinction between repression and dissociation is worth noting, since it forms a difference between Ferenczi's formulations on trauma theory.

Repression in the Freudian system refers to a hidden impulse or wish that can emerge in a more disguised (symbolic), sublimated way. The awareness of the wish or impulse is completely barred from consciousness, whereas in dissociation the impulse or wish may suddenly erupt into consciousness along with the primitive mode of experience and behavior, with little or no disguise or sublimation.

Dissociation, on the other hand, is not only an impulse or wish, but the splitting off of a whole part of the self. That portion of the self that is split off (that amounts to a person's self-image and a related way of feeling, thinking, and acting at the time of the dissociation) takes on an autonomous, quasi-independent life of its own. It becomes a kind of subsystem of the personality that can weaken and hamper the development of personality integration as a whole. It also leads to the sudden eruption of primitive, outmoded, maladaptive behavior that arises from the split-off, unintegrated part of the self.

One of the significant differences between Freud and Ferenczi was that Freud became more interested in repression than dissociation. Ferenczi's work was relevant to the concept of dissociation, especially the clinical work with sexual trauma. The interest in the concept of dissociation has been rekindled with contemporary appreciation of Ferenczi and clinical work with what are now being termed *the dissociative disorders* (Counts 1990, Gallego 1989).

Dreams and Trauma

In May 1931, Ferenczi sent Freud a copy of a paper he wished to read before the next Psycho-Analytic Congress. The paper was written on March 26, 1931. In it Ferenczi described a second function of dreams — dealing with traumatic experiences. Freud replied that he had dealt with this aspect of dream interpretation several years before (Jones 1957). Ferenczi's paper was not delivered at the next Congress. Rather, "The Confusion of Tongues" was presented (see Chapter 13).

Apparently, Ferenczi felt rebuked by Freud's comments on his "Dream" paper and therefore had a more general theory of psychoanalytic thinking to present. The paper, entitled "On the Revision of the Interpretation of Dreams," was presented posthumously, in a memorial service for Ferenczi, before the Hungarian Psychoanalytic Association on October 3, 1933. The paper was Ferenczi's last presentation and published work. It was first published in the Hungarian medical journal Gyógyászat under the title "Trauma In Psychoanalysis" (Ferenczi 1934a) and in German, entitled "Thoughts About Trauma" (Ferenczi 1934b). The first English translation of the paper appeared as "On the Revision of the Interpretation of Dreams" (Ferenczi 1934c). There were two additional reprints of the paper many years later, which made the material more available to the English-speaking analytic community (Ferenczi 1949, 1955).

Ferenczi wished to add to Freud's fundamental notion that dreams serve a wish-fulfillment transformation of the anxiety-producing experience of the day. He wished to emphasize the importance of the dream as an opportunity to repeat the trauma of the day as well as one's life. This idea is fundamental to Ferenczi's traumatic theory of neurosis. By allowing for repetition of the trauma, the dream serves a working-through function (Ferenczi 1930c).

> . . . the repetition tendency fulfills in itself a useful function in the traumatic neurosis; it endeavours to bring about a better (and if possible a final) solution than was possible at the time of the original shock. This tendency is to be assumed even where no solution results, that is, where the repetition does not lead to a better result than in the original trauma. [p. 238]

Ferenczi wished to note that the dream, in the case of traumatic neurosis, serves the crucial function of encouraging mastery over the trauma.

> Thus instead of "the dream is a wish-fulfillment," a more complete definition . . . would be: every dream, even an unpleasurable one, is an attempt at a better mastery and settling of traumatic experiences, so to speak, in the sense of an *esprit d'escalier* which is made easier in most dreams because of the diminution of the critical faculty and the predominance of the pleasure principle. [p. 238]

Anxiety dreams and nightmares are seen as the initial attempts at mastery. The residues of the day and of one's life experiences are mental impressions, needing some form of expression. Usually they are unconscious, more easily expressed in the non-censored consciousness of the dream state. Trauma aftereffects need ego mastery and, as Ferenczi wrote (1931), " . . . make use of the wish-fulfilling faculty of the dream" (p. 239).

The level of trauma, or the experience of shock, is also related to the dream state. Ferenczi wrote that "overwhelming shock acts like, as if it were, an anaesthetic" (p. 239). The sleep state encourages a dual process: the pleasure principle (wish-fulfilling function of the dream) and the return of unmastered traumatic sensory impressions that struggle for a solution (traumatolytic function of the dream).

Ferenczi (1930c) wrote that

> . . . the repetition tendency of the trauma is greater in sleep than in waking life; consequently in deep sleep it is more likely that deeply hidden, very urgent sensory impressions will return which in the first instance caused deep unconsciousness and thus remained permanently unsolved. [p. 240]

The dreamer must repeat the trauma over and over again to gain some mastery over it. But the dream work is only a beginning and a partial solution. It is in the active interaction with the analyst that the working-through process can occur.

Dream Analysis and Trauma

The function of dream analysis is to make the trauma more accessible in the waking state, to relive the events of the trauma in the analysis. Ferenczi developed a three-step approach to the retrieval of memory traces as the trauma appeared in the dream state. First, he conducted the traditional dream analysis. The aim is to deal with the narcissistic split, the split-off part of the ego, which acts as a censoring agent and allows the individual to titrate the trauma and admit to consciousness that fact of the experience that is bearable.

After the analysis of the narcissistic split, there follows a second level of dream work (Ferenczi 1930c).

> . . . there followed a second analysis in trance. In this trance one endeavors to remain in touch with the patient, which demands much tact. If the expectations of the patients are not satisfied completely they awake cross or explain to us what we ought to have said or done. The analyst must swallow a good deal and he must learn to renounce his authority as an omniscient being. This second analysis frequently makes use of some images of the dream in order to proceed through them, as it were, into the dimension of depth, i.e., into reality. [p. 242]

A third level of dream work is then developed where the process of dream work and the analysis of the trauma are integrated into the waking state of the individual.

After the trance and before the waking up it is advisable to sum up what has been lived through into one total experience and then present it to the patient. After this then follows the process of waking up which demands special precautions, e.g., it is useful after the waking up to talk over again what has happened in the session. (Here one could possibly insert the train of thought about the difference between "suggestion of content" in the earlier hypnosis and the pure suggestion of courage in the neocatharsis; the encouragement to feel and to think the traumatically interrupted mental experiences to their very end). [pp. 242–243]

Modern Trauma Theory

As discussed earlier, Freud did have a trauma theory of neurosis, both initially in discovering psychoanalysis and also in his oedipal conflict theory period, which comprised the largest span of his theoretical phase. The difference is that his trauma theories were moved away from trauma and real events as traumatogenic of neurosis. Three theories of trauma have been ascribed to Freud's thinking (McCann and Perlman 1990). The theories are:

- Unbearable affect theory, which pays attention to the emotions that bombard and overwhelm the psyche and cause disturbing aftereffects;
- Unacceptable impulse theory, in which traumatic events produce signal anxiety that can overwhelm the ego when repression fails to protect the psyche from being overwhelmed by emotions (Freud 1920, 1926); and
- Repetition of trauma theory (Freud 1939), in which the individual reexperiences or remembers the traumatic event in an attempt to master it (repetition compulsion) and in which various defense mechanisms, such as avoidance, denial, or inhibition, are employed to cope (McCann and Perlman 1990).

Ferenczi's theoretical ideas on trauma find acceptance in Henry Krystal's contemporary theory of childhood trauma. Krystal (1968, 1975, 1984) has developed a comprehensive psychoanalytic model of trauma based upon his study of survivors of extreme situations, such as the Nazi

Holocaust. Krystal discusses the differences between adult and childhood experiences of trauma. These differences deal with the capacities of a child and adult to deal with intense emotional experiences. In childhood trauma, the possibility of being easily overwhelmed or flooded with intolerable or excessive emotions is greater. Furthermore, in the earlier stages of development, emotions are primarily somatized, undifferentiated, and nonverbal. Consequently, when a child faces intense affect, it is likely to become helpless. Krystal (1968) says that adults' emotions become desomatized, differentiated from bodily states, and associated with language. Therefore, adults can better anticipate and defend themselves in situations of intense emotions. They can block the emotions before they become overwhelming. In this conceptualization, trauma is believed to be experienced differently by adults than it is by children. Krystal hypothesizes there is a surrender pattern in adults, which can include a paralysis to act, emotional blocking, and increased cognitive constriction.

THE CONFUSION OF TONGUES THEORY AND SEXUAL TRAUMA: FERENCZI'S ALTERNATE VIEW

The significance of Ferenczi's confusion of tongues theory in the history of psychoanalysis, its contribution to an understanding of his own view of neurosis, and a discussion of the phenomenon and its psychodynamics in childhood have been discussed in Chapter 13. What will be emphasized in this chapter is the role that Ferenczi assigned to sexual trauma in the etiology and treatment of psychological disorder.

It is ironic that Freud was asked to reconsider his original seduction hypothesis by his favorite student. There must have been very special reasons why Ferenczi persisted in evoking the seduction hypothesis in the final phase of his clinical career, what I have called his humanistic psychoanalysis. The confusion of tongues theory moved Ferenczi's clinical experience with sexually traumatized individuals to a new level of understanding.

Ferenczi's pioneering work in the damage and continuing effects of childhood sexual abuse is beyond anything found in the psychoanalytic literature. He provided a theoretical understanding of sexual trauma, dissociation, defense mechanisms of survival, childhood vulnerability, and the development of adult psychopathology. His understanding can be summarized as follows:

1. Difficult cases were difficult because psychoanalysis needed to view from a different perspective the traditional way of thinking about and clinically working with individuals who didn't fit the pattern of the usual neurotic.

2. Theoretically, Ferenczi wished to return to and expand Freud's seduction hypothesis. His idea was that difficult cases were suffering from the effects of childhood sexual trauma. These patients could be diagnosed today as narcissistic personality disorders, borderline personality disorders, or even psychotic disorders.

3. Ferenczi based his ideas on the observation that the patients he was treating had been sexually seduced by a parent or other significant adult. He made this observation from the histories of patients who came from privileged families; households where there were servants or fathers who were successful businessmen and professionals; and patients who were educated, sophisticated, and could afford the private practice fees for psychoanalysis.

4. What he was willing to acknowledge is that the emotional disturbances that these difficult cases showed were attributable to their reports of sexual experiences in childhood with a parent or parental figure. The seducers were the people most intimate with the child, not, as had been previously thought, strangers.

5. Ferenczi emphasized that sexual seduction was a serious psychological trauma for a child that affected the course of its personality development. In fact, the consequences were so severe as to temporarily alter the child's sense of reality and capacity to emotionally respond, as well as its state of consciousness. If the child remained untreated, this alteration would be part of the adult personality, characterized by confusion, dissociation, denial, and detachment. Because of these types of personality issues, drive and conflict analysis was not the focus of treatment. In fact, focus on the oedipal conflict would leave the incest trauma unanalyzed.

6. Ferenczi's clinical work involved the uncovering of the early childhood sexual experience and the empathic affirmation of the event as the causal factor in the individual's emotional disturbance. This affirmation of the analysand's sexual trauma was unique, courageous, and in direct contrast to the prevailing theory of Freud and the majority of his early followers. That Ferenczi was willing to place his reputation at stake for the assertion that real sexual events were the cause of psychological disorder in adulthood and, what is more, that mostly female individuals were being seduced by their fathers, who were part of the respectable

middle and upper class, was one of the emotionally courageous events in the history of psychoanalysis. Unfortunately, this courage became his undoing, as his assertions led to his political assassination and great emotional stress. Ferenczi was censured by Freud and removed from the psychoanalytic mainstream. The emotional crisis that his confusion of tongues theory caused brought Freud and Ferenczi to the breaking point of their personal and professional relationship.

It is clear now that Ferenczi's theoretical and clinical ideas about sexual abuse and its connection to the understanding and treatment of difficult cases were prophetic. Incest, which Ferenczi called the most prevalent form of sexual trauma in difficult cases, was once thought to be a rare phenomenon. In the last ten years, clinical and epidemiologic studies have demonstrated that incest is a more common occurrence than both the professional and lay communities were willing to believe. Prior to a recent study, it was thought that a 5 percent incidence of incest was the normative figure (Finkelhor and Hotaling 1984, Stone 1989, 1990). But the most current and thorough epidemiologic study of adult women showed that 19 percent had an incest history (Russell 1988).

The difficult cases of which Ferenczi spoke were, as we now know, narcissistic, borderline, and psychotic conditions. Contemporary studies also establish Ferenczi's observations that sexual trauma was an integral part of the development of a serious psychological disorder. An incest history occurs more frequently in a psychiatric population than in the population as a whole, especially among female patients hospitalized for suicidal behavior, borderline personality, or schizoaffective disorders (Stone 1989, 1990). Furthermore, the conditions of the incest experience are reflected in the nature and extent of the emotional disturbance for the victim. A variety of diagnostic categories are related to incest (e.g., borderline personality disorder, histrionic, avoidant, or paranoid personality, traumatic stress disorder [Kolb 1987], schizoaffective illness, major depressive disorder, somatization disorder, dissociative reactions, and multiple personality disorder [Stone 1989]). The percentage of an incest history is high in several subgroups—25 to 75 percent of hospitalized women with borderline personality disorder, or younger women with schizoaffective disorder or posttraumatic stress disorder (Stone 1990). A startling finding is that almost all female patients with multiple personality disorder have a history of either incestuous molestation or severe physical abuse or both (Kluft 1985). Sexual trauma is, as Ferenczi suggested, a significant factor in psychological functioning that can influence any level of personality organization. Witness a recent finding that the most intense dental phobia is manifested by women who have been sexually molested as children (Reuben 1989).

The theory of sexual trauma from a contemporary viewpoint, which integrates Ferenczi's ideas and methods in the confusion of tongues theory, can be outlined as follows:

1. An actual sexual seduction has taken place.
2. A confusion of tongues syndrome has developed.
3. A focus is developed on the recall and reexperience of the trauma.
4. The empathic method is used to create understanding, acceptance, safety, and unfolding.
5. The analyst suggests the presence of a sexual trauma if the historical, clinical, and experiential data reveal evidence.
6. An engagement is created in the relationship between analyst and analysand where caution is exercised to reduce the possibility of retraumatization. If retraumatization does occur, the analyst moves quickly to reduce the wounds by taking responsibility for the experience, uses empathy to soothe the wounds, and, when the crisis has subsided, analyzes the trauma and its relevance to the original abuse experience.
7. An awareness is developed toward the occurrence of an abusive parental transference. The sexual trauma survivor is hypersensitive to any experience in a relationship that triggers feelings of abuse, betrayal, manipulation, control, violence, or sexuality. The analysis of the transference implications only occurs after the analyst reduces the experience of abuse by empathic and humanistic interventions that soothe the psychologically wounded analysand.
8. Active measures are employed to aid in the establishment of a safe relationship, reduce the anticipation of abuse, and encourage a caring relationship, thus resolving the dissociative process and working through with the translation of insight into action.

A benign regression (Balint 1968a) is allowed to unfold where the individual can reach the archaic self in the safety of the psychoanalytic situation. An ability to function as a container is necessary (Winnicott 1951) for the negative parental introject, to tolerate the toxicity of the transference. With these considerations, the clinical work with survivors of incest trauma can, in an interesting way, return us to the most exciting period in psychoanalytic history, when both Freud and Ferenczi struggled with the significant issues in human behavior.

9. Adjunctive modalities, such as group therapy, family therapy, couple therapy, intensive individual sessions, twelve-step programs, and peer group therapy are employed to aid the analysis.

RECOVERING FROM TRAUMA

Trauma and the Psychoanalytic Situation

Ferenczi discussed the intrapsychic experience of trauma in particularly difficult cases, where the analysand cannot tolerate separation from the analyst or has the desire to have a real, permanent relation. Such desires are thwarted by the nature of the analytic relationship, which is temporary and allows for necessary intervals of separation. Even in the furthest clinical experimentation of Ferenczi's relaxation therapy, such as the mutual analysis with R.N. (Ferenczi 1932c), these needs could not realistically be satisfied.

These analysands, who suffered from traumatic pasts, experienced such restrictions in the psychoanalytic situation as a retraumatization. According to Ferenczi (1934d), the analyst's task is to help the individual develop insight into "the transference character of this situation and [trace] it back to the infantile traumatic events. . . ." (p. 30). The journey back to the infantile traumatic events necessitates the unfolding of a benign regression, as Balint would later elaborate. But in this earlier period, a distinction had not yet been drawn between benign and malignant regression (Balint 1968a). Ferenczi (1934d) described the process of malignant regression.

> Our analysis intends and apparently is also able to lead back to the first stage of the process of regression. Of course this necessitates an entire abandonment of the actual relations and a complete submergence in the traumatic past. The only bridge between the real world

and the patient in the trance state is . . . the analyst who urges the
patient to intellectual effort in the middle of the emotion instead of
his simple behaviouristic and emotional repetition, and encourages
him untiringly with questions. [p. 30]

Ferenczi went on to describe the process by which the traumatized
individual, frustrated in his attempt to gain primary love, uses splitting
and fragmentation to cope with the emotional trauma.

A surprising, but seemingly generally constant fact in the process of
the fragmentation of the self is the sudden transformation of the
object relation which has become impossible into the narcissistic
one. The individual . . . slips completely from reality and creates
another world for himself in which, unhampered by earthly difficulties, he can attain everything he wishes. If till now he was unloved,
even tortured, he splits off a part of himself which in the form of a
benevolent or kindhearted, generally motherly protector pities the
remaining tormented part of the person, cares for it, decides for it, all
this with the greatest wisdom, with penetrating intelligence. [The
split-off part, which can experience "goodness"] . . . invents fantasies
for the child who cannot otherwise be rescued. [If a new trauma
occurs] . . . there remains nothing else but suicide, unless in the last
moment something favourable turns up in reality. [pp. 30–31]

The relationship with the analyst is the lifesaving device for the individual.

This favourable element to which we are able to point as against the
suicidal impulse is the fact that in this newly occurring traumatic
struggle the patient does not stand quite alone. True, one cannot
offer him everything he would have deserved as a child, but the fact
of the possibility of help alone gives an impulse to a new life in which
the records of the irrevocable are put on the shelf and the first step
is taken toward being content with what life can still offer, and in
not throwing away what is serviceable. [p. 31]

Ferenczi felt that the analyst had a special role in the individual's
recovery from trauma:

1. Presence of a helpful person (understanding and wanting to help). Alleviation of pain.
2. Help through suggestion, when energy flags: shaking up, encouraging words . . .
3. Recollection possible only if a reconsolidated ego (integrated, or one that has become so) *resists* external influences; it is influenced but it is not fragmented by them.
4. Systems of memory scars form new tissue with its own functions: reflexes, conditioned reflexes (nervous system). This function, originally only an interrupted modification of the self/destruction), is placed in the service of *self-preservation: as alloplastically directed thought work* [Denkarbeit].
5. Repetition compulsion in the traumatized is a renewed attempt at a *better resolution.* [Ferenczi 1932c, p. 182]

Trauma and the Neo-Cathartic Method

In "Principles of Relaxation and Neo-Catharsis," presented at the Oxford Congress, Ferenczi assumed that certain traumatic memories cannot be accessed through the purely intellectual memorization process (Ferenczi 1930b). He suggests that there is a need to return to the Breuer-Freud cathartic method. As will be remembered, the original psychoanalytic method involved the encouragement of emotional release in order to reach the repressed memories and feelings. By recontacting the original feelings that were repressed at the time of the trauma, the individual would be able to work through or gain ego maturity over the residue of the emotional difficulty.

Ferenczi questioned whether the orthodox Freudian method, with its emphasis on the analysis of resistance, the encouragement of free associations and prolonged unfolding process, and the conceptualizations of the metapsychology of the patient, is really clinically helpful. He reasoned, from *his* clinical experience and not from Freudian theory, that the cathartic method was more useful in analyzing trauma (Ferenczi 1930b). "We can see then that, while the similarity of the analytical to the infantile situation impels patients to repetition, the contrast between the two encourages recollection" (p. 124).

As we have seen, Ferenczi began the technical belief in *remembering and repeating* in his criticism of the cognitive structure of Freudian psychoanalysis (Ferenczi and Rank 1925). In fact, from his earliest experiments in the active method, he heightened the emotional experience of a psychoanalytic session. Ferenczi (1930b) outlined the theoretical and clinical issues.

> . . . repressed hate often operates more strongly in the direction of fixation and arrest than openly confessed tenderness. I think I have never had this point more clearly put than by a patient whose confidence . . . I won by the method of indulgence. "Now I like you and now I can let you go," was her first spontaneous remark on the emergence of a positive affective attitude towards me. I believe it was in the analysis of the same patient that I was able to prove that relaxation lends itself particularly well to the conversion of the repetition-tendency into recollection.
>
> So long as she identified me with her hard-hearted parents, she incessantly repeated the reactions of defiance. But when I deprived her of all occasion for this attitude, she began to discriminate the present from the past and . . . to remember the psychic shocks of her childhood.
>
> *We see then that, while the similarity of the analytical to the infantile situation impels patients to repetition, the contrast between the two encourages recollection.* [pp. 123–124, italics original]

This conceptualization of Ferenczi's encourages a therapy of action. Retrieving the memory traces of childhood trauma occurs via the active Ferenczian approach. This can occur in an active measure, such as the use of drawings to retrieve memories of sexual seduction (Rachman 1990b,d, 1992a,b,f, 1993e). Remembering can also occur in a Ferenczian analysis that emphasizes relaxation therapy. The gradual unfolding of memory occurs via the creation of an empathic, safe, trusting, and non-traumatic clinical milieu in the psychoanalytic situation (Rachman 1989d, 1990d).

The therapeutic technique also involves reexperiencing the trauma in the psychoanalytic situation (Ferenczi 1930c).

> . . . to re-live the trauma (i.e., to encourage the patient to repeat and to live it out to the end—which often only succeeds after innumerable unsuccessful attempts and at first usually only piecemeal); then it may come to a new, more favourable and possibly lasting mastery of the trauma. [p. 240]

This method involves first the creation of a safe, trusting, and empathic ambience and then the appropriate introduction of active measures to aid the unfolding of the return to the original experience of trauma (Rachman, 1989b,d, 1990a,b,d).

Forgiveness and Working Through Trauma

Ferenczi described the important issue of the change in relationship between incest survivor and perpetrator that naturally occurs—once the dissociative process has been lifted, the memories of seduction are vividly experienced and the repressed rage emerges. It is an emotional struggle for all survivors that leaves them puzzled, confused, ambivalent, or ready to retaliate. Some of the countertransference reactions common to clinical work with survivors is to encourage confrontation with the abusing parent, to incite the survivor to bring a civil lawsuit against a perpetrator, or to conspicuously self-disclose outrage or anger toward the offending party. While the analysand is free to harbor and express such feelings and desires toward action, the analyst's task is to empathize with and interpret the meaning of these feelings and actions. The emotional space must be created, so that the incest survivor can, if he or she wishes, enter into a process of forgiveness toward the abuser. Although many survivors of trauma wish to maintain their anger and also may wish reparations (either financial, emotional, or interpersonal), in order to maintain permanent distance or even to destroy the toxic object, the analyst needs to maintain an empathic bond by treating each individual according to his or her needs and emotional capacities. As Ferenczi (1932c) pointed out, the issue of forgiveness must be considered in the analysis of the incest trauma.

> *Analyst* after receiving catalogue of sins, and after overcoming his defiant reaction: breakdown—"wanted the best and this is what happened!" *Patient:* in a position to *forgive.* That the first step could be taken toward forgiveness for causing the trauma indicates that they had attained insight. That it was at all *possible* to arrive at insight and communion with oneself spells the end of general *misanthropy.* Finally, it is also possible to view and *remember* the trauma with *feelings of forgiveness* and consequently *understanding.* [p. 201]

17

FERENCZI'S
CLINICAL DIARY

FERENCZI'S IDENTITY CRISIS

The *Clinical Diary* was written on the shores of the Danube during 1932. It consists of 136 spontaneous essays, or one could say free associations (Sabourin 1985). Ferenczi shared self-reflections on his clinical career, his relationship with his mentor (Freud), and the human struggle and journey he took with his difficult cases. The *Diary* was kept by Ferenczi's wife, Gizella. After his death on May 22, 1933, the diary notes were given to Balint. Ferenczi's free associations were deciphered, annotated, and translated from the German original into English.

One can liken the writing of the *Clinical Diary* to an adult version of the adolescent identity crisis in Ferenczi. An identity crisis has been attributed to a characteristic psychosocial developmental crisis of adolescence (Erikson 1950, 1956, 1959, 1968), which helps self-cohesion and aids the formation of internal structures that enable an individual to differentiate him- or herself from authority role models. When this natural process is retarded by authoritarianism, negative role models, and a lack of support in the culture, confusion prevails. When the adolescent loses direction and purpose, personality integration is threatened and group affiliation becomes tenuous. Therapeutic intervention then becomes necessary (Rachman 1975a, 1977d).

An identity crisis can reach into adulthood and force the individual to revisit the adolescent struggle toward self-definition. Erikson, the originator of this conceptualization, cited Martin Luther's identity struggle with God and the Catholic Church in a postadolescent period as an example of a protracted identity crisis in a creative and exceptional individual.

This journal was Ferenczi's creative retreat from Freud and the psychoanalytic community, which no longer understood or approved of his theories or clinical methods. Ferenczi, in his mature years, needed to return to an adolescent process, as he was suffering from an identity crisis. He could no longer use his role model, Freud, to inform his clinical work or his thinking. Having lost his role model's approval, he also lost the social network of his peers. From the chaos and crisis, it was clear that he needed to create something that would help him maintain a sense of self-cohesion, reaffirm his belief in his destiny, and solidify his identity as a psychoanalyst. Freud tried to reach out to Ferenczi, realizing that their differences were causing an emotional crisis, but he was operating from a position of power, being the parental authority as well as the sole authority in the psychoanalytic community. Freud encouraged his pupil, his "dear son," to abandon his clinical experiments in humanistic psychoanalysis and become politically involved in the International. Freud did not understand that Ferenczi was suffering from an identity crisis, provoked by Freud's rejection of him. It was a problem of relationship—the authoritarian father with the rebellious son—as well as the transferences and countertransferences that they both brought to this difficult moment in their relationship. The curative element in this psychosocial crisis was for Freud, the father, to enter into an honest, self-disclosing, and empathic dialogue with Ferenczi, the son, free of hypocrisy and any need to control, dominate, or force a prescribed solution. (It would have been even more curative if Freud could have come to Ferenczi as a wise brother, esteemed peer, or mutual analytic partner—but we know that this was impossible, since Freud could not relinquish his need to dominate, control, and exercise power over others.)

Because Freud could not relinquish his role as a stern father and Ferenczi could not relinquish his as the traumatized child, a solution needed to be found that would not cause a break between father and son, yet would allow the son to struggle toward separation, independence, and a fuller development of an identity based upon his own true self. Freud's suggested solution that Ferenczi become the president of the International was a further encouragement of a false self-experience for Ferenczi. Because Ferenczi did not want a complete rupture of his relationship with Freud, he found a solution to the relational crisis between them. He withdrew into a creative retreat; he functioned independently from Freud, developing his own identity as a psychoanalyst, gathering his own adherents. Refusing Freud's invitation to become part of the establishment by becoming more political was part of Ferenczi's emancipation proclamation. The second part of the declaration of independence was the writing of the *Clinical Diary*.

Freud/Ferenczi Relationship

Ferenczi's painful disagreements with Freud, which the *Diary* so clearly illustrated, had a history that went back to the early moments of their relationship. As mentioned in Chapter 3, a landmark in their relationship was the Sicily trip in 1910. This experience has often been cited as an incident that defined an enduring negative aspect of their relationship. The account by Jones (1955) in the Freud biography clearly implies that Ferenczi was a deeply neurotic or even psychotic partner:

> What actually happened in Sicily was merely that Ferenczi was inhibited, sulky, and unreliable in the day-to-day arrangements: Freud described his attitude as one of "bashful admiration and mute opposition." But behind those manifestations lay severe trouble in the depths of his personality . . . he was haunted by a quite inordinate and insatiable longing for his father's love. It was the dominating passion of his life and was indirectly the source of the unfortunate changes he introduced into his psychoanalytic technique twenty years later, which had the effect of estranging him from Freud (though not Freud from him). [p. 82]

The *Clinical Diary* as well as the Ferenczi/Groddeck correspondence casts a new light on the Sicily trip. The incident that caused such difficulty between Ferenczi and Freud was not fueled by Ferenczi's psychopathology, as Jones would have us believe, but by Freud's authoritarianism. During this early phase of their relationship (which was only two years old at the time), Ferenczi was looking forward to collaborating on a paper with Freud. What led to a crisis in their relationship was a complete misunderstanding as to what constitutes a collaboration. Freud suggested that they collaborate on a paper that would deal with the Schreber case. The "collaboration" meant that Ferenczi would take down Freud's dictation on his notes on the case. Ferenczi was incredulous, refusing to be Freud's flunky. Freud was angry at Ferenczi's independence and desire for mutuality (an issue that was to haunt their relationship throughout the years). Freud worked on the paper at night in his room, isolated from his friend (Ferenczi and Groddeck 1982 [letter of Christmas 1921]).

Ferenczi tried with Freud to create a mutual relationship. Unfortunately, his desire was never fulfilled. But it was not only Ferenczi's frustration. No one in the psychoanalytic community was ever able to convince Freud to relinquish his need for power and control in a relationship. Ferenczi, however, never gave up the struggle. After the failed Schreber collaboration, Ferenczi (1911) proposed a mutual experience for the analytic community. If Freud was unable to relinquish power and control, perhaps he could convince his analytic colleagues to do so.

> It would be a family in which the father enjoyed no dogmatic authority, but only that to which he was entitled by reason of his abilities and labours. His pronouncements would not be followed blindly, as if they were divine revelations, but . . . would be subject to thoroughgoing criticism, which he would accept, not with the absurd superiority of the paterfamilias, but with the attention it deserved. [p. 303]

Ferenczi continued the dialogue with Freud regarding their differences that would surface in the *Clinical Diary*. On January 17, 1930, he wrote to Freud about the clear differences that were separating them and that would form one of the themes of the *Diary* (Dupont 1988b).

> I do not share . . . your view that the therapeutic process is negligible or unimportant, and that . . . we should ignore it. I, too, have often felt "fed up" in this respect, but overcame this tendency, and I am glad to inform you that precisely in this area a whole series of questions have come into a new, a sharper focus, perhaps even the problem of repression. [p. xiii]

In a letter from Ferenczi to Freud, dated January 17, 1930, he was able to tell his mentor and analyst that Freud and he were separated by an important issue—the willingness to practice countertransference analysis (Dupont 1988b).

> What happens in the relationship between you and me (at least in me) is an entanglement of various conflicts of emotions and positions. At first you were my revered mentor and unattainable model, for whom I nourished the feelings of a pupil—always mixed, as we know. Then you became my analyst, but . . . my analysis could not

be completed. I particularly regretted that, in the course of the analysis, you did not perceive in me and did not bring to abreaction negative feelings and fantasies that were only partially transferred. It is well known that no analysand . . . could accomplish this without assistance. Painstaking self-analysis was therefore required, which I subsequently undertook. . . . Naturally this was also linked to the fact that I was able to abandon my somewhat puerile attitude and realize that I must not depend quite so *completely* on your favor — that is, that I must not overestimate my importance to you. Also, some minor incidents in the course of our travels together resulted in your inspiring certain inhibitions in me, particularly the severity with which you published my obstinate behavior over the matter of the Schreber book. . . . Wouldn't mildness and indulgence have been more appropriate from the side of the person of authority? [p. xiii]

One of the salient criticisms that Ferenczi (1932c) made in the *Diary* was his dissatisfaction with his analysis by Freud. The theme of Freud's excessive rationalism, which Ferenczi and Rank first criticized in 1925 in their monograph *Development of Psychoanalysis*, was intensified in the *Diary*.

My own analysis could not be pursued deeply enough because my analyst . . . with this strong determination to be healthy and his antipathy toward any weaknesses or abnormalities, could not follow me down in these depths, and introduced the "educational" stage too soon. Just as Freud's strength lies in firmness of education, so mine lies in the depth of the relaxation technique. [p. 62]

Ferenczi questioned whether Freud was able to enter into a mutual analysis with an analysand. Of course, Ferenczi was talking from the failure that he had experienced with his analyst.

Is Freud really convinced, or does he have a compulsion to cling too strongly to theory as a defense against self-analysis, that is, against his own doubts? . . . Freud is not the discoverer of analysis but . . . took over something ready-made, from Breuer. Perhaps he followed Breuer in a logical, intellectual fashion, and not with any emotional conviction, consequently he only analyzes others, but not himself. . . . [p. 92]

Interestingly enough, Ferenczi was echoing Jung's much earlier criticisms of Freud's appeal to authority, when Jung could not get Freud to enter into a mutual analysis with him in 1909 (see Chapter 4).

Ferenczi's focus in the *Diary* through his criticisms of Freud was also the delineation of his dissident movement away from orthodox analysis and toward his relaxation therapy and humanistic psychoanalytic method. It is his finest hour because he managed to find his independent voice, even if it was a muted one. He became the first analyst within the orthodox community to speak out about the shortcomings of Freud's conservatism and remain within the fold.

Freud thought that Ferenczi was too much under the influence of his patients. Ferenczi (1932c), on the other hand, suggested that " . . . real analysis can come about only when relaxation takes place in the child–parent relationship, that is to say, total trust and the surrender of all independence" (p. 39). Mutual analysis was Ferenczi's willingness to surrender his role as the sole authority in the therapeutic process.

HISTORY AND PRESERVATION OF FERENCZI'S CLINICAL DIARY

During a nine-month period, from January 7, 1932, until October 2, 1932, Ferenczi began to note his daily experiences with his patients during the past period of his clinical functioning. The entries were spontaneous and each one dated, so that, as Balint (1988) wrote, "one can follow how much, or how little, he could cope with on any one day" (p. 221). The details of the entries were described by Balint in the notes he prepared for the original 1969 English edition.

> The last typed entry is dated 24th August 1932. Then Ferenczi stopped working in order to go first to Vienna, where he met Freud for the last time in his life, and from there to the Wiesbaden Congress. . . . After that day there were only six more handwritten pages, all dated October 1932.
>
> If one compares the dates of the Diary: the first entry in January 1932, then fairly continuous entries until the end of August 1932, and lastly a few disjointed ones in October with the dates of the "Notes and Fragments" that were found after his death among

his papers, and published in Volume 4 of the Bausteins and subsequently in the *Final Contributions*, we find: a few experimental entries in 1920, then a continued effort through 1930 and 1931 which suddenly stops at the beginning of 1932. There is one isolated, not very interesting entry in June of that year, but a new series of entries starts mid-September in Biarritz where Ferenczi went from Wiesbaden. . . . From then on the entries continue until the end of that year. [pp. 221-222]

Balint (1988) believed that the entries of 1930 and 1931 were Ferenczi's first attempts at a clinical diary. These original entries were handwritten on all sorts of papers, including proper sheets, backs of envelopes, and half pages of pharmaceutical propaganda material.

After Ferenczi returned from the Wiesbaden Conference and the disastrous final meeting with Freud, his emotional energy was sapped. Before he left for Wiesbaden to present "The Confusion of Tongues," he had made numerous entries in the *Diary* of August 4, 7, 8, 11, 12, 13, 14, 17, 22, and 24. These entries, in number, length, and content, indicated that Ferenczi was enthusiastically preparing for his last clinical presentation. His mind and emotions were directed toward outlining his controversial theory of the confusion of tongues. Freud urged Ferenczi not to present his paper, which he refused. Consequently, Freud would not shake Ferenczi's hand in farewell. The final blow was the negative reception that "The Confusion of Tongues" received at the conference. There was only one entry in the *Diary* when Ferenczi returned from Wiesbaden, dated October 2, 1932. The entry began with an ominous note: "Further regression to being dead." Ferenczi (1932c) went on to note what appeared to be the reaction of devastation to Freud's rejection:

(. . . Is a new kind of solution to the personality problem possible after such *sinking* into the traumatic?)

In my case the blood-crisis* arose when I realized that not only can I not rely on the protection of a "higher power" but *on the contrary* I shall be trampled under foot by this indifferent power as soon as I go my own way and not his. [p. 212]

---

*Pernicious anemia, which was to cause Ferenczi's death just a few months later—Ed., Dupont 1988b, p. 215.

This more cryptic reference to the difficulties with Freud and the analytic community and the devastation it was causing Ferenczi becomes clear in the paragraphs to follow in this last *Diary* entry (Ferenczi 1932c).

> I did indeed also feel abandoned by colleagues . . . who are all too afraid of Freud to behave objectively or even sympathetically toward me, in the case of a dispute between Freud and me. A more restrained circulation of letters between Freud, Jones, and Eitingon has certainly been going on for a long time now. I am treated like a sick person who must be spared. My intervention will have to wait until I recover, so that the special "care" becomes unnecessary. [pp. 213-214]

According to Balint, Ferenczi never recovered from either his physical problems or emotional difficulties to continue writing the *Diary* after the October 2, 1932, entry. He was able to continue some writing, which eventually was published under the title "Notes and Fragments" (Ferenczi 1930c). In the winter of 1932–1933, he had to give up his practice, became bedridden, mainly because of the degeneration of his spinal cord, and finally died on May 22, 1933.

The first hint that Ferenczi was collecting material for a diary was contained in a letter from Ferenczi to Freud, dated December 25, 1929 (Dupont 1988b).

> Actually, my true affinity is for research, and, freed from all personal ambition, I have become deeply immersed . . . in the study of cases. . . . To summarize in the briefest possible way, I should like you to know the following:
>
> 1. In *all* cases where I penetrated deeply enough, I found uncovered the traumatic hysterical basis of the illness.
> 2. Where the patient and I succeeded in this, the therapeutic effect was far more significant. In many cases I had to recall previously "cured" patients for further treatment.
> 3. The critical view that I gradually formed during this period was that psychoanalysis deals far too one-sidedly with obsessive neurosis and character analysis—that is, ego psychology—while neglecting the organic/hysterical basis of the analysis. This

results from overestimating the role of fantasy, and underestimating that of traumatic reality, in pathogenesis. . . .

4. The newly acquired experiences (though in essence they refer back to the distant past) naturally also affect some particular features of technique. Certain measures are far too severe and must be tempered without completely losing sight of the secondary, educational aspect. [p. xii]

The differences that Ferenczi was referring to were his growing preoccupation with his difficult cases and the humanistic analytic method he was developing. Freud was aware that his favorite pupil was drifting away from him and the larger analytic community.

Ferenczi was continuing his clinical experiments in relaxation therapy, driven not by his psychopathology, but by an unbending motivation to heal traumatic individuals. Furthermore, he knew that Freud was growing increasingly more critical of his clinical work. Freud said that Ferenczi had a "furor sanandi" (rage to cure) (Grosskurth 1988). The real problem, therefore, was that Ferenczi could not freely communicate to his mentor about his clinical work. The only way to continue this significant work was to withdraw from the traditional analytic community (which would side with Freud's admonitions); surround himself with colleagues, analysands, and pupils who would encourage and support his deviations from Freud; and finally keep a secret journal that would preserve his final theory and method for posterity. The *Clinical Diary* allowed Ferenczi to develop his ideas independently from Freud, without suffering damaging criticisms. After all, the trauma of the "Confusion of Tongues" paper must have convinced Ferenczi that he could not risk himself any further, either personally or professionally, at the hands of Freud and the orthodox analytic community. The *Clinical Diary*, therefore, served as a lifesaving device that allowed Ferenczi to maintain self-cohesion in the face of mounting assaults on his work and person.

BALINT'S INTRODUCTION

In 1969, Balint wrote an introduction to the *Clinical Diary*, assuming that its publication was imminent and that the *Diary* and the Freud/Ferenczi correspondence would be issued simultaneously. The *Diary* was finished in October 1933, and the Freud/Ferenczi correspondence also ended in 1933. So even if this material had been published in 1969, as Balint had wished, at that time it would have indicated a thirty-six-year delay in publication. This significant delay was consistent with the successful attempt to suppress "The Confusion of Tongues," which suffered a seventeen-year delay in being published in English. It is clear, then, that the three significant Ferenczi materials, represented by "The Confusion of Tongues," the *Clinical Diary*, and the Freud/Ferenczi correspondence, were held back from publication because of the controversy they generated. Freud and his followers held back "The Confusion of Tongues" as a deliberate attempt to suppress Ferenczi's ideas. Balint, on the other hand, was delaying the publication of the *Clinical Diary* and the Freud/Ferenczi correspondence because he wanted to contribute to the healing of the wound that "The Confusion of Tongues" presentation had caused between Ferenczi, Freud, and the analytic community (Balint 1968b). "The Confusion of Tongues" is now available in the 1949 original translation by Balint (Ferenczi 1949), reprinted in Volume 3 of Ferenczi's collected papers (Ferenczi 1955), and in a retranslation by Masson (Masson 1984).

The publication of the *Clinical Diary* clearly presented a personal and professional dilemma for Balint. As Ferenczi's closest student, he was well aware of the *Diary* while it was being written in 1932. Ferenczi's sentiments at the time were as follows (Balint 1988).

> . . . during 1932 he often mentioned that he was writing it, and during his last months in 1933 he repeated time and again that, because he had to give up his practice, he could not finish the *Diary*, and how much he regretted that he could not include in it his last experiences with his patients as they, one after the other, had to leave him. [p. 219]

When Ferenczi died, Balint was burdened with the decision of whether to publish the *Diary* immediately. In consultation with Vilma Kovács and Alice Balint, it was recommended to Mrs. Ferenczi that the *Diary* not be published in 1933 and for a time thereafter. Balint wished the *Diary* to receive a more objective assessment in an atmosphere within the analytic community that could be less hostile to Ferenczi as a person and more receptive to him as an extraordinary clinician. It was a meaningful plan and indicated Balint's love for his mentor as well as his role as a healer within his own profession. Balint had been an excellent student of Ferenczi, understanding not only the healing arts in the psychoanalytic situation, but the application of this method to healing one's colleagues (an understanding Jones never possessed).

Balint's plan to heal the wounds between Freud and Ferenczi and between Ferenczi and the analytic community became complicated by factors beyond his control. In order to pass on Ferenczi's theoretical and technical legacy to psychoanalysis, the Balints and Kovács worked through the editing of his papers for the German edition, Volumes 3 and 4 of the Bausteins. Freud was aware of the project, and, according to Balint (1988), "It can be stated that he followed our work with interest, did not object to any part of the text proposed by us; on the contrary, he expressed his admiration for Ferenczi's ideas, until then unknown to him" (p. 219).

Two factors conspired to make the publication of the *Diary* difficult. One was the beginning of World War II. Balint was able to negotiate the transfer of the Ferenczi material from Vienna to Budapest and finally to neutral Switzerland, after negotiations with the Nazi authorities. The *Diary* and the Freud/Ferenczi correspondence were given to Balint by Ferenczi's widow in January 1939, when he left Budapest for England.

As ominous a force as the Nazis were, there was a still more dangerous force, ironically, within the analytic community. Balint, once again, faced Ferenczi's nemesis, Jones (Balint 1988).

> After the War my first concern became to translate and edit all the important papers by Ferenczi which had not yet appeared in English. After overcoming some resistance by Ernest Jones, the Editor of the International Psychoanalytic Library, who wanted to omit from the English edition all the papers written by Ferenczi after 1928, the *Final Contributions* appeared in 1955. The reception was not encouraging, so I decided to wait. [p. 220]

Jones, unsuccessful in totally suppressing "The Confusion of Tongues" in 1933 and the humanistic psychoanalytic papers (1928–1933) in 1955, now focused his poisoned arrow on Ferenczi's person. In the now famous character assassination attempt in Volume 3 of his Freud biography, he launched an attack on Ferenczi, accusing him of being psychotic and insinuating that his deviations from Freud were a result of his "madness" (see Chapter 6). Balint's (1988) description of how Jones continued to poison the air in the analytic community and make it difficult for the *Diary* to receive a favorable review is important to quote.

> As Jones had access to the whole Freud/Ferenczi correspondence, I could not understand how he was able to neglect the evidence

contained in it. When I asked him from what source he derived his allegations, he refused to give any information except that it was someone close to Ferenczi during his last period. When we reached this point it was already generally known that Jones was suffering from an incurable condition. Under these circumstances the only thing I felt wise to do was to agree with him to publish a correspondence in the *International Journal* (1958) in which each of us stated his point of view. [p. 220]

Balint died in 1971, and the *Diary* was not published until Dupont and Le Coq-Héron compiled the French edition in 1985.

DUPONT'S INTRODUCTION

The psychoanalytic community has been universal in its praise of Dupont's editing of the *Clinical Diary*, both the French and English editions. Her task of editing was a formidable one. In order to produce this volume, so significant to the history of psychoanalysis, Dupont had three textual sources:

1. The original manuscript in German, which contains a number of typographical errors, unusual abbreviations, sentences with missing words, neologisms, and typographical infelicities, such as unclosed parentheses. Much of the handwritten section is composed of cryptic notes that are difficult to decipher.
2. A typewritten transcription by Balint. Balint was familiar with Ferenczi's handwriting and was able to reconstruct sentences written in Ferenczi's telegraphic style. In transcribing the *Diary* he omitted several paragraphs, including two in which Ferenczi expressed his opinion of Freud. In 1969 Balint judged their publication inappropriate. It does not seem so today.
3. An English translation of the *Diary* by Balint. This work facilitated greatly the understanding of certain passages. Balint also provided notes, which have been incorporated into this edition (Dupont 1988b).

There are three areas of concentration in Ferenczi's *Diary*. Dupont (1988b) has outlined the areas under the titles: "(1) a theoretical point:

trauma; (2) a technical point (closely linked to the problem of trauma): mutual analysis; (3) a personal point: Ferenczi/Freud relationship" (p. xvii). To these three areas I would add a fourth – description of analysis with four analysands.

Although these four themes are the central contributions, the *Diary* also covers discussions on such diverse topics as paranoia, schizophrenia, homosexuality, the Oedipus complex, training analysis, termination of an analysis, the issue of emotional abreaction, and the concept of repression. These topics were all issues to which Ferenczi had devoted some aspect of his clinical functioning.

FERENCZI'S CLINICAL CASES

In the *Clinical Diary* Ferenczi described the analysis of four female analysands: R.N. (Severn), Dm. (Thompson), S.I., and B. As was the case in Freud's pioneering clinical work in psychoanalysis, when female patients such as Bertha Pappenheim helped him originate the cathartic method, Ferenczi's female patients described in the *Clinical Diary* helped him develop his relaxation therapy. We therefore again have the hidden psychodynamic of female patients contributing to the clinical method of their male doctors.

The Case of R.N.: (Elizabeth Severn)

She was the analysand who moved Ferenczi to extend the empathic method to its farthest reaches by incorporating the analyst's personality as integral to the analytic process. R.N. was perhaps the most influential analysand in Ferenczi's clinical experience who helped form his trauma theory of neurosis and the relaxation therapy method to deal with it. R.N. was the victim of severe physical, sexual, and emotional abuse as a child, which helped shape her adult personality and psychopathology. A glimpse into the horror of her childhood informs the reader of the reenactment that was triggered by being in the psychoanalytic situation with Ferenczi (1932c).

> ... the first shock occurred at the age of one and a half years (a promise by an adult, a close relative, to give her "something good" instead of which, drugged and sexually abused). At the onset of semiconsciousness, sudden awareness of something vile, total

disillusionment and helplessness, perhaps also a temporary feeling of incapacity *to exercise her own will*, that is, painful awareness of suggestibility. Persistence of this state of half-stupor; probably at her most profound depths a wish not to be alive; nevertheless, under the influence of suggestion, a normal schoolchild's existence prevails: in other words, an artificial double life, together with complete repression of her own inclination and feelings. [p. 8, italics added]

One must remember than that R.N.'s difficulty in the relationship with Ferenczi was a reenactment of a childhood trauma of such a severe nature that it could be triggered by the slightest error of interpretation, empathic failure, or nonverbal gesture perceived to be negative. Furthermore, she was interacting with a tender-minded psychoanalyst, who was beginning to practice relaxation therapy, which emphasized empathy, relaxation measure acceptance, responsiveness, love, and affection. Given Ferenczi's tender nature and his tender-mother transference clinical behavior, R.N.'s resistances to treatment and her need to evoke a mutual analysis point to Ferenczi's awareness of how severe her trauma was and how much he needed to change his behavior further in order to produce a therapeutic climate for her that would minimize retraumatization. It is clear from Ferenczi's experiments as he described them in the *Clinical Diary* that, with severe trauma based on physical and sexual abuse in early childhood, special conditions are required for a meaningful analysis.

The Case of Dm.

Dm. has been identified by Dupont to be Clara Thompson, Ferenczi's analysand, pupil, and devoted friend, who became one of the founders of the Interpersonal School of Psychoanalysis. Maurice Green, an analysand and student of Thompson and a historian and scholar of the Interpersonal School, disputes that Dm. is Thompson (Green 1993). Yet, in the *Clinical Diary* Ferenczi himself referred to "Dr. Thompson" on pages 147–148 and, on page 172, mentioned Dm. as a "psychiatrist."

Dm. was, like the other four clinical cases mentioned in the *Diary*, a victim of sexual abuse (Ferenczi 1932c).

As a child, Dm had been grossly abused sexually by her father, who was out of control; later, obviously because of the father's bad conscience and social anxiety, he reviled her, so to speak. The daughter had to take revenge on her father indirectly, by failing in her own life. [pp. 2–3]

The father seemed psychotic in that he couldn't distinguish the boundaries between himself and his daughter. Dm., in her attempts to deal with him, could not get her father to admit to his insanity. Her mother was cold "like ice." She did not receive adequate tenderness as a child from either parent.

> The principal motive in Dm: the desire to be loved by her mother. ... Her desire to become a boy was determined by the wish to eliminate her mother's dislike of her feminine inclinations. . . . This wish intensifies at the onset of puberty. . . . She is aware that her mother is displeased. . . . She seeks out masculine activities. She feels that her mother will not let her really get married. . . . When she herself falls in love with someone it ends in tragedy. She wants (dream fantasy) to be loved by the analyst. [p. 132]

The analysand's sexual abuse by the father was reenacted with Ferenczi in the abusive parental transference (Rachman 1993b). She acted out in the sessions by kissing Ferenczi and then bragging about it to other analysands and colleagues (Dupont 1988b, Rachman 1993a). Ferenczi reported his reaction to this provocative behavior.

> . . . the case of Dm; a lady who, "complying with my passivity," had allowed herself to take more and more liberties, and occasionally even kissed me. Since this behavior met with no resistance . . . she remarked quite casually in the company of other patients . . . "I am allowed to kiss Papa Ferenczi as often as I like." I first reacted to the unpleasantness that ensued with the complete impassivity with which I was conducting this analysis. But when the patient began to make herself ridiculous, ostentatiously as it were, in her sexual conduct . . . it was only through the insight and admission that my passivity had been unnatural that she was brought back to real life . . . as insight does have to reckon with social opposition. Simultaneously it became evident that here again was a case of repetition of the father–child situation. [pp. 2–3]

Dm. had developed some serious psychological symptoms as a result of her childhood trauma. She had the somatic delusion that she smelled like a corpse. Dm. felt that she had sexual odors and suffered from anal fissures (perhaps related to sexual trauma in this area of her body). Ferenczi wrote, "Patient Dm., who . . . perspires quite conspicuously and with a marked odor . . . finds a similarity between herself and the mentally ill Mrs. Smith (. . . a schizophrenic . . . penetrating smell, rather like mouse urine). Dm., on the other hand, feels that she herself exudes sexual odors" (p. 131). Ferenczi talked about being accepting of the analysand's odors and not being repelled by them, which, of course, means dealing creatively with the analyst's negative countertransference: "Naturally this provoked reactions of disgust in the analyst, which had to be overcome in the course of a prolonged period of work" (p. 132).

Ferenczi used a variety of humanistic techniques to deal with this difficult case—being a corrective self-object, mutuality, analyst self-disclosure, countertransference analysis, as well as interpretation.

> Both conditions [marked odors and anal fissures] . . . become man-ifest when she suppresses her tendency to almost manic rage. . . . The model for this whole process was infantile rage. . . . A further motive to fury was anger over the weak submission of the father to the maternal power. [p. 132]
>
> The analysis reveals that she is waiting for a hero, who will not be scared off even by these odors. The analyst must be this hero. [p. 131]
>
> If one goes too thoroughly into the positive or negative countertransference, one may avoid unpleasant experiences . . . but if one does not evade it . . . unexpected progress. . . . Dm.: Even since she sees and feels that I do not respond to her provocative actions and behavior simply with antipathy, one can have anything from her . . . enormous progress. [p. 157]
>
> Thereupon signs of resistance, which were not resolved until after she told me how disappointed she was that I did not acknowl-edge how great a sacrifice she was making of her own free will. I admitted that she was right. [p. 57]

Dm. asked for mutual analysis, but Ferenczi didn't respond in the same way to her as he did to R.N. He wrote, "Now the question: must every case be mutual?—and to what extent? . . . Dm.: Made herself independent—feels hurt because of the absence of mutuality on my part . . ." (pp. 213–214).

Perhaps Ferenczi felt that Dm. was not as severely traumatized nor in as great a resistance as R.N. In other words, Dm. was able to form a positive transference without full reversing roles; the analysis was successful without mutual analysis.

The Case of S.I.

The case of S.I. was described by Ferenczi (1932c) as one of hallucinatory psychosis.

> The patient became convinced long ago that a great many of her symptoms had been forced upon her from the outside. [p. 57]

> The content of the hallucinations: extremely abrupt shifts in time, space and objects, similar to the flight of ideas. She feels herself liberated from all the fetters and impediments of psychical distance. [p. 76]

> Human figures soon appear . . . which she calls ghosts. . . . ghosts gradually take on a frightening character. . . . "They are hitting me. . . . They are killing me!" During all of this her face is red, tears are running. . . . After several minutes . . . the whole person suddenly . . . becomes paralyzed; she lies there silent and deathly pale . . . she claims that she is no longer inside but outside her body, the body itself is dead, murdered. The figures . . . are very often the apparitions of a dead person, particularly of her brother, who died a year ago. [p. 77]

The individual's seriously disturbed behavior was clearly indicated by her attempted suicidal behavior in an analytic session.

> I suspect that the sudden change in her behavior and in her psychosis can be traced back to the following chance circumstance: when she had, in my presence, almost fatally injured herself, I became so anxious. . . . I grabbed her at once and lifted her up . . . proceeded to try to revive her. . . . [p. 128]

Ferenczi maintained his analytic stance in the introduction of physical interaction with the analysand. He realized that the embrace that was designed to bring her back to life could have been experienced as romantic, even though it was intended to be a nonsexual, loving gesture. Therefore, he analyzed the analysand's response to the embrace.

> The amount of emotion I displayed seems to have restored her sense of her own worth, as reflected by my compassion and passionate desire to help. . . . The indefatigable perseverance with which . . . I tried to understand her and so to speak bring her to life was for her really the equivalent of a man's embrace . . . on a sublimated, asexual level . . . when I could tell her that unconsciously she was waiting for a man who would not let himself be scared off even by her sexual coldness, and who would restore her self-esteem with a strong embrace. Her reply was that she would no doubt find a way to wriggle out of it. I countered this by saying that there must be an embrace that completely envelops the whole person and does not leave any exit free. [p. 128]

Ferenczi used his experience with S.I. to further understand the psychodynamics of sexual seduction.

> The result of this process is, on the one hand, the implanting of psychic contents into the psyche of the victim, dispensing unpleasure, causing pain and tension; at the same time, however, the aggressor sucks up . . . a piece of the victim . . . hence the soothing effect on an enraged person of the explosion of his rage, when he succeeds in causing pain to the other; a part of the poison is implanted in the other person. . . . at the same time (and this is what is new in what S.I. reported) the aggressor annexes the naive state of peaceful happiness, untroubled by anxiety. [p. 177]

Ferenczi described the nature and process of the toxic introject, a further elaboration of the concept he introduced in the original discussion of identification with the aggressor (Ferenczi 1933). In this work with S.I., Ferenczi became aware of the phenomenology of the experience of the victim, as his capacity to empathize with the victim was further expanded by his clinical work and his willingness to be emotionally vulnerable to his analysands. In fact, it was this willingness to be a vulnerable partner in the analytic process that allowed him to become the first psychoanalyst to specialize in working with incest survivors.

Ferenczi (1932c) further elaborated in this case on the healing power of the relationship.

> Further progress: she no longer has to be abstinent, she can drink again without any ill effects. At the same time the hallucinations assume a less terrifying character and the patient becomes better able to cope with the demands of reality, maintains that my personality has a healing effect. . . . She is also aware that at times I am bored and irritable, but that I possess the rare or even unique ability to rise above my own weaknesses. [p. 122]

This case was also an illustration of Ferenczi's humanistic method, where he self-disclosed to S.I. and entered into a mutual analysis. Furthermore, he created a therapeutic climate, through the tender-mother transference, where S.I. could develop a benign regression to her core trauma or level of basic fault.

> A new stage in mutuality refers to experiences with R.N. and S.I., especially with the latter. Through the . . . unmasking of the so-called transference and countertransference as the hiding of the most significant obstacles to the completion of all analysis, one comes to be almost convinced that no analysis can succeed as long as the false and alleged differences between the "analytical situation" and ordinary life are not overcome. . . . patients are also right in demanding from us not only that they be taken back to the traumatic experience, but also two further things: (1) real conviction . . . (2) . . . a genuine interest . . . all-conquering love . . . which alone makes life seem worth living and which constitutes a counterweight to the traumatic situation. [p. 129]

Apparently, S.I. and R.N. knew each other, with S.I. becoming involved in a delusional transference:

> . . . it was as though S.I. were demoniacally under the influence of evil spirits, which tried to devour her and terrorize her. . . . Here a link with an outburst of about three or four years ago, when . . . she suddenly came out with accusations: that I knew that R.N., a

patient she was acquainted with, was threatening her and perse-
cuting her from afar, and that I was allowing this to happen. At that
time the patient allowed herself to be placated by my sincere denial.
In the meantime . . . it has become clear to me that the patient was
right, insofar as that in the analysis of R.N. I had occasionally
identified myself with the latter, and had indeed encouraged her to
give her aggression free rein. I also knew that the patient had
expressed feelings of hatred against S.I. [p. 139]

Ferenczi accepted those aspects of the delusion that were based on
reality, rather than interpret them as psychopathological. This is an
excellent example of the further reaches of the empathic method in
treating serious emotional disturbance. The humanistic approach that
Ferenczi used in this case once again produced meaningful results. S.I. was
able to confront her childhood trauma and begin to analyze it.

The patient is now more capable of regarding the traumatic events of
her own childhood in the spirit of understanding and forgiveness,
rather than that of despair, rage, and revenge. A genuine recovery
from traumatic shock is perhaps conceivable only when the events
are not only understood but also forgiven. [p. 146]

In these statements Ferenczi outlined the process of cure and recovery
from trauma. He made it clear that the use of empathy and tenderness are
the ingredients that lead to understanding, the core of the analysis. He
also introduced one component of recovery that is just beginning to be
understood in the analysis of the incest trauma. Although not necessary as
a condition of recovery in every case, many incest survivors (as well as
other trauma survivors) feel that confronting their perpetrators is necessary, so that they can help dissolve the sense of victimization, encourage
mutuality of experience, and create the emotional atmosphere for a new
beginning with the parent.

The key to the analysis with such a difficult case is the willingness to
confront and analyze one's countertransference. Ferenczi was more willing
and more capable of entering into the inner world of countertransference
than was Freud or their contemporaries. Ferenczi made it clear in his work
with S.I. that there were emotional demands on the analyst to deal with
countertransference.

If one goes too thoroughly into the positive or negative counter-transference, one may avoid unpleasant experiences . . . but if one does not evade it . . . unexpected progress. . . . S.I. was actually someone I always liked, but she was resistant for a long time. Then the sudden shift I have often described, to serenity and sublimation. [p. 157]

The Case of B.

The fourth case that Ferenczi (1932c) referred to in detail was the case of B. This analysand described herself as having an alien inside of her, as if driven by a split-off part of herself:

> . . . the ego, B.'s innermost self, has stopped performing any independent action of its own ever since an alien will, alien decisions, were imposed on it, [and will not perform any] as long as it is prevented from protesting aloud, that is, until revived in analysis. Almost everything that has developed since the trauma is in fact the work of that alien will: "The person who does these things is not me." [p. 17]

The development of B.'s psychopathology was the result of incestuous rape. The awareness of sexual trauma first occurred through somatic memory, a characteristic experience for incest survivors.

> . . . in the course of the first session, induced by the "egg dream" complete reproduction of sensations: the smell of alcohol and tobacco as on the breath of her attacker; violent twisting of her hands at the wrists, a feeling of trying to push off with her palms the weight of a gigantic body; then a feeling of pressing weight on her chest, obstruction of her breathing by clothing, suffocation, violent stimulation . . . of her lower extremities; a most painful sensation in the abdomen with a marked rhythm, a feeling of leakage; finally the feeling of dying as though nailed to the floor, bleeding that will not stop, the sight of an evil, peering face. Then only the sight of the enormous legs of a man, arranging his clothes, leaving her to lie there. [p. 21]

Ferenczi was able to create the necessary emotional climate so that a benign regression could take place. In the climate of empathy, optimal responsiveness, and titration of anxiety, he encouraged a cathartic reenactment of the abusive experience. He would modulate the regression to maintain it at a nonmalignant level; he would allow the full emotional experience and reviving of memory. When the individual made it clear that he or she needed a response, the plea did not go unanswered. In Ferenczi's humanistic approach, pleas for responsiveness bring a reaction geared to meet the need of the individual. His capacity to deal with intense regressive phenomena is clearly revealed in this vignette from the *Clinical Diary*.

> . . . B., in certain states of relaxation, is as though paralyzed—pale, hardly breathing, eyes sunken, skin icy cold. . . . Patient describes her feeling when "expiring": "Everything turns inside-out." . . . This crust protects her from the breaking through of the repressed material hidden deep inside and sealed hermetically . . . hatred and rage play a part in the processes that precede repression. [p. 176]

There were many relaxation techniques that Ferenczi introduced to maintain the regression at a benign level and to develop a neo-cathartic experience for working through the incest trauma. The analysand wanted analysis to last twenty-four hours a day. Although Ferenczi did not maintain twenty-four-hour contact with B., there was continuous contact with R.N.

Ferenczi made house calls for B.

> The last two sessions marked by total dissatisfaction, hopelessness, tendencies to flee, above all because she has not confidence in me: in case of real need I would be neither willing nor able to help her. . . . She decided to sink into the depths of her soul, to relinquish all self-protective devices, she even permitted herself to become ill . . . *yesterday she took to her bed and sent for me* . . . she had to discover that I continued to ask stupid and boring analytic questions just as before. . . . [pp. 51–52, italics added]

The elucidation of Ferenczi's unique trauma dream technique occurred in the notes on B. Instead of using interpretation, he used the dream for intensifying the emotional experience so as to reach the incest memories and work through the trauma.

Dream interpretation during relaxation . . . instead of conscious elucidation of the dream—to take the patient back into the dream itself during the analytic session, with the aid of conscious associative material . . . quiet and simple questions. . . . one tries to remain in contact with the patients as they dream . . . this kind of submergence into a dream leads . . . to a cathartic exacerbation of the symptoms. [p. 67]

Mutual analysis is also discussed in this case, having been influenced by the clinical work with R.N. In this instance, Ferenczi said he used the "exchanged role . . . to show her what free association is, and she was to show me how the correct behavior of the analyst looked" (p. 167). Ferenczi also made some very important theoretical statements about mutual analysis.

Mutual analysis may originally have been invented by patients as a symptom of their paranoid distrust. . . . acquiescence to this work is . . . the most radical contrast to the rigid, impenetrable secrecy of their parents. Today's example: during the most recent analytical session but one, radiantly happy, pleased with herself, because for the first time she was able . . . to allow herself the pleasure of masturbation. During the next session this mood continues; actually nothing except humming to herself themes from *Tristan und Isolde*. . . . I suggest an interpretation . . . that the delights of masturbation provide a successful solution for the avoidance of the tremendous difficulties of motherhood. Strong opposition to this; every one of my assertions is rejected. Then a long pause; explanation: I feel nothing but antipathy for her. [p. 42]

The Case of N.G.

There are indications in the *Clinical Diary* that Ferenczi was moving toward mutuality in the psychoanalytic situation in an entry regarding another individual. He remembered that there was a difficulty because the analysand, N.G., requested that Ferenczi change his behavior. Ferenczi wrote of N.G. who "never tired of telling me about a teacher she found insufferable, who was very nice to her and yet always maintained a pedantic attitude, although the two lived together quite closely" (Ferenczi 1932a, p. 2).

He came to believe that "Had I understood her unspoken reproaches and accusations and altered my behavior accordingly, the patient would not have been compelled to reenact unconsciously, in her conduct toward me, the defiant attitudes of her childhood" (p. 3). The discussion of mutual analysis as it developed into a clinical technique will be found in Rachman (in press).

The Case of O.S.

Ferenczi did mention other cases in the *Diary*, including the case of O.S., a female homosexual, who was emotionally, physically, and sexually abused by a psychotic mother. The analysand suffered from phobias, an eating disorder, compulsions, manic depression, and a complete lack of affect. She was in a desperate state of dysfunction when he began to see her. Since she was in a state of intense resistance when they began the analysis, he agreed to an unusual relaxation technique—to see her homosexual partner as a part of the therapy.

> Complication: her feminine partner she has brought with her wishes to be analyzed; in view of some external problems and at the urgent request of O.S., I agree to devote half of the sessions to the partner. She is a case of sensitivity slightly tainted with paranoia: alternate attacks of excessive goodness and outbursts of hate.

Ferenczi reported some success with his relaxation therapy in treating this American woman who waited three years to see him.

> Perhaps under the influence of the sympathy she expected from me, she now found the courage—overcoming all her infantile timidity and inhibitions—to admit to a passion. It will perhaps be a less difficult task now to reunite the split-off part of the persona, affectively, with the rest of her personality. [p. 102]

The Case of Ett.

Patient Ett. was seen by Ferenczi in the United States, on her year's stay from 1926 to 1927, and then continued for about a year and a half when he returned to Budapest. It was intended to be a control analysis, but it clearly was not didactic in nature. As has been pointed out, Ferenczi argued vigorously for training analysis to be primarily an emotional experience geared to reliving and working through childhood trauma (see Chapter 16). Such a focus is clear from the following entry (Ferenczi 1932c).

> . . . I focus on her being pinned down by another woman and her extraordinary way of freeing herself. Probably this means that she not only had to endure the trauma but also had to preserve artistically the tranquil life of her mother by keeping it a secret. A second interpretation points towards mutual masturbation; she trains her mother, with whom she associated herself sexually . . . to gratify herself. It is only when she probes beyond the homosexuality that she arrives at real events . . . the heterosexual trauma. . . . One problem: what is to happen in reality to the prematurely awakened libido. [pp. 109–110]

The Case of U.

Patient U. and Case F .are the male analysands mentioned in the *Clinical Diary*. Patient U. had a sexual difficulty in that (Ferenczi 1932c) " . . . he feels no inclination for preliminary pleasure or foreplay in sexual relations, but experiences the act more like an obligation, as it were, which he seeks to get over as quickly as possible" (p. 122). Apparently he, like the female analysands, suffered from childhood sexual trauma. "He suffered a great deal from his mother's unpredictable outbursts of love as a child; it is also possible that some kind of homosexual experiences caused him to turn away from the female sex" (pp. 122–123).

The Case of F.

Case F. is also a condition of an early seduced child who suffered from the confusion of tongues syndrome, coping with the trauma by identifying completely with the aggressor. Ferenczi (1932c) discussed the internalized objects due to sexual trauma.

. . . the "perversion" of persisting infantility when the development of the libido is disturbed. In F's case the heterosexual libido, which was already developing in a normal direction in fantasy, after the shock at the age of ten splits into sadomasochism . . . and breast-fetishism accompanied by an active and passive homosexual attachment to the mother. It must be added that this was preceded by a deeply disturbing primal scene in earliest childhood (primal scene is traumatic only if life otherwise is totally asexual and hypocritical). [p. 190]

There was also an interesting issue of financial difficulty in paying for psychoanalysis. The patient claimed to be in monetary difficulty when he returned to Ferenczi for analysis.

I used the opportunity to tell him that from now on he must pay me . . . for the time being he could pay only half and continue to owe me the money for earlier treatment. Strangely enough, at the time of the first consultation I was still inclined to lend him the entire sum again . . . further reflection . . . high time to show the man the limits of reality of analysis . . . my self-analysis: identification with the coward who overcoming his fear turns into a hero, beyond good and evil. [p. 195]

The Case of G.

In Case G., Ferenczi (1932c) described the revision of the oedipal theory of neurosis that takes into account the influence of disturbed object relations due to sexual seduction by the father:

The incest situation was too passionately felt and evolved into an unbearable Oedipal complex with its inevitable repression. . . . It should be further observed how far Freud is right that the Oedipus situation is normally just a child's game and becomes a pathogenic complex only in pathological cases, under the influence of trauma. [pp. 177–178]

Besides her father's sexual behavior with her, G. was witness to her parents' having intercourse. Ferenczi described the confusion of tongues syndrome that developed from the series of sexual traumas.

The shock effect . . . goes still deeper. . . . Her entire emotional life sought refuge in regression . . . she now experiences fully and completely no emotion . . . her emotional life vanishes into unconsciousness and regresses to pure body-sensations . . . identification with the objects of terror . . . the trauma made her emotionally embryonic but at the same time wise in intellectual terms. . . . [p. 203]

. . . when she observed parents having intercourse . . . the unbearable nature of a situation leads to a sleeplike state of mind, in which all that is possible can be altered as in dreams, distorted in a negative and positive hallucinatory way . . . ego easily regress as soon as something unpleasurable occurs. [p. 202]

Ferenczi also described his self-analysis, which was necessary to maintain an empathic attitude in his humanistic approach: " . . . caught in my own theoretical postulate, I had, in a superficial and careless manner, presumed modes of feeling of an adult, sexually mature person, where probably only infantile, unrealistic erotic fantasies were involved" (pp. 205–206).

This capacity for self-scrutiny enabled Ferenczi to develop his two-person psychology and encourage the curative process in a seriously disturbed, sexually traumatized individual. There were several important lessons to be drawn from this experience.

(1) . . . analysts project . . . much of our sexual theories onto children . . . onto our patients in the question of transference . . . patients . . . they are adults . . . remain small children and just want to play with things, are frightened of reality even though they were in love with us . . . only because we analysts have these expectations or even unconscious desires. (2) We make no proper distinction between the playful, fantastic erotic velleities of children . . . (3) Fixation at the infantile stage is caused (a) by the imposition of libido of an adult kind, (b) by humiliating words of reproof, beatings, etc. for Oedipal fantasies, which in fact become real only by being taken seriously in this way. [pp. 205–206]

The Case of S.F.

In the case of S.F., Ferenczi (1932c) mentioned what appeared to be a precursor for mutual analysis when he was able to respond in a natural and sincere way to this analysand's criticisms of the orthodox Freudian approach.

He came to believe that "Had I understood her unspoken reproaches and accusations and altered my behavior accordingly, the patient would not have been compelled to reenact unconsciously, in her conduct toward me, the defiant attitudes of her childhood" (p. 3).

THE ANALYTIC COMMUNITY'S RESPONSE TO THE *CLINICAL DIARY*

The *Clinical Diary* first saw the light of day in 1985, the first publication being the French edition (Dupont 1985). It is significant that the French edition of the *Clinical Diary* was the first one to be published. The French analysts have been in the forefront of translating all of Ferenczi's work, thereby providing an opportunity for scholars to examine his life and clinical work freed from the prejudice that had existed since his death. The Ferenczi scholarship in France created a resurgence of interest in Ferenczi in Europe in the 1970s and, subsequently, in the United States.

The publication of the *Diary* has been seen as a momentous event in the history of psychoanalysis. As could be expected, the French analysts (Sabourin 1985) have been the most enthusiastic in their praise of the *Diary*:

> . . . this is a book unlike others. It is, in fact, an event which shakes all of our usual references. For psychoanalysts, it is a joyous event. . . .
>
> This body of work, which has been released from the crypt so recently, constitutes unquestionably the most formidable demonstration of psychoanalysis in action.
>
> But this body of work is also an intimate diary, the creative search of a man who sought distance from Freud's influence.

The American response to the *Clinical Diary* has also been very positive. In fact, one could say that the publication of the English version of the *Diary* in 1988 has helped spur a revival of interest in Ferenczi that was beginning to emerge as the orthodox psychoanalytic establishment was losing ground to the relational-oriented frameworks of object relations, interpersonal, and self psychology. The English edition of the *Diary* was edited by Dupont (1988b), who also provided a very useful updated introduction to supplement Balint's original 1969 essay.

Reviews of the *Diary* have appeared in professional as well as popular publications. In the professional community, three such reviews will be an example of the response to the *Diary*. One of the most traditional analytic publications, the *International Journal of Psycho-Analysis*, has published a favorable review. It will be remembered that the *International* was the journal, under Jones's editorship, that reneged on publishing "The Confusion of Tongues" paper in 1932, which aided the censorship of Ferenczi's work at the time and contributed to eventually removing it from mainstream psychoanalysis. So it is particularly welcome to see the journal that is the foremost vehicle for the Freudian tradition present a review by a Ferenczi scholar, Axel Hoffer (1990), who is also a member of the International Psychoanalytical Association. This review is a measured, enlightened, and thoughtful essay on Ferenczi's *Diary*.

> The Diary sheds some light on the essential nature of their disagreements [Freud and Ferenczi]. They are partly theoretical, based on Ferenczi's emphasis on trauma theory and on his view that infantile sexuality and the Oedipus complex are to a significant extent the unacknowledged projection of the adult's sexuality onto the vulnerable child seeking only love and tenderness. . . . The disagreements are also technical, with Freud accusing Ferenczi of a blind "furor sanandi" (passion to cure) and a professionally dangerous "technique of kissing," with Ferenczi in turn accusing Freud of a callous devotion to intellectual theorizing, indifferent to his patients' suffering. [p. 724]

Hoffer also made the significant point that the *Diary* cannot be used to demonstrate that Ferenczi was emotionally unstable, rather that his willingness to accept and understand an analysand's thoughts and feelings is a sign of his remarkable capacity to empathize with the subjective frame of reference of an analysand. He was keenly aware that Ferenczi's nontraditional behavior as reported in the *Diary* can be reviewed not only as a " 'loose cannon' on the foredeck of psychoanalysis, a man whose daring, impulsive innovations are not undone by an outpouring of 'mea culpas'; [but] as the courageous pioneer who protects his patient rather than himself, unafraid to say the emperor has no clothes" (p. 725).

One of the scholars of psychoanalytic history, Paul Roazen, has continued his understanding and praise of Ferenczi in his review of the *Clinical Diary*:

> Whatever the limitations to what Ferenczi sought to achieve, his *Clinical Diary* is full of nuggets of wisdom. For example, any kind of secrecy, whether positive or negative in character, makes the patient distrustful; he detects from little gestures . . . the presence of affects, but cannot gauge their quantity or importance; candid disclosure regarding them enables him to counteract them or to instigate countermeasures with greater certainty. [Roazen 1990a, p. 368]

The American response to Ferenczi's *Clinical Diary* has also been dramatically presented by a scholar in interpersonal psychoanalysis, Benjamin Wolstein. The interpersonal framework is closely linked to Ferenczi's life and work primarily through Thompson. Wolstein's review (1990) clearly links Ferenczi to interpersonal psychoanalysis.

Wolstein saw the historical importance of the *Diary*.

> . . . Ferenczi's *Diary* is, in my opinion, of critical historical importance. . . . For students of the history of psychoanalysis, this delay of over 50 years is a remarkable fact in itself—to which research attention must one day be paid—because this work is of major historical and clinical significance. [p. 569]

Wolstein focused on the significance of the *Diary* for the study of countertransference, especially in Ferenczi's mutual analysis of R.N.: "Most important, from the vantage point of the present is the discovery of the study of countertransference in vivo during clinical psychoanalytic inquiry of R.N." (p. 570).

Wolstein made a crucial point that distinguished Ferenczi's clinical work reported in the *Diary* in that we have a two-person psychology in action. Only those psychoanalysts who believed in a full experiential analysis for themselves and their analysands can appreciate, as Wolstein does, the significance of Ferenczi's work in relaxation therapy and mutual analysis.

Ferenczi's *Clinical Diary* has also been reviewed in nonprofessional publications. A loving tribute to it has been written by Phyllis Grosskurth (1988), the biographer of Melanie Klein (Grosskurth 1986) and the historian of psychoanalysis (Grosskurth 1991). This review, which appeared in the *New York Review of Books*, performs a very important function for the educated layman. Grosskurth provides a significant overview of Ferenczi's life, career, and relationship with Freud. Her fondness for Ferenczi is clearly illustrated in her comments.

This humility, openness and respect for the rights of the patient are unique in the annals of psychoanalysis. The child in Ferenczi was responding to the child in the patient. Through empathy (or what Melanie Klein called projective identification) Ferenczi reenacted his wishes that he had been listened to as a child and this in turn encouraged his patient to open up to him. Again and again he insists that the analyst must believe what the patient tells him. He rejoices in success; he admits failure. [p. 47]

18

FERENCZI'S CONTRIBUTION TO PSYCHOANALYSIS: AN OVERVIEW

ANALYST OF DIFFICULT CASES

Becoming the analyst of difficult cases defined Ferenczi's career and his significant contributions to psychoanalysis. He became the first analyst to address the difficulties in the analytic method when real trauma occurs rather than oedipal conflicts, and when the patient population changes from neurotic to trauma disorders, narcissistic, and borderline conditions. He was particularly suited to do this, since he had been born into a family environment that encouraged a revolutionary spirit and had developed personality characteristics during his formative years that became clinical assets.

When Ferenczi began his clinical career as a psychiatrist working with the disadvantaged he used his warmth, friendliness, spontaneity, responsiveness, and empathy to extend himself to patients who had been shunned by both society and psychiatry. Working with criminals, prostitutes, and the poor, Ferenczi fueled his capacity to be flexible, responsive, and innovative. He could integrate his own positive personality attributes into his clinical work. This idea of the clinician using his human qualities to aid the psychotherapeutic process was first fully demonstrated in one of Ferenczi's earliest cases, Rosa K. (see Chapter 2, this volume). A female transvestite homosexual, Rosa K. tested a psychiatrist's capacity to go beyond his medical training as well as community standards. Because she cross-dressed as a man, she became part of the criminal system, and was arrested and incarcerated for this behavior. If Ferenczi had stayed within the system, he would not have been able to help this woman who desperately needed some form of psychological treatment for her difficulty.

The significance of Ferenczi's treatment of Rosa K. was that the two levels of being, the clinical and the human, could be integrated into a psychotherapeutic method that helped establish the much-needed treatment relationship (which could not be a traditional psychiatric one) but allowed for the therapeutic, not judicial or inhumane, treatment of a lesbian. The humanistic psychotherapy of Rosa K. demonstrated that a clinician could use his human qualities in the clinical interaction to actually aid (not detract from) the clinical treatment. This case also helped establish the efficacy of psychotherapy with a homosexual individual, and, in particular, a transvestite.

FERENCZI'S CONTRIBUTION TO THE ANALYTIC COMMUNITY

Ferenczi made a significant contribution to the dissemination of psychoanalysis. He was instrumental in establishing psychoanalysis beyond the boundaries of Austria and Germany to Eastern Europe. As the founder of Hungarian psychoanalysis, he helped establish its scope as a treatment method and a body of knowledge. The Budapest Congress of 1918, at which the Hungarians, with Ferenczi as their leader, played host to the analytic community, highlighted the growing acceptance of Freud's contribution to the treatment and study of psychological disorders.

The establishment of the International Psychoanalytic Association was also part of Ferenczi's contribution. It is a bitter irony that the international analytic community that Ferenczi helped form would virtually ignore his work from his "Confusion of Tongues" presentation in Wiesbaden (see Chapter 13, this volume) to recent times. Clearly there is a lesson to be learned from this. Unless a clinician or theoretician can be shown to be deceitful or unethical in behavior, his ideas and methods should be examined and, when appropriate, integrated into mainstream psychoanalysis. There should be no taboo list of analysts, whose voices are silenced, whose work is suppressed, and whose ideas are unavailable for study.

Ferenczi's appointment as the first academic chair in psychoanalysis was such a significant event that it has never been duplicated to this day.

The founder of psychoanalysis, Sigmund Freud, was never granted such an honor, one he very much wished to have (and, of course, one he richly deserved). Ferenczi's appointment as a professor of psychoanalysis at the University of Budapest was based upon his achievements as a clinician, his experimental study of the treatment process, and his popularity as a teacher. The status and prestige that Ferenczi brought to psychoanalysis has never been equaled in an academic institution.

Currently, there are some signs of change. Fortunately there has been a Freudian chair in psychoanalysis at Hebrew University in Jerusalem, Israel for many years and a post-doctoral program in psychoanalysis at several universities such as Adelphi and New York University, as well as a division of psychoanalysis as part of the American Psychological Association.

ANALYTIC RELATIONSHIPS

The history of Ferenczi's relationship with Freud shows that the nature of the personal or professional relationship with Freud determined the fate of a psychoanalytic pioneer.

When Ferenczi was a loyal disciple, and specifically when he adhered to what Freud and his conservative followers considered standard analytic procedure, Ferenczi's status and significance in the mainstream analytic community was maintained. As soon as he began to experiment with his own method that did not conform to the standard or classical procedure, he was severely criticized and finally censured. Ferenczi never wanted to break away from Freud or his faithful followers. But he faced a serious dilemma that had to be confronted by many psychoanalysts who came after him who wished to move analytic theory or technique toward an evolution. How could Ferenczi remain true to the analysands he was treating who did not respond to the classical method or to approved variations in standard technique? In addition, how could he remain true to his own thinking and clinical behavior, which, through his flexibility, empathy, and daring, had proved more successful in treating the trauma victims who sought him out for treatment? Ferenczi's solution to these dilemmas was only partially successful. He did manage to continue his clinical experiments with relaxation therapy in spite of the objections of Freud and the loss of professional contact and prestige with the arbiters of analytic behavior who surrounded Freud.

This rejection by Freud and other prominent analysts of the day was an enormous price that Ferenczi had to pay for his ideas and methods. In fact, one of his prized students, Clara Thompson, was clearly concerned that the desire to please Freud while being true to his own clinical work cost Ferenczi the founding of his own school or orientation. Had he been able to overcome the need for Freud's approval, he could have carved a new path for psychoanalysis, thus reducing his personal and professional rejection and isolation, and giving him adherents who would have nourished and responded to his dissident thoughts and methods.

Thompson was able to learn this lesson well when she, Karen Horney, Erich Fromm, and others were faced with conflict and rejection by the International Psychoanalytic Association, the heir to Freud's legacy, for their views on the cultural and interpersonal aspects of psychoanalysis (Rachman in press).

Thompson was able to help found the American Academy of Psychoanalysis, which became an alternative voice to the orthodoxy of the I.P.A. This created a new community of psychoanalysts who could express their views on a variety of analytic positions. There was no longer the need to either abandon or compromise their cultural and interpersonal views or deal with the frustration and rejection of waiting for the orthodox community to finally approve of these ideas. Until that time, the ideas, methods, and innovations of such pioneers as Adler, Jung, Rank, and Ferenczi would be labeled as "not psychoanalysis" and seen as unacceptable and dissident (see Chapters 4, 5, 10, this volume).

Thompson was also able to fulfill a dream she wished for her mentor, Ferenczi. With Harry Stack Sullivan, Erich Fromm, and others, she helped found the William Alanson White Institute, where Ferenczi's work contributed significantly to the founding of the interpersonal/humanistic framework for psychoanalysis (Rachman, in press).

Another outstanding pupil of Ferenczi's and his heir to the leadership of Hungarian psychoanalysis, Michael Balint was also able to create a more positive climate for Ferenczi's ideas and methods than occurred during his teacher's lifetime. His immigration to London began a distinguished career as a contributor to the establishment of the British object relations framework as part of the Middle Group of the London Psycho-Analytic Institute (Rachman, in press). Through Balint's extensions and revisions of Ferenczi's ideas on trauma, regression, the humanistic role of the analyst, and countertransference, he helped create an alternative to orthodoxy in the post-pioneering period (Balint 1968a). He became the

European leader of the Ferenczi school as Thompson became the American leader. Unfortunately, Ferenczi's contributions to the interpersonal/ humanistic and object relations orientation were rarely acknowledged by the wider analytic community.

Balint was very sensitive to the emotional crises that had been created in the Freud/Ferenczi relationship in the 1930s, as he had become one of Ferenczi's confidants and a loyal follower. He had also witnessed "the Wiesbaden trauma" (Chapter 13, this volume) and wished to contribute to a healing process by de-emphasizing Ferenczi's relaxation therapy, which contained his most controversial ideas and methods.

Clara Thompson, who had broken away from the orthodox analytic establishment, was not as concerned with the Freud/Ferenczi crisis and its effect on mainstream psychoanalysis. Through her writings on the history of psychoanalysis, clinical papers, seminars, and supervision, she helped maintain a Ferenczian presence in the United States.

Although Balint, Thompson, and Fromm struggled to keep Ferenczi's work alive among contemporary psychoanalysts, they ultimately failed to break the "suppression barrier," and Ferenczi faded as a significant figure from the psychoanalytic scene, becoming relatively unknown for several generations of analysts. Because they broke away and established separate identities from Freud, Adler and Rank were able to maintain a certain degree of recognition in the field of psychotherapy.

One of Ferenczi's significant contributions that grew out of his early clinical experiments in the use of activity was the change in the structure and process of an analytic session and the role of the analyst. Ferenczi had always been an innovator from his earliest work as a psychiatrist. But the height of this daring and experimental orientation and discovery occurred during the latter part of Ferenczi's clinical career: Phase III, Active Psychoanalysis (1913–1923), and Phase IV, Humanistic Psychoanalysis (1924–1933).

THE ROLE OF ACTIVITY IN PSYCHOANALYTIC METHOD

In the third phase of his clinical career, Ferenczi, with Freud's approval, introduced the role of activity into psychoanalysis and began an evolutionary stage in the clinical method. Ferenczi acknowledged that the initial suggestion for his clinical experimentation came from Freud. Furthermore, Ferenczi's initial forays into changing the analytic method were spurred on by Freud's (1915 [1914]) publication "On Transference Love," in which the rule of abstinence was introduced. Freud formulated the rule of abstinence to help neophyte analytic candidates maintain their objective, neutral stance in the face of the erotic longings of female analysands. He encouraged young analysts to abstain from responding to these wishes for affection, love, or sexuality.

Ferenczi had already begun his clinical work with difficult cases and was becoming familiar with the phenomenon of the therapeutic impasse. He experienced difficulties when an analysand could not respond to the basic rule of psychoanalysis, which was to free associate. Although other analysts of the pioneering period, including Freud, were also experiencing these difficulties, Ferenczi brought unique features to their solution. Clearly, other analysts had tried to break the therapeutic impasses by intensifying the analysis of resistance. This traditional approach had serious limitations, because the more the analyst interpreted the difficulty in free association as resistance, the greater was the resistance. When the resistance was mobilized rather than reduced, the analysand might prematurely terminate the analysis.

Ferenczi began a new tradition by elasticizing the analytic process so that resistance could be addressed in a more positive way. This new active approach was characterized by several important innovations:

1. The interaction became a two-person experience in which both the analyst and analysand were active in searching for the most meaningful technique to deal with therapeutic impasses.

2. The analyst did not automatically assume the analysand is in resistance when he or she suggested a procedure or was having difficulty following standard procedure.

3. When necessary, the analyst actively intervened in the therapeutic process by encouraging abstinence, suggesting a focus, dramatizing the interaction, concentrating on experiential or emotional material, heightening the interpersonal encounter between analyst and analysand, creating psychodramatic scenarios, and focusing on changing behavior.

4. The analytic process was enhanced by the introduction of activity, as free associations were freed up and the impasse was reduced. When the activity was no longer necessary, the analyst returned to interpretation.

5. Activity was not intended to replace understanding and the development of insight.

In a clinical tour de force, Ferenczi's Case of the Female Croatian Musician launched a new era in psychotherapy (see Chapter 9, this volume). The treatment of his case incorporated a host of Ferenczi's innovations to help cure a talented individual who was riddled with a variety of serious issues. Ferenczi was so daring, creative, and flexible in his attempts to cure this opera singer of her crippling psychopathology that he set the path for a modern form of psychotherapy. Following Ferenczi's lead, psychoanalysis and psychotherapy now integrated the new therapy of action, behavior change, emotional reliving, guidance, and abstinence with the traditional analysis of transference and resistance, dream work, uncovering unconscious material, the use of interpretation, and the development of insight.

In his eagerness to implement Freud's rule of abstinence to deal successfully with difficult cases and his dedication to healing, Ferenczi realized that the continued intense application of activity could produce an adverse effect. If the analyst began to insist on the active intervention instead of continuing to interpret the resistance, the same negative effect could be produced: resistance could be solidified rather than resolved. Furthermore, a negative transference would be established, in which the analyst would be seen as a negative parental figure, that is, an intrusive, manipulative mother or a demanding, even hostile father. Ferenczi's own negative experience with activity and the criticisms of his colleagues moved him to change his focus on activity.

Although Ferenczi was to move in a very different direction by developing his relaxation therapy, the introduction of activity had contributed significantly to the evolution of the psychoanalytic method. The analytic session was restructured. The role of the analyst was expanded to include activity, emotional enlivening, directness, responsivity, and therapeutic pressure. The analysand became a more equal partner in the therapeutic process. A new method of dealing with resistance and negative transference reactions was developed.

Since Freud approved of these innovations, Ferenczi was encouraged to continue his work with difficult cases and the clinical experimentation necessary for their successful treatment.

A NEW BEGINNING FOR PSYCHOANALYSIS

All the innovations of the active analytic period paved the way for Ferenczi's new beginning for psychoanalysis, the publication of the joint monograph with Rank, *The Development of Psychoanalysis.* This monograph was the first formal critique of psychoanalysis as well as a recommendation for the future development of psychoanalytic theory and technique. The critique centered on the notion that by the middle 1920s psychoanalysis had overemphasized the intellectual side of the human mind and focused exclusively on understanding. As such, it had lost touch with its heritage, which had begun as a cathartic method. Ferenczi and Rank also felt that psychoanalysis had lost its vitality by insisting that uncovering through interpretation was the only key to the curative process. By the 1920s, this was clear to some analysts who were willing to listen to their own experience with analysands instead of trying to fit the theory and method to their experience. Furthermore, they realized that free association, uncovering unconscious material, transference and resistance analysis, and interpretation in certain instances limited the process to a cognitive focus and lengthened the treatment.

Ferenczi and Rank proposed several changes aimed at redirecting psychanalysis, which both re-anchored it in its past vitality and helped it move toward a modern analytic theory and method. Specifically, they proposed these changes:

1. The analytic process should be enlivened by encouraging the emotional expression of uncovered material. Rather than talking about it, the analytic process should encourage an experiencing of the past in the present.

2. The transference should be relived in the analytic situation as part of the working on and working through process. Interpretations of transference phenomena should occur in the context of an emotional encounter with the analyst.

3. The analyst's neutrality should be tempered with the willingness and capacity to engage the analysand in a lively, dramatic dialogue in the here and now of an analytic session. Emotion and intellect should be stimulated so that insight would be embedded in a holistic experience of mind and body.

4. Activity is necessary and useful in the analytic process to aid the formation and enhancement of the therapeutic relationship, to aid free association, help resolve impasses, provide reenactments of original trauma, and set a time limit to the therapy.

5. A time limit to the analysis, with which Freud had experimented, was seen as a helpful device. Interminable analysis is non-curative. A time

limit also helps mobilize the individual's inner resources to change and grow, lends organization and closure to the therapy, and motivates the analyst toward appropriate activity and commitment.

Rank was to develop time limits for psychotherapy as a basic ingredient, including applying the concept to each session. Rank used the publication of *The Development of Psychoanalysis* to break away from Freud. Then, Ferenczi and Rank began to differ on the role of time limits in therapy, especially since Ferenczi's work with difficult cases was requiring more rather than less time to reach the childhood sexual trauma. Under the influence of Freud and the orthodox community, Ferenczi also became critical of Rank as the latter left the fold. What had once been a personal friendship and professional collaboration ended bitterly. Once again, the politics of psychoanalysis dictated that the Society of Rings denounce Rank for deviating from the established position. Ferenczi was not able to separate himself from this kind of character assassination and became part of denouncing Rank in print. It was not Ferenczi's finest hour.

Ironically, the analytic community was to initiate the same campaign of ostracism against Ferenczi several years later, as his relaxation therapy reached its crescendo in his "Confusion of Tongues" paper. Ferenczi moved on from the separation from Rank to become more immersed in his final stage of clinical work, what became the advent of humanistic psychoanalysis.

HUMANISTIC PSYCHOANALYSIS

Although Rank left the Freudian community in a dramatic and deliberate fashion, Ferenczi became a respectful dissident who did not wish to break away from Freud or the orthodox analytic community. However, as Ferenczi immersed himself in the analysis of difficult cases, several issues, which began to separate Ferenczi's thinking and functioning from Freud's, became clear.

Childhood Seduction Theory

Ferenczi's difficult cases were survivors of childhood seduction, an observation Freud had made about his own cases when he originated psychoanalysis. It was felt that the incidence of incest Freud had originally observed was exaggerated, especially in middle- and upper-class patients. Ferenczi, however, verified Freud's original observation. A description of the cases he treated in the 1930s demonstrated that the patients were invariably suffering from childhood sexual trauma. One case in particular, the case of R.N. (Elizabeth Severn), highlighted the new psychoanalysis with an incest survivor (see Chapter 17, this volume).

Trauma Theory of Neurosis

Ferenczi also believed that a trauma theory of neurosis was needed to explain the development of psychopathology as a result of childhood seduction. He developed his confusion of tongues theory, feeling that this was a more meaningful explanation than the oedipal complex in early real trauma in the object relations of the family. Furthermore, he broadened the issue of trauma to go beyond sexual abuse to emotional disturbance in the mother–child dyad. This was one of the first attempts at developing a focus on the mother–child, pregenital issues in personality development as well as a multilevel theoretical explanation for different psychological disorders. Thus Ferenczi initiated a differentiation between psychological disorders emanating from trauma and those emanating from oedipal conflicts. His student, Michael Balint, was to take this idea and further develop a multifaceted theory of mind and psychological disorder (Balint 1968a).

A Two-Person Psychology

Ferenczi viewed human relationships as an interaction of the conscious and unconscious functioning of both parties. The real events in the object relationship are responded to as well as the intrapsychic experience of the individual. Human development occurs in an interpersonal context in which the object relations within the family, usually parental interaction with the child, is of paramount importance. One does not consider the child as a unit separate from the family process, but as an integral part of this dynamic. Any disturbance, crisis, or impasse in the therapeutic relationship is also a function of two-person experience. Both the analyst and the analysand contribute to any difficulty in the relationship. The analytic process is also viewed as an interpersonal encounter. The curative element in the disturbed relationship when empathic failures occur as a normal course of events is the parent, analyst, or teacher's willingness to own, disclose, explore, and change his or her contribution to the interaction.

The Rule of Empathy

A significant evolution in psychoanalytic theory and method occurred when Ferenczi introduced "The Rule of Empathy" (see Chapter 12, this volume). Empathy was to take its place alongside the other standard procedures of psychoanalysis (such as free association, analysis of resistances and transferences, dream exploration, etc.). Originally introduced as an intervention to overcome therapeutic impasse, freeing up "dried-up" associations, and responding to the relationship vicissitudes of difficult cases, empathy became a necessary element in the further development of Ferenczi's humanistic method. He continued to amplify and experiment with empathic interventions in his work with trauma so that it became the primary ingredient in the therapeutic relationship. The concept of resistance was redefined as an issue in the relationship between analyst and analysand. Several new interventions, such as analyst self-disclosure, countertransference analysis, and mutual analysis grew out of a new view of the therapeutic relationship as an ever-continuing process to empathize with the subjective experience of the analysand. Understanding the analysand's frame of reference led to the onset of Ferenczi's two-person psychology. Now, the relational dimension of the analytic process was being considered. The focus shifted from the study of the internal state of the analysand to the interpersonal encounter between analyst and analysand, as well as the internal process of the analyst.

The Phenomenon of Regression

A fundamental issue in Ferenczi's new psychotherapy was the phenomenon of regression. Freud had considered regression a sign of psychopathology, that the individual was returning to a primitive early childhood psychological state that was detrimental to his or her well-being. Any loss of controlled ego functioning was considered a negative therapeutic phenomenon and was a dynamic in the transference relationship. As Ferenczi pointed out in his *Clinical Diary*, Freud had abandoned his earlier work with more disturbed individuals at least in part because he did not like the clinical work with the more primitive ego states.

Ferenczi specialized in clinical work with severely disturbed individuals. He was comfortable and perhaps fearless in his capacity to work with regression. Ferenczi, and later his student Balint, had a positive view of the phenomenon of regression. They saw it as a therapeutic experience. The analyst's task was to create an ambience of empathy, trust, acceptance, and non-intrusiveness so that the individual would feel able to return emotionally to the level of the basic fault (Balint), the experiences, feelings, and thoughts that originally produced the trauma. Ferenczi demonstrated that working in the regression was essential for successful treatment of difficult cases.

Countertransference Analysis

Countertransference analysis is a central focus of a Ferenczian analysis. The analyst, accepting the two-person psychology, enters into an ongoing process of self-examination as part of the psychoanalysis. Generally speaking, this process occurs in the silence of the analyst's moment-to-moment experience in the psychoanalytic situation, using the wisdom and knowledge gained through a formal personal analysis and the culmination of a postgraduate training experience. When necessary, the analyst discloses his or her countertransference reaction in a judicious way geared to helping the individual to recover from the feelings of mistrust, dishonesty, confusion, manipulation, and abuse that contributed to his or her childhood trauma.

Relaxation Therapy and Relaxation Measures

The change in theory necessitated a change in method. Ferenczi experimented with a host of clinical innovations from the mid 1920s until his last year, 1933. It must be emphasized, however, that all of Ferenczi's humanistic clinical experiments in the analytic method were intended to free up impasses or disturbances in the object relations between analyst and analysand, in order to move the analysis to a level of understanding and insight.

In 1930, Ferenczi introduced the concept of *Nachgiebigkeit*, which was originally translated as "indulgence" but actually denotes flexibility or responsiveness to a traumatized individual (see Chapter 15, this volume).

Mutuality

Mutual analysis was clearly Ferenczi's most controversial technique. Although he made it clear it was a time-limited clinical experiment developed to deal with an intractable resistance when standard measures were futile, critics have used his mutual analytic experience with R.N. to demonstrate Ferenczi's tendency to be a "wild analyst." Mutual analysis has limitations, but there are contemporary clinicians who see the value of this courageous technique (Ragen and Aron 1993, Wolstein in press). The issue of mutual analysis can be broadened to a consideration of mutuality in the analytic relationship. One does not have to trade places with an analysand to deal therapeutically with mutuality. By creating an honest and democratic relationship, both analyst and analysand are equal partners in contributing to an understanding of the process.

EXTENSIONS OF FERENCZI'S HUMANISTIC PSYCHOANALYSIS

As a result of a twenty-five-year career of clinical psychoanalysis, Ferenczi pioneered an impressive list of theoretical and technical innovations. Of the ones discussed, there are some that were controversial in Ferenczi's time and remain so to this day. These innovations deserve greater attention in contemporary clinical circles. so we can have a meaningful dialogue about their significance in an atmosphere free of dogma, prohibitions, political intrigues, and character assassinations. There are five areas where further study is necessary.

The Incest Trauma

The analysis of the incest trauma became a new focus in psychotherapy and psychoanalysis as a result of Ferenczi's clinical work. What is needed in contemporary psychotherapy is a return to Ferenczi's thoughtful analytic approach. Ferenczi's purpose was to understand and clinically execute an analytic process that would address a neglected or little-understood focus. But he would be distressed by the present-day scene where intrusive and manipulative therapists determine the recall of memories and encourage hostility and retaliation toward alleged abusers.

Forcing recall of childhood seduction, legally suing parents for childhood abuse, forcing patients to confront their abusers is not the thoughtful, empathic, and person-centered analysis pioneered by Ferenczi. We need to return to Ferenczi's professional ethics and his thoughtful and creative analytic approach.

Judicious vs. Conspicuous Self-Disclosure

Study of the process of analyst self-disclosure is needed with a wide variety of patient populations from a clinical and empirical perspective. Hopefully, the value of such disclosures can be better appreciated when a clinical dialogue can be bolstered by attempts to demonstrate the efficacy of such interventions. Attempts to distinguish between therapeutic effects of analyst self-disclosure have recently been made in individual analysis (Rachman 1993c), in a group setting (Rachman 1990a), and with adolescents (Rachman and Ceccoli 1995). We need to move away from considering this type of intervention as non-analytic or acting-out, and recognize that it is useful and necessary in treating trauma.

Non-interpretive Behavior by the Analyst: Therapeutic Flexibility

Ferenczi experimented with a variety of relaxation measures in order to respond therapeutically to analysand so traumatized in childhood by disturbed object relations that they needed active, direct expressions of empathy and caring. These so-called non-interpretive interventions can be viewed as necessary conditions in a humanistic psychoanalysis based upon Ferenczi's work.

The therapeutic employment of relaxation measures continues to be a challenge for psychoanalysis and psychotherapy, since verbal interaction directed at the development of insight is state of the art as an intervention for most clinicians. However, clinical folklore, as revealed in informal or social gatherings, indicate that there are clinicians who employ noninterpretive behavior in the privacy of their consultations rooms, but never write about it or admit to such behavior in a scientific meeting. An anonymous study of actual clinical behavior of psychoanalysts that focuses on relaxation measures would show surprising results.

Such a study could help to dispel the idea that non-interpretive behavior is antithetical to psychoanalysis.

Power, Control, and Status

The issues of power, control, and status were addressed in Ferenczi's work by the changes he made in the structure and process of a session and the role of the analyst. Many of his clinical innovations were geared to reduce the oppressive experience of parental or authority-oriented power and control. When he did exercise power it was to initiate activity and relaxation measures. He was also aware of the inherent power, control, and status a doctor-analyst has in the analytic relationship. In fact, his awareness became acute when he realized that traumatized individuals were suffering from a confusion of tongues first experienced in childhood, then re-enacted with the analyst.

Issues of power, control, and status are now being addressed in contemporary philosophical thought (Foucault 1965, 1973, 1976) and in psychotherapy (Mack 1994).

Analysand-Informed Psychoanalysis

One of the most revolutionary experiences Ferenczi pioneered was the patient-centered psychotherapy of R.N. (Elizabeth Severn). In order to successfully treat her, Ferenczi realized that he needed to relinquish power, control, and status in this relationship and allow Elizabeth Severn, herself a therapist, to contribute to the conceptualization, process, and structure of the treatment.

Contemporary clinical experience has also demonstrated the need to foster an analysand-centered experience in which there is some mutuality regarding treatment planning. Some individuals were so severely traumatized in their object relations with one or both parents that they request more authority in how the analysis is conducted as a requirement for staying in treatment. These requests may take the form of approving of, suggesting, or creating therapeutic techniques that are of particular personal interest or value (Rachman 1981b, 1991a, 1994c,d,e). The analysis of incest survivors usually involves being responsive to the needs expressed for adjunct modalities, analyst self-disclosure, appreciation of esoteric ideas and methods, peer-group contact, concomitant therapy, bibliotherapy, and other special interests of the individual (Rachman 1990b, 1992f). Following Ferenczi's lead, an analysand's request for a parameter or a relaxation measure is not automatically seen as a resistance to doing the traditional analytic work. Rather, the analysand's request for a relaxation measure may show the analysand's psychic wisdom. As such, it should be considered, explored, and implemented when it can contribute to the recovery from trauma.

19

THE FERENCZI RENAISSANCE

What has the suppression of Ferenczi's work meant to upcoming genera-tions of psychoanalysts? Throughout this chapter, I will document how in Europe and in the United States, from Ferenczi's death and in some instances to the present day, major analytic training institutes have either ignored, suppressed, or diminished the significance of Ferenczi's work for mainstream psychoanalysis. His work was not studied and he was not considered a significant role model with whom neophyte analysts could identify. This suppression can also be documented in a study of the availability of published books and articles on Ferenczi.

The successful suppression of Ferenczi as a significant figure in psycho-analysis reinforced an unexamined dogmatic, orthodox, rigid view of psychoanalysis and removed a respectful, humanistic, and thoughtful challenge to some traditional ideas and methods. Analytic candidates, seasoned clinicians, researchers, and lay scholars were not apprised of the diversity of thought, experimentation in method, and flexibility in clinical treatment that Ferenczi originated.

In the last ten years or so, there have been attempts to rediscover Ferenczi, altering the perception of him as a forbidden or discredited analyst. A series of very recent developments have contributed to a new appreciation of Ferenczi's works, leading to what could be termed a "Ferenczi renaissance."

LITERATURE SEARCH ON THE FERENCZI MATERIALS

Recently, a literature search was conducted, as materials have become part of the computer search network (Rachman and Kahn 1994). Using the Silver Platter, Standard Psychological Abstract Literature Search, which abstracts any article in an American Psychological Association journal, some preliminary evidence was generated regarding the sparsity of Ferenczi materials. The search period now available in the Silver Platter is 1974 to 1992. Abstracted in this time period are journal articles and book chapters. An initial search period was developed for 1974 to 1986, the period that extends from the time when Ferenczi was still an unappreciated figure in psychoanalysis and psychotherapy (i.e., before the Roazen [1975] and Bergmann and Hartman [1976] books, which helped spur the beginning of a renewed interest in Ferenczi). During this period from 1974 to 1986, thirty-five references on Ferenczi were generated. A second search covered the period of 1987 to 1992, extending to the era since the rediscovery of Ferenczi in the early 1980s, including the time when Ferenczi's *Clinical Diary* was published in English (Ferenczi 1932c) and when conferences and symposiums in psychoanalytic and psychological circles were regularly including papers on Ferenczi's work. In the period from 1987 to 1992, there were eighty-five references in the literature search, over twice as many as in the first search period. So, in the literature search that covered an eighteen-year period, 1974 to 1992, 120 references to Ferenczi were generated, with a doubling of material as we entered the Ferenczi renaissance. Now that in 1993 the first publication of the long-awaited Freud/Ferenczi correspondence has appeared in English (Brabant et al. 1994), and books on Ferenczi are again being published regularly (Aron and Harris 1993, Haynal 1989, Lorin 1983, Stanton 1991), we can look forward to the finest era of interest and appreciation for Ferenczi's ideas and technical innovations.

FERENCZI'S WORK DISAPPEARS FROM PSYCHOANALYTIC CURRICULA

The attempts to suppress and censor Ferenczi's work must be considered to have been successful for more than a forty-year period (1932–1976), witnessed by the fact that the study of his clinical career, his relationship with Freud, and his ideas and techniques disappeared from psychoanalytic curricula in almost all training institutes. Analysts trained in the United States during that forty-year period did not have the opportunity to view Ferenczi as a major figure.

Generations of analytic candidates did not study Ferenczi's work as part of their institute training. Esther Menaker's description of the response to Ferenczi's death is a lost piece of information that contributes to an understanding of the suppression of Ferenczi's work by the Freudians (Menaker 1986). When she and her fellow candidates were informed of Ferenczi's death during a seminar conducted by Helene Deutsch in 1933, she remembered that "a silence fell over the class, as if to say, 'we do not speak of him.'" Menaker's experience represents a period covering September 1930 until November 1934, when she and her husband, William, were analytic candidates at the Vienna Psychoanalytic Institute. Ferenczi was alive and working in Budapest for three of the four years (1930–1933) that Menaker was in the Vienna Institute. Menaker said that Ferenczi's work was not formally studied at the Vienna Institute. The Menakers, who were independent thinkers, did, however, purchase and read several of Ferenczi's books on their own (Menaker 1994a,b).

An interesting series of experiences occurred during the period from 1940 to 1958, when the William Alanson White Institute was founded. From 1946 to 1958, Clara Thompson was the director of the White Institute. Of course, as one of Ferenczi's outstanding analysands and students, Thompson included a study of Ferenczi's work in the White Institute curriculum. Ferenczi was referred to as one of the major figures in the interpersonal framework, along with Sullivan and Fromm (Ortmeyer 1994). After 1958, Ferenczi disappeared from the training program of the White Institute. Dale Ortmeyer was a candidate at this time, and he has reported that Ferenczi was not seen as a major figure during his training experience at the White Institute. From the 1950s until about 1990, Ferenczi's influence was diminished in the training program; he was not listed on bibliographies, and there was no view of him as a major figure in psychoanalysis.

Another graduate of the White Institute, Benjamin Wolstein (1993), writes of his knowledge of Ferenczi as an analytic candidate.

> I had heard only vague and half-stated rumors during the 1950s about dangerously obscene efforts at mutual analysis, which only the mad Hungarian would think had therapeutic possibilities, yet which no self-respecting psychoanalyst would stoop to. . . . I had never heard about the existence of Ferenczi's Diary, not even during my studies at the White Institute, until its publication in 1988. [p. 180]

As of the 1990s, Ferenczi has been included in the curriculum of the White Institute. Ortmeyer (1994) reports that he is teaching a basic course in which he includes Ferenczi, Sullivan, Fromm, and Thompson. However, there is still not a major course taught there with Ferenczi as the focus.

During a period of analytic training in the early 1950s, Betty Feldman, M.S., the former head of the social work department at the Postgraduate Center for Mental Health in New York City, reported the total absence of any of Ferenczi's works in her studies to become an analyst. There was no mention of Ferenczi in any courses, nor was his name on any reading list. This occurred even though a course on the basic principles of psychoanalysis was taught by Lewis Wolberg. Besides the Freudian materials, other theorists, such as Sullivan, Horney, Alexander, and French, were studied. Feldman also reported that Franz Alexander did a clinical demonstration in the 1950s at the PGC, and no mention of Ferenczi was made in the subsequent discussion. Finally, in Feldman's analysis with Wolberg, Ferenczi was never mentioned. But the flexibility of functioning and the interpersonal warmth and responsiveness were passed down from Ferenczi to Thompson to Wolberg to Feldman. Although Feldman first heard about Ferenczi's work from me, she was an analyst who was in his tradition in her capacity for empathy, warmth, responsiveness, and flexibility.

An interesting exception to the absence of Ferenczi in his analytic studies was reported by Clifford Sager (1994). He said that Ferenczi was included in his analytic studies as part of the Society of Medical Psychoanalysis, during the period from 1946 to 1949, being mentioned in both lectures and bibliographies. Sager also read Ferenczi's writings as an analytic candidate.

The effects of the suppression of Ferenczi's work were clearly evident in my analytic training experience. My training period covered 1964 to 1968 for individual psychoanalysis, and 1968 to 1970 for group analysis, community mental health consultation, and child and adolescent analysis at the Postgraduate Center for Mental Health. Ferenczi's name was never mentioned and never appeared in a bibliography, and he was never studied in any courses taken. Furthermore, no guest lecturer ever mentioned his name or referred to his work. The absence of Ferenczi's work during this training period is especially troublesome and puzzling, since Wolberg was the founder of the PGC and an analysand of Thompson's.

Incidentally, Ferenczi's name was also never mentioned during my doctoral studies at the University of Chicago, from 1960 until 1964. This is another version of the neglect of Ferenczi's work, since Rogers, who had a major impact in the departments of clinical psychology and human development, was clearly influenced by the concept of empathy. Yet there is no mention of Ferenczi in Rogers's writings, as if Ferenczi's work on empathy did not exist.

Finally, an examination of most recent training experiences can illuminate the continual removal of Ferenczi's work from study. A recent graduate of an analytic training institute in a major metropolitan city, which she attended from 1987 to 1991, indicated that "Ferenczi was never mentioned, never on a reading list, and certainly not seen as a significant figure" (Jacobs 1994). In a discussion with an analytic candidate in training at the New York Psychoanalytic Institute, he stated that Ferenczi's work was not part of the curriculum in the two-year period of study he just completed.

It is clear that first the deliberate suppression of Ferenczi's work and then the subsequent wall of silence created a negative and damaging effect. Several generations of psychoanalysts and mental health professionals were prevented from becoming aware of Ferenczi as a major figure of psychoanalysis and from studying and extending his insights into contemporary clinical theory and practice. The present publication is an attempt to help lift the suppression barrier and wall of silence and neglect, a process that since the 1970s has begun to return Ferenczi to the rightful position as being one of the most significant figures in the history of psychoanalysis. Ferenczi's work is part of the lost history of psychoanalysis, as well as a missing link in contemporary clinical theory and practice.

Ferenczi as a Role Model

Because of the suppression of Ferenczi's work, he was also lost as an analytic role model for many generations of psychoanalysts. As Erik Erikson has shown through a lifetime of attention to the theoretical and clinical work with the developmental tasks throughout the life cycle, the development of a sense of identity is the fulcrum of adult personality. Psychoanalysts revisit the developmental task of identity formation as they struggle to integrate their educational, clinical, and personal experiences into their analytic identity. Ferenczi provides a very significant positive role model for those analysts who wish to deviate from tradition while remaining anchored to our relevant historical past.

THE FERENCZI RENAISSANCE

There are several developments that have occurred over the last thirty years to initiate a rediscovery and reevaluation of Ferenczi as a major figure in psychoanalysis. The completion of Ferenczi's *Collected Works* occurred in the 1950s, spearheaded by Balint (Ferenczi 1950, 1952, 1955).

The first step in this process was the Ferenczi number of the *International*, edited by Balint (Ferenczi 1949). In this publication, "The Confusion of Tongues" was first translated into English, as well as previously unpublished "Notes and Fragments." Publishing the COT paper in English was a landmark in modern Ferenczi scholarship, and, as well, it reversed the suppression of his major paper. Balint continued his valiant efforts to keep alive Ferenczi's work for future generations of analysands.

The next significant step was Balint's guiding the completion of Ferenczi's *Collected Works*, so that by the 1950s the Ferenczi papers were gathered in three volumes (Ferenczi 1950, 1952, 1955). In the 1950s, Izette De Forest's *Leaven of Love* (1954) kept alive Ferenczi's clinical psychoanalysis, distinguishing it from Freudian analysis. This was De Forest's elaboration of her previous outline of Ferenczi's work, during the early 1940s, shortly after Ferenczi died (De Forest 1942). Thompson (1950a,b, 1964a,b,c) must also be credited with keeping Ferenczi's work alive in her publications.

Erich Fromm (1959) was also a champion of Ferenczi, especially in discussing "The Confusion of Tongues" as one of the most significant contributions in the history of psychoanalysis, analyzing the Freud/ Ferenczi relationship, and counteracting Jones's mean-spirited attack on Ferenczi.

The 1960s showed several trends in the Ferenczi renaissance. In Germany, his work was republished in 1966 in four volumes. This significant event accorded Ferenczi's work a measure of importance and prestige and made it available to European scholars and researchers. Furthermore, John Gedo was given the task of reviewing the *Bausteine*, first presenting his assessment of Ferenczi's work in German (Gedo 1968) and then in English (Gedo 1976). Gedo's reviews move Ferenczi's work closer to mainstream psychoanalysis, even though Ferenczi is still known mainly for his dissidence (Gedo 1986a). But Gedo's position as one of the outstanding theoreticians in contemporary psychoanalysis encourages a reassessment of Ferenczi as a major figure in the field.

Balint, during the same decade, made a major contribution to the Ferenczi renaissance. In 1968, he published his now famous book *The Basic Fault*, which clarified, reorganized, and reformulated Ferenczi's ideas into an object relations framework. As such, Ferenczi's original ideas and Balint's extension of them, as well as his own contributions, became an integral part of the British object relations framework, both as part of its origins as well as its contemporary framework.

In the next decade, two significant events bolstered the rediscovery of Ferenczi and began a new era of interest in his work and life. Roazen's *Freud and His Followers*, originally published in 1975, was a major event in the history of the Ferenczi renaissance. It was based upon personal interviews with over seventy people who knew Freud personally, plus another forty or so who were either professionally interested in the history of psychoanalysis or else had participated in the early psychoanalytic movement.

In essence, Roazen was writing a new history of the psychoanalytic movement from the vantage point of the lives of the individuals who were central to its development. This was not an official document, sanctioned by the analytic establishment, the International, or Anna Freud. Roazen was a historian and political scientist foremost and owed no allegiance to the Freudian tradition. Since he was not a practicing clinician, he did not have to face any reprisals that would hinder his financial functioning.

Roazen, therefore, was free to examine the history of the analytic pioneers and not repeat Jones's hero worship of Freud, which defamed Ferenczi.

Another volume that appeared in the 1970s also contributed to furthering Ferenczi's rediscovery as a significant figure in psychoanalysis. Two established Freudian psychoanalysts and scholars, Martin S. Bergmann and Frank R. Hartman, collaborated on a book, *Evolution of Psychoanalytic Technique*, that chronicled psychoanalytic technique from 1919 through 1939, with the central contributions being by the clinical pioneers (Bergmann and Hartman 1976). More of Ferenczi's technical papers were included in this book than those of any other pioneers. Six papers by Ferenczi were included, twice as many as the nearest other featured clinician, Herman Nunberg, but five times as many as most other contributors. Technical papers from Ferenczi's work from 1919 to 1930 were featured, which spans the significant portion of his clinical career, including his controversial Relaxation Therapy. An entire section was devoted to "The Controversy Around Ferenczi's Active Technique" (pp.

110–112). Three of Ferenczi's papers significant to his development of his later alternate approach were also included. It is clear, then, from the Bergmann and Hartman book, that Ferenczi was considered one of the most significant figures in the history of the evolution of psychoanalytic technique.

For all the controversy that Jeffrey M. Masson's work and behavior have created, he made a significant contribution to the rediscovery of Ferenczi. When he succeeded Kurt Eissler as the director of the Freud Archives in or about 1980, Masson began researching the origins of psychoanalysis as a preparation for a new, officially approved unabridged version of the Freud/Fliess correspondence. When he received full access to Freud's papers from Anna Freud, he discovered unpublished letters and publications regarding the seduction theory. Masson reported that Anna Freud tried to discourage him from uncovering Freud's continued interest in the seduction theory and the suppression of Ferenczi's attempt to reintroduce the idea in his "Confusion of Tongues" paper (Masson 1984). In lectures before Hampstead Clinic in London and before the New England Psychoanalytic Society, at New Haven, in 1981, he presented his research and his conclusions. In August 1981, a series of articles was published in *The New York Times*. These lectures and the *Times* articles were not well received by the traditional psychoanalytic community.

Masson published his research and conclusions in his now controversial book, *The Assault on Truth* (1984). The latter portion of this book brings the suppression of "The Confusion of Tongues" into true focus for the first time. It also outlines a contemporary discussion of Ferenczi's significant contributions to the development of psychoanalysis. His discussion also presented material from Ferenczi's *Clinical Diary* for the first time, prior to its initial publication in French in 1985.

During the 1980s, the French and other European scholars who had been researching and translating the Ferenczi materials from German to French contributed significantly to the Ferenczi renaissance. Judith Dupont and the Le Coq-Héron (the French research and translation group composed of Dupont, Suzanne Hommel, Françoise Samson, Pierre Sabourin, and Bernard This) translated Ferenczi's papers into French, making his work available for study to the European psychoanalytic community. Dupont and her group also translated previously unpublished Ferenczi materials (Dupont had become the recipient of the Ferenczi materials). She made available the previously unpublished Ferenczi/Groddeck correspondence (Ferenczi and Groddeck 1982), his *Clinical Diary* (Ferenczi

1932b), and other early papers (Ferenczi 1902). Dupont's editorship of the *Clinical Diary* was an enormous contribution to the Ferenczi renaissance.

During the 1970s and 1980s, the French led the Ferenczi renaissance, contributing much significant material (Barande 1972, Covello 1984, Dupont 1982, 1984, 1985, 1988a,b, Lorin 1983, 1993, Sabourin 1984, Torok 1979).

In greater Europe, mention should be made of the seminal contributions of André Haynal in Switzerland. Haynal (1989, 1992, 1993a,b, in press) has published many papers on Ferenczi as well as an influential book. In addition, he is directing the translation of the Freud/Ferenczi correspondence.

At the University of Geneva Medical School, Haynal and Ernst Falzeder also organized an international conference to celebrate the 100-year anniversary of the founding of psychoanalysis (Haynal 1993a). The conference was one of several in Europe of recent origins to focus on Ferenczi. There was a Ferenczi symposium as part of the conference, featuring Dupont, Christopher Fortune, Axel Hoffer, Andrew Paskauskas, Arnold Wm. Rachman, and Judith E. Vida.

In Germany, mention should be made of the scholarship of Cremerius (1983) and Grubrich-Simitis (1986). Cremerius's examination of the "Confusion of Tongues" paper, linking the historical meaning to contemporary psychoanalysis, is a landmark in the appreciation of Ferenczi's suppressed work. During the 1980s, Grubrich-Simitis published six letters between Freud and Ferenczi that threw new light on their relationship as well as on Ferenczi's active technique. Ilse Grubrich Simitis of Frankfurt am Main is also a member of the Committee for the Publication of the Freud/Ferenczi Correspondence, whose other members included the late Enid Balint of London, Judith Dupont of Paris, Mark Paterson of London, and Arthur Rosenthal of Boston (Haynal, 1993b, p. xxxiv).

In the United Kingdom, we can note the Ferenczi scholarship of Martin Stanton. He has recently published a book on Ferenczi (Stanton 1991), the first English-language book on his work in twenty-eight years, since De Forest's seminal work (1954). Stanton has also established a department of analytic studies at Kent University, in Canterbury. In March 1992, he gave a series of lectures at the New School for Social Research in New York on Ferenczi and European psychoanalysis.

Realizing that their heritage follows a line from Ferenczi to Balint to Winnicott, the group of independent psychoanalysts of the British Psycho-Analytical Society sponsored a conference, "Ferenczi Rediscovered," on

October 15 and 16, 1993, in London. Members of the independent middle group, such as Tonnesmann and Stewart, were participants, as were the Hungarian analysts Hidas and Eros. The connection of Ferenczi to the British object relations group and the Hungarian analysts to their English counterparts is a significant part of the Ferenczi renaissance.

In Italy, there is presently a growing interest in Ferenczi. Several analysts are in the forefront of this revival—Marco Bacciagaluppi in Milan, Carlo Bonomi in Florence, and Marco Conci in Trenta. Bacciagaluppi is a Fromm and Ferenczi scholar, active in the Erich Fromm Institute in Milan. He has written extensively on Fromm, as well as on the theoretical and clinical relationship between Ferenczi and Fromm.

Bonomi is a historian of Freud's early training and clinical career, as well as a Ferenczi scholar. He presented at the Budapest congress in July 1993, and was part of the organizing committee for the IX Forum of the International Forum of Psychoanalytic Societies. As part of the IX Forum meeting in Florence, in May 1994, Bonomi organized a symposium entitled "Ferenczi's Relevance to Contemporary Psychoanalysis," featuring Haynal, Bacciagaluppi, Grey, and Rachman.

We are very fortunate, indeed, that Edith Kurzweil, a social scientist and editor of *Partisan Review*, "discovered" the Hungarian psychoanalysts in Budapest who were keeping Ferenczi's spirit and ideas alive in his homeland, shut off from the mainstream of their European and American counterparts. She has been part of a liaison between such Hungarian analysts as György Hidas and Judit Mészáros, the president and vice-president of the Sándor Ferenczi Society. They and other Hungarian analysts, such as Läszlo Benedek and Bea Ehmann, organized the Fourth International Conference of the Sándor Ferenczi Society, entitled, "The Talking Therapy: Ferenczi and the Psychoanalytic Vocation," July 18–21, 1993, in Budapest. Over 120 Ferenczi enthusiasts from fourteen countries gathered to pay tribute to Ferenczi's ideas, methods, and life. Three days of papers were interwoven with friendship and fellowship among colleagues from South America, Europe, Asia, the Middle East, and North America. A highlight of the gathering was a gala reception at the Hotel Gellért, the site of the Budapest Congress of 1918. A very special trip was arranged to visit Ferenczi's gravesite in the Jewish cemetery outside of Budapest, where flowers were placed on his grave and a memorial service was conducted.

The United States has been an important center for Ferenczi research and scholarship since the 1940s. In the late 1980s and now 1990s, there is a new Ferenczi scholarship in the United States, centered in the

Northeast, in places such as New York University, the William Alanson White Institute, and the American Academy of Psychoanalysis.

NYU's postdoctoral program in psychoanalysis, especially the relational orientation, is a university-based training program in psychoanalysis that has several Ferenczi scholars in its department, including Lewis Aron, Adrienne Harris, Sue Shapiro, Arnold Wm. Rachman, and Benjamin Wolstein. The relational orientation has included Ferenczi's work in courses and bibliographies and considers him to be one of the founding fathers of its orientation as well as one of the significant figures in psychoanalysis.

The American Academy of Psychoanalysis has been very cordial to Ferenczi's ideas and methods through its history, I think in part because it was founded by Thompson and Karen Horney as well as other psychoanalysts who were protesting the orthodoxy and rigidity of the traditional analytic establishment. Of course, Thompson's intimate connection to Ferenczi was another significant factor.

In the last decade or so, the American Academy's annual conferences and its publication, the *Journal of the American Academy of Psychoanalysis*, have sponsored symposiums and printed many articles relevant to Ferenczi. Among the Academy fellows who have been very encouraging of this Ferenczi study and scholarship are Zvi Lothane, Samuel Slipp, and Saul Tuttman.

The first international conference in the United States dedicated to Ferenczi's work occurred May 17–18, 1991, at the New York Academy of Medicine. Organized by Aron and Harris and sponsored jointly by the Department of Psychiatry, St. Luke's/Roosevelt Hospital Center, and the Section on Psychiatry, the New York Academy of Medicine, the theme was "The Theoretical and Clinical Contributions of Sándor Ferenczi." This conference served a very significant function in the Ferenczi renaissance. Capitalizing on the publication of Ferenczi's *Clinical Diary* in English in 1988 and the gathering interest in the upcoming publication of the Freud/Ferenczi correspondence, it was the first major conference to focus on Ferenczi's theoretical and clinical work for contemporary psychoanalysis while bringing together major figures in Ferenczian scholarship in Europe with their American counterparts. This conference brought the Hungarian analysts who have courageously kept alive Ferenczi's legacy, in isolation in Eastern Europe, into meaningful intellectual and interpersonal contact with the mainstream of European and American psychoanalysis.

We can even note that the American Psychoanalytic Association has opened the door for Ferenczi. In recent years, they have begun a new series entitled *Classics Revisited*, where in a symposium format a paper that is considered to be of great historical significance and a lasting contribution to psychoanalysis is brought into focus. In 1991, a Classics Revisited Symposium was organized at the A.P.A. meeting in New York City, with the topic Ferenczi and Rank's *The Development of Psychoanalysis*. Gedo was one of the participants, and his paper will be published as part of a Ferenczi number in an upcoming issue of *Psychoanalytic Inquiry* (Gedo in press).

SANDOR FERENCZI INSTITUTE, NEW YORK CITY

In an attempt to cure the confusion of tongues in the psychotherapy community, so that Ferenczi's ideas and methods do not suffer again from suppression, neglect, or derision and will continue to be available to future generations of analysts and psychotherapists, an opportunity is now provided for the study and dissemination of all his materials. To ths end, I founded the Sándor Ferenczi Institute in 1993.

The purposes of the Ferenczi Institute are to train psychoanalysts, psychotherapists, and mental health professionals in the theories and methods of Ferenczi's pioneering work; to provide seminars and symposiums to the professional community; to encourage research in Ferenczi's ideas and clinical methods; to become a depository for materials of interest to Ferenczi scholars and students of the history of psychoanalysis; and to encourage study, treatment, and research in areas of humanistic psychoanalysis and psychotherapy that Ferenczi pioneered.

REFERENCES

Alexander, F. (1933). On Ferenczi's relaxation principle. *International Journal of Psycho-Analysis* 14:183–192.

—— (1935). The problem of psychoanalytic technique. *Psychoanalytic Quarterly* 4:588–611.

—— (1965). Unexplored areas in psychoanalytic theory and treatment. In *New Perspectives in Psychoanalysis: Sándor Rado Lectures 1957–1963*, ed. G. Danube. New York: Grune & Stratton.

Alexander, F., French, T. M., Bacon, C. L., et al. (1946). *Psychoanalytic Therapy: Principles and Application.* New York: Ronald Press.

Allen, F. H. (1942). *Psychotherapy with Children.* New York: Norton.

Anzieu, D. (1975). *L'auto-analyse de Freud et la decouverte de la psychanalyse*, vol. I. Paris: Presses Universitaires de France.

Aron, L. (1990). One-person and two-person psychologies and the method of psychoanalysis. *Psychoanalytic Psychology* 7:475–485.

—— (1992). From Ferenczi to Searles and contemporary relational approaches. *Psychoanalytic Dialogues* 2:181–190.

Aron, L., and Harris, A. (1993). *Sándor Ferenczi's Clinical and Theoretical Contributions.* Hillsdale, NJ: Analytic Press.

Bacal, H. A. (1987). British object-relations theorists and self psychology: some critical reflections. *International Journal of Psycho-Analysis* 68:81–98.

—— (1990). The elements of a corrective selfobject experience. *Psychoanalytic Inquiry* 10:347–372.

Bacal, H. A., and Newman, K. M. (1990). *Theories of Object Relations: Bridges to Self Psychology.* New York: Columbia University Press.

Bacciagaluppi, M. (1989). Erich Fromm's views on psychoanalytic "technique." *Contemporary Psychoanalysis* 25:2, 226–243.

—— (1992). A workshop on Erich Fromm. *Academy Forum* 36:1, 2, 12–13, Spring/Summer.

Balint, A., and Balint, M. (1939). On transference and countertransference. *Journal of Psycho-Analysis* 20:223–230.

Balint, M. (1932). Character analysis and new beginning. In *Primary Love and Psycho-analytic Technique*, pp. 157–164. London: Hogarth.

_____ (1933). Dr. Sándor Ferenczi (obituary). *International Journal of Psycho-Analysis* 30:4, 215–219, 1949.

_____ ed. (1949). Sándor Ferenczi number. *International Journal of Psycho-Analysis* 30: entire no. 4.

_____ (1958). Letter to the editor. Sándor Ferenczi's last years. *International Journal of Psycho-Analysis* 39:68.

_____ (1959). *Thrills and Regressions*. London: Hogarth.

_____ (1968a). *The Basic Fault: Therapeutic Aspects of Regression*. London: Tavistock.

_____ (1968b). The disagreement between Freud and Ferenczi and its repercussions. In *The Basic Fault: Therapeutic Aspects of Regression*, pp. 149–156. London: Tavistock.

_____ (1969). Trauma and object relationship. *International Journal of Psycho-Analysis* 50:4, 429–435.

_____ (1970). Introduction to *Schriften zur Psychoanalyse* by Sándor Ferenczi: Frankfurt Fischer.

_____ (1988). Draft/notes for a preface introduction. In *The Clinical Diary of Sándor Ferenczi*, ed. J. Dupont, pp. 219–222. Cambridge, MA: Harvard University Press.

Barande, I. (1972). *Sándor Ferenczi*. Paris: Payot.

Basch, M. F. (1984). The selfobject theory of motivation and the history of psychoanalysis. In *Kohut's Legacy: Contributions to Self Psychology*, ed. P. E. Stepansky and A. Goldberg, pp. 3–17. Hillsdale, NJ: Analytic Press.

Bergmann, M. S., and Hartman, F. R., eds. (1976). *The Evolution of Psychoanalytic Technique*. New York: Basic Books.

Bettelheim, B. (1982). *Freud and Man's Soul*. New York: Alfred A. Knopf.

Boyer, L. B., and Giovaccini, P. L. (1967). *Psychoanalytic Treatment of Characterological and Schizophrenic Disorders*. New York: Science House.

Brabant, E., Falzeder, E., and Giampieri-Deutsch, P., eds. (1993a). *Sigmund Freud/Sándor Ferenczi. Briefwechsel. Band 1/1, 1908–1911*. Vienna: Böhlau Verlag.

_____ (1993b). *Sigmund Freud/Sándor Ferenczi. Correspondence. Tome 1, 1908–1914*. Paris: Calmann-Lévy.

_____ (1993c). *Sigmund Freud/Sándor Ferenczi Lettere. Volume primo, 1908–1914*. Milan: Raffaello Cortina.

_____ (1993d). *The Correspondence of Sigmund Freud and Sándor Ferenczi*, vol. 1, 1908–1914. Cambridge, MA: The Belknap Press of Harvard

University.

_____ (in press) (1994). *Sigmund Freud/Sándor Ferenczi. Briefwechsel. Band I/2, 1912–1914*. Vienna: Böhlau Verlag.

Brunswick, R. M. (1929). A note on the childish theory of coitus a tergo. *International Journal of Psycho-Analysis* 10:93–95.

Burgess, A. W., Groth, N. A., Holmstrom, L. L., and Sgroi, S. S. (1978). *Sexual Assault of Children and Adolescents*. Lexington, MA: D. C. Heath.

Burgess, A. W., and Holmstrom, L. L. (1974). Rape trauma syndrome. *American Journal of Psychiatry* 131:981–985.

Chessick, R. D. (1985a). *Psychology of the Self and the Treatment of Narcissism*. New York: Jason Aronson.

_____ (1985b). Self and object: Fairbairn, Winnicott, Balint, and R. D. Laing. In *Psychology of the Self and the Treatment of Narcissism*, pp. 93–102. New York: Jason Aronson.

Clark, R. W. (1980a). Sigmund Freud's sortie to America. *American Heritage*, April/May, pp. 34–43.

_____ (1980b). *Freud: The Man and the Cause*. New York: Random House.

Collins Publishers (1981). *Collins German-English Dictionary*. London: Collins.

Coltrera, J. T. and Rosa, N. C. (1967). Freud's psychoanalytic techniques—from the beginnings to 1923. In *Psychoanalytic Techniques*, ed. B. B. Wolman. New York: Basic Books.

Corbett, L. (1989). Kohut and Jung: a comparison of theory and therapy. In *Self Psychology: Comparisons and Contrasts*, ed. D. W. Detrick and S. P. Detrick. Hillsdale, NJ: Analytic Press.

Counts, R. M. (1990). The concept of dissociation. *Journal of the American Academy of Psychoanalysis* 18:3, Fall.

Covello, A. (1984). Lettres de Freud: du scenario de Jones au diagnostic sur Ferenczi. *Confrontation* 12:63–78.

Cremerius, J. (1983). Die Sprache der Zärtlichkeit und der Leindenschaft: Reflexionen zur Sándor Ferenczi's Wiesbadener Vortrag von 1932. Sándor Ferenczi's Bedeutung fur Theorie und Therapie der Psychoanalyse. (The language of tenderness and passion: reflections on Sándor Ferenczi's presentation at the Wiesbaden Conference of 1932. The meaning of Sándor Ferenczi's work for the theory and therapy of psychoanalysis). *Psyche* 37:11, 988–1015.

Decker, H. S. (1990). *Freud, Dora, and Vienna 1900*. New York: Free Press.

De Forest, I. (1942). The therapeutic technique of Sándor Ferenczi.

International Journal of Psycho-Analysis 23:1, 121–139.

_____ (1954). *The Leaven of Love: A Development of the Psychoanalytic Theory and Technique of Sándor Ferenczi.* New York: Harper & Row.

Donn, L. (1988). *Freud and Jung: Years of Friendship, Years of Loss.* New York: Charles Scribner's Sons.

Doorley, L. (1982). When Freud came to Worcester. *Yankee*, December, pp. 2–6.

Dupont, J. (1982). The source of inventions. In *Ferenczi/ Groddeck Correspondence*, (1921–1933), pp. 11–37. Traduction, notes et commentaires par le Groupe de traduction du Coq-Héron. Paris: Payot.

_____ (1984). Entre Freud et Ferenczi: Groddeck. *Confrontation* 12:33–42, Automne.

_____ (1985). Ferenczi's Journal Clinique Janvier–Octobre 1932. Paris: Payot.

_____ (1988a). Ferenczi's "madness." *Contemporary Psychoanalysis* 24:2, 250–261.

_____ ed. (1988b). *The Clinical Diary of Sándor Ferenczi.* Cambridge, MA: Harvard University Press.

Eisenstein, S. (1966). Otto Rank, 1884–1939: The myth of the birth of the hero. In *Psychoanalytic Pioneers*, ed. F. Alexander, S. Eisenstein, and M. Grotjahn, pp. 36–50. New York: Basic Books.

Eissler, K. R. (1953). The effect of the structure of the ego on psychoanalytic technique. *Journal of the American Psycho-Analytic Association* 1:104–143.

_____ (1965). A critical assessment of the future of psychoanalysis: a view from within. Panel reported by I. Miller. *Journal of the American Psychoanalytic Association* 23:151.

Epstein, L., and Feiner, A. H., eds. (1979). *Countertransference.* New York: Jason Aronson.

Erikson, E. H. (1950). *Childhood and Society.* New York: Norton.

_____ (1956). The problem of ego identity. In *Identity: Youth and Crisis*, pp. 142–207, 208–231. New York: Norton, 1968.

_____ (1959). Identity and the life cycle. *Psychological Issues.* Monograph No. 1. New York: International Universities Press.

_____ (1968). *Identity: Youth and Crisis.* New York: Norton.

Fairbairn, W. R. D. (1952). A synthesis of the development of the author's views regarding the structure of the personality. In *Psychoanalytic Studies of the Personality.* London: Routledge & Kegan Paul.

_____ (1954). *An Object Relations Theory of the Personality.* New York: Basic

Books.

Falzeder, E. (1995). Personal comunication, January 19.

Federn, P. (1933). Sándor Ferenczi, born July 16, 1873, died May 22, 1933. *International Journal of Psycho-Analysis* 14:467–485.

Ferenczi, S. (1902). Homosexualitas feminina (female homosexuality). *Gyópgyászat*, 11:167–168. [English translation by Gabor Kalman.]

———— (1908a). The analytic conception of the psycho-neuroses. In *Further Contributions to the Theory and Technique of Psycho-Analysis*, ed. J. Rickman, pp. 15–30. New York: Brunner/Mazel, 1980.

———— (1908b). Actual and psycho-neuroses in the light of Freud's investigations and psycho-analysis. In *Further Contributions to the Theory and Technique of Psycho-Analysis*, ed. J. Rickman, pp. 30–55. New York: Brunner/Mazel, 1980.

———— (1909). Introjection and transference. In *First Contributions to Psycho-Analysis*, ed. E. Jones, pp. 35–93. New York: Brunner/Mazel, Vol. I, 1980.

———— (1911). On the organization of the psychoanalytic movement. In *Final Contributions to the Problems and Methods of Psycho-Analysis*, ed. M. Balint, pp. 299–307. New York: Brunner/Mazel, 1980.

———— (1912a). On the part played by homosexuality in the pathogenesis of paranoia. In *First Contributions to Psycho-Analysis*, vol. 1, ed. E. Jones, pp. 154–184. New York: Brunner/Mazel, 1980.

———— (1912b). On transitory symptom construction during the analysis (transitory conversion, substitution, illusion, hallucination, "character-regression," and "expression-displacement). In *First Contributions to Psycho-Analysis*, vol. 1 ed. E. Jones, pp. 193–212. New York: Brunner/Mazel, 1980.

———— (1914). The nosology of male homosexuality. In *First Contributions to Psycho-Analysis*, vol. 1, ed. E. Jones, pp. 154–184. New York: Brunner/Mazel, 1980.

———— (1916–17). Dreams of the unsuspecting. In *Further Contributions to the Theory and Technique of Psycho-Analysis*, ed. J. Rickman, pp. 346–348. New York: Brunner/Mazel, 1980.

———— (1917). Review of "Die Psychische Bedingheit Und Psychoanalytische Behandlung Organischen Leiden." In *Final Contributions to the Problems and Methods of Psycho-Analysis*, ed. M. Balint, pp. 342–343. New York: Brunner/Mazel, 1980.

———— (1919a). On the technique of psycho-analysis. In *Further Contributions to the Theory and Technique of Psycho-Analysis*, vol. 2, ed. J.

Rickman, pp. 177–189. New York: Brunner/Mazel, 1980.

_____ (1919b). Technical difficulties in the analysis of a case of hysteria: including observations on larval forms of onanism and onanistic equivalents. In *Further Contributions to the Theory and Technique of Psycho-Analysis*, vol. 2, ed. J. Rickman, pp. 189–197. New York: Brunner/Mazel, 1980.

_____ (1919c). On influencing of the patient in psychoanalysis. In *Further Contributions to the Theory and Technique of Psycho-Analysis*, vol. 2, ed. J. Rickman, pp. 235–237. New York: Brunner/Mazel, 1980.

_____ (1920). The further development of the active therapy in psychoanalysis. In *Further Contributions to the Theory and Technique of Psycho-Analysis*, vol. 2, ed. J. Rickman, pp. 198–217. New York: Brunner/Mazel, 1980.

_____ (1921a). Review of "Der Seelensucher: Ein Psychoanalytischer Roman" by Georg Groddeck. In *Final Contributions to the Problems and Methods of Psycho-Analysis*, ed. M. Balint, pp. 344–348. New York: Brunner/Mazel, 1980.

_____ (1921b). Psycho-analytical observations on tic. In *Further Contributions to the Theory and Technique of Psycho-Analysis*, ed. J. Rickman, pp. 142–174. New York: Brunner/Mazel, 1980.

_____ (1924a). *Thalassa: A Theory of Genitality*. New York: *Psychoanalytic Quarterly*, monograph, 1938.

_____ (1924b). On forced phantasies: activity in the association technique. In *Further Contributions to the Theory and Technique of Psycho-Analysis*, vol. 2, ed. J. Rickman, pp. 68–77. New York: Brunner Mazel, 1980.

_____ (1925a). Contraindications to the 'active' psychoanalytic technique. In *Further Contributions to the Theory and Technique of Psycho-Analysis*, vol. 2, ed. J. Rickman, pp. 217–230. New York: Brunner/Mazel, 1980.

_____ (1925b). Psycho-analysis of sexual habits. In *Further Contributions to the Theory and Technique of Psycho-Analysis*, vol. 2, ed. J. Rickman, pp. 257–297. New York: Brunner/Mazel, 1980.

_____ (1926a). Gulliver phantasies. In *Final Contributions to the Problems and Methods of Psycho-Analysis*, ed. M. Balint, pp. 41–60. New York: Brunner/Mazel, 1980.

_____ (1926b). Present-day problems in psycho-analysis. In *Final Contributions to the Problems and Methods of Psycho-Anaysis*, ed. M. Balint, pp. 29–40. New York: Brunner/Mazel, 1980.

_____ (1926c). The problem of acceptance of unpleasant ideas – advances in knowledge of the sense of reality. *Further Contributions to the Theory and Technique of Psycho-Analysis*, vol. 2, ed. J. Rickman, pp. 366–379. New York: Brunner/Mazel, 1980.

_____ (1926d). Freud's importance for the mental hygiene movement. In *Final Contributions to the Problems and Methods of Psycho-Analysis*, ed. M. Balint, pp. 18–21. New York: Brunner/Mazel, 1980.

_____ (1927a). The problem of the termination of the analysis. In *Final Contributions to the Problems and Methods of Psycho-Analysis*, vol. 3, ed. M. Balint, pp. 77–86. New York: Brunner/Mazel, 1980.

_____ (1927b). Review of O. Rank's *Technique of Psychoanalysis*. *International Journal of Psycho-Analysis* 8:93–100.

_____ (1928a). Die Elastitizität der psychoanalytischen Technik. *Internationale Zeitschrift für Psychoanalyse. XIV. Band. Heft 2*, pp. 197–209.

_____ (1928b). The elasticity of psychoanalytic technique. In *Final Contributions to the Problems and Methods of Psycho-Analysis*, vol. 3, ed. M. Balint, pp. 87–102. New York: Brunner/Mazel, 1980.

_____ (1930a). Relaxationsprinzip und Neokatharsis. *Internationale Zeitschrift für Psychoanalyse. XIV. Band. Heft 2*, pp. 149–164.

_____ (1930b). The principle of relaxation and neo-catharsis. *Final Contributions to the Problems and Methods of Psycho-Analysis*, vol. 3, ed. M. Balint, pp. 108–125. New York: Brunner/Mazel, 1980.

_____ (1930c). Notes and fragments. In *Final Contributions to the Problems and Methods of Psycho-Analysis*, ed. M. Balint, pp. 216–279. New York: Brunner/Mazel, 1980.

_____ (1931). Child analysis in the analysis of adults. In *Final Contributions to the Problems and Methods of Psycho-Analysis*, vol. 3, ed. M. Balint, pp. 126–142. New York: Brunner/Mazel, 1980.

_____ (1932a). Notes and fragments, 11/24/32. In *Final Contributions to the Problems and Methods of Psycho-Analysis*, vol. 3, ed. M. Balint, p. 272. New York: Brunner/Mazel, 1980.

_____ (1932b). *Journal Clinique: Janvier-Octobre 1932*, ed. Le Groupe du Coq-Héron. Paris: Payot, 1985. [French edition – appeared before English edition.]

_____ (1932c). *The Clinical Diary of Sándor Ferenczi*, ed. J. Dupont. Trans. M. Balint and N. Z. Jackson. Cambridge, MA: Harvard University Press, 1988.

_____ (1933). The confusion of tongues between adults and children: the language of tenderness and passion. In *Final Contributions to the*

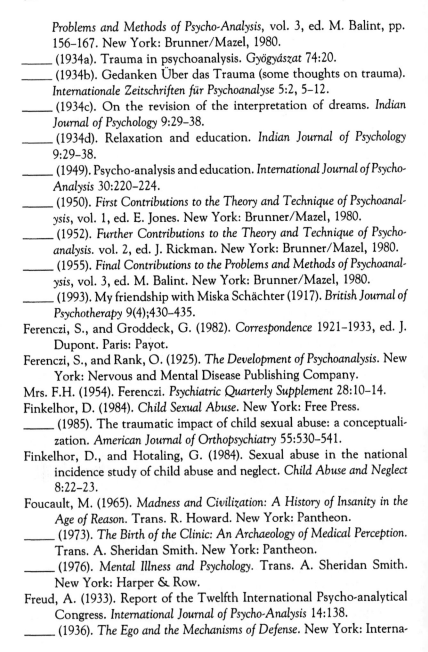

Problems and Methods of Psycho-Analysis, vol. 3, ed. M. Balint, pp. 156–167. New York: Brunner/Mazel, 1980.

_____ (1934a). Trauma in psychoanalysis. *Gyógyászat* 74:20.

_____ (1934b). Gedanken Über das Trauma (some thoughts on trauma). *Internationale Zeitschriften für Psychoanalyse* 5:2, 5–12.

_____ (1934c). On the revision of the interpretation of dreams. *Indian Journal of Psychology* 9:29–38.

_____ (1934d). Relaxation and education. *Indian Journal of Psychology* 9:29–38.

_____ (1949). Psycho-analysis and education. *International Journal of Psycho-Analysis* 30:220–224.

_____ (1950). *First Contributions to the Theory and Technique of Psychoanalysis*, vol. 1, ed. E. Jones. New York: Brunner/Mazel, 1980.

_____ (1952). *Further Contributions to the Theory and Technique of Psychoanalysis*. vol. 2, ed. J. Rickman. New York: Brunner/Mazel, 1980.

_____ (1955). *Final Contributions to the Problems and Methods of Psychoanalysis*, vol. 3, ed. M. Balint. New York: Brunner/Mazel, 1980.

_____ (1993). My friendship with Miska Schächter (1917). *British Journal of Psychotherapy* 9(4);430–435.

Ferenczi, S., and Groddeck, G. (1982). *Correspondence 1921–1933*, ed. J. Dupont. Paris: Payot.

Ferenczi, S., and Rank, O. (1925). *The Development of Psychoanalysis*. New York: Nervous and Mental Disease Publishing Company.

Mrs. F.H. (1954). Ferenczi. *Psychiatric Quarterly Supplement* 28:10–14.

Finkelhor, D. (1984). *Child Sexual Abuse*. New York: Free Press.

_____ (1985). The traumatic impact of child sexual abuse: a conceptualization. *American Journal of Orthopsychiatry* 55:530–541.

Finkelhor, D., and Hotaling, G. (1984). Sexual abuse in the national incidence study of child abuse and neglect. *Child Abuse and Neglect* 8:22–23.

Foucault, M. (1965). *Madness and Civilization: A History of Insanity in the Age of Reason*. Trans. R. Howard. New York: Pantheon.

_____ (1973). *The Birth of the Clinic: An Archaeology of Medical Perception*. Trans. A. Sheridan Smith. New York: Pantheon.

_____ (1976). *Mental Illness and Psychology*. Trans. A. Sheridan Smith. New York: Harper & Row.

Freud, A. (1933). Report of the Twelfth International Psycho-analytical Congress. *International Journal of Psycho-Analysis* 14:138.

_____ (1936). *The Ego and the Mechanisms of Defense*. New York: International Universities Press, 1966.

———— (1967). *The Writings of Anna Freud,* vol. 2. New York: International Universities Press.

Freud, S. (1896a). Further remarks on the neuro-psychosis of defense. *Standard Edition* 3:157–185.

———— (1896b). The aetiology of hysteria. *Standard Edition* 3:191–221.

———— (1905a). Fragment of an analysis of a case of hysteria. *Standard Edition* 7.

———— (1905b). Three essays on the theory of sexuality. *Standard Edition* 7:125–248.

———— (1910a). The future prospects of psychoanalytic therapy. *Standard Edition* 11:139–152.

———— (1910b). Preface to Sándor Ferenczi's *Psychoanalysis: Essays in the field of psycho-analysis. Standard Edition* 9:252.

———— (1911). Psycho-analytic notes on an autobiographical account of a case of paranoia (dementia paranoides). Part III. On the mechanism of paranoia. *Standard Edition* 12.

———— (1912a). The dynamics of transference. *Standard Edition* 12:97–108.

———— (1912b). Recommendations to physicians practicing psycho-analysis. *Standard Edition* 12:109–120.

———— (1913a). The disposition to obsessional neurosis. *Standard Edition* 12:313–326.

———— (1913b). On beginning the treatment (further recommendations on the technique of psycho-analysis I). *Standard Edition* 12:121–144.

———— (1914a). On the history of the psychoanalytic movement. *Standard Edition* 14:3–66.

———— (1914b). Remembering, repeating and working-through (further recommendations on the technique of psycho-analysis II). *Standard Edition* 12:145–146.

———— (1915 [1914]). Observations on transference-love (further recommendations on the technique of psycho-analysis III). *Standard Edition* 12:157–171.

———— (1915–1916). Introductory lectures on psychoanalysis. Lecture XI: The dreamwork. *Standard Edition* 15:170–183.

———— (1918). From the history of an infantile neurosis. *Standard Edition* 17:3–104.

———— (1919 [1918]). Lines of advance in psycho-analytic therapy. *Standard Edition* 17:157–168.

———— (1920). Beyond the pleasure principle. *Standard Edition* 18:3–64.

_____ (1921). Group psychology and the analysis of the ego. *Standard Edition* 18:67–143.

_____ (1923a). Dr. Sándor Ferenczi on his 50th birthday. *Standard Edition* 19:267–269.

_____ (1923b). The ego and the id. *Standard Edition* 19:12–66.

_____ (1926). The question of lay analysis: conversations with an impartial person, postscript (1927). *Standard Edition* 20:179–251.

_____ (1931). Female sexuality. *Standard Edition* 21:223–243.

_____ (1933a) Sándor Ferenczi (obituary). *International Zeitschrift für Psychoanalyse* 19:301–304.

_____ (1933b). Sándor Ferenczi. *International Journal of Psycho-Analysis* 14:3, 297–299.

_____ (1933c). Sándor Ferenczi. *Standard Edition* 22:227–229.

_____ (1933d). New introductory lectures on psycho-analysis. Lecture XXXIII: Femininity. *Standard Edition* 22.

_____ (1937). Analysis terminable and interminable. *Standard Edition* 23:209–253.

_____ (1939). Moses and monotheism. *Standard Edition* 23:3–140.

_____ (1954). *The Origins of Psychoanalysis: Letters to Wilhelm Fliess, Drafts and Notes: 1887–1902.* New York: Basic Books.

_____ (1966). *The Complete Introductory Lectures on Psychoanalysis.* New York: Norton.

Freud Museum (1987). The Freud Museum Ring Pamphlet. London: The Freud Museum.

Fromm, E. (1959). *Sigmund Freud's Mission.* New York: Harper & Row.

_____ (1963). *The Dogma of Christ.* New York: Holt, Rinehart & Winston.

_____ (1964). Foreword. In *Interpersonal Psychoanalysis: The Selected Papers of Clara M. Thompson,* ed. M. Green. New York: Basic Books.

_____ (1970). *The Crisis of Psychoanalysis: Essays On Freud, Marx and Social Psychology.* New York: Holt, Rinehart & Winston.

Fromm-Reichmann, F. (1950). *Principles of Intensive Psychotherapy.* Chicago: University of Chicago Press.

Gallego, M. A. (1989). The manifest content of dreams. *American Journal of Psychoanalysis* 49:2, June.

Gay, P. (1988). *Freud: A Life For Our Time.* New York: Norton.

Gedo, J. (1968). Noch einmal der Gelehrte Saugling. *Psyche* 22: 301–319.

_____ (1976). The wise baby reconsidered. In *Freud: The Fusion of Science and Humanism,* ed. J. E. Gedo and G. H. Pollock, pp. 357–378. New York: International Universities Press.

_____ (1986a). *Conceptual Issues in Psychoanalysis: Essays in History and Method.* Hillsdale, NJ: Analytic Press.

_____ (1986b). Ferenczi: psychoanalysis' first dissident. In *Conceptual Issues in Psychoanalysis: Essays in History and Method,* pp. 36–50. Hillsdale, NJ: Analytic Press.

_____ (1986c). A hero of our time: the dissidence of Heinz Kohut. In *Conceptual Issues in Psychoanalysis: Essays in History and Method.* Hillsdale, NJ: Analytic Press.

_____ (1986d). Heinz Kohut in the wilderness. In *Conceptual Issues in Psychoanalysis: Essays in History and Method.* Hillsdale, NJ: Analytic Press.

_____ (in press). Ferenczi as the orthodox vizier. In *A favorite son: the legacy of Sándor Ferenczi,* ed. A. W. Rachman. *Psychoanalytic Inquiry.*

Gill, M. M. (1979a). The analysis of the transference. *Journal of the American Psychoanalytic Association, Supplement* 27:263–288.

_____ (1979b). *Psychoanalysis and psychotherapy—1954–1977.* Paper presented at the symposium on Psychoanalysis and Psychotherapy—Similarities and Differences—a 25-Year Perspective, Atlanta, GA: October 20. (Unpublished, cited in Stone, L., Some thoughts on the "here and now" in psychoanalytic technique and process, *Psychoanalytic Quarterly* 1:4, 709–733, 1981.)

Glover, E. (1924). "Active therapy" and psycho-analysis: a critical review. *International Journal of Psycho-Analysis* 5:3, 269–311, July.

_____ (1955). Active technique. In *The Technique of Psychoanalysis,* pp. 165–184. New York: International Universities Press.

Goldberg, A. (1978). *The Psychology of the Self: A Casebook.* New York: International Universities Press.

Goldwert, M. (1986). Childhood seduction and the spiritualization of psychology: the case of Jung and Rank. *Child Abuse and Neglect* 10:555–557.

Gorkin, M. (1987). *The Uses of Countertransference.* New York: Jason Aronson.

Green, M. R. (1993). Personal communication. April.

Greenson, R. (1965). The working alliance and the transference neurosis. *Psychoanalytic Quarterly* 34:155–181.

Groddeck, G. (1928). *The Book of the It.* New York: Nervous and Mental Diseases Publishing Company.

_____ (1928/1929). Physical treatment of organic disease. *British Journal of*

Medical Psychology 9:179.

_____ (1929). *Exploring the Unconscious*. London: C. W. Daniel.

_____ (1933). Der Mensch als Symbol. *Internationaler Psychoanalytischer.* Vienna: Verlag Gesellschaft.

_____ (1934). *The World of Men*. London: C. W. Daniel.

Grosskurth, P. (1986). *Melanie Klein: Her World and Her Work*. Cambridge, MA: Harvard University Press.

_____ (1988). The lovable analyst—the clinical diary of Sándor Ferenczi. *The New York Review of Books*, December 8, pp. 45–47.

_____ (1991). *The Secret Ring: Freud's Inner Circle and the Politics of Psychoanalysis*. New York: Addison-Wesley.

Grossman, C. M., and Grossman, S. (1965). *The Wild Analyst*. New York: George Braziller.

Groth, N. A., and Birnbaum, J. H. (1979). *Men Who Rape: The Psychology of the Offender*. New York: Plenum.

Grotjahn, M. (1945). Georg Groddeck and his teachings about man's innate need for symbolization. *Psychoanalytic Review* 32:9–24.

_____ (1966). Georg Groddeck 1866–1934: the untamed analyst. In *Psychoanalytic Pioneers*, ed. F. Alexander, S. Eisenstein, and M. Grotjahn, pp. 308–320. New York: Basic Books.

_____ (1971). Collectors items from the correspondence between Sigmund Freud and Otto Rank: and from the first "rundbriefe" of the "ring holders." *Journal of the Otto Rank Association* 6:1, 7–31, June.

_____ (1973). Notes on reading the "rundbriefe." *Journal of the Otto Rank Association* 8:2, 35–88.

Grubrich-Simitis, I. (1986). Six letters of Sigmund Freud and Sándor Ferenczi on the interrelationship of psycho-analytic theory and technique. *International Review of Psycho-Analysis* 13:259–277.

Grünberger, B. (1980). From the "active technique" to the "confusion of tongues": on Ferenczi's deviation. In *Psychoanalysis In France*, ed. S. Lebovici and D. Widlocher, pp. 127–152. New York: International Universities Press.

Guntrip, H. (1961). *Personality Structure and Human Interaction*. New York: International Universities Press.

_____ (1969). *Schizoid Phenomena, Object Relations, and the Self*. New York: International Universities Press.

_____ (1971). *Psychoanalytic Theory, Therapy and the Self*. New York: Basic Books.

Hajós, K. (1930). Behavior of various extraxts of stomach and duodenum used to induce remissions. *Gyógyászat* 70: 1056–1058.

Haynal, A. (1987). *La technique en question: Controverses en psychoanalyse.* Paris: Payot.

_____ (1989). *Controversies in Psychoanalytic Method: From Freud and Ferenczi to Michael Balint.* New York: New York University Press.

_____ (1992). *Historical factors related to Ferenczi's clinical diary.* Paper presented at the American Academy of Psychoanalysis, Washington, DC, May 3.

_____ (1993a). *100 Years of Psychoanalysis.* Paper presented at the International Conference, University of Geneva Medical School, Geneva, Switzerland, September 17–18.

_____ (1993b). Introduction. In *The Correspondence of Sigmund Freud and Sándor Ferenczi,* vol. 1, 1908–1914, ed. E. Brabant, E. Falzeder, and P. Giampieri-Deutsch. Cambridge, MA: The Belknap Press of Harvard University.

_____ (in press). For a metapsychology of the analyst: Sándor Ferenczi's quest. *Psychoanalytic Inquiry.*

Heimann, P. (1950). On countertransference. *International Journal of Psycho-Analysis* 31:81–84.

Hoffer, A. (1990). Review of *The Clinical Diary of Sándor Ferenczi. International Journal of Psycho-Analysis* 71:4, 723–727.

_____ (1994). Personal communication. March 8.

Jacobs, L. (1994). Personal communication.

Jacoby, R. (1983). *The Repression of Psychoanalysis: Otto Fenichel and the Political Freudians.* New York: Basic Books.

James, B., and Nasjleti, M. (1983). *Treating Sexually Abused Children and Their Families.* Palo Alto, CA: Consulting Psychologists Press.

Jones, E. (1953). *The Life and Work of Sigmund Freud: Vol. 1. The Formative Years and the Great Discoveries.* New York: Basic Books.

_____ (1955). *The Life and Work of Sigmund Freud: Vol. 2. Years of Maturity, 1901–1919.* New York: Basic Books.

_____ (1957). *The Life and Work of Sigmund Freud: Vol. 3. The Last Phase: 1919–1939.* New York: Basic Books.

_____ (1958). Letter to the editor: Dr. Ernest Jones comments. *International Journal of Psycho-Analysis* 39:68.

_____ (1959). *Free Associations: Memories of a Psychoanalyst.* New York: Basic Books.

Jung, C. (1912). The theory of psychoanalysis. In *The Collected Works of C. G. Jung,* vol. 4. New York: Pantheon, 1961.

_____ (1969). Psychology and religion: west and east. In *The Collected Works of C. G. Jung*, vol. 2, p. 338. Princeton, NJ: Princeton University Press.

Kahn, E. (1985). Heinz Kohut and Carl Rogers: a timely comparison. *American Psychologist* 40:8, 893–904.

Kaplan, A. G. (1975). Sex in psychotherapy: the myth of Sándor Ferenczi. *Contemporary Psychoanalysis* II:175–187.

Karpfe, F. B. (1953). *The Psychology and Psychotherapy of Otto Rank*. New York: Philosophical Library.

Kass, L. (1976). *Pernicious Anemia*. Philadelphia: Saunders.

Kernberg, O. (1974). Further contributions to the treatment of narcissistic personalities. *International Journal of Psycho-Analysis* 55:215–240.

_____ (1975). *Borderline Conditions and Pathological Narcissism*. New York: Jason Aronson.

Khan, M. M. R. (1969). On the clinical provision of frustrations, recognitions, and failures in the analytic situation – an essay on Dr. Michael Balint's researches on the theory of psychoanalytic technique. *International Journal of Psycho-Analysis* 50:237–248.

_____ (1974). *Privacy of the Self*. London: Hogarth.

Klein, M. I. (1981). Freud's seduction theory: its implications for fantasy and memory in psychoanalytic theory. *Bulletin of the Menninger Clinic* 45:185–208.

Klein, M., and Tribich, D. (1982). Blame the child: Freud's blindness to the damaging influence of parents' personalities. *New York Academy of Sciences* 22:8, 14–20.

Kluft, R., ed. (1985). *Incest and Multiple Personality*. Washington, DC: American Psychiatric Press.

Koelsch, W. A. (1970). Freud discovers America. *Virginia Quarterly Review* 46:1, 115–132, Winter.

Kohut, H. (1959). Introspection, empathy and psychoanalysis: an examination of the relationship between mode of observation and theory. In *The Search for the Self*, pp. 205–232. New York: International Universities Press, 1978.

_____ (1968). The psychoanalytic treatment of narcissistic personality disorders: outline of a systematic approach. *Psychoanalytic Study of the Child*, 23:86–113. New York: International Universities Press.

_____ (1971). *The Analysis of the Self*. New York: International Universities Press.

_____ (1977). *The Restoration of the Self*. New York: International Universities Press.

_____ (1978a). Introspection, empathy, and psychoanalysis: an examination of the relationship between mode of observation and theory. In *The Search for the Self*, vol. 1., ed. P. H. Ornstein, pp. 205–232. New York: International Universities Press.

_____ (1978b). *The Search for the Self: Selected Writings of Heinz Kohut 1950–1958*, vols. 1 and 2, ed. P. Ornstein. New York: International Universities Press.

_____ (1979). The two analyses of Mr. Z. *International Journal of Psycho-Analysis* 60:3–27.

_____ (1983). Selected problems of self psychological theory. In *Reflections on Self Psychology*, ed. J. D. Lichtenberg and S. Kaplan, pp. 387–416. Hillsdale, NJ: Lawrence Erlbaum.

_____ (1984a). *How Does Analysis Cure?* ed. A. Goldberg and P. E. Stepansky. Chicago: The University of Chicago Press.

_____ (1984b). The role of empathy in psychoanalytic cure. In *How Does Analysis Cure?* ed. A. Goldberg and P. E. Stepansky, pp. 172–191. Chicago: University of Chicago Press.

Kohut, H., and Wolf, E. (1978). The disorders of the self and their treatment: an outline. *International Journal of Psycho-Analysis* 59:413–425.

Kolb, L. C. (1987). A neuropsychological hypothesis explaining post-traumatic stress disorder. *American Journal of Psychiatry* 144:989–995.

Krüll, M. (1979). *Freud Und Sien Vater, Die Entehung Der Psychoanalyse Und Freuds Ungeloste Vaterbingung*. Munich: C. H. Beck.

_____ (1986). *Freud and His Father*. New York: Norton.

Krystal, H. (1968). *Massive Psychic Trauma*. New York: International Universities Press.

_____ (1975). Affect tolerance. *The Annual of Psychoanalysis 3*. New York: International Universities Press.

_____ (1984). Psychoanalytic views on human emotional damages. In *Post-traumatic Stress Disorder: Psychological and Biological Sequelae*, ed. B. A. van der Kolk, pp. 1–28. Washington, DC: American Psychiatric Press.

Larivière, M. (1994a). Personal communication. March 5.

_____ (1994b). Personal communication. March 8.

_____ (1994c). Personal communication. March 12.

Larson, L. R. (1993). Betrayal and repetition: understanding aggression in sexually abused girls. *Clinical Social Work Journal* 21(2)137–149.

Levine, H. B., ed. (1990). *Adult Analysis and Childhood Sexual Abuse*. Hillsdale, NJ: Analytic Press.

Levy, S. T. (1985). Empathy and psychoanalytic technique. *Journal of the American Psychoanalytic Association* 2:33, 353–378.

Lewis, H. B. (1984). Review of *The Assault on Truth: Freud's Suppression of the Seduction Theory* by Jeffrey Moussaieff Masson. *Psychoanalytic Psychology* 4:349–355.

Lieberman, E. J. (1985). *Acts of Will: The Life and Work of Otto Rank.* New York: Free Press.

Little, M. (1951). Countertransference and the patient's response to it. *International Journal of Psycho-Analysis* 32:32–40.

_____ (1957). "R" – the analyst's response to his patient's needs. *International Journal of Psycho-Analysis* 38:240–254.

_____ (1960). Countertransference. *British Journal of Medical Psychology* 33:29–31.

Loftus, E. F., and Ketcham, K. (1991). *Witness for the Defense.* New York: St. Martin's Press.

Lorand, S. (1966). Sándor Ferenczi 1873–1933: pioneer of pioneers. In *Psychoanalytic Pioneers*, ed. F. Alexander, S. Eisenstein, and M. Grotjahn, pp. 14–35. New York: Basic Books.

_____ (1975–76). The founding of the Psychoanalytic Institute of the State University of New York Downstate Medical Center: an autobiographical history. *Psychoanalytic Review* 62:4, 677–714.

Lorin, C. (1983). *Le Jeune Ferenczi: Premiers Ecrits: 1899–1906.* Paris: Aubier-Montaigne.

_____ (1993). *Sándor Ferenczi de la Médecine à la Psychanalyse.* Paris: Presses Universitaires de France.

Ludmer, R. I. (1988). Creativity and the true self. *Contemporary Psychoanalysis* 24:2, 234–239.

Mack, J. E. (1994). Power, powerlessness, and empowerment in psychotherapy. *Psychiatry* 57:178–197.

Malcolm, J. (1981). *Psychoanalysis: The Impossible Profession.* New York: Alfred A. Knopf.

_____ (1983a). Trouble in the archives. *The New Yorker*, December.

_____ (1983b). *In the Freud Archives.* New York: Alfred A. Knopf.

Marthe, R. (1966). *The Psychoanalytic Revolution: Sigmund Freud's Life of Achievement.* New York: Harcourt, Brace & World.

Masson, J. M. (1984). *The Assault on Truth: Freud's Suppression of the Seduction Theory.* New York: Farrar, Straus & Giroux.

Masterson, J. (1976). *Psychotherapy of the Borderline Adult.* New York: Brunner/Mazel.

Mattick, P. (1994). Personal communication. March 11.

McCann, L. I., and Perlman, L. A. (1990). *Psychological Trauma and the Adult Survivor.* New York: Brunner/Mazel.

McGrath, W. J. (1986). *Freud's Discovery of Psychoanalysis: The Politics of Hysteria.* Ithaca, NY: Cornell University Press.

McGuire, W., ed. (1974). *The Freud/Jung Letters.* Trans. by R. Manheim and R. F. C. Hull. Princeton, NJ: Princeton University Press.

Menaker, E. (1982). *Otto Rank: A Rediscovered Legacy.* New York: Columbia University Press.

_____ (1983). Self, will and empathy. *Contemporary Psychoanalysis* 10:3, 460–469.

_____ (1986). Personal communication. April.

_____ (1991). Otto Rank and self psychology. In *Self Psychology: Comparison and Contrast*, ed. D. Detrick and S. Detrick, pp. 75–87. Hillsdale, NJ: Analytic Press.

_____ (1994a). Personal communication. January 12.

_____ (1994b). Personal communication. March 11.

Mészáros, J. (1993). Ferenczi's preanalytic period embedded in the cultural streams of the Fin de Siècle. In *The Legacy of Sándor Ferenczi*, ed. L. Aron and A. Harris, pp. 41–51. Hillsdale, NJ: Analytic Press.

_____ (1995). Personal communication, September 13.

Nemes, L. (1988). Freud and Ferenczi: a possible interpretation of their relationship. *Contemporary Psychoanalysis* 24:2, 240–249.

New York Psychoanalytic Institute Archives (1927). The 109th Meeting of the New York Psychoanalytic Society. Tuesday, April 26th.

Newton, C. (1925). Translator's preface. In S. Ferenczi and O. Rank *The Development of Psychoanalysis.* New York: Nervous and Mental Disease Publishing Company.

Ortmeyer, D. (1994). Personal communication.

Perry, H. S. (1982a). *Psychiatrist of America: The Life of Harry Stack Sullivan.* Cambridge, MA: Harvard University Press.

_____ (1982b). Clara Thompson – "Dear Friend and Colleague." In *Psychiatrist of America: The Life of Harry Stack Sullivan.* pp. 201–214. Cambridge, MA: Harvard University Press.

Putnam, J. J. (1909). Personal impressions of Sigmund Freud and his work. In *Addresses on Psychoanalysis.* London: Hogarth, 1951.

Quen, J. M., and Carlson, E. T. (1978). *American Psychoanalysis: Origins and Development.* New York: Brunner/Mazel.

Rachman, A. W. (1975). *Identity Group Psychotherapy with Adolescents.*

438   References

Springfield, IL: Charles C Thomas.

_____ (1977a). Interviews with Dr. Sándor Lorand about Dr. Sándor Ferenczi. October 4, 1977, and December 27, 1977.

_____ (1977b). Encounter techniques in analytic group psychotherapy with adolescents. *International Journal of Group Psychotherapy* 21:3, 319–329.

_____ (1978a). *The first encounter session: Ferenczi's case of the female Croatian musician.* Paper presented at the American Group Psychotherapy Association Convention. New Orleans, LA, February.

_____ (1978b). *Humanistic analysis in groups.* Unpublished manuscript.

_____ (1980a). *Freud's deviation from classical technique: his introduction of "activity" into psychoanalysis.* Paper presented at Invited Lecture Series, Pine Rest Christian Hospital, Grand Rapids, MI, April.

_____ (1981a). Humanistic analysis in groups. *Psychotherapy: Theory, Research and Practice* 18:4, 457–477.

_____ (1981b). Clinical meditation in groups. *Psychotherapy: Theory, Research, Practice* 18:2, 252–258, Summer.

_____ (1982). *Judicious self-disclosure in group psychotherapy.* Paper presented at the American Group Psychotherapy Association Conference, New York City, February.

_____ (1984a). *Freud and Ferenczi: a relationship that changed the course of psychoanalysis.* Paper presented at the Psychoanalytic Institute, Postgraduate Center for Mental Health, New York City, March.

_____ (1984b). *An outline of Ferenczian psychoanalysis.* Paper presented at the Psychoanalytic Institute, Postgraduate Center for Mental Health, New York City, March.

_____ (1987). *Confusion of tongues: the Ferenczian metaphor for childhood seduction and emotional truama.* Paper presented at the American Academy of Psychoanalysis, Chicago, IL, May 8.

_____ (1988a). The rule of empathy: Sándor Ferenczi's pioneering contributions to the empathic method in psychoanalysis. *Journal of the American Academy of Psychoanalysis* 16:1, 1–27, January.

_____ (1988b). Liberating the creative self through active combined psychotherapy. In *Borderline and Narcissistic Patients in Therapy*, ed. N. Slavinska-Holy. New York: International Universities Press.

_____ (1988c). *Sándor Ferenczi's influence in modern psychoanalysis.* Paper presented at the History of Psychoanalysis Course, Institute for Modern Psychoanalysis, New York, February 25.

_____ (1989a). Confusion of tongues: the Ferenczian metaphor for childhood seduction and emotional trauma. *Journal of the American Academy of Psychoanalysis* 17:2, 182–205.

——— (1989b). Ferenczi's contributions to the evolution of a self psychology framework in psychoanalysis. In *Self Psychology: Comparison and Contrast*, ed. D. W. Dietrich and S. P. Dietrich, pp. 81–100. Hillsdale, NJ: Analytic Press.

——— (1989c). Identity group psychotherapy with adolescents: a reformulation. In *Adolescent Group Psychotherapy*, ed. F. Azima-Cramer and L. H. Richmond, pp. 21–41. New York: International Universities Press.

——— (1989d). *The analysis of the incest trauma.* Paper presented at Grand Rounds, Brookdale Hospital, Brooklyn, NY, October.

——— (1990a). Judicious self-disclosure in group analysis. *Group* 14:3, 132–144.

——— (1990b). *The retrieval of the incest trauma through the use of drawings.* Paper presented at the Psychology Department, Bellevue Hospital, November.

——— (1990c). *A humanistic view of confrontation in the treatment of addiction.* Paper presented at the Conference: Recovery Groups—The Use of Dynamic Group Therapy in the Treatment of Addictive Disorders, Psychoanalytic Institute, Postgraduate Center for Mental Health, New York City, March.

——— (1990d). *Countertransference and the analysis of the incest trauma.* Paper presented at the Group Therapy Department, Psychoanalytic Institute Postgraduate Center for Mental Health, New York City, March.

——— (1991a). An oedipally conflicted patient. In *Psychopathology of the Submerged Personality*, ed. A. Wolf and L. Kutash, pp. 215–238. Northvale, NJ: Jason Aronson.

——— (1991b). *Dreams of incest: the literal interpretation.* Paper presented at The Royal Road to the Unconscious: A Conference on Dreams, C. G. Jung Foundation of New York, New York City, January 26.

——— (1991c). *Ferenczi's early treatment of a female homosexual transvestite: the case of Rosa K. (1902).* Unpublished manuscript.

——— (1991d). *Psychoanalysis, sexual seduction and the contemporary analysis of incest.* Paper presented at the American Academy of Psychoanalysis, New York City, December 19.

——— (1992a). *The seduction of the child.* Paper presented at the Jungian Foundation, New York City, January.

_____ (1992b). *The analysis of the incest trauma in group analysis.* Paper presented at the American Group Psychotherapy Association Conference, New York City, February.

_____ (1992c). *Ferenczi's discovery of the confusion of tongues theory—division of psychoanalysis.* Paper presented at the American Psychological Association, April, Philadelphia, PA.

_____ (1992d). *Ferenczi's clinical diary.* Paper presented at the American Academy of Psychoanalysis, Washington, DC, May.

_____ (1992e). *The confusion of tongues between Hedda Nussbaum and Joel Steinberg: dynamics of an abusive relationship.* Paper presented at the International Conference of the Psycho-History Society, John Jay College, New York City, June.

_____ (1992f). *Reviving and retrieving incest memories.* Paper presented at the Psychology Department, New York University-Bellevue Hospital Medical Center, New York City, November.

_____ (1993a). Ferenczi and sexuality. In *The Theoretical and Clinical Contributions of Sándor Ferenczi,* ed. L. Aron and S. Harris, pp. 81–100. Hillsdale, NJ: Analytic Press.

_____ (1993b). *The abusive parental transference in group analysis of the incest trauma.* Paper presented at the American Group Psychotherapy Association Conference, San Diego, CA, February 19.

_____ (1993c). *Judicious self-disclosure by the psychoanalyst.* Paper presented at the Fourth International Ferenczi Conference, Budapest, Hungary, July 19.

_____ (1993d). *The use of group analysis in the retrieval of incest memories.* Paper presented at the American Academy of Psychoanalysis, New York City, December.

_____ (1993e). *Theoretical issues in the treatment of childhood sexual trauma in spinal cord injured patients: the confusion of tongues theory of childhood seduction.* Paper presented at the American Association of Spinal Cord Injury Psychologists and Social Workers, Las Vegas, NV, September 8.

_____ (1994a). The confusion of tongues theory: Ferenczi's legacy to psychoanalysis. In *100 years of Psychoanalysis,* ed. A. Haynal and E. Falzeder, pp. 235–255. London: Karnac.

_____ (1994b). *The examination and analysis of the psychotherapist's emotional reactions to a "difficult analysand."* Paper presented at the Sándor Ferenczi Study Group, Grand Rapids, MI, January 29.

_____ (1994c). *Non-interpretative behavior by the psychoanalyst in the psycho-*

analytic situation. Paper presented at the Ferenczi Symposium, IX Forum of International Federation of Psychoanalytic Societies, Florence, Italy, May 14.

_____ (1994d). *Ferenczi's humanistic psychoanalysis: the challenge for analytic treatment in the 21st century.* Paper presented at the Encontro Internacional Peropectivas Psicanaliticas, Sao Paulo, Brazil, August 16.

_____ (1994e). *Oedipus from Brooklyn: a Ferenczian analysis.* Paper presented at the Arculo Brasiliano de Psicanalise, Belo Horozonti, Brazil, August 18.

_____ (in press). *Sándor Ferenczi's Humanistic Psychotherapy: Contemporary Clinical Applications.* Northvale, NJ: Jason Aronson.

Rachman, A. W., and Ceccoli, V. C. (1995). Judicious self-disclosure in adolescent group psychotherapy. In *Group Therapy with Children and Adolescents,* ed. P. Kymisis and D. Halperin. Washington, DC: American Psychiatric Press.

Rachman, A. W., and Kahn, S. R. (1994). *A preliminary study of citations of Ferenczi's work in the analytic literature.* Unpublished manuscript.

Rachman, A. W., and Mattick, P. (1994). *The confusion of tongues between Freud and Dora: the need for tenderness not sexuality.* Unpublished manuscript.

Racker, H. (1953b). A contribution to the problem of countertransference. *International Journal of Psycho-Analysis* 37:360–366.

_____ (1957). The meaning and use of contertransference. *Psychoanalytic Quarterly* 26:303–357.

_____ (1968). *Transference and Countertransference.* New York: International Universities Press.

Rado, S. (1933). In memoriam: Sándor Ferenczi, 1873–1933. *Psychoanalytic Quarterly* 2:356–358.

Ragen, T., and Aron, L. (1993). Abandoned workings: Ferenczi's mutual analysis. In *The Legacy of Sándor Ferenczi,* ed. L. Aron and A. Harris, pp. 217–226. Hillsdale, NJ: Analytic Press.

Rank, O. (1907). *Der Kuenstler* (The Artist). Vienna: Heller.

_____ (1924). The trauma of birth. *Psychoanalytic Review,* July.

_____ (1926). *Technik der Psychoanlayse 1: Die Analytische Situation.* Vienna: Deuticke.

_____ (1932). *Art and Artist.* New York: Alfred A. Knopf.

_____ (1945a). *Will Therapy and Truth and Reality.* New York: Alfred A. Knopf.

_____ (1945b). *Will Therapy,* vol. 3. (One-volume edition of *Will Therapy* published in 1945.) New York: Alfred A. Knopf.

Rapaport, D. (1959). The structure of psychoanalytic theory: a systematizing attempt. In *Psychology: A Study of a Science*, vol. 3, ed. S. Koch, pp. 55–183. New York: McGraw-Hill.

Reich, A. (1951). On counter-transference. *International Journal of Psycho-Analysis* 32:25–31.

_____ (1966). Empathy and countertransference. In *Psychoanalytic Contributions*, pp. 344–360. New York: International Universities Press.

Reuben, C. (1989). On the cuspid. *Ms. Magazine*, pp. 16–20.

Roazen, P. (1969). *Brother Animal: The Story of Freud and Tausk*. New York: New York University Press.

_____ (1975). *Freud and His Followers*. New York: Alfred A. Knopf.

_____ (1990a). Review of *The Clinical Diary of Sándor Ferenczi*. *American Journal of Psychoanalysis* 50:4, 367–371.

_____ (1990b). *The history of the psychoanalytic movement*. Paper presented at Symposium on Jung, Freud, Ferenczi, Sullivan: their relationship and their contributions, Jungian Institute, New York City, January 28.

_____ (1993). *Meeting Freud's Family*. Amherst, MA: University of Massachusetts Press.

Rogers, C. R. (1942). *Counseling and Psychotherapy*. Cambridge, MA: Houghton Mifflin.

_____ (1951). *Client-Centered Therapy: Its Current Practice Implications and Theory*. Boston: Houghton Mifflin.

_____ (1959a). Client-centered therapy. In *American Handbook of Psychiatry*, vol. 3, ed. S. Arieti, pp. 183–200. New York: Basic Books.

_____ (1959b). A theory of therapy, personality, and interpersonal relationships as developed in the client-centered framework. In *Psychology: A Study of Science*, vol. 3, ed. S. Koch, pp. 184–256. New York: McGraw-Hill.

_____ (1961). *On Becoming a Person*. Boston: Houghton Mifflin.

_____ (1967). Client-centered therapy. In *Comprehensive Textbook of Psychiatry*, ed. A. M. Freedman and H. I. Kaplan, pp. 1225–1228. Baltimore: Williams & Wilkins.

_____ (1975). Empathetic: an unappreciated way of being. *The Counseling Psychologist* 5:2, 2–10.

_____ (1980). *A Way of Being*. Boston: Houghton Mifflin.

_____ (1986a). Client-centered therapy. In *Psychotherapist's Handbook*, ed. I. L. Kutash and A. Wolf, pp. 197–208. San Francisco: Jossey-Bass.

_____ (1986b). Rogers, Kohut, and Erickson: a personal perspective on some similarities and differences. *Person-Centered Review* 1:125–140.

Rush, F. (1980). *The Best Kept Secret: Sexual Abuse of Children.* New York: McGraw-Hill.

Russell, D. E. H. (1988). *The Secret Trauma.* New York: Basic Books.

Sabourin, P. (1984). *Ferenczi, Paladin et Grand Vizir Secret.* Paris: Editions Universitaires.

_____ (1985). Mutual pardon/final success: epilogue. In *Ferenczi's Journal Clinique: Janvier–Octobre 1932,* pp. 289–294. Paris: Payot.

Sachs, H. (1944). *Freud: Master and Friend.* Cambridge, MA: Harvard University Press.

Sager, C. (1994). Personal communication.

Schachet, L. (1977). *The Meaning of Illness: Selected Psychological Writings of G. Groddeck.* New York: International Universities Press.

Schur, M. (1972). *Freud: Living and Dying.* New York: International Universities Press.

Searles, H. F. (1975). The patient as therapist to his analyst. In *Tactics and Techniques in Psychoanalytic Therapy: Vol. 2. Countertransference,* ed. P. L. Giovacchini. New York: Jason Aronson.

_____ (1979a). *Countertransference and Related Subjects.* New York: International Universities Press.

_____ (1979b). The patient as therapist to his analyst. In *Countertransference and Related Subjects.* New York: International Universities Press.

Severn, E. (1913). *Psycho-Therapy: Its Doctrine and Practice.* London: Rider.

_____ (1920). *The Psychology of Behavior.* New York: Dodd, Mead.

_____ (1934). *The Discovery of the Self: A Study of Psychological Cure.* Philadelphia: David McKay.

Simmel, E. (1926). Georg Groddeck zum sechzigsten Geburtstag. *Internationale Zeitschrift für Psychoanalyse* 12:591.

Simon, E. (1984). Lecture de Ferenczi autour de Thalassa (Ferenczi's Lecture about Thalassa). *Confrontation* 12:43–61, Autumn.

Slakter, E. (1987). *Countertransference: A Comprehensive View of Those Reactions of the Therapist to the Patient that May Help or Hinder Treatment.* New York: Jason Aronson.

Spotnitz, H. (1979). Narcissistic countertransference. In *Countertransference,* ed. L. Epstein and A. H. Feiner, pp. 329–343. New York: Jason Aronson.

Stanton, M. (1991). *Sándor Ferenczi: Reconsidering Active Intervention.*

Northvale, NJ: Jason Aronson.

Stolorow, R. (1976). Psychoanalytic reflections on client-centered therapy in the light of modern conceptions of narcissism. *Psychotherapy: Theory, Research and Practice* 13:26-29.

Stolorow, R., Brandchaft, B., and Atwood, G. (1983). Intersubjectivity in psychoanalytic treatment, with special reference to archaic states. *Bulletin of the Menninger Clinic* 47:117-128.

Stolorow, R., and Lachmann, F. (1980). *Psychoanalysis of Developmental Arrests*. New York: International Universities Press.

Stone, L. (1954). The widening scope of indications for psychoanalysis. *Journal of the American Psychoanalytic Association* 2:567-594.

_____ (1981a). Some thoughts on the "here and now" in psychoanalytic technique and process. *Psychoanalytic Quarterly* 1:4, 709-733.

_____ (1981b). Notes on the noninterpretive elements in the psychoanalytic situation and process. *Journal of the American Psychoanalytic Association* 29:89-118.

Stone, M. H. (1989). Individual psychotherapy with victims of incest. *Psychiatric Clinics of North America* 12:2, 237-255, June.

_____ (1990). Incest in the borderline patient. In *Incest-Related Syndrome of Adult Psychopathology*, ed. R.P. Kluft, pp. 183-204. Washington, DC: American Psychiatric Press.

Sugerman, A. (1977). Psychoanalysis as a humanistic psychology. *Psychotherapy: Theory, Research and Practice* 14:3, 204-211.

Sullivan, H. S. (1940). *Conceptions of Modern Psychiatry*. New York: Norton.

_____ (1953). *The Interpersonal Theory of Psychiatry*. New York: Norton.

_____ (1954). *The Psychiatric Interview*. New York: Norton.

Sulloway, F. (1979). *Freud: Biologist of the Mind*. New York: Basic Books.

Sylwan, B. (1984). An untoward event: Òu la Guerre du Trauma de Breuer à Freud de Jones à Ferenczi. *Cahiers Confrontation* 12:101-122, Automne.

Taft, J. (1945). Translator's introduction. In O. Rank, *Will Therapy and Truth and Reality*. New York: Alfred A. Knopf.

_____ (1958). *Otto Rank: A Biographical Study Based on Notebooks, Letters, Collected Writings, Therapeutic Achievements, and Personal Associations*. New York: Julian.

_____ (1962). *The Dynamics of Therapy in a Controlled Relationship*. New York: Dover.

Tavris, C. (1993). Beware the incest-survivor machine. *The New York*

Times, January 3, pp. C1, C16–C17.

Thompson, C. (1942). The therapeutic technique of Sándor Ferenczi. *International Journal of Psycho-Analysis* 23:120–134.

_____ (1943). The therapeutic technique of Sándor Ferenczi: a comment. *International Journal of Psycho-Analysis* 16:64, 66.

_____ (1944). Ferenczi's contribution to psychoanalysis. *Psychiatry* 7:245–252.

_____ (1950a). *Psychoanalysis: Evolution and Development, A Review of Theory and Therapy*. New York: Hermitage House.

_____ (1950b). Deviations and new developments in the 1920s. In *Psychoanalysis: Evolution and Development*. New York: Hermitage House.

_____ (1950c). Introduction. In S. Ferenczi, *Sex In Psychoanalysis*. New York: Basic Books.

_____ (1964a). Ferenczi's relaxation method. In *Interpersonal Psychoanalysis: Papers of Clara M. Thompson*, ed. M. R. Green, pp. 67–82. New York: Basic Books.

_____ (1964b). Sándor Ferenczi, 1873–1933. In *Interpersonal Psychoanalysis: Papers of Clara M. Thompson*, ed. M. R. Green, pp. 65–66. New York: Basic Books.

_____ (1964c). Sándor Ferenczi, 1873–1933. *Contemporary Psychoanalysis* 24:2, 182–195, 1988.

Torok, M. (1979). L'os de la fin. *Cahiers Confrontation* I:163–186.

_____ (1984). La correspondence Ferenczi-Freud. La vie de la lettre dans l'historie de la psychoanalyse. *Confrontation* 12:79–100.

Vida, J. E. (1991). Sándor Ferenczi on female sexuality. *Journal of the American Academy of Psychoanalysis* 19:271–281.

Winnicott, D. W. (1949). Hate in the countertransference. *International Journal of Psycho-Analysis* 30:69–75.

_____ (1951). Transitional objects and transitional phenomena. In *Collected Papers: Through Paediatrics to Psychoanalysis*, pp. 229–242. New York: Basic Books, 1958.

_____ (1958). *Collected Papers*. London: Tavistock.

_____ (1960a). Countertransference. *British Journal of Medical Psychology* 33:17–21.

_____ (1960b). Ego distortion in terms of true and false self. In *The Maturational Processes and the Facilitating Environment*, pp. 140–152. New York: International Universities Press, 1965.

_____ (1960c). Parent–infant relationship. In *The Maturational Processes and the Facilitating Environment*. New York: International Universities Press, 1965.

_____ (1965a). *The Maturational Processes and the Facilitating Environment.* New York: International Universities Press.

_____ (1965b). *The Family and Individual Development.* New York: Basic Books.

Wolf, A., and Kutash, I. (1991). *Psychotherapy of the Submerged Personality.* Northvale, NJ: Jason Aronson.

Wolstein, B. (1959). *Countertransference.* New York: Grune & Stratton.

_____ (1967). *Theory of Psychoanalytic Therapy.* New York: Grune & Stratton.

_____ (1989). Ferenczi, Freud, and the origins of American interpersonal relations. *Contemporary Psychoanalysis* 25:672–685.

_____ (1990). The therapeutic experience of psychoanalytic inquiry. *Psychoanalytic Psychology* 7:4, 565–580.

_____ (1993). Sándor Ferenczi and American interpersonal relations: historical and personal reflections. In *The Legacy of Sándor Ferenczi,* ed. L. Aron and A. Harris, pp. 175–184. Hillsdale, NJ: Analytic Press.

_____ (in press). Countertransference, the frame and other themes related to Ferenczi and RN's mutual analysis. *Psychoanalytic Inquiry.*

Yalom, I. D. (1975). *The Theory and Practice of Group Psychotherapy.* New York: Basic Books.

Young-Bruehl, E. (1988). *Anna Freud: A Biography.* New York: Summit Books.

CREDITS

INDEX

ABOUT THE AUTHOR

Arnold Wm. Rachman, Ph.D., F.A.G.P.A., is Clinical Professor of Psychology at the Derner Institute of Adelphi University, Garden City, New York; Associate Clinical Professor of Psychiatry, New York University Medical Center; Training and Supervising Analyst, Postgraduate Center for Mental Health, New York City; and Supervising Analyst, New York University Postdoctoral Program in Psychoanalysis. Dr. Rachman is a fellow of the American Group Psychotherapy Association and a member of both the American Psychological Association and the Sandor Ferenczi Society in Budapest, Hungary. He is the founder of The Ferenczi Institute in New York City, and is in the private practice of individual and group psychoanalysis, also in New York City.